The Works of Samuel Johnson
by Samuel Johnson

Address:
HardPress
8345 NW 66TH ST #2561
MIAMI FL 33166-2626
USA
Email: info@hardpress.net

ESTO SOL TESTIS

Walter J. H. Jones.
Esquire.

THE
WORKS

OF

SAMUEL JOHNSON, LL.D.

A NEW EDITION

IN TWELVE VOLUMES.

WITH

AN ESSAY ON HIS LIFE AND GENIUS,

By ARTHUR MURPHY, Esq.

VOLUME THE FIFTH.

LONDON:

PRINTED FOR F. C. AND J. RIVINGTON; G. AND W. NICOL; T. EGERTON; LONGMAN, HURST, REES, ORME, AND BROWN; T. CADELL; J. NUNN; J. CUTHELL; J. AND W. T. CLARKE; J. BOOKER; J. CARPENTER; JEFFERY AND SON; J. AND A. ARCH; J. BOOTH; J. RICHARDSON; HATCHARD AND SON; W. GINGER; R. H. EVANS; J. MAWMAN; R. SCHOLEY; BALDWIN, CRADOCK, AND JOY; SHERWOOD AND JONES; T. HAMILTON; J. ROBINSON; R. SAUNDERS; HARDING, MAVOR, AND LEPARD; G. AND W. B. WHITTAKER; LLOYD AND SON; J. BOHN; T. TEGG; T. WILKIE; OGLE AND CO.; SIMPKIN AND MARSHALL; KINGSBURY, PARBURY, AND ALLEN; G. MACKIE; J. PORTER; G. GREENLAND; W. MASON; J. COLLINGWOOD; W. WOOD; HURST AND ROBINSON: J. RACKHAM; AND DEIGHTON AND SONS, CAMBRIDGE; BRODIE, DOWDING, AND CO. SALISBURY; AND BELL AND BRADFUTE; AND J. FAIRBAIRN, AT EDINBURGH.

1823

LONDON:

PRINTED BY S. AND R. BENTLEY, DORSET STREET.

CONTENTS

OF

THE FIFTH VOLUME.

THE IDLER.

Numb.		Page
1	IDLER's character	1
2	Invitation to correspondents	5
3	Idler's reason for writing	9
4	Charities and Hospitals	13
5	Proposals for a female army	17
6	Lady's performance on horseback	21
7	Scheme for news-writers	25
8	Plan of military discipline	29
9	Progress of idleness	33
10	Political credulity	37
11	Discourses on the weather	41
12	Marriages why advertised	45
13	The imaginary housewife	49
14	Robbery of time	53
15	Treacle's complaint of his wife	56
16	Drugget's retirement	60
17	Expedients of Idlers	64
18	Drugget vindicated	67
19	Whirler's character	71
20	Louisbourg's history	75
21	Linger's history of listlessness	80
22	Imprisonment of debtors	84
23	Uncertainty of friendship	88
24	Man does not always think	92
25	New actors on the theatre	96
26	Betty Broom's history	100
27	Power of habits	105
28	Wedding day—Grocer's wife—Chairman	109

Numb.		Page
29	Betty Broom's history	113
30	Corruption of news-writers	117
31	Disguises of idleness. Sober's character	121
32	Sleep	125
33	Journal of a fellow of a college	129
34	Punch and conversation	134
35	Auction hunter	138
36	The terrific diction	142
37	Iron and gold	146
38	Debtors in prison	150
39	The bracelet	155
40	Art of advertising	159
41	On the death of a friend	163
42	Perdita's complaint of her father	167
43	Monitions on the flight of time	171
44	Use of memory	175
45	Portraits defended	178
46	Molly Quick's complaint of her mistress	182
47	Deborah Ginger's account of city wits	186
48	The bustles of idleness	191
49	Marvel's journey	194
50	Marvel paralleled	198
51	Domestick greatness unattainable	202
52	Self-denial necessary	206
53	Mischiefs of good company	210
54	Mrs. Savecharges' complaint	215
55	Author's mortifications	220
56	Virtuosos whimsical	224
57	Character of Sophron the prudent	228
58	Expectations of pleasure frustrated	232
59	Books fall into neglect	235
60	Minim the critick	238
61	Minim the critick	244
62	Ranger's account of the vanity of riches	248
63	Progress of arts and language	252
64	Ranger's complaint concluded	255
65	Fate of posthumous works	259
66	Loss of antient writings	263
67	Scholar's journal	266

Numb.		Page
68	History of translations	272
69	History of translations	275
70	Hard words defended	279
71	Dick Shifter's rural excursion	283
72	Regulation of memory	288
73	Tranquil's use of riches	292
74	Memory rarely deficient	296
75	Gelaleddin of Bassora	300
76	False criticisms on painting	304
77	Easy writing	308
78	Steady, Snug, Startle, Solid, and Misty	312
79	Grand style of painting	317
80	Ladies' journey to London	321
81	Indian's speech to his countrymen	325
82	The true idea of beauty	329
83	Scruple, Wormwood, Sturdy, and Gentle	335
84	Biography how best performed	339
85	Books multiplied by useless compilations	343
86	Miss Heartless's want of a lodging	346
87	Amazonian bravery revived	350
88	What have ye done?	354
89	Physical evil moral good	357
90	Rhetorical action considered	361
91	Sufficiency of the English language	364
92	Nature of cunning	368
93	Sam Softly's history	372
94	Obstructions of learning	375
95	Tim Wainscot's son a fine gentleman	378
96	Hacho of Lapland	382
97	Narratives of travellers considered	386
98	Sophia Heedful	390
99	Ortogrul of Basra	393
100	The good sort of woman	396
101	Omar's plan of life	401
102	Authors inattentive to themselves	405
103	Horrour of the last	408

HISTORY of RASSELAS, Prince of Abissinia . 417

ADVERTISEMENT.

—————

THE IDLER having omitted to distinguish the Essays of his Correspondents by any particular signature, thinks it necessary to inform his Readers, that from the ninth, the fifteenth, thirty-third, forty-second, fifty-fourth, sixty-seventh, seventy-sixth, seventy-ninth, eighty-second, ninety-third, ninety-sixth, and ninety-eighth Papers, he claims no other praise than that of having given them to the Publick.*

* The names of the authors of these Papers, as far as known, will be given in the course of the present edition.

I D L E R.

NUMB. 1.   SATURDAY, *April* 15, 1758. *

Vacui sub umbra
Lusimus.   HOR.

THOSE who attempt periodical essays   seem to be often stopped in the beginning, by the difficulty of finding a proper title.   Two writers, since the time of the Spectator, have assumed his name, without any pretensions to lawful inheritance ; an effort was once made to revive the Tatler ; and the strange appellations, by which other papers have been called, show that the authors were distressed, like the natives of America, who come to the Europeans to beg a name.

It will be easily believed of the Idler, that if his title had required any search, he never would have found it.   Every mode of life has its conveniences. The Idler, who habituates himself to be satisfied with what he can most easily obtain, not only escapes

* Originally published in " The Universal Chronicle, or Weekly Gazette," a newspaper projected by Mr. John Newbery.   C.

labours which are often fruitless, but sometimes succeeds better than those who despise all that is within their reach, and think every thing more valuable as it is harder to be acquired.

If similitude of manners be a motive to kindness, the Idler may flatter himself with universal patron-age. There is no single character under which such numbers are comprised. Every man is, or hopes to be, an Idler. Even those who seem to differ most from us are hastening to increase our fraternity; as peace is the end of war, so to be idle is the ultimate purpose of the busy.

There is perhaps no appellation by which a writer can better denote his kindred to the human species. It has been found hard to describe man by an adequate definition. Some philosophers have called him a reasonable animal; but others have considered reason as a quality of which many creatures partake. He has been termed likewise a laughing animal; but it is said that some men have never laughed. Perhaps man may be more properly distinguished as an idle animal; for there is no man who is not sometimes idle. It is at least a definition from which none that shall find it in this paper can be excepted; for who can be more idle than the reader of the Idler?

That the definition may be complete, idleness must be not only the general, but the peculiar characteristick of man; and perhaps man is the only being that can properly be called idle, that does by others what he might do himself, or sacrifices duty or pleasure to the love of ease.

Scarcely any name can be imagined from which less envy or competition is to be dreaded. The Idler has no rivals or enemies. The man of business forgets him ; the man of enterprise despises him ; and though such as tread the same track of life fall commonly into jealousy and discord, Idlers are always found to associate in peace ; and he who is most famed for doing nothing, is glad to meet another as idle as himself.

What is to be expected from this paper, whether it will be uniform or various, learned or familiar, serious or gay, political or moral, continued or interrupted, it is hoped that no reader will enquire. That the Idler has some scheme, cannot be doubted, for to form schemes is the Idler's privilege. But though he has many projects in his head, he is now grown sparing of communication, having observed, that his hearers are apt to remember what he forgets himself ; that his tardiness of execution exposes him to the encroachments of those who catch a hint and fall to work ; and that very specious plans, after long contrivance and pompous displays, have subsided in weariness without a trial, and without miscarriage have been blasted by derision.

Something the Idler's character may be supposed to promise. Those that are curious after diminutive history, who watch the revolutions of families, and the rise and fall of characters either male or female, will hope to be gratified by this paper ; for the Idler is always inquisitive and seldom retentive. He that delights in obloquy and satire, and wishes to see clouds gathering over any reputation that dazzles him with its brightness, will snatch up the Idler's essays with a beating heart. The Idler is naturally censorious; those who attempt nothing themselves, think every thing easily performed, and consider the unsuccessful always as criminal.

I think it necessary to give notice, that I make no contract, nor incur any obligation. If those who depend on the Idler for intelligence and entertainment, should suffer the disappointment which commonly follows ill-placed expectations, they are to lay the blame only on themselves.

Yet hope is not wholly to be cast away. The Idler, though sluggish, is yet alive, and may sometimes be stimulated to vigour and activity. He may descend into profoundness, or tower into sublimity; for the diligence of an Idler is rapid and impetuous, as ponderous bodies forced into velocity move with violence proportionate to their weight.

But these vehement exertions of intellect cannot be frequent, and he will therefore gladly receive help from any correspondent, who shall enable him to please without his own labour. He excludes no style, he prohibits no subject; only let him that writes to the Idler remember, that his letters must not be long; no words are to be squandered in declarations of esteem, or confessions of inability; conscious dulness has little right to be prolix, and praise is not so welcome to the Idler as quiet.

NUMB. 2.   SATURDAY, *April 22, 1758.*

Toto vix quater anno
Membranam.   HOR.

MANY positions are often on the tongue, and
seldom in the mind; there are many truths which
every human being acknowledges and forgets.   It is
generally known, that he who expects much will be
often disappointed; yet disappointment seldom cures
us of expectation, or has any other effect than that
of producing a moral sentence, or peevish exclamation.   He that embarks in the voyage of life, will
always wish to advance rather by the impulse of the
wind, than the strokes of the oar; and many founder in the passage, while they lie waiting for the
gale that is to waft them to their wish.

It will naturally be suspected that the Idler has
lately suffered some disappointment, and that he does
not talk thus gravely for nothing.   No man is required to betray his own secrets.   I will, however,
confess, that I have now been a writer almost a week,
and have not yet heard a single word of praise, nor
received one hint from any correspondent.

Whence this negligence proceeds I am not able
to discover.   Many of my predecessors have thought
themselves obliged to return their acknowledgments
in the second paper, for the kind reception of the
first; and in a short time, apologies have become
necessary to those ingenious gentlemen and ladies,

whose performances, though in the highest degree elegant and learned, have been unavoidably delayed.

What then will be thought of me, who, having experienced no kindness, have no thanks to return ; whom no gentleman or lady has yet enabled to give any cause of discontent, and who have therefore no opportunity of showing how skilfully I can pacify resentment, extenuate negligence, or palliate rejection.

I have long known that splendor of reputation is not to be counted among the necessaries of life, and therefore shall not much repine if praise be withheld till it is better deserved. But surely I may be allowed to complain, that, in a nation of authors, not one has thought me worthy of notice after so fair an invitation.

At the time when the rage of writing has seized the old and young, when the cook warbles her lyricks in the kitchen, and the thrasher vociferates his heroicks in the barn ; when our traders deal out knowledge in bulky volumes, and our girls forsake their samplers to teach kingdoms wisdom ; it may seem very unnecessary to draw any more from their proper occupations, by affording new opportunities of literary fame.

I should be indeed unwilling to find that, for the sake of corresponding with the Idler, the smith's iron had cooled on the anvil, or the spinster's distaff stood unemployed. I solicit only the contributions of those who have already devoted themselves to literature, or, without any determinate intention, wander at large through the expanse of life, and wear out the day in hearing at one place what they utter at another.

Of these, a great part are already writers. One has a friend in the country upon whom he exercises his powers; whose passions he raises and depresses; whose understanding he perplexes with paradoxes, or strengthens by argument; whose admiration he courts, whose praises he enjoys; and who serves him instead of a senate or a theatre; as the young soldiers in the Roman camp learned the use of their weapons by fencing against a post in the place of an enemy.

Another has his pockets filled with essays and epigrams, which he reads from house to house, to select parties; and which his acquaintances are daily entreating him to withhold no longer from the impatience of the publick.

If among these any one is persuaded, that, by such preludes of composition, he has qualified himself to appear in the open world, and is yet afraid of those censures which they who have already written, and they who cannot write, are equally ready to fulminate against public pretenders to fame, he may, by transmitting his performances to the Idler, make a cheap experiment of his abilities, and enjoy the pleasure of success, without the hazard of miscarriage.

Many advantages not generally known arise from this method of stealing on the public. The standing author of the paper is always the object of critical malignity. Whatever is mean will be imputed to him, and whatever is excellent be ascribed to his assistants. It does not much alter the event, that the author and his correspondents are equally unknown; for the author, whoever he be, is an individual, of whom every reader has some fixed idea, and whom he is therefore unwilling to gratify with applause ; but the praises given to his correspondents are scattered in the air, none can tell on whom they will light, and therefore none are unwilling to bestow them.

He that is known to contribute to a periodical work, needs no other caution than not to tell what particular pieces are his own ; such secrecy is indeed very difficult ; but if it can be maintained, it is scarcely to be imagined at how small an expence he may grow considerable.

A person of quality, by a single paper, may engross the honour of a volume. Fame is indeed dealt with a hand less and less bounteous through the subordinate ranks, till it descends to the professed author, who will find it very difficult to get more than he deserves ; but every man who does not want it, or who needs not value it, may have liberal allowances ; and, for five letters in the year sent to the Idler, of which perhaps only two are printed, will be promoted to the first rank of writers by those who are weary of the present race of wits, and wish to sink them into obscurity before the lustre of a name not yet known enough to be detested.

Numb. 3.　Saturday, *April* 29, 1758.

Otia vitæ
Solamur cantu.　　　　　　Stat.

It has long been the complaint of those who frequent the theatres, that all the dramatick art has been long exhausted, and that the vicissitudes of fortune, and accidents of life, have been shown in every possible combination, till the first scene informs us of the last, and the play no sooner opens, than every auditor knows how it will conclude.　When a conspiracy is formed in a tragedy, we guess by whom it will be detected ; when a letter is dropt in a comedy, we can tell by whom it will be found.　Nothing is now left for the poet but character and sentiment, which are to make their way as they can, without the soft anxiety of suspense, or the enlivening agitation of surprize.

A new paper lies under the same disadvantages as a new play.　There is danger lest it be new without novelty.　My earlier predecessors had their choice of vices and follies, and selected such as were most likely to raise merriment or attract attention ; they had the whole field of life before them, untrodden and unsurveyed ; characters of every kind shot up in their way and those of the most luxuriant growth, or most conspicuous colours, were naturally cropt by the first sickle.　They that follow are forced to peep into neglected corners, to note the casual varieties of the same species, and to recommend themselves by minute industry, and distinctions too subtle for common eyes.

Sometimes it may happen, that the haste or negligence of the first inquirers has left enough behind to reward another search ; sometimes new objects start up under the eye, and he that is looking for one kind of matter, is amply gratified by the discovery of another.   But still it must be allowed, that, as more is taken, less can remain : and every truth brought newly to light impoverishes the mine, from which succeeding intellects are to dig their treasures.

Many philosophers imagine, that the elements themselves may be in time exhausted ; that the sun, by shining long, will effuse all its light ; and that, by the continual waste of aqueous particles, the whole earth will at last become a sandy desert.

I would not advise my readers to disturb themselves by contriving how they shall live without light and water.   For the days of universal thirst and perpetual darkness are at a great distance.   The ocean and the sun will last our time, and we may leave posterity to shift for themselves.

But if the stores of nature are limited, much more narrow bounds must be set to the modes of life ; and mankind may want a moral or amusing paper, many years before they shall be deprived of drink or day-light.   This want, which to the busy and the inventive may seem easily remediable by some substitute or other, the whole race of Idlers will feel with all the sensibility that such torpid animals can suffer.

When I consider the innumerable multitudes that, having no motive of desire, or determination of will, lie freezing in perpetual inactivity, till some external impulse puts them in motion; who awake in the morning, vacant of thought, with minds gaping for the intellectual food, which some kind essayist has been accustomed to supply; I am moved by the commiseration with which all human beings ought to behold the distresses of each other, to try some expedients for their relief, and to inquire by what methods the listless may be actuated, and the empty be replenished.

There are said to be pleasures in madness known only to madmen. There are certainly miseries in idleness, which the Idler only can conceive. These miseries I have often felt and often bewailed. I know by experience, how welcome is every avocation that summons the thoughts to a new image; and how much languor and lassitude are relieved by that officiousness which offers a momentary amusement to him who is unable to find it for himself.

It is naturally indifferent to this race of men what entertainment they receive, so they are but entertained. They catch, with equal eagerness, at a moral lecture, or the memoirs of a robber; a prediction of the appearance of a comet, or the calculation of the chances of a lottery.

They might therefore easily be pleased, if they consulted only their own minds; but those who will not take the trouble to think for themselves, have always somebody that thinks for them; and the difficulty in writing is to please those from whom others learn to be pleased.

Much mischief is done in the world with very little interest or design. He that assumes the character of a critick, and justifies his claim by perpetual censure, imagines that he is hurting none but the author, and him he considers as a pestilent animal, whom every other being has a right to persecute; little does he think how many harmless men he involves in his own guilt, by teaching them to be noxious without malignity, and to repeat objections which they do not understand; or how many honest minds he debars from pleasure, by exciting an artificial fastidiousness, and making them too wise to concur with their own sensations. He who is taught by a critick to dislike that which pleased him in his natural state, has the same reason to complain of his instructor, as the madman to rail at his doctor, who, when he thought himself master of Peru, physicked him to poverty.

If men will struggle against their own advantage, they are not to expect that the Idler will take much pains upon them; he has himself to please as well as them, and has long learned, or endeavoured to learn, not to make the pleasure of others too necessary to his own.

Numb. 4. Saturday, *May* 6, 1758.

Πάντας γὰρ φιλέεσκε. Hom.

CHARITY, or tenderness for the poor, which is now justly considered, by a great part of mankind, as inseparable from piety, and in which almost all the goodness of the present age consists, is, I think, known only to those who enjoy, either immediately or by transmission, the light of revelation.

Those ancient nations who have given us the wisest models of government, and the brightest examples of patriotism, whose institutions have been transcribed by all succeeding legislatures, and whose history is studied by every candidate for political or military reputation, have yet left behind them no mention of alms-houses or hospitals, of places where age might repose, or sickness be relieved.

The Roman emperors, indeed, gave large donatives to the citizens and soldiers, but these distributions were always reckoned rather popular than virtuous: nothing more was intended than an ostentation of liberality, nor was any recompence expected, but suffrages and acclamations.

Their beneficence was merely occasional; he that ceased to need the favour of the people, ceased likewise to court it; and, therefore, no man thought it either necessary or wise to make any standing provision for the needy, to look forwards to the wants of posterity, or to secure successions of charity, for successions of distress.

Compassion is by some reasoners, on whom the name of philosophers has been too easily conferred, resolved into an affection merely selfish, an involuntary perception of pain at the involuntary sight of a being like ourselves languishing in misery. But this sensation, if ever it be felt at all from the brute instinct of uninstructed nature, will only produce effects desultory and transient; it will never settle into a principle of action, or extend relief to calamities unseen, in generations not yet in being.

The devotion of life or fortune to the succour of the poor, is a height of virtue, to which humanity has never risen by its own power. The charity of the Mahometans is a precept which their teacher evidently transplanted from the doctrines of Christianity; and the care with which some of the Oriental sects attend, as is said, to the necessities of the diseased and indigent, may be added to the other arguments, which prove Zoroaster to have borrowed his institutions from the law of Moses.

The present age, though not likely to shine hereafter among the most splendid periods of history, has yet given examples of charity, which may be very properly recommended to imitation. The equal distribution of wealth, which long commerce has produced, does not enable any single hand to raise edifices of piety like fortified cities, to appropriate manors to religious uses, or deal out such large and lasting beneficence as was scattered over the land in ancient times, by those who possessed counties or provinces. But no sooner is a new species of misery

brought to view, and a design of relieving it professed, than every hand is open to contribute something,
every tongue is busied in solicitation, and every art of
pleasure is employed for a time in the interest of
virtue.

The most apparent and pressing miseries incident
to man, have now their peculiar houses of reception
and relief; and there are few among us, raised bowever
little above the danger of poverty, who may not justly
claim, what is implored by the Mahometans in their
most ardent benedictions, the prayers of the poor.

Among those actions which the mind can most
securely review with unabated pleasure, is that of
having contributed to an hospital for the sick. Of
some kinds of charity the consequences are dubious:
some evils which beneficence has been busy to remedy,
are not certainly known to be very grievous to the
sufferer, or detrimental to the community; but no
man can question whether wounds and sickness are
not really painful; whether it be not worthy of a
good man's care to restore those to ease and usefulness, from whose labour infants and women expect
their bread, and who, by a casual hurt, or lingering
disease, lie pining in want and anguish, burthen-
some to others, and weary of themselves.

Yet as the hospitals of the present time subsist
only by gifts bestowed at pleasure, without any
solid fund of support, there is danger lest the blaze
of charity, which now burns with so much heat and
splendor, should die away for want of lasting fuel:
lest fashion should suddenly withdraw her smile,
and inconstancy transfer the publick attention to

something which may appear more eligible, because it will be new.

Whatever is left in the hands of chance must be subject to vicissitude; and when any establishment is found to be useful, it ought to be the next care to make it permanent.

But man is a transitory being, and his designs must partake of the imperfections of their author. To confer duration is not always in our power. We must snatch the present moment, and employ it well, without too much solicitude for the future, and content ourselves with reflecting that our part is performed. He that waits for an opportunity to do much at once, may breathe out his life in idle wishes, and regret, in the last hour, his useless intentions, and barren zeal.

The most active promoters of the present schemes of charity cannot be cleared from some instances of misconduct, which may awaken contempt or censure, and hasten that neglect which is likely to come too soon of itself. The open competitions between different hospitals, and the animosity with which their patrons oppose one another, may prejudice weak minds against them all. For it will not be easily believed, that any man can, for good reasons, wish to exclude another from doing good. The spirit of charity can only be continued by a reconciliation of these ridiculous feuds; and therefore, instead of contentions who shall be the only benefactors to the needy, let there be no other struggle than who shall be the first.

NUMB. 5.   SATURDAY, *May* 13, 1758.

Κάλλος
'Αντ' ἐγκίων ἀπάντων
'Αντ' ἀσπίδων ἀπασῶν.   ANAC.

Our military operations are at last begun; our troops are marching in all the pomp of war, and a camp is marked out on the Isle of Wight; the heart of every Englishman now swells with confidence, though somewhat softened by generous compassion for the consternation and distresses of our enemies.

This formidable armament and splendid march produce different effects upon different minds, according to the boundless diversities of temper, occupation, and habits of thought.

Many a tender maiden considers her lover as already lost, because he cannot reach the camp but by crossing the sea; men of a more political understanding are persuaded that we shall now see, in a few days, the ambassadors of France supplicating for pity. Some are hoping for a bloody battle, because a bloody battle makes a vendible narrative; some are composing songs of victory; some planning arches of triumph; and some are mixing fireworks for the celebration of a peace.

Of all extensive and complicated objects different parts are selected by different eyes; and minds are variously affected, as they vary their attention. The care of the publick is now fixed upon our soldiers, who are leaving their native country to wander, none can tell how long, in the pathless desarts of the Isle of Wight. The tender sigh for their sufferings, and the gay drink to their success. I, who look, or believe myself to look, with more philosophic eyes on human affairs, must confess, that I saw the troops march with little emotion; my thoughts were fixed upon other scenes, and the tear stole into my eyes, not for those who were going away, but for those who were left behind.

We have no reason to doubt but our troops will proceed with proper caution; there are men among them who can take care of themselves. But how shall the ladies endure without them? By what arts can they, who have long had no joy but from the civilities of a soldier, now amuse their hours, and solace their separation?

Of fifty thousand men, now destined to different stations, if we allow each to have been occasionally necessary only to four women, a short computation will inform us, that two hundred thousand ladies are left to languish in distress; two hundred thousand ladies, who must run to sales and auctions without an attendant; sit at the play, without a critick to direct their opinion; buy their fans by their own judgment; dispose shells by their own invention; walk in the Mall without a gallant; go to the gardens without a protector; and shuffle cards with vain impatience, for want of a fourth to complete the party.

Of these ladies, some, I hope, have lap-dogs, and some monkies; but they are unsatisfactory companions. Many useful offices are performed by men of scarlet, to which neither dog nor monkey has adequate abilities. A parrot, indeed, is as fine as a colonel, and, if he has been much used to good company, is not wholly without conversation; but a parrot, after all, is a poor little creature, and has neither sword nor shoulder-knot, can neither dance nor play cards.

Since the soldiers must obey the call of their duty, and go to that side of the kingdom which faces France, I know not why the ladies, who cannot live without them, should not follow them. The prejudices and pride of man have long presumed the sword and spindle made for different hands, and denied the other sex to partake the grandeur of military glory. This notion may be consistently enough received in France, where the salick law excludes females from the throne; but we, who allow them to be sovereigns, may surely suppose them capable to be soldiers.

It were to be wished that some man, whose experience and authority might enforce regard, would propose that our encampments for the present year should comprise an equal number of men and women, who should march and fight in mingled bodies. If proper colonels were once appointed, and the drums ordered to beat for female volunteers, our regiments would soon be filled without the reproach or cruelty of an impress.

Of these heroines, some might serve on foot under the denomination of the *Female Buffs*, and some on horseback, with the title of *Lady Hussars*.

What objections can be made to this scheme I have endeavoured maturely to consider; and cannot find that a modern soldier has any duties, except that of obedience, which a lady cannot perform. If the hair has lost its powder, a lady has a puff; if a coat be spotted, a lady has a brush. Strength is of less importance since fire-arms have been used; blows of the hand are now seldom exchanged; and what is there to be done in the charge or the retreat beyond the powers of a sprightly maiden?

Our masculine squadrons will not suppose themselves disgraced by their auxiliaries, till they have done something which women could not have done. The troops of Braddock never saw their enemies, and perhaps were defeated by women. If our American general had headed an army of girls, he might still have built a fort and taken it. Had Minorca been defended by a female garrison, it might have been surrendered, as it was, without a breach; and I cannot but think, that seven thousand women might have ventured to look at Rochfort. sack a village, rob a vineyard, and return in safety.

NUMB. 6. SATURDAY, *May* 20, 1758.

Ταμεῖον ἀρετῆς γεναία γυνή.   GR. PRO.

THE lady who had undertaken to ride on one horse a thousand miles in a thousand hours, has completed her journey in little more than two-thirds of the time stipulated, and was conducted through the last mile with triumphal honours. Acclamation shouted before her, and all the flowers of the spring were scattered in her way.

Every heart ought to rejoice when true merit is distinguished with public notice. I am far from wishing either to the amazon or her horse any diminution of happiness or fame, and cannot but lament that they were not more amply and suitably rewarded.

There was once a time when wreaths of bays or oak were considered as recompences equal to the most wearisome labours and terrific dangers, and when the miseries of long marches and stormy seas were at once driven from the remembrance by the fragrance of a garland.

If this heroine had been born in ancient times, she might perhaps have been delighted with the simplicity of ancient gratitude ; or if any thing was wanting to full satisfaction, she might have supplied the deficiency with the hope of deification, and anticipated the altars that would be raised, and the vows that would be made, by future candidates for equestrian glory, to the patroness of the race and the goddess of the stable.

But fate reserved her for a more enlightened age,

which has discovered leaves and flowers to be transitory things; which considers profit as the end of honour; and rates the event of every undertaking only by the money that is gained or lost. In these days, to strew the road with daisies and lilies, is to mock merit, and delude hope. The toyman will not give his jewels, nor the mercer measure out his silks, for vegetable coin. A primrose, though picked up under the feet of the most renowned courser, will neither be received as a stake at cards, nor procure a seat at an opera, nor buy candles for a rout, nor lace for a livery. And though there are many virtuosos, whose sole ambition is to possess something which can be found in no other hand, yet some are more accustomed to store their cabinets by theft than purchase, and none of them would either steal or buy one of the flowers of gratulation till he knows that all the rest are totally destroyed.

Little therefore did it avail this wonderful lady to be received, however joyfully, with such obsolete and barren ceremonies of praise. Had the way been covered with guineas, though but for the tenth part of the last mile, she would have considered her skill and diligence as not wholly lost; and might have rejoiced in the speed and perseverance which had left her such superfluity of time, that she could at leisure gather her reward without the danger of Atalanta's miscarriage.

So much ground could not indeed have been paved with gold but at a large expence, and we are at present engaged in a war, which demands and enforces frugality. But common rules are made only for common life, and some deviation from general policy may be allowed in favour of a lady that rode a thousand miles in a thousand hours.

Since the spirit of antiquity so much prevails amongst us, that even on this great occasion we have given flowers instead of money, let us at least complete our imitation of the ancients, and endeavour to transmit to posterity the memory of that virtue, which we consider as superior to pecuniary recompence. Let an equestrian statue of this heroine be erected, near the starting-post on the heath of Newmarket, to fill kindred souls with emulation, and tell the grand-daughters of our grand-daughters what an English maiden has once performed.

. As events, however illustrious, are soon obscured if they are intrusted to tradition, I think it necessary, that the pedestal should be inscribed with a concise account of this great performance. The composition of this narrative ought not to be committed rashly to improper hands. If the rhetoricians of Newmarket, who may be supposed likely to conceive in its full strength the dignity of the subject, should undertake to express it, there is danger lest they admit some phrases which, though well understood at present, may be ambiguous in another century. If posterity should read on a public monument, that *the lady carried her horse a thousand miles in a thousand hours*, they may think that the statue and inscription are at variance, because one will represent the horse as carrying his lady, and the other tell that the lady carried her horse.

Some doubts likewise may be raised by speculatists,

and some controversies be agitated among historians, concerning the motive as well as the manner of the action. As it will be known, that this wonder was performed in a time of war, some will suppose that the lady was frighted by invaders, and fled to preserve her life or her chastity : others will conjecture, that she was thus honoured for some intelligence carried of the enemy's designs : some will think that she brought news of a victory ; others, that she was commissioned to tell of a conspiracy ; and some will congratulate themselves on their acuter penetration, and find, that all these notions of patriotism and publick spirit are improbable and chimerical ; they will confidently tell, that she only ran away from her guardians, and that the true causes of her speed were fear and love.

. Let it therefore be carefully mentioned, that by this performance *she won her wager ;* and, lest this should, by any change of manners, seem an inadequate or incredible incitement, let it be added, that at this time the original motives of human actions had lost their influence ; that the love of praise was extinct ; the fear of infamy was become ridiculous; and the only wish of an Englishman was, *to win his wager.**

* The incident, so pleasingly ridiculed in this paper, happened in 1758; and the newspapers of the time gave it due importance . C.

NUMB. 7. SATURDAY, *May* 27, 1758.

ONE of the principal amusements of the *Idler* is to read the works of those minute historians the writers of news, who, though contemptuously over-looked by the composers of bulky volumes, are yet necessary in a nation where much wealth produces much leisure, and one part of the people has nothing to do but to observe the lives and fortunes of the other.

To us, who are regaled every morning and evening with intelligence, and are supplied from day to day with materials for conversation, it is difficult to conceive how man can subsist without a newspaper, or to what entertainment companies can assemble, in those wide regions of the earth that have neither *Chronicles* nor *Magazines,* neither *Gazettes* nor *Advertisers,* neither *Journals* nor *Evening Posts.*

There are never great numbers in any nation, whose reason or invention can find employment for their tongues, who can raise a pleasing discourse from their own stock of sentiments and images ; and those few who have qualified themselves by speculation for general disquisitions are soon left without an audience. The common talk of men must relate to facts in which the talkers have, or think they have, an interest ; and where such facts cannot be known, the pleasures of society will be merely sensual. Thus the natives of the Mahometan empires, who approach most nearly to European civility, have no higher pleasure at their convivial assemblies than to bear a piper, or gaze upon a tumbler, and no company can keep together longer than they are diverted by sounds or shows.

All foreigners remark, that the knowledge of the common people of England is greater than that of any other vulgar. This superiority we undoubtedly owe to the rivulets of intelligence, which are continually trickling among us, which every one may catch, and of which every one partakes.

This universal diffusion of instruction is, perhaps, not wholly without its inconveniences; it certainly fills the nation with superficial disputants; enables those to talk who were born to work; and affords information sufficient to elate vanity, and stiffen obstinacy, but too little to enlarge the mind into compléte skill for full comprehension.

Whatever is found to gratify the publick, will be multiplied by the emulation of venders beyond necessity or use. This plenty indeed produces cheapness, but cheapness always ends in negligence and depravation.

The compilation of newspapers is often committed to narrow and mercenary minds, not qualified for the task of delighting or instructing; who are content to fill their paper, with whatever matter, without industry to gather, or discernment to select.

Thus journals are daily multiplied without increase of knowledge. The tale of the morning paper is told again in the evening, and the narratives of the evening are bought again in the morning. These repetitions, indeed, waste time, but they do not shorten it. The most eager peruser of news is tired before he has completed his labour;

and many a man, who enters the coffee-house in his night-gown and slippers, is called away to his shop, or his dinner, before he has well considered the state of Europe.

It is discovered by Reaumur, that spiders might make silk, if they could be persuaded to live in peace together. The writers of news, if they could be confederated, might give more pleasure to the publick. The morning and evening authors might divide an event between them; a single action, and that not of much importance, might be gradually discovered, so as to vary a whole week with joy, anxiety, and conjecture.

We know that a French ship of war was lately taken by a ship of England; but this event was suffered to burst upon us all at once, and then what we knew already was echoed from day to day, and from week to week.

Let us suppose these spiders of literature to spin together, and enquire to what an extensive web such another event might be regularly drawn, and how six morning and six evening writers might agree to retail their articles.

On *Monday Morning* the Captain of a ship might arrive, who left the *Friseur* of *France*, and the *Bull-dog*, Captain *Grim*, in sight of one another, so that an engagement seemed unavoidable.

Monday Evening. A sound of cannon was heard off Cape Finisterre, supposed to be those of the Bull-dog and Friseur.

Tuesday Morning. It was this morning reported that the Bull-dog engaged the Friseur, yard-arm and yard-arm, three glasses and a half, but was obliged to sheer off for want of powder. It is hoped that enquiry will be made into this affair in a proper place.

Tuesday Evening. The account of the engagement between the Bull-dog and Friseur was premature.

Wednesday Morning. Another express is arrived, which brings news, that the Friseur had lost all her masts, and three hundred of her men, in the late engagement; and that Captain Grim is come into harbour much shattered.

Wednesday Evening. We hear that the brave Captain Grim, having expended his powder, proposed to enter the Friseur sword in hand; but that his lieutenant, the nephew of a certain nobleman, remonstrated against it.

Thursday Morning. We wait impatiently for a full account of the late engagement between the Bull-dog and Friseur.

Thursday Evening. It is said the order of the Bath will be sent to Captain Grim.

Friday Morning. A certain Lord of the Admiralty has been heard to say of a certain Captain, that if he had done his duty, a certain French ship might have been taken. It was not thus that merit was rewarded in the days of Cromwell.

Friday Evening. There is certain information at the Admiralty, that the Friseur is taken, after a resistance of two hours.

Saturday Morning. A letter from one of the gunners of the Bull-dog mentions the taking of the Friseur, and attributes their success wholly to the bravery and resolution of Captain Grim, who never owed any of his advancement to borough-jobbers, or any other corrupters of the people.

Saturday Evening. Captain Grim arrived at the Admiralty, with an account that he engaged the Friseur, a ship of equal force with his own, off Cape Finisterre, and took her after an obstinate resistance, having killed one hundred and fifty of the French, with the loss of ninety-five of his own men.

NUMB. 8. SATURDAY, *June 3*, 1758.

TO THE IDLER.

SIR,

IN the time of public danger, it is every man's duty to withdraw his thoughts in some measure from his private interest, and employ part of his time for the general welfare. National conduct ought to be the result of national wisdom, a plan formed by mature consideration and diligent selection out of all the schemes which may be offered, and all the information which can be procured.

In a battle, every man should fight as if he was the single champion; in preparations for war, every man should think, as if the last event depended on his counsel. None can tell what discoveries are within his reach, or how much he may contribute to the public safety.

Full of these considerations, I have carefully reviewed the process of the war, and find, what every other man has found, that we have hitherto added nothing to our military reputation : that at one time we have been beaten by enemies whom we did not see ; and, at another, have avoided the sight of enemies lest we should be beaten.

Whether our troops are defective in discipline or in courage, is not very useful to enquire; they evidently want something necessary to success ; and he that shall supply that want will deserve well of his country.

To learn of an enemy has always been accounted politick and honourable ; and therefore I hope it will raise no prejudices against my project, to confess that I borrowed it from a Frenchman.

When the Isle of Rhodes was, many centuries ago, in the hands of that military order now called the Knights of Malta, it was ravaged by a dragon, who inhabited a den under a rock, from which he issued forth when he was hungry or wanton, and without fear or mercy devoured men and beasts as they came in his way. Many councils were held, and many devices offered, for his destruction ; but as his back was armed with impenetrable scales, none would venture to attack him. At last Dudon, a French knight, undertook the deliverance of the island. From some place of security, he took a view of the dragon, or, as a modern soldier would say, *reconnoitred* him, and observed that his belly was naked and vulnerable. He then returned home to make his *arrangements* ; and, by a very exact imitation of nature, made a dragon of pasteboard, in the belly of which he put beef and mutton, and accustomed two sturdy mastiffs to feed themselves by tearing their way to the concealed flesh. When his dogs were well practised in this method of plunder, he marched out with them at his heels, and shewed them the dragon; they rushed upon him in quest of their dinner; Dudon battered his scull, while they lacerated his belly; and neither his sting nor claws were able to defend him.

Something like this might be practised in our present state. Let a fortification be raised on Salisbury Plain, resembling Brest, or Toulon, or Paris itself, with all the usual preparation for defence; let the inclosure be filled with beef and ale: let the soldiers, from some proper eminence, see shirts waving upon lines, and here and there a plump landlady hurrying about with pots in her hands. When they are sufficiently animated to advance, lead them in exact order, with fife and drum, to that side whence the wind blows, till they come within the scent of roast meat and tobacco. Contrive that they may approach the place fasting about an hour after dinner-time, assure them that there is no danger, and command an attack.

If nobody within either moves or speaks, it is not unlikely that they may carry the place by storm; but if a panick should seize them, it will be proper to defer the enterprize to a more hungry hour. When they have entered, let them fill their bellies and return to the camp.

On the next day let the same place be shewn them again, but with some additions of strength or terror. I cannot pretend to inform our generals through what gradations of danger they should train their men to fortitude. They best know what the soldiers and what themselves can bear. It will be proper that the war should every day vary its appearance. Sometimes, as they mount the rampart, a cook may throw fat upon the fire, to accustom them to a sudden blaze ; and sometimes, by the clatter of empty pots, they may be inured to formidable noises. But let it never be forgotten, that victory must repose with a full belly.

In time it will be proper to bring our French prisoners from the coast, and place them upon the walls in martial order. At their first appearance their hands must be tied, but they may be allowed to grin. In a month they may guard the place with their hands loosed, provided that on pain of death they be forbidden to strike.

By this method our army will soon be brought to look an enemy in the face. But it has been lately observed, that fear is received by the ear as well as the eyes; and the Indian war-cry is represented as too dreadful to be endured ; as a sound that will force the bravest veteran to drop his weapon, and desert his rank ; that will deafen his ear, and chill his breast ; that will neither suffer him to hear orders or to feel shame, or retain any sensibility but the dread of death.

That the savage clamours of naked barbarians should thus terrify troops disciplined to war, and ranged in array with arms in their hands, is surely strange. But this is no time to reason. I am of opinion, that by a proper mixture of asses, bulls, turkeys, geese, and tragedians, a noise might be procured equally horrid with the war-cry. When our men have been encouraged by frequent victories, nothing will remain but to qualify them for extreme danger, by a sudden concert of terrific vociferation. When they have endured this last trial, let them be led to action, as men who are no longer to be frightened ; as men who can bear at once the grimaces of the Gauls, and the howl of the Americans.

NUMB. 9. SATURDAY, *June* 10, 1758.

TO THE IDLER.

SIR,

I HAVE read you ; that is a favour few authors can boast of having received from me besides yourself. My intention in telling you of it is to inform you, that you have both pleased and angered me. Never did writer appear so delightful to me as you did when you adopted the name of the *Idler*. But what a falling-off was there when your first production was brought to light ! A natural irresistible attachment to that favourable passion, *idling*, had led me to hope for indulgence from the *Idler*, but I find him a stranger to the title.

What rules has he proposed totally to unbrace the slackened nerve ; to shade the heavy eye of inattention ; to give the smooth feature and the uncontracted muscle ; or procure insensibility to the whole animal composition ?

These were some of the placid blessings I promised myself the enjoyment of, when I committed violence upon myself by mustering up all my strength to set about reading you ; but I am disappointed in them

all, and the stroke of eleven in the morning is still as
terrible to me as before, and I find putting on my
clothes still as painful and laborious.   Oh that our
climate would permit that original nakedness which
the thrice happy Indians to this day enjoy! How
many unsolicitous hours should I bask away, warmed
in bed by the sun's glorious beams, could I, like them
tumble from thence in a moment, when necessity
obliges me to endure the torment of getting upon my
legs.

But wherefore do I talk to you upon subjects of
this delicate nature? you who seem ignorant of the
inexpressible charms of the elbow-chair, attended
with a soft stool for the elevation of the feet! Thus,
vacant of thought, do I indulge the live-long day.

You may define happiness as you please; I em-
brace that opinion which makes it consist in the absence of pain.   To reflect is pain; to stir is pain;
therefore I never reflect or stir but when I cannot
help it.   Perhaps you will call my scheme of life indolence, and therefore think the *Idler* excused from
taking any notice of me; but I have always looked
upon indolence and idleness as the same; and so desire you will now and then, while you profess yourself of our fraternity, take some notice of me, and
others in my situation, who think they have a right
to your assistance; or relinquish the name.

You may publish, burn, or destroy this, just as
you are in the humour; it is ten to one but I forget
that I wrote it, before it reaches you.   I believe you
may find a motto for it in Horace, but I cannot
reach him without getting out of my chair; that is

a sufficient reason for my not affixing any.——And
being obliged to sit upright to ring the bell for my
servant to convey this to the penny-post, if I slip
the opportunity of his being now in the room, makes
me break off abruptly.*

THIS correspondent, whoever he be, is not to be
dismissed without some tokens of regard.   There is
no mark more certain of a genuine Idler, than uneasiness without molestation, and complaint without
a grievance.

Yet my gratitude to the contributor of half a paper shall not wholly overpower my sincerity.   I must
inform you, that, with all his pretensions, he that
calls for directions to be idle, is yet but in the rudi-
ments of idleness, and has attained neither the practice nor theory of wasting life.   The true nature of
idleness he will know in time, by continuing to be
idle.   Virgil tells us of an impetuous and rapid being, that acquires strength by motion.   The Idler
acquires weight by lying still.

The *vis inertiæ,* the quality of resisting all external impulses, is hourly increasing; the restless and
troublesome faculties of attention and distinction, reflection on the past, and solicitude for the future, by
a long indulgence of idleness, will, like tapers in un-
elastic air, be gradually extinguished; and the officious lover, the vigilant soldier, the busy trader, may,
by a judicious composure of his mind, sink into a
state approaching to that of brute matter; in which

* By an unknown correspondent.   C.

he shall retain the consciousness of his own existence, only by an obtuse languor and drowsy discontent.

This is the lowest stage to which the favourites of idleness can descend; these regions of undelighted quiet can be entered by few. Of those that are prepared to sink down into their shade, some are roused into action by avarice or ambition, some are awakened by the voice of fame, some allured by the smile of beauty, and many withheld by the importunities of want. Of all the enemies of idleness, want is the most formidable. Fame is soon found to be a sound, and love a dream; avarice and ambition may be justly suspected of privy confederacies with idleness; for when they have for a while protected their votaries, they often deliver them up to end their lives under her dominion. Want always struggles against idleness, but Want herself is often overcome; and every hour shews the careful observer those who had rather live in ease than in plenty.

So wide is the region of Idleness, and so powerful her influence. But she does not immediately confer all her gifts. My correspondent, who seems, with all his errors, worthy of advice, must be told, that he is calling too hastily for the last effusion of total insensibility. Whatever he may have been taught by unskilful Idlers to believe, labour is necessary in his initiation to idleness. He that never labours may know the pains of idleness, but not the pleasure. The comfort is, that if he devotes himself to insensibility, he will daily lengthen the intervals of idleness, and shorten those of labour, till at last he will lie down to rest, and no longer disturb the world or himself by bustle or competition.

Thus I have endeavoured to give him that information which, perhaps, after all, he did not want; for a true Idler often calls for that which he knows is never to be had, and asks questions which he does not desire ever to be answered.

NUMB. 10.   SATURDAY, *June* 17, 1758.

CREDULITY, or confidence of opinion too great for the evidence from which opinion is derived, we find to be a general weakness imputed by every sect and party to all others, and indeed by every man to every other man.

Of all kinds of credulity, the most obstinate and wonderful is that of political zealots; of men, who being numbered, they know not how or why, in any of the parties that divide a state, resign the use of their own eyes and ears, and resolve to believe nothing that does not favour those whom they profess to follow.

The bigot of philosophy is seduced by authorities which he has not always opportunities to examine, is entangled in systems by which truth and falsehood are inextricably complicated, or undertakes to talk on subjects which nature did not form him able to comprehend.

The Cartesian, who denies that his horse feels the spur, or that the hare is afraid when the hounds approach her; the disciple of Malbranche, who maintains that the man was not hurt by the bullet, which, according to vulgar apprehension, swept away his legs; the follower of Berkeley, who while he sits writing at his table, declares that he has neither table, paper, nor fingers; have all the honour at least of being deceived by fallacies not easily detected, and may plead that they did not forsake truth, but for appearances which they were not able to distinguish from it.

But the man who engages in a party has seldom to do with any thing remote or abstruse. The present state of things is before his eyes; and, if he cannot be satisfied without retrospection, yet he seldom extends his views beyond the historical events of the last century. All the knowledge that he can want is within his attainment, and most of the arguments which he can hear are within his capacity.

Yet so it is that an Idler meets every hour of his life with men who have different opinions upon every thing past, present, and future; who deny the most notorious facts, contradict the most cogent truths, and persist in asserting to-day what they asserted yesterday, in defiance of evidence, and contempt of confutation.

Two of my companions, who are grown old in idleness, are Tom Tempest and Jack Sneaker. Both of them consider themselves as neglected by their parties, and therefore entitled to credit; for why should they favour ingratitude? They are both men of integrity, where no factious interest is to be promoted; and both lovers of truth, when they are not heated with political debate.

Tom Tempest is a steady friend to the house of Stuart. He can recount the prodigies that have appeared in the sky, and the calamities that have afflicted the nation every year from the Revolution ; and is of opinion, that, if the exiled family had continued to reign, there would have neither been worms in our ships nor caterpillars in our trees. He wonders that the nation was not awakened by the hard frost to a revocation of the true king, and is hourly afraid that the whole island will be lost in the sea. He believes that king William burned Whitehall that he might steal the furniture ; and that Tillotson died an atheist. Of queen Anne he speaks with more tenderness, owns that she meant well, and can tell by whom and why she was poisoned. In the succeeding reigns all has been corruption, malice and design. He believes that nothing ill has ever happened for these forty years by chance or error ; he holds that the battle of Dettingen was won by mistake, and that of Fontenoy lost by contract ; that the Victory was sunk by a private order ; that Cornhill was fired by emissaries from the council ; and the arch of Westminster-bridge was so contrived as to sink on purpose that the nation might be put to charge. He considers the new road to Islington as an encroachment on liberty, and often asserts that *broad wheels* will be the ruin of England.

Tom is generally vehement and noisy, but nevertheless has some secrets which he always communicates in a whisper. Many and many a time has Tom told me, in a corner, that our miseries were almost at an end, and that we should see, in a month, another monarch on the throne ; the time elapses without a revolution ; Tom meets me again with new intelligence, the whole scheme is now settled, and we shall see great events in another month.

Jack Sneaker is an hearty adherent to the present establishment; he has known those who saw the bed into which the Pretender was conveyed in a warming-pan. He often rejoices, that the nation was not enslaved by the Irish. He believes that king William never lost a battle, and that if he had lived one year longer he would have conquered France. He holds that Charles the First was a Papist. He allows there were some good men in the reign of queen Anne, but the peace of Utrecht brought a blast upon the nation, and has been the cause of all the evil that we have suffered to the present hour. He believes that the scheme of the South Sea was well intended, but that it miscarried by the influence of France. He considers a standing army as the bulwark of liberty, thinks us secured from corruption by septennial parliaments, relates how we are enriched and strengthened by the electoral dominions, and declares that the publick debt is a blessing to the nation.

Yet amidst all this prosperity, poor Jack is hourly disturbed by the dread of Popery. He wonders that some stricter laws are not made against Papists, and is sometimes afraid that they are busy with French gold among the bishops and judges.

He cannot believe that the Nonjurors are so quiet for nothing, they must certainly be forming some plot for the establishment of Popery; he does not think the present oaths sufficiently binding, and wishes that some better security could be found for the succession of Hanover. He is zealous for the naturalization of foreign Protestants, and rejoiced at the admission of the Jews to the English privileges, because he thought a Jew would never be a Papist.

NUMB. 11.   SATURDAY, *June* 24, 1758.

IT is commonly observed, that when two Englishmen meet, their first talk is of the weather; they are in haste to tell each other, what each must already know, that it is hot or cold, bright or cloudy, windy or calm.

There are, among the numerous lovers of subtilties and paradoxes, some who derive the civil institutions of every country from its climate, who impute freedom and slavery to the temperature of the air, can fix the meridian of vice and virtue, and tell at what degree of latitude we are to expect courage or timidity, knowledge or ignorance.

From these dreams of idle speculation, a slight survey of life, and a little knowledge of history, is sufficient to awaken any inquirer, whose ambition of distinction has not overpowered his love of truth. Forms of government are seldom the result of much deliberation; they are framed by chance in popular assemblies, or in conquered countries by despotick authority. Laws are often occasional, often capricious, made always by a few, and sometimes by a single voice. Nations have changed their characters; slavery is now no where more patiently endured, than in countries once inhabited by the zealots of liberty.

But national customs can arise only from general agreement; they are not imposed, but chosen, and are continued only by the continuance of their cause. An Englishman's notice of the weather is the natural consequence of changeable skies and uncertain seasons. In many parts of the world, wet weather and dry are regularly expected at certain periods; but in our island every man goes to sleep, unable to guess whether he shall behold in the morning a bright or cloudy atmosphere, whether his rest shall be lulled by a shower, or broken by a tempest. We therefore rejoice mutually at good weather, as at an escape from something that we feared; and mutually complain of bad, as of the loss of something that we hoped.

Such is the reason of our practice; and who shall treat it with contempt? Surely not the attendant on a court, whose business is to watch the looks of a being weak and foolish as himself, and whose vanity is to recount the names of men, who might drop into nothing, and leave no vacuity; nor the proprietor of funds, who stops his acquaintance in the street to tell him of the loss of half-a-crown; nor the inquirer after news, who fills his head with foreign events, and talks of skirmishes and sieges, of which no consequence will ever reach his hearers or himself. The weather is a nobler and more interesting subject; it is the present state of the skies and of the earth, on which plenty and famine are suspended, on which millions depend for the necessaries of life.

The weather is frequently mentioned for another reason, less honourable to my dear countrymen. Our dispositions too frequently change with the colour of the sky; and when we find ourselves cheerful and good-natured, we naturally pay our acknowledgments to the powers of sunshine; or, if we sink into dulness and peevishness, look round the horizon for an excuse, and charge our discontent upon an easterly wind or a cloudy day.

Surely nothing is more reproachful to a being endowed with reason, than to resign its powers to the influence of the air, and live in dependence on the weather and the wind, for the only blessings which nature has put into our power, tranquillity and benevolence. To look up to the sky for the nutriment of our bodies, is the condition of nature; to call upon the sun for peace and gaiety, or deprecate the clouds lest sorrow should overwhelm us, is the cowardice of idleness, and the idolatry of folly.

Yet even in this age of inquiry and knowledge, when superstition is driven away, and omens and prodigies have lost their terrors, we find this folly countenanced by frequent examples. Those that laugh at the portentous glare of a comet, and hear a crow with equal tranquillity from the right or left, will yet talk of times and situations proper for intellectual performances, will imagine the fancy exalted by vernal breezes, and the reason invigorated by a bright calm.

If men who have given up themselves to fanciful credulity would confine their conceits in their own minds, they might regulate their lives by the barometer, with inconvenience only to themselves; but to fill the world with accounts of intellects subject to ebb and flow, of one genius that awakened in the spring, and another that ripened in the autumn, of one mind expanded in the summer, and of another concentrated in the winter, is no less dangerous than to tell children of bugbears and goblins. Fear will find every house haunted; and idleness will wait for ever for the moment of illumination.

This distinction of seasons is produced only by imagination operating on luxury. To temperance every day is bright, and every hour is propitious to diligence. He that shall resolutely excite his faculties, or exert his virtues, will soon make himself superior to the seasons, and may set at defiance the morning mist, and the evening damp, the blasts of the east, and the clouds of the south.

It was the boast of the Stoick philosophy, to make man unshaken by calamity, and unelated by success, incorruptible by pleasure, and invulnerable by pain; these are heights of wisdom which none ever attained, and to which few can aspire; but there are lower degrees of constancy necessary to common virtue: and every man, however he may distrust himself in the extremes of good or evil, might at least struggle against the tyranny of the climate, and refuse to enslave his virtue or his reason to the most variable of all variations, the changes of the weather.

NUMB. 12.   SATURDAY, *July* 1, 1758.

THAT every man is important in his own eyes, is a position of which we all either voluntarily or unwarily at least once an hour confess the truth; and it will unavoidably follow, that every man believes himself important to the publick.

The right which this importance gives us to general notice and visible distinction, is one of those disputable privileges which we have not always courage to assert; and which we therefore suffer to lie dormant till some elation of mind, or vicissitude of fortune, incites us to declare our pretensions and enforce our demands. And hopeless as the claim of vulgar characters may seem to the supercilious and severe, there are few who do not at one time or other endeavour to step forward beyond their rank, who do not make some struggles for fame, and shew that they think all other conveniencies and delights imperfectly enjoyed without a name.

To get a name, can happen but to few. A name, even in the most commercial nation, is one of the few things which cannot be bought. It is the free gift of mankind, which must be deserved before it will be granted, and is at last unwillingly bestowed. But this unwillingness only increases desire in him who believes his merit sufficient to overcome it.

There is a particular period of life, in which this fondness for a name seems principally to predominate in both sexes. Scarce any couple comes together but the nuptials are declared in the newspapers with encomiums on each party. Many an eye, ranging over the page with eager curiosity in quest of states- men and heroes, is stopped by a marriage celebrated between Mr. Buckram, an eminent salesman in Threadneedle-street, and Miss Dolly Juniper, the only daughter of an eminent distiller, of the parish of St. Giles's in the Fields, a young lady adorned with every accomplishment that can give happiness to the married state. Or we are told, amidst our impatience for the event of a battle, that on a certain day Mr. Winker, a tide-waiter at Yarmouth, was married to Mrs. Cackle, a widow lady of great accomplishments, and that as soon as the ceremony was performed they set out in a post-chaise for Yarmouth.

Many are the inquiries which such intelligence must undoubtedly raise, but nothing in this world is lasting. When the reader has contemplated with envy, or with gladness, the felicity of Mr. Buckram and Mr. Winker, and ransacked his memory for the names of Juniper and Cackle, his attention is di- verted to other thoughts, by finding that Mirza will not cover this season ; or that a spaniel has been lost or stolen, that answers to the name of Ranger.

Whence it arises that on the day of marriage all agree to call thus openly for honours, I am not able to discover. Some, perhaps, think it kind, by a publick declaration, to put an end to the hopes of rivalry and the fears of jealousy, to let parents know that they may set their daughters at liberty whom they have locked up for fear of the bridegroom, or to dismiss to their counters and their offices the amorous youths that had been used to hover round the dwelling of the bride.

These connubial praises may have another cause. It may be the intention of the husband and wife to dignify themselves in the eyes of each other, and, according to their different tempers or expectations, to win affection, or enforce respect.

It was said of the family of Lucas, that it was *noble, for all the brothers were valiant, and all the sisters were virtuous.* What would a stranger say of the *English* nation, in which on the day of marriage all the men are *eminent,* and all the women *beautiful, accomplished,* and *rich?*

How long the wife will be persuaded of the eminence of her husband, or the husband continue to believe that his wife has the qualities required to make marriage happy, may reasonably be questioned. I am afraid that much time seldom passes before each is convinced that praises are fallacious, and particularly those praises which we confer upon ourselves.

I should therefore think, that this custom might be omitted without any loss to the community ; and that the sons and daughters of lanes and allies might go hereafter to the next church, with no witnesses of their worth or happiness but their parents and their friends ; but if they cannot be happy on the bridal day without some gratification of their vanity, I hope they will be willing to encourage a friend of mine who proposes to devote his powers to their service.

Mr. Settle, a man whose *eminence* was once allowed by the *eminent,* and whose *accomplishments* were confessed by the *accomplished,* in the latter part of a long life supported himself by an uncommon expedient. He had a standing elegy and epithalamium, of which only the first and last were leaves varied occasionally, and the intermediate pages were, by general terms, left applicable alike to every character. When any marriage became known, Settle ran to the bridegroom with his epithalamium; and when he heard of any death, ran to the heir with his elegy.

Who can think himself disgraced by a trade that was practised so long by the rival of Dryden, by the poet whose " Empress of Morocco" was played before princes by ladies of the court?

My friend purposes to open an office in the Fleet for matrimonial panegyricks, and will accommodate all with praise who think their own powers of expression inadequate to their merit. He will sell any man or woman the virtue or qualification which is most fashionable or most desired; but desires his customers to remember, that he sets beauty at the highest price, and riches at the next, and, if he be well paid, throws in virtue for nothing.

NUMB. 13. SATURDAY, *July* 8, 1758.

TO THE IDLER.

DEAR MR. IDLER,

THOUGH few men of prudence are much inclined
to interpose in disputes between man and wife, who
commonly make peace at the expence of the arbitra-
tor; yet I will venture to lay before you a controversy,
by which the quiet of my house has been long disturbed, and which, unless you can decide it, is likely
to produce lasting evils, and embitter those hours
which nature seems to have appropriated to tenderness and repose.

I married a wife with no great fortune, but of a
family remarkable for domestick prudence, and elegant frugality. I lived with her at ease, if not with
happiness, and seldom had any reason of complaint.
The house was always clean, the servants were active
and regular, dinner was on the table every day at the
same minute, and the ladies of the neighbourhood
were frightened when I invited their husbands, lest
their own economy should be less esteemed.

During this gentle lapse of life, my dear brought
me three daughters. I wished for a son, to continue
the family; but my wife often tells me, that boys
are dirty things, and are always troublesome in a
house; and declares that she has hated the sight of
them ever since she saw lady Fondle's eldest son ride
over a carpet with his hobby-horse all mire.

I did not much attend to her opinion, but knew that girls could not be made boys; and therefore composed myself to bear what I could not remedy, and resolved to bestow that care on my daughters, to which only the sons are commonly thought entitled.

But my wife's notions of education differ widely from mine. She is an irreconcileable enemy to idleness, and considers every state of life as idleness, in which the hands are not employed, or some art acquired, by which she thinks money may be got or saved.

In pursuance of this principle, she calls up her daughters at a certain hour, and appoints them a task of needle-work to be performed before breakfast. They are confined in a garret, which has its window in the roof, both because work is best done at a skylight, and because children are apt to lose time by looking about them.

They bring down their work to breakfast, and as they deserve are commended or reproved; they are then sent up with a new task till dinner; if no company is expected, their mother sits with them the whole afternoon, to direct their operations, and to draw patterns, and is sometimes denied to her nearest relations when she is engaged in teaching them a new stitch.

By this continual exercise of their diligence, she has obtained a very considerable number of laborious performances. We have twice as many fire-skreens as chimneys, and three flourished quilts for every bed. Half the rooms are adorned with a kind of *sutile pictures*, which imitate tapestry. But all their work is not set out to shew ; she has boxes filled with knit garters and braided shoes. She has twenty covers for side-saddles embroidered with silver flowers, and has curtains wrought with gold in various figures, which she resolves some time or other to hang up. All these she displays to her company whenever she is elate with merit, and eager for praise ; and amidst the praises which her friends and herself bestow upon her merit, she never fails to turn to me, and ask what all these would cost, if I had been to buy them.

I sometimes venture to tell her, that many of the ornaments are superfluous ; that what is done with so much labour might have been supplied by a very easy purchase ; that the work is not always worth the materials ; and that I know not why the children should be persecuted with useless tasks, or obliged to make shoes that are never worn. She answers with a look of contempt, that men never care how money goes, and proceeds to tell of a dozen new chairs for which she is contriving covers, and of a couch which she intends to stand as a monument of needle-work.

In the mean time, the girls grow up in total ignorance of every thing past, present, and future. Molly asked me the other day, whether Ireland was in France, and was ordered by her mother to mend her hem. Kitty knows not, at sixteen, the difference between a Protestant and a Papist, because she has been employed three years in filling the side of a closet with a hanging that is to represent Cranmer in the flames. And Dolly, my eldest girl, is now unable to read a chapter in the Bible, having spent all the time, which other children pass at school, in working the interview between Solomon and the queen of Sheba.

About a month ago, *Tent* and *Turkey*-stitch seemed at a stand; my wife knew not what new work to introduce; I ventured to propose that the girls should now learn to read and write, and mentioned the necessity of a little arithmetick; but, unhappily, my wife has discovered that linen wears out, and has bought the girls three little wheels, that they may spin hukkaback for the servants' table. I remonstrated, that with larger wheels they might dispatch in an hour what must now cost them a day; but she told me, with irresistible authority, that any business is better than idleness; that when these wheels are set upon a table, with mats under them, they will turn without noise, and keep the girls upright; that great wheels are not fit for gentlewomen; and that with these, small as they are, she does not doubt but that the three girls, if they are kept close, will spin every year as much cloth as would cost five pounds if one were to buy it.

NUMB. 14. SATURDAY, *July* 15, 1758.

WHEN Diogenes received a visit in his tub from Alexander the Great, and was asked, according to the ancient forms of royal courtesy, what petition he had to offer: "I have nothing," said he, "to ask, but that you would remove to the other side, that you may not, by intercepting the sunshine, take from me what you cannot give me."

Such was the demand of Diogenes from the greatest monarch of the earth, which those, who have less power than Alexander, may, with yet more propriety, apply to themselves. He that does much good, may be allowed to do sometimes a little harm. But if the opportunities of beneficence be denied by fortune, innocence should at least be vigilantly preserved.

It is well known, that time once past never returns; and that the moment which is lost, is lost for ever. Time therefore ought, above all other kinds of property, to be free from invasion; and yet there is no man who does not claim the power of wasting that time which is the right of others.

This usurpation is so general, that a very small part of the year is spent by choice; scarcely any thing is done when it is intended, or obtained when it is desired. Life is continually ravaged by invaders; one steals away an hour, and another a day; one conceals the robbery by hurrying us into business, another by lulling us with amusement; the depredation is continued through a thousand vicissitudes of tumult and tranquillity, till, having lost all, we can lose no more.

This waste of the lives of men has been very frequently charged upon the Great, whose followers linger from year to year in expectations, and die at last with petitions in their hands. Those who raise envy will easily incur censure. I know not whether statesmen and patrons do not suffer more reproaches than they deserve, and may not rather themselves complain, that they are given up a prey to pretensions without merit, and to importunity without shame.

The truth is, that the inconveniences of attendance are more lamented than felt. To the greater number solicitation is its own reward. To be seen in good company. to talk of familiarities with men of power, to be able to tell the freshest news, to gratify an inferior circle with predictions of increase or decline of favour, and to be regarded as a candidate for high offices, are compensations more than equivalent to the delay of favours, which perhaps he that begs them has hardly confidence to expect.

A man conspicuous in a high station, who multiplies hopes that he may multiply dependants, may be considered as a beast of prey, justly dreaded, but easily avoided; his den is known, and they who would not be devoured, need not approach it. The great danger of the waste of time is from caterpillars and moths, who are not resisted, because they are not feared, and who work on with unheeded mischiefs, and invisible encroachments.

He, whose rank or merit procures him the notice of mankind, must give up himself, in a great measure to the convenience or humour of those who surround him. Every man, who is sick of himself, will fly to him for relief; he that wants to speak will require him to hear; and he that wants to hear will expect him to speak. Hour passes after hour, the noon succeeds to morning, and the evening to noon, while a thousand objects are forced upon his attention, which he rejects as fast as they are offered, but which the custom of the world requires to be received with appearance of regard.

If we will have the kindness of others, we must endure their follies. He who cannot persuade himself to withraw from society, must be content to pay a tribute of his time to a multitude of tyrants; to the loiterer, who makes appointments which he never keeps; to the consulter, who asks advice which he never takes; to the boaster, who blusters only to be praised; to the complainer, who whines only to be pitied; to the projector, whose happiness is to entertain his friends with expectations which all but himself know to be vain; to the economist, who tells of bargains and settlements; to the politician, who predicts the fate of battles and breach of alliances; to the usurer, who compares the different funds; and to the talker, who talks only because he loves to be talking.

To put every man in possession of his own time,

and rescue the day from this succession of usurpers, is beyond my power, and beyond my hope. Yet, perhaps some stop might be put to this unmerciful persecution, if all would seriously reflect, that whoever pays a visit that is not desired, or talks longer than the hearer is willing to attend, is guilty of an injury which he cannot repair, and takes away that which he cannot give.

NUMB. 15.   SATURDAY, *July* 22, 1758.

TO THE IDLER.

SIR,

I HAVE the misfortune to be a man of business; that, you will say, is a most grievous one; but what makes it the more so to me, is, that my wife has nothing to do: at least she had too good an education, and the prospect of too good a fortune in reversion when I married her, to think of employing herself either in my shop-affairs, or the management of my family.

Her time, you know, as well as my own, must be filled up some way or other. For my part, I have enough to mind, in weighing my goods out, and waiting on my customers: but my wife, though she could be of as much use as a shopman to me, if she would put her hand to it, is now only in my

way.   She walks all the morning sauntering about
the shop with her arms through her pocket-holes, or
stands gaping at the door-sill, and looking at every
person that passes by.   She is continually asking me a
thousand frivolous questions about every customer that
comes in and goes out; and all the while that I am
entering any thing in my day-book, she is lolling over
the counter, and staring at it, as if I was only scrib-
bling or drawing figures for her amusement.   Sometimes, indeed, she will take a needle : but as she
always works at the door, or in the middle of the
shop, she has so many interruptions, that she is
longer hemming a towel, or darning a stocking, than
I am in breaking forty loaves of sugar, and making
it up into pounds.

In the afternoon I am sure likewise to have her
company, except she is called upon by some of her
acquaintance : and then, as we let out all the upper
part of our house, and have only a little room back-
wards for ourselves, they either keep such a chatter-
ing, or else are calling out every moment to me, that
I cannot mind my business for them.

My wife, I am sure, might do all the little matters
our family requires ; and I could wish that she would
employ herself in them ; but, instead of that, we
have a girl to do the work, and look after a little boy
about two years old, which I may fairly say is the
mother's own child.   The brat must be humoured in
every thing : he is therefore suffered constantly to
play in the shop, pull all the goods about, and
clamber up the shelves to get at the plums and sugar.
I dare not correct him ; because, if I did, I should

have wife and maid both upon me at once. As to the latter, she is as lazy and sluttish as her mistress; and because she complains she has too much work, we can scarcely get her to do any thing at all : nay, what is worse than that, I am afraid she is hardly honest; and as she is intrusted to buy all our provisions, the jade, I am sure, makes a market-penny out of every article.

But to return to my deary.——The evenings are the only time when it is fine weather, that I am left to myself; for then she generally takes the child out to give it milk in the park. When she comes home again, she is so fatigued with walking, that she cannot stir from her chair : and it is an hour, after shop is shut, before I can get a bit of supper, while the maid is taken up in undressing and putting the child to bed.

But you will pity me much more when I tell you the manner in which we generally pass our Sundays. In the morning she is commonly too ill to dress herself to go to church; she therefore never gets up till noon ; and what is still more vexatious, keeps me in bed with her, when I ought to be busily engaged in better employment. It is well if she can get her things on by dinner-time ; and when that is over, I am sure to be dragged out by her, either to *Georgia*, or Hornsey Wood, or the White Conduit House. Yet even these near excursions are so very fatiguing to her, that, besides what it costs me in tea and hot rolls, and syllabubs, and cakes for the boy, I am frequently forced to take a hackney-coach, or drive them out in a one-horse chair. At other times, as my wife is rather of the fattest, and a very poor walker, besides bearing her whole weight upon my arm, I am obliged to carry the child myself.

Thus, Sir, does she constantly drawl out her time, without either profit or satisfaction ; and, while I see my neighbours' wives helping in the shop, and almost earning as much as their husbands, I have the mortification to find, that mine is nothing but a dead weight upon me.   In short, I do not know any greater misfortune can happen to a plain hard-working tradesman, as I am, than to be joined to such a woman, who is rather a clog than an help-mate to him.

I am, Sir,

Your humble servant,

ZACHARY TREACLE.*

* An unknown correspondent.

NUMB. 16.   SATURDAY, *July* 29, 1758.

I PAID a visit yesterday to my old friend Ned Drugget, at his country-lodgings. Ned began trade with a very small fortune ; he took a small house in an obscure street, and for some years dealt only in remnants. Knowing that *light gains make a heavy purse,* he was content with moderate profit ; having observed or heard the effects of civility, he bowed down to the counter edge at the entrance and departure of every customer, listened without impatience to the objections of the ignorant, and refused without resentment the offers of the penurious. His only recreation was to stand at his own door and look into the street. His dinner was sent him from a neighbouring alehouse, and he opened and shut the shop at a certain hour with his own hands.

His reputation soon extended from one end of the street to the other ; and Mr. Drugget's exemplary conduct was recommended by every master to his apprentice, and by every father to his son. Ned was not only considered as a thriving trader, but as a man of elegance and politeness, for he was remarkably neat in his dress, and would wear his coat threadbare, without spotting it ; his hat was always brushed, his shoes glossy, his wig nicely curled, and his stockings without a wrinkle. With such qualifications it was not very difficult for him to gain the heart of Miss Comfit, the only daughter of Mr. Comfit the confectioner.

Ned is one of those whose happiness marriage has encreased. His wife had the same disposition with himself; and his method of life was very little changed, except that he dismissed the lodgers from the first floor, and took the whole house into his own hands.

He had already, by his parsimony, accumulated a considerable sum, to which the fortune of his wife was now added. From this time he began to grasp at greater acquisitions, and was always ready, with money in his hand, to pick up the refuse of a sale, or to buy the stock of a trader who retired from business. He soon added his parlour to his shop, and was obliged a few months afterwards to hire a warehouse.

He had now a shop splendidly and copiously furnished with every thing that time had injured, or fashion had degraded, with fragments of tissues, odd yards of brocade, vast bales of faded silk, and innumerable boxes of antiquated ribbons. His shop was soon celebrated through all quarters of the town, and frequented by every form of ostentatious poverty. Every maid, whose misfortune it was to be taller than her lady, matched her gown at Mr. Drugget's; and many a maiden, who had passed a winter with her aunt in London, dazzled the rusticks, at her return, with cheap finery which Drugget had supplied. His shop was often visited in a morning by ladies who left their coaches in the next street, and crept through the alley in linen gowns. Drugget knows the rank of his customers by their bashfulness; and when he finds them unwilling to be seen, invites them up stairs, or retires with them to the back window.

I rejoiced at the encreasing prosperity of my friend, and imagined, that as he grew rich, he was growing happy. His mind has partaken the enlargement of his fortune. When I stepped in for the first five years, I was welcomed only with a shake of the hand; in the next period of his life, he beckoned across the way for a pot of beer; but for six years past, he invites me to dinner; and if he bespeaks me the day before, never fails to regale me with a fillet of veal.

His riches neither made him uncivil nor negligent; he rose at the same hour, attended with the same assiduity, and bowed with the same gentleness. But for some years he has been much inclined to talk of the fatigues of business, and the confinement of a shop, and to wish that he had been so happy as to have renewed his uncle's lease of a farm, that he might havo lived without noise and hurry, in a pure air, in the artless society of honest villagers, and the contemplation of the works of nature.

I soon discovered the cause of my friend's philosophy. He thought himself grown rich enough to have a lodging in the country, like the mercers on Ludgate-hill, and was resolved to enjoy himself in the decline of life. This was a revolution not to be made suddenly. He talked three years of the pleasures of the country, but passed every night over his own shop. But at last he resolved to be happy, and hired a lodging in the country, that he may steal some hours in the week from business; for, says he, *when a man advances in life, he loves to entertain himself sometimes with his own thoughts.*

I was invited to this seat of quiet and contemplation among those whom Mr. Drugget considers as his most reputable friends, and desires to make the first witnesses of his elevation to the highest dignities of a shopkeeper. I found him at Islington, in a room which overlooked the high road, amusing himself with looking through the window, which the clouds of dust would not suffer him to open. He embraced me, told me I was welcome into the country, and asked me, if I did not feel myself refreshed. He then desired that dinner might be hastened, for fresh air always sharpened his appetite, and ordered me a toast and a glass of wine after my walk. He told me much of the pleasure he found in retirement, and wondered what had kept him so long out of the country. After dinner, company came in, and Mr. Drugget again repeated the praises of the country, recommended the pleasures of meditation, and told them, that he had been all the morning at the window, counting the carriages as they passed before him.

Numb. 17.   Saturday, *August* 5, 1758.

THE rainy weather, which has continued the last month, is said to have given great disturbance to the inspectors of barometers. The oraculous glasses have deceived their votaries; shower has succeeded shower, though they predicted sunshine and dry skies; and by fatal confidence in these fallacious promises, many coats have lost their gloss, and many curls been moistened to flaccidity.

This is one of the distresses to which mortals subject themselves by the pride of speculation. I had no part in this learned disappointment, who am content to credit my senses, and to believe that rain will fall when the air blackens, and that the weather will be dry when the sun is bright. My caution indeed does not always preserve me from a shower. To be wet, may happen to the genuine Idler; but to be wet in opposition to theory, can befal only the Idler that pretends to be busy. Of those that spin out life in trifles and die without a memorial, many flatter themselves with high opinions of their own importance, and imagine that they are every day adding some improvement to human life. To be idle and to be poor, have always been reproaches, and therefore every man endeavours, with his utmost care, to hide his poverty from others, and his *idleness* from himself.

Among those whom I never could persuade to rank themselves with Idlers, and who speak with indignation of my morning sleeps and nocturnal rambles; one passes the day in catching spiders, that he may count their eyes with a microscope; another erects his head, and exhibits the dust of a marigold separated from the flower with a dexterity worthy of Leeuwenhoeck himself. Some turn the wheel of electricity; some suspend rings to a load-stone, and find that what they did yesterday they can do again to-day. Some register the changes of the wind, and die fully convinced that the wind is changeable.

There are men yet more profound, who have heard that two colourless liquors may produce a colour by union, and that two cold bodies will grow hot if they are mingled; they mingle them, and produce the effect expected, say it is strange, and mingle them again.

The Idlers that sport only with inanimate nature may claim some indulgence; if they are useless, they are still innocent: but there are others, whom I know not how to mention without more emotion than my love of quiet willingly admits. Among the inferior professors of medical knowledge, is a race of wretches, whose lives are only varied by varieties of cruelty; whose favourite amusement is to nail dogs to tables and open them alive; to try how long life may be continued in various degrees of mutilation, or with the excision or laceration of the vital parts; to examine whether burning irons are felt more acutely by the bone or tendon; and whether the more lasting agonies are produced by poison forced into the mouth, or injected into the veins.

It is not without reluctance that I offend the sensibility of the tender mind with images like these. If such cruelties were not practised, it were to be desired that they should not be conceived ; but, since they are published every day with ostentation, let me be allowed once to mention them, since I mention them with abhorrence.

Mead has invidiously remarked of Woodward, that he gathered shells and stones, and would pass for a philosopher. With pretensions much less reasonable, the anatomical novice tears out the living bowels of an animal, and styles himself physician, prepares himself by familiar cruelty for that profession which he is to exercise upon the tender and the helpless, upon feeble bodies and broken minds, and by which he has opportunities to extend his arts of torture, and continue those experiments upon infancy and age, which he has hitherto tried upon cats and dogs.

What is alledged in defence of these hateful practices, every one knows ; but the truth is, that by knives, fire, and poison, knowledge is not always sought, and is very seldom attained. The experiments that have been tried, are tried again ; he that burned an animal with irons yesterday, will be willing to amuse himself with burning another tomorrow. I know not, that by living dissections any discovery has been made by which a single malady is more easily cured. And if the knowledge of physiology has been · somewhat encreased, he surely buys knowledge dear, who learns the use of the lacteals at the expence of his humanity. It is time that universal resentment should arise against these horrid operations, which tend to harden the heart, extinguish those sensations which give man confidence in man, and make the physician more dreadful than the gout or stone.

NUMB. 18. SATURDAY, *August* 12, 1758.

TO THE IDLER.

SIR,

IT commonly happens to him who endeavours to obtain distinction by ridicule, or censure, that he teaches others to practise his own arts against himself; and that, after a short enjoyment of the applause paid to his sagacity, or of the mirth excited by his wit, he is doomed to suffer the same severities of scrutiny, to hear inquiry detecting his faults, and exaggeration sporting with his failings.

The natural discontent of inferiority will seldom fail to operate in some degree of malice against him who professes to superintend the conduct of others, especially if he seats himself uncalled in the chair of judicature, and exercises authority by his own commission.

You cannot, therefore, wonder that your observations on human folly, if they produce laughter at one time, awaken criticism at another; and that among the numbers whom you have taught to scoff at the retirement of Drugget, there is one who offers his apology.

The mistake of your old friend is by no means peculiar. The publick pleasures of far the greater part of mankind are counterfeit. Very few carry their philosophy to places of diversion, or are very careful to analyse their enjoyments. The general condition of life is so full of misery, that we are glad to catch delight without inquiring whence it comes, or by what power it is bestowed.

The mind is seldom quickened to very vigorous operations but by pain, or the dread of pain. We do not disturb ourselves with the detection of fallacies which do us no harm, nor willingly decline a pleasing effect to investigate its cause. He that is happy, by whatever means, desires nothing but the continuance of happiness, and is no more solicitous to distribute his sensations into their proper species, than the common gazer on the beauties of the spring to separate light into its original rays.

Pleasure is therefore seldom such as it appears to others, nor often such as we represent it to ourselves. Of the ladies that sparkle at a musical performance, a very small number has any quick sensibility of harmonious sounds. But every one that goes has her pleasure. She has the pleasure of wearing fine clothes, and of shewing them, of outshining those whom she suspects to envy her; she has the pleasure of appearing among other ladies in a place whither the race of meaner mortals seldom intrudes, and of reflecting that, in the conversations of the next morning, her name will be mentioned among those that sat in the first row ; she has the pleasure of returning courtesies, or refusing to return them, of receiving compliments with civility, or rejecting them with disdain. She has the pleasure of meeting some of her acquaintance, of guessing why the rest are absent, and of telling them that she saw the opera, on pretence of inquiring why they would miss it. She has the pleasure of being supposed to be pleased with a refined amusement, and of hoping to be numbered among the votaresses of harmony. She has the pleasure of escaping for two hours the superiority of a sister, or the controul of a husband ; and from all these pleasures she concludes, that heavenly musick is the balm of life.

All assemblies of gaiety are brought together by motives of the same kind. The theatre is not filled with those that know or regard the skill of the actor, nor the ball-room by those who dance, or attend to the dancers. To all places of general resort, where the standard of pleasure is erected, we run with equal eagerness, or appearance of eagerness, for very different reasons. One goes that he may say he has been there, another because he never misses. This man goes to try what he can find, and that to discover what others find. Whatever diversion is costly will be frequented by those who desire to be thought rich ; and whatever has, by any accident, become fashionable, easily continues its reputation, because every one is ashamed of not partaking it.

To every place of entertainment we go with expectation and desire of being pleased ; we meet others who are brought by the same motives ; no one will be the first to own the disappointment; one face reflects the smile of another, till each believes the rest delighted, and endeavours to catch and transmit the circulating rapture.   In time all are deceived by the cheat to which all contribute.   The fiction of happiness is propagated by every tongue, and confirmed by every look, till at last all profess the joy which they do not feel, consent to yield to the general delusion; and when the voluntary dream is at an end, lament that bliss is of so short a duration.

If Drugget pretended to pleasures of which he had no perception, or boasted of one amusement where he was indulging another, what did he which is not done by all those who read his story? of whom some pretend delight in conversation, only because they dare not be alone; some praise the quiet of solitude, because they are envious of sense, and impatient of folly; and some gratify their pride, by writing characters which expose the vanity of life.

I am, Sir,
Your humble Servant.

NUMB. 19.   SATURDAY, *August* 19, 1758.

SOME of those ancient sages that have exercised their abilities in the inquiry after the *supreme good*, have been of opinion, that the highest degree of earthly happiness is quiet ; a calm repose both of mind and body, undisturbed by the sight of folly or the noise of business, the tumults of publick commotion, or the agitations of private interest ; a state in which the mind has no other employment, but to observe and regulate her own motions, to trace thought from thought, combine one image with another, raise systems of science, and form theories of virtue.

To the scheme of these solitary speculatists, it has been justly objected, that if they are happy, they are happy only by being useless. That mankind is one vast republick, where every individual receives many benefits from the labours of others, which, by labouring in his turn for others, he is obliged to repay ; and that where the united efforts of all are not able to exempt all from misery, none have a right to withdraw from their task of vigilance, or to be indulged in idle wisdom or solitary pleasures.

It is common for controvertists, in the heat of disputation, to add one position to another till they reach the extremities of knowledge, where truth and falsehood lose their distinction. Their admirers follow them to the brink of absurdity, and then start back from each side towards the middle

point.   So it has happened in this great disquisition.   Many perceive alike the force of the contrary
arguments, find quiet shameful, and business dangerous, and therefore pass their lives between them,
in bustle without business, and negligence without
quiet.

Among the principal names of this moderate set
is that great philosopher Jack Whirler, whose business keeps him in perpetual motion, and whose
motion always eludes his business ; who is always to
do what he never does, who cannot stand still because
he is wanted in another place, and who is wanted in
many places because he stays in none.

Jack has more business than he can conveniently transact in one house ; he has therefore one habitation near Bow-Church, and another about a mile
distant.   By this ingenious distribution of himself
between two houses, Jack has contrived to be found
at neither.   Jack's trade is extensive, and he has
many dealers ; his conversation is sprightly, and he
has many companions ; his disposition is kind, and
he has many friends.   Jack neither forbears pleasure
for business, nor omits business for pleasure, but
is equally invisible to his friends and his customers ;
to him that comes with an invitation to a club, and
to him that waits to settle an account.

When you call at his house, his clerk tells you,
that Mr. Whirler was just stept out, but will be at
home exactly at two ; you wait at a coffee-house till
two, and then find that he has been at home, and is
gone out again, but left word that he should be at
the Half-moon tavern at seven, where he hopes

to meet you.   At seven you go to the tavern.   At eight in comes Mr. Whirler to tell you, that he is glad to see you, and only begs leave to run for a few minutes to a gentleman that lives near the Exchange, from whom he will return before supper can be ready.   Away he runs to the Exchange, to tell those who are waiting for him, that he must beg them to defer their business till to-morrow, because his time is come at the Half-moon.

Jack's cheerfulness and civility rank him among those whose presence never gives pain, and whom all receive with fondness and caresses.   He calls often on his friends, to tell them that he will come again to-morrow; on the morrow he comes again, to tell them how an unexpected summons hurries him away.——When he enters a house, his first declaration is, that he cannot sit down; and so short are his visits, that he seldom appears to have come for any other reason but to say, He must go.

The dogs of Egypt, when thirst brings them to the Nile, are said to run as they drink for fear of the crocodiles.   Jack Whirler always dines at full speed.   He enters, finds the family at table, sits familiarly down, and fills his plate; but while the first morsel is in his mouth, hears the clock strike, and rises; then goes to another house, sits down again, recollects another engagement; has only time to taste the soup, makes a short excuse to the company, and continues through another street his desultory dinner.

But, overwhelmed as he is with business, his chief desire is to have still more.   Every new proposal takes possession of his thoughts; he soon balances probabilities, engages in the project, brings it almost to completion, and then forsakes it for another, which he catches with some alacrity, urges with the same vehemence, and abandons with the same coldness.

Every man may be observed to have a certain strain of lamentation, some peculiar theme of complaint on which he dwells in his moments of dejection. Jack's topick of sorrow is the want of time. Many an excellent design languishes in empty theory for want of time. For the omission of any civilities, want of time is his plea to others; for the neglect of any affairs, want of time is his excuse to himself. That he wants time, he sincerely believes; for he once pined away many months with a lingering distemper, for want of time to attend his health.

Thus Jack Whirler lives in perpetual fatigue without proportionate advantage, because he does not consider that no man can see all with his own eyes, or do all with his own hands; that whoever is engaged in multiplicity of business, must transact much by substitution, and leave something to hazard; and that he who attempts to do all, will waste his life in doing little.

NUMB. 20. SATURDAY, *August* 26, 1758.

THERE is no crime more infamous than the violation of truth. It is apparent that men can be social beings no longer than they believe each other. When speech is employed only as the vehicle of falsehood, every man must disunite himself from others, inhabit his own cave, and seek prey only for himself.

Yet the law of truth, thus sacred and necessary, is broken without punishment, without censure, in compliance with inveterate prejudice and prevailing passions. Men are willing to credit what they wish, and encourage rather those who gratify them with pleasure, than those that instruct them with fidelity.

For this reason every historian discovers his country; and it is impossible to read the different accounts of any great event, without a wish that truth had more power over partiality.

Amidst the joy of my countrymen for the acquisition of Louisbourg, I could not forbear to consider how differently this revolution of American power is not only now mentioned by the contending nations, but will be represented by the writers of another century.

The English historian will imagine himself barely

doing justice to English virtue, when he relates the capture of Louisbourg in the following manner:

" The English had hitherto seen with great indignation, their attempts baffled and their force defied by an enemy, whom they considered themselves as entitled to conquer by the right of prescription, and whom many ages of hereditary superiority had taught them to despise. Their fleets were more numerous, and their seamen braver, than those of France; yet they only floated useless on the ocean, and the French derided them from their ports. Misfortunes, as is usual, produced discontent, the people murmured at the ministers, and the ministers censured the commanders.

" In the summer of this year, the English began to find their success answerable to their cause. A fleet and an army were sent to America to dislodge the enemies from the settlements which they had so perfidiously made, and so insolently maintained, and to repress that power which was growing more every day by the association of the Indians, with whom these degenerate Europeans intermarried, and whom they secured to their party by presents and promises.

" In the beginning of June the ships of war and vessels containing the land-forces appeared before Louisbourg, a place so secured by nature that art was almost superfluous, and yet fortified by art as if nature had left it open. The French boasted that it was impregnable, and spoke with scorn of all attempts that could be made against it. The garrison was numerous, the stores equal to the longest siege, and their engineers and commanders high in reputation. The mouth of the harbour was so narrow, that three ships within might easily defend it against all attacks from the sea. The French had, with that caution which cowards borrow from fear, and attribute to policy, eluded our fleets, and sent into that port, five great ships and six smaller, of which they sunk four in the mouth of the passage, having raised batteries, and posted troops at all the places where they thought it possible to make a descent. The English, however, had more to dread from the roughness of the sea, than from the skill or bravery of the defendants. Some days passed before the surges, which rise very high round that island, would suffer them to land. At last their impatience could be restrained no longer; they got possession of the shore with little loss by the sea, and with less by the enemy. In a few days the artillery was landed, the batteries were raised, and the French had no other hope than to escape from one post to another. A shot from the batteries fired the powder in one of their largest ships, the flame spread to the two next, and all three were destroyed; the English admiral sent his boats against the two large ships yet remaining, took them without resistance, and terrified the garrison to an immediate capitulation."

Let us now oppose to this English narrative the relation which will be produced, about the same time, by the writer of the age of Louis XV.

"About this time the English admitted to the conduct of affairs a man who undertook to save from destruction that ferocious and turbulent people, who, from the mean insolence of wealthy traders, and the lawless confidence of successful robbers, were now sunk in despair and stupified with horror. He called in the ships which had been dispersed over the ocean to guard their merchants, and sent a fleet and an army, in which almost the whole strength of England was comprised, *to secure their* possessions in America, which were endangered alike by the French arms and the French virtue. We had taken the English fortresses by force, and gained the Indian nations by humanity. The English, wherever they come, are sure to have the natives for their enemies; for the only motive of their settlements is avarice, and the only consequence of their success is oppression. In this war they acted like other barbarians, and, with a degree of outrageous cruelty, which the gentleness of our manners scarcely suffers us to conceive, offered rewards by open proclamation to those who should bring in the scalps of Indian women and children. A trader always makes war with the cruelty of a pirate.

"They had long looked with envy and with terror upon the influence which the French exerted over all the northern regions of America by the possession of Louisbourg, a place naturally strong and new fortified with some slight outworks. They hoped to surprise the garrison unprovided; but that sluggishness which always defeats their malice, gave us time to send supplies, and to station ships for the defence of the harbour. They came before Louisbourg in June, and were for some time in doubt whether they should land. But the commanders, who had lately seen an admiral beheaded for not having done what he had not power to do, durst not leave the place unassaulted. An Englishman has no ardour for honour, nor zeal for duty ; he neither values glory nor loves his king, but balances one danger with another, and will fight rather than be hanged. They therefore landed, but with great loss ; their engineers had, in the last war with the French, learned something of the military science, and made their approaches with sufficient skill : but all their efforts had been without effect, had not a ball unfortunately fallen into the powder of one of our ships, which communicated the fire to the rest, and, by opening the passage of the harbour, obliged the garrison to capitulate. Thus was Louisbourg lost, and our troops marched out with the admiration of their enemies, who durst hardly think themselves masters of the place."

Numb. 21.   Saturday, *September* 2, 1758.

TO THE IDLER.

DEAR MR. IDLER,

THERE is a species of misery, or of disease, for which our language is commonly supposed to be without a name, but which I think is emphatically enough denominated *listlessness*, and which is commonly termed a want of something to do.

Of the unhappiness of this state I do not expect all your readers to have an adequate idea.   Many are overburdened with business, and can imagine no comfort but in rest ; many have minds so placid, as willingly to indulge a voluntary lethargy ; or so narrow, as easily to be filled to their utmost capacity.   By these I shall not be understood, and therefore cannot be pitied.   Those only will sympathize with my complaint, whose imagination is active and resolution weak, whose desires are ardent, and whose choice is delicate ; who cannot satisfy themselves with standing still, and yet cannot find a motive to direct their course.

I was the second son of a gentleman, whose estate was barely sufficient to support himself and his heir in the dignity of killing game.   He therefore made use of the interest which the alliances of his family afforded him, to procure me a post in the army.   I passed some years in the most contemptible of all human stations, that of a soldier in time of peace. I wandered with the regiment as the quarters were changed, without opportunity for business, taste for knowledge, or money for pleasure. Wherever I came, I was for some time a stranger without curiosity, and afterwards an acquaintance without friendship. Having nothing to hope in these places of fortuitous residence, I resigned my conduct to chance; I had no intention to offend, I had no ambition to delight.

I suppose every man is shocked when he hears how frequently soldiers are wishing for war. The wish is not always sincere; the greater part are content with sleep and lace, and counterfeit an ardour which they do not feel; but those who desire it most are neither prompted by malevolence nor patriotism; they neither pant for laurels, nor delight in blood; but long to be delivered from the tyranny of idleness, and restored to the dignity of active beings.

I never imagined myself to have more courage than other men, yet was often involuntarily wishing for a war, but of a war at that time I had no prospect; and being enabled, by the death of an uncle, to live without my pay, I quitted the army, and resolved to regulate my own motions.

I was pleased, for a while, with the novelty of independence, and imagined that I had now found what every man desires. My time was in my own power, and my habitation was wherever my choice should fix it. I amused myself for two years in passing from place to place, and comparing one convenience with another; but being at last ashamed of inquiry, and weary of uncertainty, I purchased a house, and established my family.

I now expected to begin to be happy, and was happy for a short time with that expectation.   But I soon perceived my spirits to subside, and my imagination to grow dark.   The gloom thickened every day round me.   I wondered by what malignant power my peace was blasted, till I discovered at last that I had nothing to do.

Time, with all its celerity, moves slowly to him whose whole employment is to watch its flight.   I am forced upon a thousand shifts to enable me to endure the tediousness of the day.   I rise when I can sleep no longer, and take my morning walk; I see what I have seen before, and return.   I sit down, and persuade myself that I sit down to think, find it impossible to think without a subject, rise up to inquire after news, and endeavour to kindle in myself an artificial impatience for intelligence of events, which will never extend any consequence to me, but that a few minutes they abstract me from myself.

When I have heard any thing that may gratify curiosity, I am busied for a while in running to relate it.   I hasten from one place of concourse to another, delighted with my own importance, and proud to think that I am doing something, though I know that another hour would spare my labour.

I had once a round of visits, which I paid very regularly; but I have now tired most of my friends. When I have sat down I forget to rise, and have more than once overheard one asking another when I would be gone.   I perceive the company tired, I observe the mistress of the family whispering to her servants, I find orders given to put off business till to-morrow, I see the watches frequently inspected, and yet cannot withdraw to the vacuity of solitude, or venture myself in my own company.

Thus burdensome to myself and others, I form many schemes of employment which may make my life useful or agreeable, and exempt me from the ignominy of living by sufferance. This new course I have long designed, but have not yet begun. The present moment is never proper for the change, but there is always a time in view when all obstacles will be removed, and I shall surprize all that know me with a new distribution of my time. Twenty years have past since I have resolved a complete amendment, and twenty years have been lost in delays. Age is coming upon me ; and I should look back with rage and despair upon the waste of life, but that I am now beginning in earnest to begin a reformation.

I am, Sir,

Your humble servant,

DICK LINGER.

NUMB. 22.   SATURDAY, *September* 16, 1758.

TO THE IDLER.

SIR,

As I was passing lately under one of the gates of this city, I was struck with horror by a rueful cry, which summoned me *to remember the poor debtors*.

The wisdom and justice of the English laws are, by Englishmen at least, loudly celebrated : but scarcely the most zealous admirers of our institutions can think that law wise, which, when men are capable of work, obliges them to beg ; or just, which exposes the liberty of one to the passions of another.

The prosperity of a people is proportionate to the number of hands and minds usefully employed.   To the community, sedition is a fever, corruption is a gangrene, and idleness an atrophy.   Whatever body, and whatever society, wastes more than it acquires, must gradually decay ; and every being that continues to be fed, and ceases to labour, takes away something from the publick stock.

The confinement, therefore, of any man in the sloth and darkness of a prison, is a loss to the nation, and no gain to the creditor.   For of the multitudes who are pining in those cells of misery, a very small part is suspected of any fraudulent act by which they retain what belongs to others.   The rest are imprisoned by the wantonness of pride, the malignity of revenge, or the acrimony of disappointed expectation.

If those who thus rigorously exercise the power which the law has put into their hands, be asked, why they continue to imprison those whom they know to be unable to pay them; one will answer, that his debtor once lived better than himself; another, that his wife looked above her neighbours, and his children went in silk clothes to the dancing-school; and another, that he pretended to be a joker and a wit. Some will reply, that if they were in debt, they should meet with the same treatment; some, that they owe no more than they can pay, and need therefore give no account of their actions. Some will confess their resolution, that their debtors shall rot in jail; and some will discover, that they hope, by cruelty to wring the payment from their friends.

The end of all civil regulations is to secure private happiness from private malignity; to keep individuals from the power of one another; but this end is apparently neglected, when a man, irritated with loss, is allowed to be the judge of his own cause, and to assign the punishment of his own pain; when the distinction between guilt and happiness, between casualty and design, is entrusted to eyes blind with interest, to understandings depraved by resentment.

Since poverty is punished among us as a crime, it ought at least to be treated with the same lenity as other crimes; the offender ought not to languish at the will of him whom he has offended, but to be allowed some appeal to the justice of his country. There can be no reason why any debtor should be imprisoned, but that he may be compelled to payment; and a term should therefore be fixed, in which the creditor should exhibit his accusation of concealed property. If such property can be discovered, let it be given to the creditor ; if the charge is not offered, or cannot be proved, let the prisoner be dismissed.

Those who made the laws have apparently supposed, that every deficiency of payment is the crime of the debtor. But the truth is, that the creditor always shares the act, and often more than shares the guilt, of improper trust. It seldom happens that any man imprisons another but for debts which he suffered to be contracted in hope of advantage to himself, and for bargains in which he proportioned his profit to his own opinion of the hazard ; and there is no reason, why one should punish the other for a contract in which both concurred.

Many of the inhabitants of prisons may justly complain of harder treatment. He that once owes more than he can pay, is often obliged to bribe his creditor to patience, by encreasing his debt. Worse and worse commodities, at a higher and higher price, are forced upon him ; he is impoverished by compulsive traffick, and at last overwhelmed, in the common receptacles of misery, by debts, which, without his own consent, were accumulated on his head. To the relief of this distress, no other objection can be made, but that by an easy dissolution of debts fraud will be left without punishment, and imprudence without awe ; and that when insolvency should be no longer punishable, credit will cease.

The motive to credit is the hope of advantage. Commerce can never be at a stop, while one man wants what another can supply; and credit will never be denied, while it is likely to be repaid with profit. He that trusts one whom he designs to sue, is criminal, by the act of trust; the cessation of such insidious traffick is to be desired, and no reason can be given why a change of the law should impair any other.

We see nation trade with nation, where no payment can be compelled. Mutual convenience produces mutual confidence; and the merchants continue to satisfy the demands of each other, though they have nothing to dread but the loss of trade.

It is vain to continue an institution, which experience shews to be ineffectual. We have now imprisoned one generation of debtors after another, but we do not find that their numbers lessen. We have now learned that rashness and imprudence will not be deterred from taking credit; let us try whether fraud and avarice may be more easily restrained from giving it.

I am, Sir, &c.*

---

* This number was substituted for the original No. 22, which we have reprinted at the end of this volume.   C.

Numb. 23.   Saturday, *September 23, 1758.*

Life has no pleasure higher or nobler than that of friendship.   It is painful to consider, that this sublime enjoyment may be impaired or destroyed by innumerable causes, and that there is no human possession of which the duration is less certain.

Many have talked in very exalted language, of the perpetuity of friendship, of invincible constancy, and unalienable kindness ; and some examples have been seen of men who have continued faithful to their earliest choice, and whose affection has predominated over changes of fortune, and contrariety of opinion.

But these instances are memorable, because they are rare.   The friendship which is to be practised or expected by common mortals, must take its rise from mutual pleasure, and must end when the power ceases of delighting each other.

Many accidents therefore may happen, by which the ardour of kindness will be abated, without criminal baseness or contemptible inconstancy on either part.   To give pleasure is not always in our power ; and little does he know himself, who believes that he can be always able to receive it.

Those who would gladly pass their days together may be separated by the different course of their affairs; and friendship, like love, is destroyed by long absence, though it may be encreased by short intermissions. What we have missed long enough to want it, we value more when it is regained; but that which has been lost till it is forgotten, will be found at last with little gladness, and with still less if a substitute has supplied the place. A man deprived of the companion to whom he used to open his bosom, and with whom he shared the hours of leisure and merriment, feels the day at first hanging heavy on him; his difficulties oppress, and his doubts distract him; he sees time come and go without his wonted gratification, and all is sadness within, and solitude about him. But this uneasiness never lasts long; necessity produces expedients, new amusements are discovered, and new conversation is admitted.

No expectation is more frequently disappointed, than that which naturally arises in the mind from the prospect of meeting an old friend after long separation. We expect the attraction to be revived, and the coalition to be renewed; no man considers how much alteration time has made in himself, and very few inquire what effect it has had upon others. The first hour convinces them, that the pleasure, which they had formerly enjoyed, is for ever at an end; different scenes have made different impressions; the opinions of both are changed; and that similitude of manners and sentiment is lost, which confirmed them both in the approbation of themselves.

Friendship is often destroyed by opposition of interest, not only by the ponderous and visible interest which the desire of wealth and greatness forms and maintains, but by a thousand secret and slight competitions, scarcely known to the mind upon which they operate. There is scarcely any man without some favourite trifle which he values above greater attainments, some desire of petty praise which he cannot patiently suffer to be frustrated. This minute ambition is sometimes crossed before it is known, and sometimes defeated by wanton petulance; but such attacks are seldom made without the loss of friendship; for whoever has once found the vulnerable part will always be feared, and the resentment will burn on in secret, of which shame hinders the discovery.

This, however, is a slow malignity, which a wise man will obviate as inconsistent with quiet, and a good man will repress as contrary to virtue; but human happiness is sometimes violated by some more sudden strokes.

A dispute begun in jest upon a subject which a moment before was on both parts regarded with careless indifference, is continued by the desire of conquest, till vanity kindles into rage, and opposition rankles into enmity. Against this hasty mischief, I know not what security can be obtained: men will be sometimes surprized into quarrels; and though they might both hasten to reconciliation, as soon as their tumult had subsided, yet two minds will seldom be found together, which can at once subdue their discontent, or immediately enjoy the sweets of peace without remembering the wounds of the conflict.

Friendship has other enemies. Suspicion is always hardening the cautious, and disgust repelling the delicate.   Very slender differences will sometimes part those whom long reciprocation of civility or beneficence has united.   Lonelove and Ranger retired into the country to enjoy the company of each other, and returned in six weeks cold and petulant ; Ranger's pleasure was to walk in the fields, and Lonelove's to sit in a bower ; each had complied with the other in his turn, and each was angry that compliance had been exacted.

The most fatal disease of friendship is gradual decay, or dislike hourly encreased by causes too slender for complaint, and too numerous for removal.——Those who are angry may be reconciled ; those who have been injured may receive a recompence : but when the desire of pleasing and willingness to be pleased is silently diminished, the renovation of friendship is hopeless : as, when the vital powers sink into languor, there is no longer any use of the physician.

NUMB. 24. SATURDAY, *September 30, 1758.*

WHEN man sees one of the inferior creatures perched upon a tree, or basking in the sunshine, without any apparent endeavour or pursuit, he often asks himself, or his companions, *On what that animal can be supposed to be thinking?*

Of this question, since neither bird nor beast can answer it, we must be content to live without the resolution. We know not how much the brutes recollect of the past, or anticipate of the future; what power they have of comparing and preferring: or whether their faculties may not rest in motionless indifference, till they are moved by the presence of their proper object, or stimulated to act by corporal sensations.

I am the less inclined to these superfluous inquiries, because I have always been able to find sufficient matter for curiosity in my own species. It is useless to go far in quest of that which may be found at home; a very narrow circle of observation will supply a sufficient number of men and women, who might be asked, with equal propriety, *On what they can be thinking?*

It is reasonable to believe, that thought, like every thing else, has its causes and effects; that it must proceed from something known, done, or suffered; and must produce some action or event. Yet how great is the number of those in whose mind no source of thought has ever been opened,

in whose life no consequence of thought is ever discovered; who have learned nothing upon which they
can reflect; who have neither seen nor felt any thing
which could leave its traces on the memory; who
neither foresee nor desire any change of their condition, and have therefore neither fear, hope, nor design and yet are supposed to be thinking beings.

To every act a subject is required. He that
thinks must think upon something. But tell me,
ye that pierce deepest into nature, ye that take the
widest surveys of life, inform me, kind shades of
Malbranche and of Locke, what that something can
be which excites and continues thought in maiden
aunts with small fortunes; in younger brothers
that live upon annuities; in traders retired from
business; in soldiers absent from their regiments;
or in widows that have no children?

Life is commonly considered as either active or
contemplative; but surely this division, how long
soever it has been received, is inadequate and fallacious. There are mortals whose life is certainly
not active, for they do neither good nor evil; and
whose life cannot be properly called contemplative,
for they never attend either to the conduct of men,
or the works of nature, but rise in the morning,
look round them till night in careless stupidity, go
to bed and sleep, and rise again in the morning.

It has been lately a celebrated question in the
schools of philosophy, *Whether the soul always
thinks?* Some have defined the soul to be the *power
of thinking*; concluded that its essence consists in
act; that if it should cease to act, it would cease

to be; and that cessation of thought is but another name for extinction of mind. This argument is subtle, but not conclusive; because it supposes what cannot be proved, that the nature of mind is properly defined. Others affect to disdain subtilty, when subtilty will not serve their purpose, and appeal to daily experience. We spend many hours, they say, in sleep, without the least remembrance of any thoughts which then passed in our minds; and since we can only by our own consciousness be sure that we think, why should we imagine that we have had thought of which no consciousness remains?

This argument, which appeals to experience, may from experience be confuted. We every day do something which we forget when it is done, and know to have been done only by consequence. The waking hours are not denied to have been passed in thought; yet he that shall endeavour to recollect on one day the ideas of the former, will only turn the eye of reflection upon vacancy; he will find, that the greater part is irrevocably vanished, and wonder how the moments could come and go, and leave so little behind them.

To discover only that the arguments on both sides are defective, and to throw back the tenet into its former uncertainty, is the sport of wanton or malevolent scepticism, delighting to see the sons of philosophy at work upon a task which never can be decided. I shall suggest an argument hitherto overlooked, which may perhaps determine the controversy.

If it be impossible to think without materials, there must necessarily be minds that do not always think; and whence shall we furnish materials for the meditation of the glutton between his meals, of the sportsman in a rainy month, of the annuitant between the days of quarterly payment, of the politician when the mails are detained by contrary winds?

But how frequent soever may be the examples of existence without thought, it is certainly a state not much to be desired. He that lives in torpid insensibility, wants nothing of a carcase but putrefaction. It is the part of every inhabitant of the earth to partake the pains and pleasures of his fellow beings; and, as in a road through a country desart and uniform, the traveller languishes for want of amusement, so the passage of life will be tedious and irksome to him who does not beguile it by diversified ideas.

NUMB. 25.   SATURDAY, *October* 7, 1758.

TO THE IDLER.

SIR,

I AM a very constant frequenter of the playhouse, a place to which I suppose the *Idler* not much a stranger, since he can have no where else so much entertainment with so little concurrence of his own endeavour.   At all other assemblies, he that comes to receive delight, will be expected to give it ; but in the theatre nothing is necessary to the amusement of two hours, but to sit down and be willing to be pleased.

The last week has offered two new actors to the town.   The appearance and retirement of actors are the great events of the theatrical world ; and their first performances fill the pit with conjecture and prognostication, as the first actions of a new monarch agitate nations with hope or fear.

What opinion I have formed of the future excellence of these candidates for dramatick glory, it is not necessary to declare.   Their entrance gave me a higher and nobler pleasure than any borrowed character can afford.   I saw the ranks of the theatre emulating each other in candour and humanity, and contending who should most effectually assist the struggles of endeavour, dissipate the blush of diffidence, and still the flutter of timidity.

This behaviour is such as becomes a people, too tender to repress those who wish to please, too generous to insult those who can make no resistance. A publick performer is so much in the power of spectators, that all unnecessary severity is restrained by that general law of humanity which forbids us to be cruel where there is nothing to be feared.

In every new performer something must be pardoned. No man can, by any force of resolution, secure to himself the full possession of his own powers under the eye of a large assembly. Variation of gesture, and flexion of voice, are to be obtained only by experience.

There is nothing for which such numbers think themselves qualified as for theatrical exhibition. Every human being has an action graceful to his own eye, a voice musical to his own ear, and a sensibility which nature forbids him to know that any other bosom can excel. An art in which such numbers fancy themselves excellent, and which the publick liberally rewards, will excite many competitors, and in many attempts there must be many miscarriages.

The care of the critick should be to distinguish error from inability, faults of inexperience from defects of nature. Action irregular and turbulent may be reclaimed; vociferation vehement and confused may be restrained and modulated; the stalk of the tyrant may become the gait of the man; the yell of inarticulate distress may be reduced to human lamentation. All these faults should be for a time overlooked, and afterwards censured with gentleness and candour. But if in an actor there appears an utter vacancy of meaning, a frigid equality, a stupid languor, a torpid apathy, the greatest kindness that can be shewn him, is a speedy sentence of expulsion.

I am, Sir, &c.

THE plea which my correspondent has offered for young actors, I am very far from wishing to invalidate.   I always considered those combinations which are sometimes formed in the playhouse, as acts of fraud and cruelty ; he that applauds him who does not deserve praise, is endeavouring to deceive the publick ; he that hisses in malice or sport, is an oppressor and a robber.

But surely this laudable forbearance might be justly extended to young poets.   The art of the writer, like that of the player, is attained by slow degrees.   The power of distinguishing and discriminating comick characters, or of filling tragedy with poetical images, must be the gift of nature, which no instruction nor labour can supply ; but the art of dramatick disposition, the contexture of the scenes, the opposition of characters, the involution of the plot, the expedients of suspension, and the stratagems of surprize, are to be learned by practice ; and it is cruel to discourage a poet for ever, because he has not from genius what only experience can bestow.

Life is a stage.   Let me likewise solicit candour for the young actor on the stage of life.   They that enter into the world are too often treated with unreasonable rigour by those that were once as ignorant and heady as themselves; and distinction is not always made between the faults which require speedy and violent eradication, and those that will gradually drop away in the progression of life. Vicious solicitations of appetite, if not checked, will grow more importunate ; and mean arts of profit or ambition will gather strength in the mind, if they are not early suppressed. But mistaken notions of superiority, desires of useless show, pride of little accomplishments, and all the train of vanity, will be brushed away by the wing of time.

Reproof should not exhaust its power upon petty failings; let it watch diligently against the incursion of vice, and leave foppery and futility to die of themselves.

NUMB. 26. SATURDAY, *October* 14, 1758.

MR. IDLER,

I NEVER thought that I should write any thing to be printed ; but having lately seen your first essay, which was sent down into the kitchen, with a great bundle of gazettes and useless papers, I find that you are willing to admit any correspondent, and there-fore hope you will not reject me. If you publish my letter, it may encourage others, in the same con-dition with myself, to tell their stories, which may be perhaps as useful as those of great ladies.

I am a poor girl. I was bred in the country at a charity-school, maintained by the contributions of wealthy neighbours. The ladies, or patronesses, vi-sited us from time to time, examined how we were taught, and saw that our clothes were clean. We lived happily enough, and were instructed to be thankful to those at whose cost we were educated. I was always the favourite of my mistress; she used to call me to read and shew my copy-book to all strangers, who never dismissed me without commen-dation, and very seldom without a shilling.

At last the chief of our subscribers, having passed a winter in London, came down full of an opinion new and strange to the whole country. She held it little less than criminal to teach poor girls to read and write. They who are born to poverty, she said, are born to ignorance, and will work the harder the less they know. She told her friends, that London was in confusion by the insolence of servants ; that scarcely a wench was to be got for *all work,* since education had made such numbers of fine ladies, that nobody would now accept a lower title than that of a waiting-maid, or something that might qualify her to wear laced shoes and long ruffles, and to sit at work in the parlour window. But she was resolved, for her part, to spoil no more girls ; those who were to live by their hands, should neither read nor write out of her pocket ; the world was bad enough already, and she would have no part in making it worse.

She was for a short time warmly opposed ; but she persevered in her notions, and withdrew her subscription. Few listen without a desire of conviction to those who advise them to spare their money. Her example and her arguments gained ground daily ; and in less than a year the whole parish was convinced, that the nation would be ruined, if the children of the poor were taught to read and write.

Our school was now dissolved : my mistress kissed me when we parted, and told me, that, being old and helpless, she could not assist me, advised me to seek a service, and charged me not to forget what I had learned.

My reputation for scholarship, which had hitherto recommended me to favour, was, by the adherents to the new opinion, considered as a crime ; and, when I offered myself to any mistress, I had no other answer than, " Sure, child, you would not work !

hard work is not fit for a pen-woman; a scrubbing-brush would spoil your hand, child!"

I could not live at home; and while I was considering to what I should betake me, one of the girls, who had gone from our school to London, came down in a silk gown, and told her acquaintance how well she lived, what fine things she saw, and what great wages she received. I resolved to try my fortune, and took my passage in the next week's waggon to London. I had no snares laid for me at my arrival, but came safe to a sister of my mistress, who undertook to get me a place. She knew only the families of mean tradesmen; and I, having no high opinion of my own qualifications, was willing to accept the first offer.

My first mistress was wife of a working watch-maker, who earned more than was sufficient to keep his family in decency and plenty; but it was their constant practice to hire a chaise on Sunday, and spend half the wages of the week on Richmond Hill; of Monday he commonly lay half in bed, and spent the other half in merriment; Tuesday and Wednesday consumed the rest of his money; and three days every week were passed in extremity of want by us who were left at home, while my master lived on trust at an alehouse. You may be sure, that of the sufferers the maid suffered most; and I left them, after three months, rather than be starved.

I was then maid to a hatter's wife. There was no want to be dreaded, for they lived in perpetual luxury. My mistress was a diligent woman, and rose early in the morning to set the journeymen to work ; my master was a man much beloved by his neighbours, and sat at one club or other every night. I was obliged to wait on my master at night, and on my mistress in the morning.   He seldom came home before two, and she rose at five.   I could no more live without sleep than without food, and therefore entreated them to look out for another servant.

My next removal was to a linen-draper's, who had six children.   My mistress, when I first entered the house, informed me, that I must never contradict the children, nor suffer them to cry.   I had no desire to offend, and readily promised to do my best. But when I gave them their breakfast, I could not help all first; when I was playing with one in my lap, I was forced to keep the rest in expectation. That which was not gratified always resented the injury with a loud outcry, which put my mistress in a fury at me, and procured sugar-plumbs to the child. I could not keep six children quiet, who were bribed to be clamorous ; and was therefore dismissed, as a girl honest, but not good-natured.

I then lived with a couple that kept a petty shop of remnants and cheap linen.   I was qualified to make a bill, or keep a book ; and being therefore often called, at a busy time, to serve the customers, expected that I should now be happy, in proportion as I was useful.   But my mistress appropriated every day part of the profit to some private use, and, as she grew bolder in her theft, at last deducted such sums, that my master began to wonder how he sold so much, and gained so little.   She pretended to assist his inquiries, and began, very gravely, to hope that "Betty was honest, and yet those sharp girls were apt to be lightfingered." You will believe that I did not stay there much longer.

The rest of my story I will tell you in another letter; and only beg to be informed, in some paper, for which of my places, except perhaps the last, I was disqualified by my skill in reading and writing.

I am, Sir,

Your very humble servant,

BETTY BROOM.

NUMB. 27. SATURDAY, *October* 21, 1758.

IT has been the endeavour of all those whom the world has reverenced for superior wisdom, to persuade man to be acquainted with himself, to learn his own powers and his own weakness, to observe by what evils he is most dangerously beset, and by what temptations most easily overcome.

This counsel has been often given with serious dignity, and often received with appearance of conviction; but, as very few can search deep into their own minds without meeting what they wish to hide from themselves, scarcely any man persists in cultivating such disagreeable acquaintance, but draws the veil again between his eyes and his heart, leaves his passions and appetites as he found them, and advises others to look into themselves.

This is the common result of inquiry even among those that endeavour to grow wiser or better: but this endeavour is far enough from frequency; the greater part of the multitudes that swarm upon the earth have never been disturbed by such uneasy curiosity, but deliver themselves up to business or to pleasure, plunge into the current of life, whether placid or turbulent, and pass on from one point of prospect to another, attentive rather to any thing

than the state of their minds; satisfied, at an easy
rate, with an opinion, that they are no worse than
others, that every man must mind his own interest,
or that their pleasures hurt only themselves, and are
therefore no proper subjects of censure.

Some, however, there are, whom the intrusion of
scruples, the recollection of better notions, or the latent reprehension of good examples, will not suffer to
live entirely contented with their own conduct; these
are forced to pacify the mutiny of reason with fair
promises, and quiet their thoughts with designs of
calling all their actions to review, and planning a new
scheme for the time to come.

There is nothing which we estimate so fallaciously
as the force of our own resolutions, nor any fallacy
which we so unwillingly and tardily detect. He
that has resolved a thousand times, and a thousand times deserted his own purpose, yet suffers no
abatement of his confidence, but still believes himself his own master; and able, by innate vigour of
soul, to press forward to his end, through all the
obstructions that inconveniences or delights can put
in his way.

That this mistake should prevail for a time, is
very natural. When conviction is present, and
temptation out of sight, we do not easily conceive
how any reasonable being can deviate from his true
interest. What ought to be done, while it yet hangs
only in speculation, is so plain and certain, that
there is no place for doubt; the whole soul yields
itself to the predominance of truth, and readily de-

termines to do what, when the time of action comes, will be at last omitted.

I believe most men may review all the lives that have passed within their observation, without remembering one efficacious resolution, or being able to tell a single instance of a course of practice suddenly changed in consequence of a change of opinion, or an establishment of determination.   Many indeed alter their conduct, and are not at fifty what they were at thirty ; but they commonly varied imperceptibly from themselves, followed the train of external causes, and rather suffered reformation than made it.

It is not uncommon to charge the difference between promise and performance, between profession and reality, upon deep design and studied deceit ; but the truth is, that there is very little hypocrisy in the world ; we do not so often endeavour or wish to impose on others as on ourselves ; we resolve to do right, we hope to keep our resolutions, we declare them to confirm our own hope, and fix our own inconstancy by calling witnesses of our actions ; but at last habit prevails, and those whom we invited to our triumph, laugh at our defeat.

Custom is commonly too strong for the most resolute resolver, though furnished for the assault with all the weapons of philosophy. " He that endeavours to free himself from an ill habit," says Bacon, " must not change too much at a time, lest he should be discouraged by difficulty ; nor too little, for then he will make but slow advances."   This is a precept which may be applauded in a book, but will fail in the trial, in which every change will be found too

great or too little. Those who have been able to
conquer habit, are like those that are fabled to have
returned from the realms of Pluto :

> " Pauci, quos æquus amavit
> Jupiter, atque ardens evexit ad æthera virtus."

They are sufficient to give hope, but not security ;
to animate the contest, but not to promise victory.

Those who are in the power of evil habits must
conquer them as they can ; and conquered they must
be, or neither wisdom nor happiness can be attained :
but those who are not yet subject to their influence
may, by timely caution, preserve their freedom ; they
may effectually resolve to escape the tyrant, whom
they will very vainly resolve to conquer.

NUMB. 28.   SATURDAY, *October* 28, 1758.

TO THE IDLER.

SIR,

IT is very easy for a man who sits idle at home, and has nobody to please but himself, to ridicule or to censure the common practices of mankind ; and those who have no present temptation to break the rules of propriety, may applaud his judgment, and join in his merriment ; but let the author or his readers mingle with common life, they will find themselves irresistibly borne away by the stream of custom, and must submit, after they have laughed at others, to give others the same opportunity of laughing at them.

There is no paper published by the *Idler* which I have read with more approbation than that which censures the practice of recording vulgar marriages in the newspapers. I carried it about in my pocket, and read it to all those whom I suspected of having published their nuptials, or of being inclined to publish them, and sent transcripts of it to all the couples that transgressed your precepts for the next fortnight. I hoped that they were all vexed, and pleased myself with imagining their misery.

But short is the triumph of malignity. I was married last week to Miss Mohair, the daughter of a salesman; and at my first appearance after the wedding night, was asked by my wife's mother, whether I had sent our marriage to the *Advertiser!* I endeavoured to shew how unfit it was to demand the attention of the publick to our domestick affairs; but she told me, with great vehemence, " That she would not have it thought to be a stolen match; that the blood of the Mohairs should never be disgraced; that her husband had served all the parish offices but one; that she had lived five-and-thirty years at the same house, had paid every body twenty shillings in the pound, and would have me know, though she was not as fine and as flaunting as Mrs. Ginghum, the deputy's wife, she was not ashamed to tell her name, and would shew her face with the best of them; and since I had married her daughter——" At this instant entered my father-in-law, a grave man, from whom I expected succour; but upon hearing the case, he told me, " That it would be very imprudent to miss such an opportunity of advertising my shop; and that when notice was given of my marriage, many of my wife's friends would think themselves obliged to be my customers." I was subdued by clamour on one side, and gravity on the other, and shall be obliged to tell the town, that " three days ago Timothy Mushroom, an eminent oilman in Sea-Coal Lane, was married to Miss Polly Mobair of Lothbury, a beautiful young lady, with a large fortune."

I am, Sir, &c.

SIR,

I am the unfortunate wife of the grocer whose letter you published about teu weeks ago, in which he complains, like a sorry fellow, that I loiter in the shop with my needle-work in my hand, and that I oblige him to take me out on Sundays, and keep a girl to look after the child. Sweet Mr. Idler, if you did but know all, you would give no encouragement to such an unreasonable grumbler. I brought him three hundred pounds, which set him up in a shop, and bought-in a stock, on which, with good management, we might live comfortably; but now I have given him a shop, I am forced to watch him and the shop too. I will tell you, Mr. Idler, how it is. There is an alehouse over the way with a ninepin alley, to which he is sure to run when I turn my back, and there loses his money, for he plays at ninepins as he does every thing else. While he is at this favourite sport, he sets a dirty boy to watch his door, and call him to his customers; but he is so long in coming, and so rude when he comes, that our custom falls off every day.

Those who cannot govern themselves, must be governed. I have resolved to keep him for the future behind his counter, and let him bounce at his customers if he dares. I cannot be above stairs and below at the same time, and have therefore taken a girl to look after the child and dress the dinner; and, after all, pray who is to blame?

On a Sunday, it is true, I make him walk abroad, and sometimes carry the child; I wonder who should carry it! But I never take him out till after church-time, nor would do it then, but that, if he is left alone, he will be upon the bed. On a Sunday, if he stays at home, he has six meals, and, when he can eat no longer, has twenty stratagems to escape from me to the alehouse; but I commonly keep the door locked, till Monday produces something for him to do.

This is the true state of the case, and these are the provocations for which he has written his letter to you. I hope you will write a paper to shew, that, if a wife must spend her whole time in watching her husband, she cannot conveniently tend her child, or sit at her needle.

I am, Sir, &c.

SIR,

THERE is in this town a species of oppression which the law has not hitherto prevented or redressed.

I am a chairman. You know, Sir, we come when we are called, and are expected to carry all who require our assistance. It is common for men of the most unwieldy corpulence to crowd themselves into a chair, and demand to be carried for a shilling as far as an airy young lady whom we scarcely feel upon our poles. Surely we ought to be paid like all other mortals in proportion to our labour. Engines should be fixed in proper places to weigh chairs as they weigh waggons; and those, whom ease and plenty have made unable to carry themselves, should give part of their superfluities to those who carry them.

I am, Sir, &c.

NÚMB. 29.　SATURDAY, *November* 4, 1758.

TO THE IDLER.

SIR,

I HAVE often observed, that friends are lost by discontinuance of intercourse without any offence on either part, and have long known, that it is more dangerous to be forgotten than to be blamed; I therefore make haste to send you the rest of my story, lest, by the delay of another fortnight, the name of Betty Broom might be no longer remembered by you or your readers.

Having left the last place in haste to avoid the charge or the suspicion of theft, I had not secured another service, and was forced to take a lodging in a back street. I had now got good clothes. The woman who lived in the garret opposite to mine was very officious, and offered to take care of my room and clean it, while I went round to my acquaintance to inquire for a mistress. I knew not why she was so kind, nor how I could recompense her; but in a few days I missed some of my linen, went to another lodging, and resolved not to have another friend in the next garret.

In six weeks I became under-maid at the house of a mercer in Cornhill, whose son was his apprentice. The young gentleman used to sit late at the tavern, without the knowledge of his father; and I was ordered by my mistress to let him in silently to his bed under the counter, and to be very careful to take away his candle. The hours which I was obliged to watch, whilst the rest of the family was in bed, I considered as supernumerary, and, having no business assigned for them, thought myself at liberty to spend them my own way: I kept myself awake with a book, and for some time liked my state the better for this opportunity of reading. At last, the upper-maid found my book, and shewed it to my mistress, who told me, that wenches like me might spend their time better; that she never knew any of the readers that had good designs in their heads: that she could always find something else to do with her time, than to puzzle over books; and did not like that such a fine lady should sit up for her young master.

This was the first time that I found it thought criminal or dangerous to know how to read. I was dismissed decently, lest I should tell tales, and had a small gratuity above my wages.

I then lived with a gentlewoman of a small fortune. This was the only happy part of my life. My mistress, for whom publick diversions were too expensive, spent her time with books, and was pleased to find a maid who could partake her amusements. I rose early in the morning, that I might have time in the afternoon to read or listen, and was suffered to tell my opinion, or express my delight. Thus fifteen months stole away, in which I did not repine that I was born to servitude. But a burning fever seized my mistress, of whom I shall say no more, than that her servant wept upon her grave.

I had lived in a kind of luxury, which made me very unfit for another place; and was rather too delicate for the conversation of a kitchen; so that when I was hired in the family of an East India director, my behaviour was so different, as they said, from that of a common servant, that they concluded me a gentlewoman in disguise, and turned me out in three weeks, on suspicion of some design which they could not comprehend.

I then fled for refuge to the other end of the town, where I hoped to find no obstruction from my new accomplishments, and was hired under the house-keeper in a splendid family. Here I was too wise for the maids, and too nice for the footmen; yet I might have lived on without much uneasiness, had not my mistress, the housekeeper, who used to employ me in buying necessaries for the family, found a bill which I had made of one day's expences. I suppose it did not quite agree with her own book, for she fiercely declared her resolution, that there should be no pen and ink in that kitchen but her own.

She had the justice, or the prudence, not to injure my reputation; and I was easily admitted into another house in the neighbourhood, where my business was to sweep the rooms and make the beds. Here I was, for some time, the favourite of Mrs. Simper, my lady's woman, who could not bear the vulgar girls, and was happy in the attendance of a young woman of some education. Mrs. Simper loved a novel, though she could not read hard words, and therefore, when her lady was abroad, we always laid hold on her books. At last, my abilities became so much celebrated, that the house-steward used to employ me in keeping his accounts. Mrs. Simper then found out, that my sauciness was grown to such a height that nobody could endure it, and told my lady, that there never had been a room well swept since Betty Broom came into the house.

I was then hired by a consumptive lady, who wanted a maid that could read and write. I attended her four years, and though she was never pleased, yet when I declared my resolution to leave her, she burst into tears, and told me that I must bear the peevishness of a sick bed, and I should find myself remembered in her will. I complied, and a codicil was added in my favour; but in less than a week, when I set her gruel before her, I laid the spoon on the left side, and she threw her will into the fire. In two days she made another, which she burnt in the same manner, because she could not eat her chicken. A third was made, and destroyed because she heard a mouse within the wainscot, and was sure that I should suffer her to be carried away alive. After this I was for some time out of favour, but as her illness grew upon her, resentment and sullenness gave way to kinder sentiments. She died, and left me five hundred pounds; with this fortune I am going to settle in my native parish, where I resolve to spend some hours every day in teaching poor girls to read and write.

I am, Sir,
Your humble Servant,
BETTY BROOM.

NUMB. 30.　SATURDAY, *November* 11, 1758.

THE desires of man increase with his acquisitions; every step which he advances brings something within his view, which he did not see before, and which, as soon as he sees it, he begins to want. Where necessity ends, curiosity begins; and no sooner are we supplied with every thing that nature can demand, than we sit down to contrive artificial appetites.

By this restlessness of mind, every populous and wealthy city is filled with innumerable employments, for which the greater part of mankind is without a name; with artificers, whose labour is exerted in producing such petty conveniences, that many shops are furnished with instruments, of which the use can hardly be found without inquiry, but which he that once knows them quickly learns to number among necessary things.

Such is the diligence with which, in countries completely civilized, one part of mankind labours for another, that wants are supplied faster than they can be formed, and the idle and luxurious find life stagnate for want of some desire to keep it in motion. This species of distress furnishes a new set of occupations; and multitudes are busied, from day to day, in finding the rich and the fortunate something to do.

It is very common to reproach those artists as useless, who produce only such superfluities as neither accommodate the body, nor improve the mind; and of which no other effect can be imagined, than that they are the occasions of spending money, and consuming time.

But this censure will be mitigated, when it is seriously considered that money and time are the heaviest burdens of life, and that the unhappiest of all mortals are those who have more of either than they know how to use. To set himself free from these incumbrances, one hurries to Newmarket; another, travels over Europe; one pulls down his house and calls architects about him; another buys a seat in the country, and follows his hounds over hedges and through rivers; one makes collections of shells; and another searches the world for tulips and carnations.

He is surely a public benefactor who finds employment for those to whom it is thus difficult to find it for themselves. It is true, that this is seldom done merely from generosity or compassion; almost every man seeks his own advantage in helping others, and therefore it is too common for mercenary officiousness to consider rather what is grateful, than what is right.

We all know that it is more profitable to be loved than esteemed; and ministers of pleasure will always be found, who study to make themselves necessary, and to supplant those who are practising the same arts.

One of the amusements of idleness is reading without the fatigue of close attention, and the world therefore swarms with writers whose wish is not to be studied, but to be read.

No species of literary men has lately been so much multiplied as the writers of news. Not many years ago the nation was content with one gazette; but now we have not only in the metropolis papers for every morning and every evening, but almost every large town has its weekly historian, who regularly circulates his periodical intelligence, and fills the villages of his district with conjectures on the events of war, and with debates on the true interest of Europe.

To write news in its perfection requires such a combination of qualities, that a man completely fitted for the task is not always to be found. In Sir Henry Wotton's jocular definition, *An ambassador is said to be a man of virtue sent abroad to tell lies for the advantage of his country;* a news-writer is *a man without virtue, who writes lies at home for his own profit.* To these compositions is required neither genius nor knowledge, neither industry nor sprightliness; but contempt of shame and indifference to truth are absolutely necessary. He who by a long familiarity with infamy has obtained these qualities, may confidently tell to-day what he intends to contradict to-morrow; he may affirm fearlessly what he knows that he shall be obliged to recant, and may write letters from Amsterdam or Dresden to himself.

In a time of war the nation is always of one mind, eager to hear something good of themselves and ill of the enemy. At this time the task of news-writers is easy : they have nothing to do but to tell that a battle is expected, and afterwards that a battle has been fought, in which we and our friends, whether conquering or conquered, did all, and our enemies did nothing.

Scarcely any thing awakens attention like a tale of cruelty. The writer of news never fails in the intermission of action to tell how the enemies murdered children and ravished virgins ; and, if the scene of action be somewhat distant, scalps half the inhabitants of a province.

Among the calamities of war may be justly numbered the diminution of the love of truth, by the falsehoods which interest dictates, and credulity encourages. A peace will equally leave the warrior and relator of wars destitute of employment ; and I know not whether more is to be dreaded from streets filled with soldiers accustomed to plunder, or from garrets filled with scribblers accustomed to lie.

NUMB. 31.   SATURDAY, *November* 18, 1758.

MANY moralists have remarked, that pride has of all human vices the widest dominion, appears in the greatest multiplicity of forms, and lies hid under the greatest variety of disguises; of disguises, which, like the moon's *veil of brightness,* are both its *lustre and its shade,* and betray it to others, though they hide it from ourselves.

It is not my intention to degrade pride from this pre-eminence of mischief; yet I know not whether idleness may not maintain a very doubtful and obstinate competition.

There are some that profess idleness in its full dignity, who call themselves the *Idle,* as Busiris in the play calls himself the *Proud;* who boast that they do nothing, and thank their stars that they have nothing to do; who sleep every night till they can sleep no longer, and rise only that exercise may enable them to sleep again; who prolong the reign of darkness by double curtains, and never see the sun but to *tell him how they hate his beams;* whose whole labour is to vary the posture of indulgence, and whose day differs from their night but as a couch or chair differs from a bed.

These are the true and open votaries of idleness, for whom she weaves the garlands of poppies, and into whose cup she pours the waters of oblivion; who exist in a state of unruffled stupidity, forgetting and forgotten; who have long ceased to live, and at whose death the survivors can only say, that they have ceased to breathe.

But idleness predominates in many lives where it is not suspected; for, being a vice which terminates in itself, it may be enjoyed without injury to others; and it is therefore not watched like fraud, which endangers property; or like pride, which naturally seeks its gratifications in another's inferiority. Idleness is a silent and peaceful quality, that neither raises envy by ostentation, nor hatred by opposition; and therefore nobody is busy to censure or detect it.

As pride sometimes is hid under humility, idleness is often covered by turbulence and hurry. He that neglects his known duty and real employment, naturally endeavours to crowd his mind with something that may bar out the remembrance of his own folly, and does any thing but what he ought to do with eager diligence, that he may keep himself in his own favour.

Some are always in a state of preparation, occupied in previous measures, forming plans, accumulating materials, and providing for the main affair. These are certainly under the secret power of idleness. Nothing is to be expected from the workman whose tools are for ever to be sought. I was once told by a great master, that no man ever excelled in painting, who was eminently curious about pencils and colours.

There are others to whom idleness dictates another expedient, by which life may be passed unprofitably away without the tediousness of many vacant hours.

The art is, to fill the day with petty business, to have always something in hand which may raise curiosity, but not solicitude, and keep the mind in a state of action, but not of labour.

This art has for many years been practised by my old friend Sober with wonderful success. Sober is a man of strong desires and quick imagination, so exactly balanced by the love of ease, that they can seldom stimulate him to any difficult undertaking; they have, however, so much power, that they will not suffer him to lie quite at rest; and though they do not make him sufficiently useful to others, they make him at least weary of himself.

Mr. Sober's chief pleasure is conversation; there is no end of his talk or his attention; to speak or to hear is equally pleasing; for he still fancies that he is teaching or learning something, and is free for the time from his own reproaches.

But there is one time at night when he must go home, that his friends may sleep; and another time in the morning, when all the world agrees to shut out interruption. These are the moments of which poor Sober trembles at the thought. But the misery of these tiresome intervals he has many means of alleviating. He has persuaded himself that the manual arts are undeservedly overlooked; he has observed in many trades the effects of close thought, and just ratiocination. From speculation he proceeded to practice, and supplied himself with the tools of a carpenter, with which he mended his coal-box very successfully, and which he still continues to employ, as he finds occasion.

He has attempted at other times the crafts of the shoemaker, tinman, plumber, and potter; in all these arts he has failed, and resolves to qualify himself for them by better information. But his daily amusement is chemistry. He has a small furnace, which he employs in distillation, and which has long been the solace of his life. He draws oils and waters, and essences and spirits, which he knows to be of no use; sits and counts the drops as they come from his retort, and forgets that, whilst a drop is falling, a moment flies away.

Poor Sober! I have often teized him with reproof, and he has often promised reformation; for no man is so much open to conviction as the Idler, but there is none on whom it operates so little. What will be the effect of this paper I know not; perhaps he will read it and laugh, and light the fire in his furnace; but my hope is, that he will quit his trifles, and betake himself to rational and useful diligence.*

* In *Mr. Sober,* we have many undoubted traits of Dr. Johnson's character. No man was ever more sensible of his own weaknesses. C.

NUMB. 32.   SATURDAY, *November* 25, 1758.

AMONG the innumerable mortifications that way-lay human arrogance on every side, may well be reckoned our ignorance of the most common objects and effects, a defect of which we become more sensible, by every attempt to supply it. Vulgar and inactive minds confound familiarity with knowledge, and conceive themselves informed of the whole nature of things when they are shewn their form or told their use; but the speculatist, who is not content with superficial views, harasses himself with fruitless curiosity, and still as he inquires more, perceives only that he knows less.

Sleep is a state in which a great part of every life is passed. No animal has been yet discovered whose existence is not varied with intervals of insensibility; and some late philosophers have extended the empire of sleep over the vegetable world.

Yet of this change, so frequent, so great, so general, and so necessary, no searcher has yet found either the efficient or fiual cause; or can tell by what power the mind and body are thus chained down in irresistible stupefaction; or what benefits the animal receives from this alternate suspension of its active powers.

Whatever may be the multiplicity or contrariety of opinions upon this subject, nature has taken sufficient care that theory shall have little influence on practice. The most diligent inquirer is not able long to keep his eyes open; the most eager disputant will begin about midnight to desert his argument; and, once in four and twenty-hours, the gay and the gloomy, the witty and the dull, the clamorous and the silent, the busy and the idle, are all overpowered by the gentle tyrant, and all lie down in the equality of sleep.

Philosophy has often attempted to repress insolence, by asserting, that all conditions are levelled by death; a position which, however it may deject the happy, will seldom afford much comfort to the wretched. It is far more pleasing to consider, that sleep is equally a leveller with death; that the time is never at a great distance, when the balm of rest shall be diffused alike upon every head, when the diversities of life shall stop their operation, and the high and the low shall lie down together.

It is somewhere recorded of Alexander, that in the pride of conquests, and intoxication of flattery, he declared that he only perceived himself to be a man by the necessity of sleep. Whether he considered sleep as necessary to his mind or body, it was indeed a sufficient evidence of human infirmity; the body which required such frequency of renovation, gave but faint promises of immortality; and the mind which, from time to time, sunk gladly into insensibility, had made no very near approaches to the felicity of the supreme and self-sufficient nature.

I know not what can tend more to repress all the passions that disturb the peace of the world, than the consideration that there is no height of happiness or honour, from which man does not eagerly descend to a state of unconscious repose; that the best condition of life is such, that we contentedly quit its good to be disentangled from its evils; that in a few hours splendour fades before the eye, and praise itself deadens in the ear; the senses withdraw from their objects, and reason favours the retreat.

What then are the hopes and prospects of covetousness, ambition, and rapacity? Let him that desires most have all his desires gratified, he never shall attain a state which he can for a day and a night, contemplate with satisfaction, or from which, if he had the power of perpetual vigilance, he would not long for periodical separations.

All envy would be extinguished, if it were universally known that there are none to be envied, and surely none can be much envied who are not pleased with themselves. There is reason to suspect, that the distinctions of mankind have more shew than value, when it is found that all agree to be weary alike of pleasures and of cares; that the powerful and the weak, the celebrated and obscure, join in one common wish, and implore from nature's hand the nectar of oblivion.

Such is our desire of abstraction from ourselves, that very few are satisfied with the quantity of stupefaction which the needs of the body force upon the mind. Alexander himself added intemperance to sleep, and solaced with the fumes of wine the sovereignty of the world: and almost every man has some art by which he steals his thoughts away from his present state.

It is not much of life that is spent in close attention to any important duty. Many hours of every day are suffered to fly away without any traces left upon the intellects. We suffer phantoms to rise up before us, and amuse ourselves with the dance of airy images, which, after a time, we dismiss for ever, and know not how we have been busied.

Many have no happier moments than those that they pass in solitude, abandoned to their own imagination, which sometimes puts sceptres in their hands or mitres on their heads, shifts the scene of pleasure with endless variety, bids all the forms of beauty sparkle before them, and gluts them with every change of visionary luxury.

It is easy in these semi-slumbers to collect all the possibilities of happiness, to alter the course of the sun, to bring back the past, and anticipate the future, to unite all the beauties of all seasons, and all the blessings of all climates, to receive and bestow felicity, and forget that misery is the lot of man. All this is a voluntary dream, a temporary recession from the realities of life to airy fictions; and habitual subjection of reason to fancy.

Others are afraid to be alone, and amuse themselves by a perpetual succession of companions: but the difference is not great; in solitude we have our dreams to ourselves, and in company we agree to dream in concert. The end sought in both is forgetfulness of ourselves.

NUMB. 33.　SATURDAY, *December* 2, 1758.

[I hope the author of the following letter* will excuse the omission of some parts, and allow me to
remark, that the Journal of the Citizen in the
Spectator has almost precluded the attempt of any
future writer.]

> ————*Non ita Romuli*
> *Præscriptum, & intonsi Catonis*
> 　*Auspiciis, veterumque normâ.*　　HOR.

SIR,

YOU have often solicited correspondence. I have
sent you the Journal of a Senior Fellow, or Genuine
Idler, just transmitted from Cambridge by a face-
tious correspondent, and warranted to have been
transcribed from the common-place book of the jour-
nalist.

Monday, Nine o'Clock. Turned off my bed-
maker for waking me at eight. Weather rainy.
Consulted my weather-glass. No hopes of a ride
before dinner.

Ditto, Ten. After breakfast, transcribed half a
sermon from Dr. Hickman. *N. B.* Never to transcribe any more from Calamy ; Mrs. Pilcocks, at my
curacy, having one volume of that author lying in
her parlour-window.

Ditto, Eleven. Went down into my cellar. *Mem.*
My Mountain will be fit to drink in a month's time.
N. B. To remove the five-year-old port into the new
bin on the left hand.

　　　　　* Mr. Thomas Warton.　C.

Ditto Twelve. Mended a pen. Looked at my weather-glass again. Quicksilver very low. Shaved. Barber's hand shakes.

Ditto, One. Dined alone in my room on a sole. *N. B.* The shrimp-sauce not so good as Mr. H. of Peterhouse and I used to eat in London last winter at the Mitre in Fleet-street. Sat down to a pint of Madeira. Mr. H. surprised me over it. We finished two bottles of port together, and were very cheerful. *Mem.* To dine with Mr. H. at Peter-house next Wednesday. One of the dishes a leg of pork and pease, by my desire.

Ditto, Six. Newspaper in the common-room.

Ditto, Seven. Returned to my room. Made a tiff of warm punch, and to bed before nine; did not fall asleep till ten, a young fellow-commoner being very noisy over my head.

Tuesday, Nine. Rose squeamish. A fine morning. Weather-glass very high.

Ditto, Ten. Ordered my horse, and rode to the five-mile stone on the Newmarket road. Appetite gets better. A pack of hounds, in full cry, crossed the road, and startled my horse.

Ditto, Twelve. Drest. Found a letter on my table to be in London the 19th inst. Bespoke a new wig.

Ditto, One. At dinner in the hall. Too much water in the soup. Dr. Dry always orders the beef to be salted too much for me.

Ditto, Two. In the common-room. Dr. Dry gave us an instance of a gentleman who kept the gout out of his stomach by drinking old Madeira.

Conversation chiefly on the expeditions. Company broke up at four. Dr. Dry and myself played at back-gammon for a brace of snipes. Won.

Ditto, Five. At the coffee-house. Met Mr. H. there. Could not get a sight of the *Monitor.*

Ditto, Seven. Returned home, and stirred my fire. Went to the common-room, and supped on the snipes with Dr. Dry.

Ditto, Eight. Began the evening in the common-room. Dr. Dry told several stories. Were very merry. Our new fellow, that studies physick, very talkative toward twelve. Pretends he will bring the youngest Miss —— to drink tea with me soon. Impertinent blockhead !

Wednesday, Nine. Alarmed with a pain in my ancle. Q. The gout ? Fear I can't dine at Peterhouse ; but I hope a ride will set all to rights. Weather-glass below FAIR.

Ditto, Ten. Mounted 'my horse, though the weather suspicious. Pain in my ancle entirely gone. Catched in a shower coming back. Convinced that my weather-glass is the best in Cambridge.

Ditto, Twelve. Drest. Sauntered up to the Fishmonger's hill. Met Mr. H. and went with him to Peterhouse. Cook made us wait thirty-six minutes beyond the time. The company, some of my Emanuel friends. For dinner, a pair of soles, a leg of pork and pease, among other things. *Mem.* Pease-pudding not boiled enough. Cook reprimanded and sconced in my presence.

Ditto, after dinner. Pain in my ancle returns. Dull all the afternoon. Rallied for being no com-

pany.   Mr. H.'s account of the accommodations on
the road in his Bath journey.

Ditto, Six.   Got into spirits.   Never was more
chatty.   We sat late at whist.   Mr. H. and self
agreed at parting to take a gentle ride, and dine at
the old house on the London road to-morrow.

Thursday, Nine.   My sempstress.   She has lost
the measure of my wrist.   Forced to be measured
again.   The baggage has got a trick of smiling.

Ditto, Ten to Eleven.   Made some rappee-snuff.
Read the magazines.   Received a present of pickles
from Miss Pilcocks.   *Mem.* To send in return some
collared eel, which I know both the old lady and
miss are fond of.

Ditto, Eleven. Glass very high.   Mounted at the
gate with Mr. H.   Horse skittish, and wants exercise.   Arrive at the old house.   All the provisions
bespoke by some rakish fellow-commoner in the next
room, who had been on a scheme to Newmarket.
Could get nothing but mutton-chops off the worst
end.   Port very new.   Agree to try some other
house to-morrow.

HERE the Journal breaks off: for the next morning, as my friend informs me, our genial academick
was waked with a severe fit of the gout; and, at
present, enjoys all the dignity of that disease.   But
I believe we have lost nothing by this interruption :
since a continuation of the remainder of the Journal,
through the remainder of the week, would most
probably have exhibited nothing more than a re-

peated relation of the same circumstances of *idling* and luxury.

I hope it will not be concluded, from this specimen of academick life, that I have attempted to decry our universities.   If literature is not the essential requisite of the modern academick, I am yet persuaded, that Cambridge and Oxford, however degenerated, surpass the fashionable *academies* of our metropolis, and the *gymnasia* of foreign countries. The number of learned persons in these celebrated seats is still considerable, and more conveniences and opportunities for study still subsist in them, than in any other place.   There is at least one very powerful incentive to learning ; I mean the GENIUS *of the place*.   It is a sort of inspiring deity, which every youth of quick sensibility and ingenuous disposition creates to himself, by reflecting, that he is placed under those venerable walls, where a HOOKER and a HAMMOND, a BACON and a NEWTON, once pursued the same course of science, and from whence they soared to the most elevated heights of literary fame.   This is that incitement which Tully, according to his own testimony, experienced at Athens, when he contemplated the porticos where Socrates sat, and the laurel-groves where Plato disputed. But there are other circumstances, and of the highest importance, which render our colleges superior to all other places of education.   Their institutions, although somewhat fallen from their primæval simplicity, are such as influence in a particular manner, the moral conduct of their youth ; and in this general depravity of manners and laxity of principles, pure religion is no where more strongly inculcated. The *academies,* as they are presumptuously styled, are too low to be mentioned ; and foreign seminaries are likely to prejudice the unwary mind with Calvinism. But English universities render their students virtuous, at least by excluding all opportunities of vice; and, by teaching them the principles of the *Church of England,* confirm them in those of true christianity.

NUMB. 34. SATURDAY, *December* 9, 1758.

To illustrate one thing by its resemblance to another, has been always the most popular and efficacious art of instruction. There is indeed no other method of teaching that of which any one is ignorant but by means of something already known; and a mind so enlarged by contemplation, and inquiry, that it has always many objects within its view, will seldom be long without some near and familiar image through which an easy transition may be made to truths more distant and obscure.

Of the parallels which have been drawn by wit and curiosity, some are literal and real, as between poetry and painting, two arts which pursue the same end, by the operation of the same mental faculties, and which differ only as the one represents things by marks permanent and natural, the other by signs accidental and arbitrary. The one therefore is more easily and generally understood, since similitude of form is immediately perceived; the other is capable of conveying more ideas, for men have thought and spoken of many things which they do not see.

Other parallels are fortuitous and fanciful, yet these have sometimes been extended to many particulars of resemblance by a lucky concurrence of diligence and chance. The animal *body* is composed of many members, united under the direction of one mind : any number of individuals, connected for some common purpose, is therefore called a body. From this participation of the same appellation arose the comparison of the *body* natural and *body* politick, of which, how far soever it has been deduced, no end has hitherto been found.

In these imaginary similitudes, the same word is used at once in its primitive and metaphorical sense. Thus health, ascribed to the body natural, is opposed to sickness ; but attributed to the body politick stands as contrary to adversity. These parallels therefore have more of genius, but less of truth ; they often please, but they never convince.

Of this kind is a curious speculation frequently indulged by a philosopher of my acquaintance, who had discovered, that the qualities requisite to conversation are very exactly represented by a bowl of punch.

Punch, says this profound investigator, is a liquor compounded of spirit and acid juices, sugar and water. The spirit, volatile and fiery, is the proper emblem of vivacity and wit ; the acidity of the lemon will very aptly figure pungency of raillery, and acrimony of censure ; sugar is the natural representative of luscious adulation and gentle complaisance ; and water is the proper hieroglyphick of easy prattle, innocent and tasteless.

Spirit alone is too powerful for use. It will produce madness rather than merriment ; and instead of quenching thirst will inflame the blood. Thus wit, too copiously poured out, agitates the hearer with emotions rather violent than pleasing ; every one shrinks from the force of its oppression, the company sits entranced and overpowered; all are astonished, but nobody is pleased.

The acid juices give this genial liquor all its power of stimulating the palate. Conversation would become dull and vapid, if negligence were not sometimes roused, and sluggishness quickened, by due severity of reprehension. But acids unmixed will distort the face and torture the palate ; and he that has no other qualities than penetration and asperity, he whose constant employment is detection and censure, who looks only to find faults, and speaks only to punish them, will soon be dreaded, hated and avoided.

The taste of sugar is generally pleasing, but it cannot long be eaten by itself. Thus meekness and courtesy will always recommend the first address, but soon pall and nauseate, unless they are associated with more sprightly qualities. The chief use of sugar is to temper the taste of other substances ; and softness of behaviour in the same manner mitigates the roughness of contradiction, and allays the bitterness of unwelcome truth.

Water is the universal vehicle by which are conveyed the particles necessary to sustenance and growth, by which thirst is quenched, and all the wants of life and nature are supplied. Thus all the business of the world is transacted by artless and easy talk, neither sublimed by fancy, nor discoloured by affectation, without either the harshness of satire, or the lusciousness of flattery. By this limpid vein of language, curiosity is gratified, and all the knowledge is conveyed which one man is required to impart for the safety or convenience of another. Water is the only ingredient in punch which can be used alone, and with which man is content till fancy has framed an artificial want. Thus while we only desire to have our ignorance informed, we are most delighted with the plainest diction; and it is only in the moments of idleness or pride, that we call for the gratifications of wit or flattery.

He only will please long, who, by tempering the acidity of satire with the sugar of civility, and allaying the heat of wit with the frigidity of humble chat, can make the true punch of conversation; and as that punch can be drunk in the greatest quantity which has the largest proportion of water, so that companion will be oftenest welcome, whose talk flows out with inoffensive copiousness, and unenvied insipidity.

NUMB. 35.   SATURDAY, *December* 16, 1758.

TO THE IDLER.

MR. IDLER,

IF it be difficult to persuade the idle to be busy, it is likewise, as experience has taught me, not easy to convince the busy that it is better to be idle. When you shall despair of stimulating sluggishness to motion, I hope you will turn your thoughts towards the means of stilling the bustle of pernicious activity.

I am the unfortunate husband of a *buyer of bargains.* My wife has somewhere heard, that a good housewife *never* has any thing to *purchase when it is wanted.* This maxim is often in her mouth, and always in her head. She is not one of those philosophical talkers that speculate without practice; and learn sentences of wisdom only to repeat them; she is always making additions to her stores; she never looks into a broker's shop, but she spies something that may be wanted some time; and it is impossible to make her pass the door of a house where she hears *goods selling by auction.*

Whatever she thinks cheap, she holds it the duty of an œconomist to buy; in consequence of this maxim, we are incumbered on every side with useless lumber. The servants can scarcely creep to their beds through the chests and boxes that surround them. The carpenter is employed once a week in building closets, fixing cupboards, and fastening shelves; and my house has the appearance of a ship stored for a voyage to the colonies.

I had often observed that advertisements set her on fire; and therefore, pretending to emulate her laudable frugality, I forbade the newspaper to be taken any longer; but my precaution is vain; I know not by what fatality, or by what confederacy, every catalogue of *genuine furniture* comes to her hand, every advertisement of a warehouse newly opened, is in her pocket-book, and she knows before any of her neighbours when the stock of any man *leaving off trade* is to be *sold cheap for ready money*.

Such intelligence is to my dear one the Syren's song. No engagement, no duty, no interest, can withhold her from a sale, from which she always returns congratulating herself upon her dexterity at a bargain; the porter lays down his burden in the hall; she displays her new acquisitions, and spends the rest of the day in contriving where they shall be put.

As she cannot bear to have any thing uncomplete, one purchase necessitates another; she has twenty feather-beds more than she can use, and a late sale has supplied her with a proportionable number of Whitney blankets, a large roll of linen for sheets, and five quilts for every bed, which she bought because the seller told her, that if she would clear his hands he would let her have a bargain.

Thus by hourly encroachments my habitation is made narrower and narrower; the dining-room is so crowded with tables, that dinner scarcely can be served; the parlour is decorated with so many piles of china, that I dare not step within the door; at every turn of the stairs I have a clock, and half the windows of the upper floors are darkened, that shelves may be set before them.

This, however, might be borne, if she would gratify her own inclinations without opposing mine. But I who am idle am luxurious, and she condemns me to live upon salt provision. She knows the loss of buying in small quantities, we have therefore whole hogs and quarters of oxen. Part of our meat is tainted before it is eaten, and part is thrown away because it is spoiled; but she persists in her system, and will never buy any thing by single pennyworths.

The common vice of those who are still grasping at more, is to neglect that which they already possess, but from this failing my charmer is free. It is the great care of her life that the pieces of beef should be boiled in the order in which they are bought; that the second bag of pease should not be opened till the first are eaten; that every feather-bed shall be lain on in its turn; that the carpets should be taken out of the chests once a month and brushed, and the rolls of linen opened now and then before the fire. She is daily inquiring after the best traps for mice, and keeps the rooms always scented by fumigations to destroy the moths. She employs workmen, from time to time, to adjust six clocks that never go, and clean five jacks that rust in the garret; and a woman in the next alley lives by scouring the brass and pewter, which are only laid up to tarnish again.

She is always imagining some distant time in which she shall use whatever she accumulates : she has four looking-glasses which she cannot hang up in her house, but which will be handsome in more lofty rooms ; and pays rent for the place of a vast copper in some warehouse, because when we live in the country we shall brew our own beer.

Of this life I have long been weary, but know not how to change it : all the married men whom I consult advise me to have patience ; but some old bachelors are of opinion that since she loves sales so well, she should have a sale of her own ; and I have, I think, resolved to open her hoards, and advertise an auction.

I am, Sir,

Your very humble servant,

PETER PLENTY.

NUMB. 36. SATURDAY, *December* 23, 1758.

THE great differences that disturb the peace of mankind are not about ends, but means. We have all the same general desires, but how those desires shall be accomplished will for ever be disputed. The ultimate purpose of government is temporal, and that of religion is eternal happiness. Hitherto we agree; but here we must part, to try, according to the endless varieties of passion and understanding combined with one another, every possible form of government, and every imaginable tenet of religion.

We are told by Cumberland that *rectitude*, applied to action or contemplation, is merely metaphorical; and that as a *right* line describes the shortest passage from point to point, so a *right* action effects a good design by the fewest means; and so likewise a *right* opinion is that which connects distant truths by the shortest train of intermediate propositions.

To find the nearest way from truth to truth, or from purpose to effect, not to use more instruments where fewer will be sufficient, not to move by wheels and levers what will give way to the naked hand, is the great proof of a healthful and vigorous mind, neither feeble with helpless ignorance, nor overburdened with unwieldy knowledge.

But there are men who seem to think nothing so much the characteristick of a genius, as to do common things in an uncommon manner; like Hudibras, to *tell the clock by algebra*; or like the lady in Dr.

Young's satires, *to drink tea by stratagem* ; to quit the beaten track only because it is known, and take a new path, however crooked or rough, because the strait was found out before.

Every man speaks and writes with intent to be understood ; and it can seldom happen but he that understands himself might convey his notions to another, if, content to be understood, he did not seek to be admired ; but when once he begins to contrive how his sentiments may be received, not with most ease to his reader, but with most advantage to himself, he then transfers his consideration from words to sounds, from sentences to periods, and as he grows more elegant becomes less intelligible.

It is difficult to enumerate every species of authors whose labours counteract themselves ; the man of exuberance and copiousness, who diffuses every thought through so many diversities of expression, that it is lost like water in a mist ; the ponderous dictator of sentences, whose notions are delivered in the lump, and are, like uncoined bullion, of more weight than use ; the liberal illustrator, who shews by examples and comparisons what was clearly seen when it was first proposed ; and the stately son of demonstration, who proves with mathematical formality what no man has yet pretended to doubt.

There is a mode of style for which I know not that the masters of oratory have yet found a name ; a style by which the most evident truths are so obscured, that they can no longer be perceived, and the most familiar propositions so disguised that they cannot be known. Every other kind of eloquence is the dress of sense; but this is the mask by which a true master of his art will so effectually conceal it, that a man will as easily mistake his own positions, if he meets them thus transformed, as he may pass in a masquerade his nearest acquaintance.

This style may be called the *terrifick*, for its chief intention is to terrify and amaze; it may be termed the *repulsive*, for its natural effect is to drive away the reader; or it may be distinguished, in plain English, by the denomination of the *bugbear style*, for it has more terror than danger, and will appear less formidable as it is more nearly approached.

A mother tells her infant, that *two and two make four*; the child remembers the proposition, and is able to count four to all the purposes of life, till the course of his education brings him among philosophers, who fright him from his former knowledge, by telling him, that four is a certain aggregate of units; that all numbers being only the repetition of an unit, which, though not a number itself, is the parent, root, or original of all number, *four* is the denomination assigned to a certain number of such repetitions. The only danger is, lest, when he first hears these dreadful sounds, the pupil should run away; if he has but the courage to stay till the conclusion, he will find that, when speculation has done its worst, two and two still make four.

An illustrious example of this species of eloquence may be found in " Letters concerning Mind." The author begins by declaring, that " the sorts of things are things that now are, have been, and shall be, and the things that strictly ARE." In this position, except the last clause, in which he uses something of the scholastick language, there is nothing but what every man has heard and imagines himself to know. But who would not believe that some wonderful novelty is presented to his intellect, when he is afterwards told, in the true bugbear style, that " the *ares,* in the former sense, are things that lie between the *have-beens* and *shall-bes.* The *have-beens* are things that are past ; the *shall-bes* are things that are to come ; and things that ARE, *in the latter sense,* are things that have not been, nor shall be, nor stand in the midst of such as are before them, or shall be after them. The things that have been, and shall be, have respect to present, past, and future. Those likewise that now ARE have moreover place ; that for instance, which is here, that which is to the east, that which is to the west."*

All this, my dear reader, is very strange ; but though it be strange, it is not new ; survey these wonderful sentences again, and they will be found to contain nothing more than very plain truths, which till this Author arose had always been delivered in plain language.

* These "Letters on Mind" were written by a Mr. Petvin, who some years afterwards published another tract, entitled a " Summary of the Soul's Perceptive Faculties," 1768. He was at that time compared to the subtle doctor, who, when he grew old, wept because he could not understand his own books. C.

NUMB. 37.   SATURDAY, *December* 30, 1758.

THOSE who are skilled in the extraction and preparation of metals, declare, that iron is every where to be found; and that not only its proper ore is copiously treasured in the caverns of the earth, but that its particles are dispersed throughout all other bodies.

If the extent of the human view could comprehend the whole frame of the universe, I believe it would be found invariably true, that Providence has given that in greatest plenty, which the condition of life makes of greatest use; and that nothing is penuriously imparted or placed far from the reach of man, of which a more liberal distribution, or more easy acquisition, would increase real and rational felicity.

Iron is common, and gold is rare. Iron contributes so much to supply the wants of nature, that its use constitutes much of the difference between savage and polished life, between the state of him that slumbers in European palaces, and him that shelters himself in the cavities of a rock from the chilness of the night, or the violence of the storm. Gold can never be hardened into saws or axes; it can neither furnish instruments of manufacture, utensils of agriculture, nor weapons of defence; its only quality is to shine, and the value of its lustre arises from its scarcity.

Throughout the whole circle, both of natural and moral life, necessaries are as iron, and superfluities as gold. What we really need we may readily obtain; so readily, that far the greater part of mankind has, in the wantonness of abundance, confounded natural with artificial desires, and invented necessities for the sake of employment, because the mind is impatient of inaction, and life is sustained with so little labour, that the tediousness of idle time cannot otherwise be supported.

Thus plenty is the original cause of many of our needs; and even the poverty, which is so frequent and distressful in civilized nations, proceeds often from that change of manners which opulence has produced. Nature makes us poor only when we want necessaries; but custom gives the name of poverty to the want of superfluities.

When Socrates passed through shops of toys and ornaments, he cried out, "How many things are here which I do not need!" And the same exclamation may every man make who surveys the common accommodations of life.

Superfluity and difficulty begin together. To dress food for the stomach is easy, the art is to irritate the palate when the stomach is sufficed. A rude hand may build walls, form roofs, and lay floors, and provide all that warmth and security require; we only call the nicer artificers to carve the cornice, or to paint the ceilings. Such dress as may enable the body to endure the different seasons, the most unenlightened nations have been able to procure; but the work of science begins in the ambition of distinction, in variations of fashion, and emulation of elegance. Corn grows with easy culture; the gardener's experiments are only employed to exalt the flavours of fruits, and brighten the colours of flowers.

Even of knowledge, those parts are most easy which are generally necessary. The intercourse of society is maintained without the elegances of language. Figures, criticisms, and refinements, are the work of those whom idleness makes weary of themselves. The commerce of the world is carried on by easy methods of computation. Subtilty and study are required only when questions are invented merely to puzzle, and calculations are extended to shew the skill of the calculator. The light of the sun is equally beneficial to him whose eyes tell him that it moves, and to him whose reason persuades him that it stands still; and plants grow with the same luxuriance, whether we suppose earth or water the parent of vegetation.

If we raise our thoughts to nobler inquiries, we shall still find facility concurring with usefulness. No man needs stay to be virtuous till the moralists have determined the essence of virtue; our duty is made apparent by its approximate consequences, though the general and ultimate reason should never be discovered. Religion may regulate the life of him to whom the *Scotists* and *Thomists* are alike unknown; and the assertors of fate and free-will, however different in their talk, agree to act in the same manner.

It is not my intention to depreciate the politer arts or abstruser studies. That curiosity which always succeeds ease and plenty, was undoubtedly given us as a proof of capacity which our present state is not able to fill, as a preparative for some better mode of existence, which shall furnish employment for the whole soul, and where pleasure shall be adequate to our powers of fruition. In the mean time, let us gratefully acknowledge that goodness which grants us ease at a cheap rate, which changes the seasons where the nature of heat and cold has not been yet examined, and gives the vicissitudes of day and night to those who never marked the tropicks, or numbered the constellations.

NUMB. 38.   SATURDAY, *January* 6, 1759.

SINCE the publication of the letter concerning the condition of those who are confined in gaols by their creditors, an inquiry is said to have been made, by which it appears that more than twenty thousand * are at this time prisoners for debt.

We often look with indifference on the successive parts of that, which if the whole were seen together, would shake us with emotion.   A debtor is dragged to prison, pitied for a moment, and then forgotten ; another follows him, and is lost alike in the caverns of oblivion ; but when the whole mass of calamity rises up at once, when twenty thousand reasonable beings are heard all groaning in unnecessary misery, not by the infirmity of nature, but the mistake or negligence of policy, who can forbear to pity and lament, to wonder and abhor !

There is here no need of declamatory vehemence : we live in an age of commerce and computation ; let us therefore coolly inquire what is the sum of evil which the imprisonment of debtors brings upon our country.

It seems to be the opinion of the later computists, that the inhabitants of England do not exceed six millions, of which twenty thousand is the three-

* This number was at that time confidently published ; but the author has since found reason to question the calculation.

hundredth part. What shall we say of the humanity or the wisdom of a nation that voluntarily sacrifices one in every three hundred to lingering destruction !

The misfortunes of an individual do not extend their influence to many; yet if we consider the effects of consanguinity and friendship, and the general reciprocation of wants and benefits, which make one man dear or necessary to another, it may reasonably be supposed, that every man languishing in prison gives trouble of some kind to two others who love or need him. By this multiplication of misery we see distress extended to the hundredth part of the whole society.

If we estimate at a shilling a day what is lost by the inaction and consumed in the support of each man thus chained down to involuntary idleness, the publick loss will rise in one year to three hundred thousand pounds; in ten years to more than a sixth part of our circulating coin.

I am afraid that those who are best acquainted with the state of our prisons will confess that my conjecture is too near the truth, when I suppose that the corrosion of resentment, the heaviness of sorrow, the corruption of confined air, the want of exercise, and sometimes of food, the contagion of diseases, from which there is no retreat, and the severity of tyrants, against whom there can be no resistance, and all the complicated horrors of a prison, put an end every year to the life of one in four of those that are shut up from the common comforts of human life.

Thus perish yearly five thousand men, overborne

with sorrow, consumed by famine, or putrified by filth; many of them in the most vigorous and useful part of life; for the thoughtless and imprudent are commonly young, and the active and the busy are seldom old.

According to the rule generally received, which supposes that one in thirty dies yearly, the race of man may be said to be renewed at the end of thirty years. Who would have believed till now, that of every English generation, an hundred and fifty thousand perish in our gaols! that in every century, a nation eminent for science, studious of commerce, ambitious of empire, should willingly lose, in noisome dungeons, five hundred thousand of its inhabitants; a number greater than has ever been destroyed in the same time by the pestilence and sword!

A very late occurrence may shew us the value of the number which we thus condemn to be useless; in the re-establishment of the trained bands, thirty thousand are considered as a force sufficient against all exigencies. While, therefore, we detain twenty thousand in prison, we shut up in darkness and uselessness two-thirds of an army which ourselves judge equal to the defence of our country.

The monastick institutions have been often blamed, as tending to retard the increase of mankind. And perhaps retirement ought rarely to be permitted, except to those whose employment is consistent with abstraction, and who, though solitary, will not be idle; to those whom infirmity makes useless to the commonwealth, or to those who have paid their due proportion to society, and who, having lived for others, may be honourably dismissed to live for themselves. But whatever be the evil or the folly of these retreats, those have no right to censure them whose prisons contain greater numbers than the monasteries of other countries. It is, surely, less foolish and less criminal to permit inaction than compel it; to comply with doubtful opinions of happiness, than condemn to certain and apparent misery; to indulge the extravagancies of erroneous pity, than to multiply and enforce temptation to wickedness.

The misery of gaols is not half their evil: they are filled with every corruption which poverty and wickedness can generate between them; with all the shameless and profligate enormities that can be produced by the impudence of ignominy, the rage of want, and the malignity of despair. In a prison the awe of the publick eye is lost, and the power of the law is spent; there are few fears, there are no blushes. The lewd inflame the lewd, the audacious harden the audacious. Every one fortifies himself as he can against his own sensibility, endeavours to practise on others the arts which are practised on himself; and gains the kindness of his associates by similitude of manners.

Thus some sink amidst their misery, and others survive only to propagate villainy. It may be hoped, that our lawgivers will at length take away from us this power of starving and depraving one another; but, if there be any reason why this inveterate evil should not be removed in our age, which true policy has enlightened beyond any former time, let those, whose writings form the opinions and the practices of their contemporaries, endeavour to transfer the reproach of such imprisonment from the debtor to the creditor, till universal infamy shall pursue the wretch whose wantonness of power, or revenge of disappointment, condemns another to torture and to ruin ; till he shall be hunted through the world as an enemy to man, and find in riches no shelter from contempt.

Surely, he whose debtor has perished in prison, although he may acquit himself of deliberate murder, must at least have his mind clouded with discontent, when he considers how much another has suffered from him ; when he thinks on the wife bewailing her husband, or the children begging the bread which their father would have earned.   If there are any made so obdurate by avarice or cruelty, as to revolve these consequences without dread or pity, I must leave them to be awakened by some other power, for I write only to human beings.

NUMB. 39.   SATURDAY, *January* 13, 1759.

TO THE IDLER.

SIR,

As none look more diligently about them than those who have nothing to do, or who do nothing, I suppose it has not escaped your observation, that the bracelet, an ornament of great antiquity, has been for some years revived among the English ladies.

The genius of our nation is said, I know not for what reason, to appear rather in improvement than invention. The bracelet was known in the earliest ages; but it was formerly only a hoop of gold, or a cluster of jewels, and shewed nothing but the wealth or vanity of the wearer, till our ladies, by carrying pictures on their wrists, made their ornaments works of fancy and exercises of judgment.

This addition of art to luxury is one of the innumerable proofs that might be given of the late increase of female erudition; and I have often congratulated myself that my life has happened at a time when those, on whom so much of human felicity depends, have learned to think as well as speak, and when respect takes possession of the ear, while love is entering at the eye.

I have observed, that, even by the suffrages of their own sex, those ladies are accounted wisest, who do not yet disdain to be taught; and therefore I shall offer a few hints for the completion of the bracelet, without any dread of the fate of Orpheus.

To the ladies who' wear the pictures of their husbands or children, or any other relations, I can offer nothing more decent or more proper. It is reasonable to believe that she intends at least to perform her duty, who carries a perpetual excitement to recollection and caution, whose own ornaments must upbraid her with every failure, and who, by an open violation of her engagements, must for ever forfeit her bracelet.

Yet I know not whether it is the interest of the husband to solicit very earnestly a place on the bracelet. If his image be not in the heart, it is of small avail to hang it on the hand. A husband encircled with diamonds and rubies may gain some esteem, but will never excite love. He that thinks himself most secure of his wife, should be fearful of persecuting her continually with his presence. The joy of life is variety; the tenderest love requires to be rekindled by intervals of absence; and Fidelity herself will be wearied with transferring her eye only from the same man to the same picture.

In many countries the condition of every woman is known by her dress. Marriage is rewarded with some honourable distinction, which celibacy is forbidden to usurp. Some such information a bracelet might afford. The ladies might enroll themselves in distinct classes, and carry in open view the emblems of their order. The bracelet of the authoress may exhibit the Muses in a grove of laurel; the housewife may shew Penelope with her web; the votress of a single life may carry Ursula with her troop of virgins; the gamester may have Fortune with her wheel; and those women *that have no character at all* may display a field of white enamel, as imploring help to fill up the vacuity.

There is a set of ladies who have outlived most animal pleasures, and, having nothing rational to put in their place, solace with-cards the loss of what time has taken away, and the want of what wisdom, having never been courted, has never given. For these I know not how to provide a proper decoration. They cannot be numbered among the gamesters; for though they are always at play, they play for nothing, and never rise to the dignity of hazard or the reputation of skill. They neither love nor are loved, and cannot be supposed to contemplate any human image with delight. Yet, though they despair to please, they always wish to be fine, and therefore cannot be without a bracelet. To this sisterhood I can recommend nothing more likely to please them than the king of clubs, a personage very comely and majestick, who will never meet their eyes without reviving the thought of some past or future party, and who may be displayed in the act of dealing with grace and propriety.

But the bracelet which might be most easily introduced into general use is a small convex mirror, in which the lady may see herself whenever she shall lift her hand. This will be a perpetual source of delight. Other ornaments are of use only in publick, but this will furnish gratifications to solitude. This will shew a face that must always please; she who is followed by admirers will carry about her a perpetual justification of the publick voice ; and she who passes without notice may appeal from prejudice to her own eyes.

But I know not why the privilege of the bracelet should be confined to women ; it was in former ages worn by heroes in battle ; and as modern soldiers are always distinguished by splendour of dress, I should rejoice to see the bracelet added to the cockade.

In hope of this ornamental innovation, I have spent some thoughts upon military bracelets. There is no passion more heroick than love ; and therefore I should be glad to see the sons of England marching in the field, every man with the picture of a woman of honour bound upon his hand. But since in the army, as every where else, there will always be men who love nobody but themselves, or whom no woman of honour will permit to love her, there is a necessity of some other distinctions and devices.

I have read of a prince who, having lost a town, ordered the name of it to be every morning shouted in his ear till it should be recovered. For the same purpose I think the prospect of Minorca might be properly worn on the hands of some of our generals : others might delight their countrymen, and dignify themselves, with a view of Rochfort as it appeared to them at sea : and those that shall return from the conquest of America, may exhibit the warehouse of Frontenac, with an inscription denoting, that it was taken in less than three years by less than twenty thousand men.

I am, Sir, &c.

TOM TOY.

NUMB. 40. SATURDAY, *January* 20, 1759.

THE practice of appending to the narratives of publick transactions more minute and domestick intelligence, and filling the newspapers with advertisements, has grown up by slow degrees to its present state.

Genius is shewn only by invention. The man who first took advantage of the general curiosity that was excited by a siege or battle, to betray the readers of news into the knowledge of the shop where the best puffs and powder were to be sold, was undoubtedly a man of great sagacity, and profound skill in the nature of man. But when he had once shewn the way, it was easy to follow him ; and every man now knows a ready method of informing the publick of all that he desires to buy or sell, whether his wares be material or intellectual; whether he makes clothes or teaches the mathematicks, whether he be a tutor that wants a pupil, or a pupil that wants a tutor.

Whatever is common is despised. Advertisements are now so numerous that they are very negligently perused, and it is therefore become necessary to gain attention by magnificence of promises, and by eloquence sometimes sublime and sometimes pathetick.

Promise, large promise, is the soul of an advertisement. I remember a *wash-ball* that had a quality truly wonderful—It gave *an exquisite edge to the razor*. And there are now to be sold *for ready money only*, some *duvets for bed-coverings, of down, beyond comparison superior to what is called otter-down,* and indeed such, that its *many excellencies cannot be here set forth.* With one excellence we are made acquainted — *it is warmer than four or five blankets, and lighter than one.*

There are some, however, that know the prejudice of mankind in favour of modest sincerity. The vender of the *beautifying fluid* sells a lotion that repels pimples, washes away freckles, smooths the skin, and plumps the flesh ; and yet, with a generous abhorrence of ostentation, confesses, that it will not *restore the bloom of fifteen to a lady of fifty.*

The true pathos of advertisements must have sunk deep into the heart of every man that remembers the zeal shewn by the seller of the *anodyne necklace,* for the ease and safety *of poor toothing infants,* and the affection with which he warned every mother, that *she would never forgive herself* if her infant should perish without a necklace.

I cannot but remark to the celebrated author, who gave in his notifications of the camel and dromedary, so many specimens of the genuine sublime, that there is now arrived another subject yet more worthy of his pen. *A famous Mohawk Indian warrior, who took Dieskaw the French general prisoner, dressed in the same manner with the native Indians when they go to war, with his face and body painted, with his scalping-knife, tom-ax, and all other implements of war ! a sight worthy the curiosity of every true Briton !* This is a very powerful description ; but a critick of great refinement would say, that it conveys rather *horror* than *terror.*

An Indian, dressed as he goes to war, may bring company together ; but if he carries the scalping knife and tom-ax, there arc many true Britons that will never be persuaded to see him but through a grate.

It has been remarked by the severer judges, that the salutary sorrow of tragick scenes is too soon effaced by the merriment of the epilogue ; the same inconvenience arises from the improper disposition of advertisements. The noblest objects may be so associated as to be made ridiculous. The camel and dromedary themselves might have lost much of their dignity between *the true flower of mustard* and the *original Daffy's elixir ;* and I could not but feel some indignation when I found this illustrious Indian warrior immediately succeeded by *a fresh parcel of Dublin butter.*

The trade of advertising is now so near to perfection, that it is not easy to propose any improvement. But as every art ought to be exercised in due subordination to the publick good, I cannot but propose it as a moral question to these masters of the publick ear, Whether they do not sometimes play too wantonly with our passions, as when the registrar of lottery tickets invites us to his shop by an account of the prize which he sold last year ; and whether the advertising controvertists do not indulge asperity of language without any adequate provocation ; as in the dispute about *straps for razors,* now happily subsided, and in the altercation which at present subsists concerning *eau de luce?*

In an advertisement it is allowed to every man to speak well of himself, but I know not why he should assume the privilege of censuring his neighbour. He may proclaim his own virtue or skill, but ought not to exclude others from the same pretensions.

Every man that advertises his own excellence should write with some consciousness of a character which dares to call the attention of the publick. He should remember that his name is to stand in the same paper with those of the king of Prussia and the emperor of Germany, and endeavour to make himself worthy of such association.

Some regard is likewise to be paid to posterity. There are men of diligence and curiosity who treasure up the papers of the day merely because others neglect them, and in time they will be scarce. When these collections shall be read in another century, how will numberless contradictions be reconciled? and how shall fame be possibly distributed among the taylors and boddice-makers of the present age?

Surely these things deserve consideration. It is enough for me to have hinted my desire that these abuses may be rectified; but such is the state of nature, that what all have the right of doing, many will attempt without sufficient care or due qualifications.

NUMB. 41.   SATURDAY, *January* 27, 1759.

THE following letter relates to an affliction perhaps not necessary to be imparted to the publick;
but I could not persuade myself to suppress it, because I think I know the sentiments to be sincere,
and I feel no disposition to provide for this day any
other entertainment.

> *At tu quisquis eris, miseri qui cruda poetæ*
>   *Credideris fletu funera digna tuo,*
> *Hæc postrema tibi sit flendi causa, fluatque*
> *Lenis inoffenso vitaque morsque gradu.*

MR. IDLER,

NOTWITHSTANDING the warnings of philosophers,
and the daily examples of losses and misfortunes
which life forces upon our observation, such is the
absorption of our thoughts in the business of the
present day, such the resignation of our reason to
empty hopes of future felicity, or such our unwillingness to foresee what we dread, that every calamity
comes suddenly upon us, and not only presses us as
a burden, but crushes as a blow.

There are evils which happen out of the common
course of nature, against which it is no reproach not
to be provided. A flash of lightning intercepts the
traveller in his way. The concussion of an earth-
quake heaps the ruins of cities upon their inhabitants. But other miseries time brings, though silently yet visibly, forward by its even lapse, which
yet approach us unseen because we turn our eyes

away, and seize us unresisted because we could not arm ourselves against them but by setting them before us.

That it is vain to shrink from what cannot be avoided, and to hide that from ourselves which must some time be found, is a truth which we all know, but which all neglect, and perhaps none more than the speculative reasoner, whose thoughts are always from home, whose eye wanders over life, whose fancy dances after meteors of happiness kindled by itself, and who examines every thing rather than his own state.

Nothing is more evident than that the decays of age must terminate in death; yet there is no man, says Tully, who does not believe that he may yet live another year; and there is none who does not, upon the same principle, hope another year for his parent or his friend: but the fallacy will be in time detected; the last year, the last day, must come. It has come, and is past. The life which made my own life pleasant is at an end, and the gates of death are shut upon my prospects.

The loss of a friend upon whom the heart was fixed, to whom every wish and endeavour tended, is a state of dreary desolation, in which the mind looks abroad impatient of itself, and finds nothing but emptiness and horror. The blameless life, the artless tenderness, the pious simplicity, the modest resignation, the patient sickness, and the quiet death, are remembered only to add value to the loss, to aggravate regret for what cannot be amended, to deepen sorrow for what cannot be recalled.

These are the calamities by which Providence gradually disengages us from the love of life. Other evils fortitude may repel, or hope may mitigate; but irreparable privation leaves nothing to exercise resolution or flatter expectation. The dead cannot return, and nothing is left us here but languishment and grief.

Yet such is the course of nature, that whoever lives long must outlive those whom he loves and honours. Such is the condition of our present existence, that life must one time lose its associations, and every inhabitant of the earth must walk downward to the grave alone and unregarded, without any partner of his joy or grief, without any interested witness of his misfortunes or success.

Misfortune, indeed, he may yet feel; for where is the bottom of the misery of man? But what is success to him that has none to enjoy it? Happiness is not found in self-contemplation; it is perceived only when it is reflected from another.

We know little of the state of departed souls, because such knowledge is not necessary to a good life. Reason deserts us at the brink of the grave and can give no further intelligence. Revelation is not wholly silent. "There is joy in the angels of Heaven over one sinner that repenteth;" and surely this joy is not incommunicable to souls disentangled from the body, and made like angels.

Let hope therefore dictate, what revelation does not confute, that the union of souls may still remain; and that we who are struggling with sin, sorrow, and infirmities, may have our part in the attention and kindness of those who have finished their course, and are now receiving their reward.

These are the great occasions which force the mind to take refuge in religion : when we have no help in ourselves, what can remain but that we look up to a higher and a greater Power? and to what hope may we not raise our eyes and hearts, when we consider that the greatest POWER is the BEST?

Surely there is no man who, thus afflicted, does not seek succour in the *gospel,* which has brought *life and immortality to light.* The precepts of Epicurus, who teaches us to endure what the laws of the universe make necessary, may silence, but not content us. The dictates of Zeno, who commands us to look with indifference on external things, may dispose us to conceal our sorrow, but cannot assuage it. Real alleviation of the loss of friends, and rational tranquillity in the prospect of our own dissolution, can be received only from the promises of Him in whose hands are life and death, and from the assurance of another and better state, in which all tears will be wiped from the eyes, and the whole soul shall be filled with joy. Philosophy may infuse stubbornness, but Religion only can give patience.

I am, &c.*

---

* This paper was written by Dr. Johnson on the death of his mother, He wrote his " Rasselas," with the affectionate purpose of defraying the expences of her funeral, and paying a few small debts which she left.   C.

NUMB. 42. SATURDAY, *February* 3, 1759.

THE subject of the following letter is not wholly unmentioned by the RAMBLER. The SPECTATOR has also a letter containing a case not much different. I hope my correspondent's performance is more an effort of genius, than effusion of the passions; and that she hath rather attempted to paint some possible distress, than really feels the evils which she has described.

TO THE IDLER.

SIR,

THERE is a cause of misery, which, though certainly known both to you and your predecessors, has been little taken notice of in your papers; I mean the snares that the bad behaviour of parents extends over the paths of life which their children are to tread after them; and as I make no doubt but the *Idler* holds the shield for virtue, as well as the glass for folly, that he will employ his leisure hours as much to his own satisfaction in warning his readers against a danger, as in laughing them out of a fashion: for this reason I am tempted to ask admittance for my story in your paper, though it has nothing to recommend it but truth, and the honest wish of warning others to shun the track which I am afraid may lead me at last to ruin.

I am the child of a father, who, having always lived in one spot in the country where he was born, and having had no genteel education himself, thought no qualifications in the world desirable but as they led up to fortune, and no learning necessary to happiness but such as might most effectually teach me to make the best market of myself. I was unfortunately born a beauty, to a full sense of which my father took care to flatter me; and having, when very young, put me to a school in the country, afterwards transplanted me to another in town, at the instigation of his friends, where his ill-judged fondness let me remain no longer than to learn just enough experience to convince me of the sordidness of his views, to give me an idea of perfections which my present situation will never suffer me to reach, and to teach me sufficient morals to dare to despise what is bad, though it be in a father.

Thus equipped (as he thought completely) for life, I was carried back into the country, and lived with him and my mother in a small village, within a few miles of the county-town; where I mixed, at first with reluctance, among company which, though I never despised, I could not approve, as they were brought up with other inclinations, and narrower views than my own. My father took great pains to shew me every where, both at his own house, and at such publick diversions as the country afforded: he frequently told the people all he had was for his daughter; took care to repeat the civilities I had received from all his friends in London; told how much I was admired, and all his little ambition could suggest to set me in a stronger light.

Thus have I continued tricked out for sale, as I may call it, and doomed, by parental authority, to a state little better than that of prostitution. I look on myself as growing cheaper every hour, and am losing all that honest pride, that modest confidence, in which the virgin dignity consists. Nor does my misfortune stop here : though many would be too generous to impute the follies of a father to a child whose heart has set her above them ; yet I am afraid the most charitable of them will hardly think it possible for me to be a daily spectatress of his vices without tacitly allowing them, and at last consenting to them, as the eye of the frighted infant is, by degrees, reconciled to the darkness of which at first it was afraid. It is a common opinion, he himself must very well know, that vices, like diseases, are often hereditary ; and that the property of the one is to infect the manners, as the other poisons the springs of life.

Yet this, though bad, is not the worst ; my father deceives himself the hopes of the very child he has brought into the world ; he suffers his house to be the seat of drunkenness, riot, and irreligion : who seduces, almost in my sight, the menial servant, converses with the prostitute, and corrupts the wife ! Thus I, who from my earliest dawn of reason was taught to think that at my approach every eye sparkled with pleasure, or was dejected as conscious of superior charms, am excluded from society, through fear lest I should partake, if not of my father's crimes, at least of his reproach. Is a parent, who is so little

solicitous for the welfare of a child, better than a
pirate who turns a wretch adrift in a boat at sea,
without a star to steer by, or an anchor to hold it
fast?   Am I not to lay all my miseries at those
doors which ought to have opened only for my protection?   And if doomed to add at last one more to
the number of those wretches whom neither the world
nor its law befriends, may I not justly say that I have
been awed by a parent into ruin?   But though a parent's power is screened from insult and violation by
the very words of Heaven, yet surely no laws divine or
human, forbid me to remove myself from the malignant shade of a plant that poisons all around it, blasts
the bloom of youth, checks its improvements, and
makes all its flowrets fade; but to whom can the
wretched, can the dependant fly?   For me to fly a
father's house, is to be a beggar: I have only one
comforter amidst my anxieties, a pious relation, who
bids me appeal to Heaven for a witness to my just
intentions, fly as a deserted wretch to its protection;
and, being asked who my father is, point, like the
antient philosopher, with my finger to the heavens.

The hope in which I write this, is, that you will
give it a place in your paper; and, as your essays
sometimes find their way into the country, that my
father may read my story there; and, if not for his
own sake, yet for mine, spare to perpetuate that
worst of calamities to me, the loss of character,
from which all his dissimulation has not been able
to rescue himself.   Tell the world, Sir, that it is
possible for virtue to keep its throne unshaken without any other guard than itself; that it is possible to

maintain that purity of thought so necessary to the completion of human excellence even in the midst of temptations; when they have no friend within, nor are assisted by the voluntary indulgence of vicious thoughts.

If the insertion of a story like this does not break in on the plan of your paper, you have it in your power to be a better friend than her father to

PERDITA. *

NUMB. 43.   SATURDAY, *February* 10, 1759.

THE natural advantages which arise from the position of the earth which we inhabit with respect to the other planets, afford much employment to mathematical speculation, by which it has been discovered, that no other conformation of the system could have given such commodious distributions of light and heat, or imparted fertility and pleasure to so great a part of a revolving sphere.

It may be perhaps observed by the moralist, with equal reason, that our globe seems particularly fitted for the residence of a being, placed here only for a short time, whose task is to advance himself to a higher and happier state of existence, by unremitted vigilance of caution, and activity of virtue.

* An unknown correspondent.   C.

The duties required of man are such as human nature does not willingly perform, and such as those are inclined to delay who yet intend some time to fulfil them.   It was therefore necessary that this universal reluctance should be counteracted, and the drowsiness of hesitation wakened into resolve; that the danger of procrastination should be always in view, and the fallacies of security be hourly detected.

To this end all the appearances of nature uniformly conspire.   Whatever we see on every side reminds us of the lapse of time and the flux of life. The day and night succeed each other, the rotation of seasons diversifies the year, the sun rises, attains the meridian, declines, and sets; and the moon every night changes its form.

The day has been considered as an image of the year, and the year as the representation of life. The morning answers to the spring, and the spring to childhood and youth; the noon corresponds to the summer, and the summer to the strength of manhood.   The evening is an emblem of autumn, and autumn of declining life.   The night with its silence and darkness shews the winter, in which all the powers of vegetation are benumbed; and the winter points out the time when life shall cease, with its hopes and pleasures.

He that is carried forward however swiftly, by a motion equable and easy, perceives not the change of place but by the variation of objects.   If the wheel of life, which rolls thus silently along, passed on through undistinguishable uniformity, we should never mark its approaches to the end of the course.   If one hour were like another ; if the passage of the sun did not shew that the day is wasting ; if the change of seasons did not impress upon us the flight of the year ; quantities of duration equal to days and years would glide unobserved.   If the parts of time were not variously coloured, we should never discern their departure or succession, but should live thoughtless of the past, and careless of the future, without will, and perhaps without power, to compute the periods of life, or to compare the time which is already lost with that which may probably remain.

But the course of time is so visibly marked, that it is observed even by the birds of passage, and by nations who have raised their minds very little above animal instinct : there are human beings whose language does not supply them with words by which they can number five, but I have read of none that have not names for day and night, for summer and winter.

Yet it is certain, that these admonitions of nature, however forcible, however importunate, are too often vain ; and that many who mark with such accuracy the course of time, appear to have little sensibility of the decline of life.   Every man has something to do which he neglects ; every man has faults to conquer which he delays to combat.

So little do we accustom ourselves to consider the effects of time, that things necessary and certain often surprise us like unexpected contingencies.   We leave the beauty in her bloom, and, after an absence of twenty years, wonder, at our return, to find her faded. We meet those whom we left children, and can scarcely persuade ourselves to treat them as men. The traveller visits in age those countries through which he rambled in his youth, and hopes for merriment at the old place. The man of business, wearied with unsatisfactory prosperity, retires to the town of his nativity, and expects to play away the last years with the companions of his childhood, and recover youth in the fields where he once was young.

From this inattention, so general and so mischievous, let it be every man's study to exempt himself. Let him that desires to see others happy make haste to give while his gift can be enjoyed, and remember that every moment of delay takes away something from the value of his benefaction. And let him, who purposes his own happiness, reflect, that while he forms his purpose the day rolls on, and *the night cometh when no man can work.*

NUMB. 44. SATURDAY, *February* 17, 1759.

MEMORY is, among the faculties of the human mind, that of which we make the most frequent use, or rather that of which the agency is incessant, or perpetual. Memory is the primary and fundamental power, without which there could be no other intellectual operation. Judgment and ratiocination suppose something already known, and draw their decisions only from experience. Imagination selects ideas from the treasures of remembrance, and produces novelty only by varied combinations. We do not even form conjectures of distant, or anticipations of future events, but by concluding what is possible from what is past.

The two offices of memory are collection and distribution ; by one images are accumulated, and by the other produced for use. Collection is always the employment of our first years ; and distribution commonly that of our advanced age.

To collect and reposite the various forms of things, is far the most pleasing part of mental occupation. We are naturally delighted with novelty, and there is a time when all that we see is new. When first we enter into the world, whithersoever we turn our eyes, they meet knowledge with pleasure at her side ; every diversity of nature pours ideas in .upon the soul ; neither search nor labour are necessary ; we have nothing more to do than to open our eyes, and curiosity is gratified.

Much of the pleasure which the first survey of the world affords, is exhausted before we are conscious of our own felicity, or able to compare our condition with some possible state. We have therefore few traces of the joy of our earliest discoveries ; yet we all remember a time when nature had so many untasted gratifications, that every excursion gave delight which can now be found no longer, when the noise of a torrent, the rustle of a wood, the song of birds, or the play of lambs, had power to fill the attention, and suspend all perception of the course of time.

But these easy pleasures are soon at an end ; we have seen in a very little time so much, that we call out for new objects of observation, and endeavour to find variety in books and life. But study is laborious, and not always satisfactory ; and conversation has its pains as well as pleasures ; we are willing to learn, but not willing to be taught ; we are pained by ignorance, but pained yet more by another's knowledge.

From the vexation of pupillage men commonly set themselves free about the middle of life, by shutting up the avenues of intelligence, and resolving to rest in their present state ; and they, whose ardour of inquiry continues longer, find themselves insensibly forsaken by their instructors. As every man advances in life, the proportion between those that are younger and that are older than himself is continually changing ; and he that has lived half a century finds few that do not require from him that information which he once expected from those that went before him.

Then it is that the magazines of memory are opened, and the stores of accumulated knowledge are displayed by vanity or benevolence, or in honest commerce of mutual interest. Every man wants others, and is therefore glad when he is wanted by them.   And as few men will endure the labour of intense meditation without necessity, he that has learned enough for his profit or his honour, seldom endeavours after further acquisitions.

The pleasure of recollecting speculative notions would not be much less than that of gaining them, if they could be kept pure and unmingled with the passages of life; but such is the necessary concatenation of our thoughts, that good and evil are linked together, and no pleasure recurs but associated with pain.   Every revived idea reminds us of a time when something was enjoyed that is now lost, when some hope was not yet blasted, when some purpose had yet not languished into sluggishness or indifference.

Whether it be that life has more vexations than comforts, or what is in the event just the same, that evil makes deeper impression than good, it is certain that few can review the time past without heaviness of heart.   He remembers many calamities incurred by folly, many opportunities lost by negligence.   The shades of the dead rise up before him; and he laments the companions of his youth, the partners of his amusements, the assistants of his labours, whom the hand of death has snatched away.

When an offer was made to Themistocles of teach-

ing him the art of memory, he answered, that he
would rather wish for the art of forgetfulness. He
felt his imagination haunted by phantoms of misery
which he was unable to suppress, and would gladly
have calmed his thoughts with some *oblivious anti-
dote.* In this we all resemble one another; the hero
and the sage are, like vulgar mortals, overburdened
by the weight of life; all shrink from recollection,
and all wish for an art of forgetfulness.

NUMB. 45.   SATURDAY, *February* 24, 1759.

THERE is in many minds a kind of vanity exerted
to the disadvantage of themselves; a desire to be
praised for superior acuteness discovered only in the
degradation of their species, or censure of their
country.

Defamation is sufficiently copious. The general
lampooner of mankind may find long exercise for his
zeal or wit, in the defects of nature, the vexations
of life, the follies of opinion, and the corruptions of
practice. But fiction is easier than discernment;
and most of these writers spare themselves the labour
of enquiry, and exhaust their virulence upon imaginary crimes, which, as they never existed, can never
be amended.

That the painters find no encouragement among
the English for many other works than portraits,
has been imputed to national selfishness. 'Tis vain,
says the satirist, to set before any Englishman the

scenes of landscape, or the heroes of history; nature and antiquity are nothing in his eye; he has no value but for himself, nor desires any copy but of his own form.

Whoever is delighted with his own picture must derive his pleasure from the pleasure of another. Every man is always present to himself, and has, therefore, little need of his own resemblance, nor can desire it, but for the sake of those whom he loves, and by whom he hopes to be remembered. This use of the art is a natural and reasonable consequence of affection; and though, like other human actions, it is often complicated with pride, yet even such pride is more laudable than that by which palaces are covered with pictures, that, however excellent, neither imply the owner's virtue, nor excite it.

Genius is chiefly exerted in historical pictures; and the art of the painter of portraits is often lost in the obscurity of his subject. But it is in painting as in life; what is greatest is not always best. I should grieve to see Reynolds transfer to heroes and to goddesses, to empty splendour and to airy fiction, that art which is now employed in diffusing friendship, in reviving tenderness, in quickening the affections of the absent, and continuing the presence of the dead.

Yet in a nation great and opulent there is room, and ought to be patronage, for an art like that of painting through all its diversities; and it is to be wished, that the reward now offered for an historical picture may excite an honest emulation, and give beginning to an English school.

It is not very easy to find an action or event that can be efficaciously represented by a painter.

He must have an action not successive but instantaneous; for the time of a picture is a single moment. For this reason, the death of Hercules cannot well be painted, though at the first view it flatters the imagination with very glittering ideas: the gloomy mountain, overhanging the sea, and covered with trees, some bending to the wind, and some torn from their roots by the raging hero; the violence with which he rends from his shoulders the invenomed garment; the propriety with which his muscular nakedness may be displayed; the death of Lycas whirled from the promontory; the gigantic presence of Philoctetes; the blaze of the fatal pile, which the deities behold with grief and terror from the sky.

All these images fill the mind, but will not compose a picture, because they cannot be united in a single moment. Hercules must have rent his flesh at one time, and tossed Lycas into the air at another; he must first tear up the trees, and then lie down upon the pile.

The action must be circumstantial and distinct. There is a passage in the Iliad which cannot be read without strong emotions. A Trojan prince, seized by Achilles in the battle, falls at his feet, and in moving terms supplicates for life. " How can a wretch like thee," says the haughty Greek, " intreat to live, when thou knowest that the time must come when Achilles is to die ?" This cannot be painted, because no peculiarity of attitude or disposition can so supply the place of language as to impress the sentiment.

The event painted must be such as excites passion, and different passions in the several actors, or a tumult of contending passions in the chief.

Perhaps the discovery of Ulysses by his nurse is of this kind. The surprise of the nurse mingled with joy; that of Ulysses checked by prudence, and clouded by solicitude; and the distinctness of the action by which the scar is found; all concur to complete the subject. But the picture, having only two figures, will want variety.

A much nobler assemblage may be furnished by the death of Epaminondas. The mixture of gladness and grief in the face of the messenger who brings his dying general an account of the victory; the various passions of the attendants; the sublimity of composure in the hero, while the dart is by his own command drawn from his side, and the faint gleam of satisfaction that diffuses itself over the languor of death; are worthy of that pencil which yet I do not wish to see employed upon them.

If the design were not too multifarious and extensive, I should wish that our painters would attempt the dissolution of the parliament by Cromwell. The point of time may be chosen when Cromwell, looking round the Pandæmonium with contempt, ordered the bauble to be taken away; and Harrison laid hands on the Speaker to drag him from the chair.

The various appearances, which rage, and terror, and astonishment, and guilt, might exhibit in the faces of that hateful assembly, of whom the principal persons may be faithfully drawn from portraits or prints; the irresolute repugnance of some, the hypocritical submissions of others, the ferocious insolence of Cromwell, the rugged brutality of Harrison, and the general trepidation of fear and wickedness, would, if some proper disposition could be contrived, make a picture of unexampled variety, and irresistible instruction.

NUMB. 46.   SATURDAY, *March 3*, 1759.

MR. IDLER,

I am encouraged, by the notice you have taken of Betty Broom, to represent the miseries which I suffer from a species of tyranny which, I believe, is not very uncommon, though perhaps it may have escaped the observation of those who converse little with fine ladies, or see them only in their publick characters.

To this method of venting my vexation I am the more inclined, because if I do not complain to you, I must burst in silence; for my mistress has teazed me and teazed me till I can hold no longer, and yet I must not tell her of her tricks. The girls that live in common services can quarrel, and give warning, and find other places; but we that live with great ladies, if we once offend them, have nothing left but to return into the country.

I am waiting-maid to a lady who keeps the best company, and is seen at every place of fashionable resort. I am envied by all the maids in the square, for few countesses leave off so many clothes as my mistress, and nobody shares with me: so that I supply two families in the country with finery for the assizes and horse-races, besides what I wear myself. The steward and house-keeper have joined against me to procure my removal, that they may advance a relation of their own; but their designs are found out by my lady, who says I need not fear them, for she will never have dowdies about her.

You will think, Mr. Idler, like others, that I am very happy, and may well be contented with my lot. But I will tell you. My lady has an odd humour. She never orders any thing in direct words, for she loves a sharp girl that can take a hint.

I would not have you suspect that she has any thing to hint which she is ashamed to speak at length; for none can have greater purity of sentiment, or rectitude of intention. She has nothing to hide, yet nothing will she tell. She always gives her directions obliquely and allusively, by the mention of something relative or consequential, without any other purpose than to exercise my acuteness and her own.

It is impossible to give a notion of this style otherwise than by examples. One night, when she had sat writing letters till it was time to be dressed, *Molly*, said she, *the Ladies are all to be at Court to-night in white aprons.* When she means that I should send to order the chair, she says, *I think the streets are clean, I may venture to walk.* When she would have something put into its place, she bids me *lay it on the floor.* If she would have me snuff the candles, she asks *whether I think her eyes are like a cat's?* If she thinks her chocolate delayed, she talks of *the benefit of abstinence.* If any needle-work is forgotten, she supposes *that I have heard of the lady who died by pricking her finger.*

She always imagines that I can recall every thing past from a single word. If she wants her head from the milliner, she only says, *Molly, you know Mrs. Tape.* If she would have the mantua-maker sent for, she remarks *that Mr. Taffety, the mercer, was here last week.* She ordered, a fortnight ago, that the first time she was abroad all day I should chuse her a new set of coffee-cups at the china-shop : of this she reminded me yesterday, as she was going down stairs, by saying, *You can't find your way now to Pall-mall.*

All this would never vex me, if, by increasing my trouble, she spared her own; but, dear Mr. Idler, is it not as easy to say *coffee-cups,* as *Pall-mall?* and to tell me in plain words what I am to do, and when it is to be done, as to torment her own head with the labour of finding hints, and mine with that of understanding them ?

When first I came to this lady, I had nothing like the learning that I have now; for she has many books, and I have much time to read; so that of late I seldom have missed her meaning : but when she first took me I was an ignorant girl; and she, who, as is very common, confounded want of knowledge with want of understanding, began once to despair of bringing me to any thing, because, when I came into her chamber at the call of her bell, she asked me, *Whether we lived at Zembla* ; and I did not guess the meaning of her enquiry, but modestly answered, that *I could not tell.* She had happened to ring once when I did not hear her, and meant to put me in mind of that country where sounds are said to be congealed by the frost.

Another time, as I was dressing her head, she began to talk on a sudden of *Medusa,* and *snakes,* and *men turned into stone, and maids that, if they were not watched, would let their mistresses be Gorgons.* I looked round me half frightened, and quite bewildered ; till at last, finding that her literature was thrown away upon me, she bid me with great vehemence, reach the curling-irons.

It is not without some indignation, Mr. Idler, that I discover in these artifices of vexation, something worse than foppery or caprice ; a mean delight in superiority, which knows itself in no danger of reproof or opposition ; a cruel pleasure in seeing the perplexity of a mind obliged to find what is studiously concealed, and a mean indulgence of petty malevolence, in the sharp censure of involuntary, and very often of inevitable, failings. When, beyond her expectation, I hit upon her meaning, I can perceive a sudden cloud of disappointment spread over her face ; and have sometimes been afraid, lest I should lose her favour by understanding her when she means to puzzle me.

This day, however, she has conquered my sagacity. When she went out of her dressing-room, she said nothing, but, *Molly, you know,* and hastened to her chariot. What I am to know is yet a secret ;

but if I do not know, before she comes back, what I yet have no means of discovering, she will make my dullness a pretence for a fortnight's ill humour, treat me as a creature devoid of the faculties necessary to the common duties of life, and perhaps give the next gown to the housekeeper.

I am, Sir,

Your humble Servant.

MOLLY QUICK.

NUMB. 47. SATURDAY, *March* 10, 1759.

TO THE IDLER.

MR. IDLER,

I AM the unfortunate wife of a city wit, and cannot but think that my case may deserve equal compassion with any of those which have been represented in your paper.

I married my husband within three months after the expiration of his apprenticeship; we put our money together, and furnished a large and splendid shop, in which he was for five years and a half diligent and civil. The notice which curiosity or kindness commonly bestows on beginners, was continued by confidence and esteem; one customer, pleased with his treatment and his bargain, recommended another; and we were busy behind the counter from morning to night.

Thus every day increased our wealth and our reputation. My husband was often invited to dinner

openly on the Exchange by hundred thousand pounds
men ; and whenever I went to any of the halls, the
wives of the aldermen made me low courtesies.   We
always took up our notes before the day, and made
all considerable payments by draughts upon our
banker.

You will easily believe that I was well enough
pleased with my condition ; for what happiness can
be greater than that of growing every day richer and
richer ?   I will not deny, that, imagining myself
likely to be in a short time the sheriff's lady, I broke
off my acquaintance with some of my neighbours ;
and advised my husband to keep good company, and
not to be seen with men that were worth nothing.

In time he found that ale disagreed with his constitution, and went every night to drink his pint at a
tavern, where he met with a set of cricticks, who disputed upon the merit of the different theatrical performers.   By these idle fellows he was taken to the
play, which at first he did not seem much to heed ;
for he owned, that he very seldom knew what they
were doing, and that, while his companions would
let him alone, he was commonly thinking on his last
bargain.

Having once gone, however, he went again and
again, though I often told him that three shillings
were thrown away ; at last he grew uneasy if he
missed a night, and importuned me to go with him.
I went to a tragedy which they called Macbeth ; and,
when I came home, told him, that I could not bear
to see men and women make themselves such fools,
by pretending to be witches and ghosts, generals and

kings, and to walk in their sleep when they were as much awake as those that looked at them. He told me, that I must get higher notions, and that a play was the most rational of all entertainments, and most proper to relax the mind after the business of the day.

By degrees he gained knowledge of some of the players; and, when the play was over, very frequently treated them with suppers; for which he was admitted to stand behind the scenes.

He soon began to lose some of his morning hours in the same folly, and was for one winter very diligent in his attendance on the rehearsals; but of this species of idleness he grew weary, and said that the play was nothing without the company.

His ardour for the diversion of the evening increased; he bought a sword, and paid five shillings a night to sit in the boxes; he went sometimes into a place which he calls the green-room, where all the wits of the age assemble; and, when he had been there, could do nothing for two or three days, but repeat their jests, or tell their disputes.

He has now lost his regard for every thing but the play-house; he invites, three times a week, one or other to drink claret, and talk of the drama. His first care in the morning is to read the play-bills; and, if he remembers any lines of the tragedy which is to be represented, walks about the shop, repeating them so loud, and with such strange gestures, that the passengers gather round the door.

His greatest pleasure when I married him was to hear the situation of his shop commended, and to be told how many estates have been got in it by the same trade; but of late he grows peevish at any mention of business, and delights in nothing so much as to be told that he speaks like Mossop.

Among his new associates he has learned another language, and speaks in such a strain that his neighbours cannot understand him. If a customer talks longer than he is willing to hear, he will complain that he has been excruciated with unmeaning verbosity; he laughs at the letters of his friends for their tameness of expression, and often declares himself weary of attending to the *minutiæ* of a shop.

It is well for me that I know how to keep a book, for of late he is scarcely ever in the way. Since one of his friends told him that he had a genius for tragick poetry, he has locked himself in an upper room six or seven hours a day; and, when I carry him any paper to be read or signed, I hear him talking vehemently to himself, sometimes of love and beauty, sometimes of friendship and virtue, but more frequently of liberty and his country.

I would gladly, Mr. Idler, be informed, what to think of a shopkeeper, who is incessantly talking about liberty; a word, which, since his acquaintance with polite life, my husband has always in his mouth; he is, on all occasions, afraid of our liberty, and declares his resolution to hazard all for liberty. What can the man mean? I am sure he has liberty enough: it were better for him and me if his liberty was lessened.

He has a friend, whom he calls a critick, that comes twice a week to read what he is writing.

This critick tells him that his piece is a little irregular, but that some detached scenes will shine prodigiously, and that in the character of Bombulus he is wonderfully great. My scribbler then squeezes his hand, calls him the best of friends, thanks him for his sincerity, and tells him that he hates to be flattered. I have reason to believe that he seldom parts with his dear friend without lending him two guineas, and am afraid that he gave bail for him three days ago.

By this course of life our credit as traders is lessened; and I cannot forbear to suspect, that my husband's honour as a wit is not much advanced, for he seems to be always the lowest of the company, and is afraid to tell his opinion till the rest have spoken. When he was behind his counter, he used to be brisk, active, and jocular, like a man that knew what he was doing, and did not fear to look another in the face; but among wits and criticks he is timorous and awkward, and hangs down his head at his own table. Dear Mr. Idler, persuade him, if you can, to return once more to his native element. Tell him, that wit will never make him rich, but that there are places where riches will always make a wit.

I am, Sir, &c.

DEBORAH GINGER.

NUMB. 48. SATURDAY, *March* 17, 1759.

THERE is no kind of idleness, by which we are so easily seduced, as that which dignifies itself by the appearance of business, and by making the loiterer imagine that he has something to do which must not be neglected, keeps him in perpetual agitation, and hurries him rapidly from place to place.

He that sits still, or reposes himself upon a couch, no more deceives himself than he deceives others; he knows that he is doing nothing, and has no other solace of his insignificance than the resolution, which the lazy hourly make, of changing his mode of life.

To do nothing every man is ashamed; and to do much almost every man is unwilling or afraid. Innumerable expedients have therefore been invented to produce motion without labour, and employment without solicitude. The greater part of those whom the kindness of fortune has left to their own direction, and whom want does not keep chained to the counter or the plough, play throughout life with the shadows of business, and know not at last what they have been doing.

These imitators of action are of all denominations. Some are seen at every auction without intention to purchase; others appear punctually at the Exchange, though they are known there only by their faces. Some are always making parties to visit collections for which they have no taste; and some neglect every pleasure and every duty to hear questions, in which they have no interest, debated in parliament.

These men never appear more ridiculous than in the distress which they imagine themselves to feel, from some accidental interruption of those empty pursuits. A tiger newly imprisoned is indeed more formidable, but not more angry, than Jack Tulip withheld from a florist's feast, or Tom Distich hindered from seeing the first representation of a play.

As political affairs are the highest and most extensive of temporal concerns; the mimick of a politician is more busy and important than any other trifler. Monsieur le Noir, a man who, without property or importance in any corner of the earth, has, in the present confusion of the world, declared himself a steady adherent to the French, is made miserable by a wind that keeps back the packet-boat, and still more miserable by every account of a Malouin privateer caught in his cruize; he knows well that nothing can be done or said by him which can produce any effect but that of laughter, that he can neither hasten nor retard good or evil, that his joys and sorrows have scarcely any partakers; yet such is his zeal, and such his curiosity, that he would run barefooted to Gravesend, for the sake of knowing first that the English had lost a tender, and would ride out to meet every mail from the continent if he might be permitted to open it.

Learning is generally confessed to be desirable, and there are some who fancy themselves always busy in acquiring it. Of these ambulatory students, one of the most busy is my friend Tom Restless.

Tom has long had a mind to be a man of knowledge, but he does not care to spend much time among authors; for he is of opinion that few books deserve the labour of perusal, that they give the mind an unfashionable cast, and destroy that freedom of thought and easiness of manners indispensably requisite to acceptance in the world. Tom has therefore found another way to wisdom. When he rises he goes into a coffee-house, where he creeps so near to men whom he takes to be reasoners as to hear their discourse, and endeavours to remember something which, when it has been strained through Tom's head, is so near to nothing, that what it once was cannot be discovered. This he carries round from friend to friend through a circle of visits, till, hearing what each says upon the question, he becomes able at dinner to say a little himself; and, as every great genius relaxes himself among his inferiors, meets with some who wonder how so young a man can talk so wisely.

At night he has a new feast prepared for his intellects; he always runs to a disputing society, or a speaking club, where he half hears what, if he had heard the whole, he would but half understand; goes home pleased with the consciousness of a day well spent, lies down full of ideas, and rises in the morning empty as before.

I SUPPED three nights ago with my friend Will Marvel. His affairs obliged him lately to take a journey into Devonshire. from which he has just returned. He knows me to be a very patient hearer, and was glad of my company. as it gave him an opportunity of disburdening himself by a minute relation of the casualties of his expedition.

Will is not one of those who go out and return with nothing to tell. He has a story of his travels, which will strike a home-bred citizen with horror, and has in ten days suffered so often the extremes of terror and joy. that he is in doubt whether he shall ever again expose either his body or mind to such danger and fatigue.

When he left London the morning was bright, and a fair day was promised. But Will is born to struggle with difficulties. That happened to him, which has sometimes, perhaps, happened to others. Before he had gone more than ten miles, it began to rain. What course was to be taken? His soul disdained to turn back. He did what the King of Prussia might have done: he flapped his hat, buttoned up his cape, and went forwards. fortifying his mind by the stoical consolation, that whatever is violent will be short.

His constancy was not long tried; at the distance of about half a mile he saw an inn, which he entered wet and weary, and found civil treatment and proper refreshment. After a respite of about two hours, he looked abroad, and seeing the sky clear, called for his horse, and passed the first stage without any other memorable accident.

Will considered, that labour must be relieved by pleasure, and that the strength which great undertakings require must be maintained by copious nutriment ; he therefore ordered himself an elegant supper, drank two bottles of claret, and passed the beginning of the night in sound sleep ; but, waking before light, was forewarned of the troubles of the next day, by a shower beating against his windows with such violence as to threaten the dissolution of nature. When he arose, he found what he expected, that the country was under water. He joined himself, however, to a company that was travelling the same way, and came safely to the place of dinner, though every step of his horse dashed the mud into the air.

In the afternoon, having parted from his company, he set forward alone, and passed many collections of water, of which it was impossible to guess the depth, and which he now cannot review without some censure of his own rashness ; but what a man undertakes he must perform, and Marvel hates a coward at his heart.

Few that lie warm in their beds think what others undergo, who have perhaps been as tenderly educated, and have as acute sensations as themselves. My friend was now to lodge the second night almost fifty miles from home, in a house which he never had seen before, among people to whom he was totally a stranger, not knowing whether the next man he should meet would prove good or bad ; but seeing an inn of a good appearance, he rode resolutely into the yard ; and knowing that respect is often paid in proportion as it is claimed, delivered his injunction to the hostler with spirit, and entering the house, called vigorously about him.

On the third day up rose the sun and Mr. Marvel. His troubles and his dangers were now such as he wishes no other man ever to encounter. The ways were less frequented, and the country more thinly inhabited. He rode many a lonely hour through mire and water, and met not a single soul for two miles together with whom he could exchange a word. He cannot deny that, looking round upon the dreary region, and seeing nothing but bleak fields and naked trees, hills obscured by fogs, and flats covered with inundations, he did for some time suffer melancholy to prevail upon him, and wished himself again safe at home. One comfort he had, which was, to consider that none of his friends were in the same distress, for whom, if they had been with him, he should have suffered more than for himself ; he could not forbear sometimes to consider how happily the Idler is settled in an easier condition, who, surrounded like him with terrours, could have done nothing but lie down and die.

Amidst these reflections he came to a town and found a dinner which disposed him to more cheerful sentiments : but the joys of life are short, and its miseries are long ; he mounted and travelled fifteen miles more through dirt and desolation.

At last the sun set, and all the horrors of darkness came upon him. He then repented the weak indulgence in which he had gratified himself at noon with too long an interval of rest: yet he went forward along a path which he could no longer see, sometimes rushing suddenly into water, and sometimes incumbered with stiff clay, ignorant whither he was going, and uncertain whether his next step might not be the last.

In this dismal gloom of nocturnal peregrination his horse unexpectedly stood still. Marvel had heard many relations of the instinct of horses, and was in doubt what danger might be at hand. Sometimes he fancied that he was on the bank of a river still and deep, and sometimes that a dead body lay across the track. He sat still awhile to recollect his thoughts; and as he was about to alight and explore the darkness, out stepped a man with a lantern, and opened the turnpike. He hired a guide to the town, arrived in safety, and slept in quiet.

The rest of his journey was nothing but danger. He climbed and descended precipices on which vulgar mortals tremble to look; he passed marshes like the *Serbonian bog, where armies would have sunk;* he forded rivers where the current roared like the Egre of the Severn; or ventured himself on bridges that trembled under him, from which he looked down on foaming whirlpools, or dreadful abysses; he wandered over houseless heaths, amidst all the rage of elements, with the snow driving in his face, and the tempest howling in his ears.

Such are the colours in which Marvel paints his adventures. He has accustomed himself to sounding words and hyperbolical images, till he has lost

the power of true description.   In a road through
which the heaviest carriages pass without difficulty,
and the post-boy every day and night goes and returns, he meets with hardships like those which are
endured in Siberian deserts, and misses nothing of
romantick danger but a giant and a dragon.   When
his dreadful story is told in proper terms, it is only
that the way was dirty in winter, and that he experienced the common vicissitudes of rain and sunshine.

NUMB. 50,   SATURDAY, *March* 31, 1759.

THE character of Mr. Marvel has raised the merriment of some and the contempt of others, who do
not sufficiently consider how often they hear and
practise the same arts of exaggerated narration.

There is not, perhaps, among the multitudes of
all conditions that swarm upon the earth, a single
man who does not believe that he has something extraordinary to relate of himself; and who does not,
at one time or other, summon the attention of his
friends to the casualties of his adventures and the
vicissitudes of his fortune; casualties and vicissitudes that happen alike in lives uniform and diversified; to the commander of armies and the writer at a
desk; to the sailor who resigns himself to the wind
and water, and the farmer whose longest journey is
to the market.

In the present state of the world man may pass
through Shakespeare's seven stages of life, and meet

nothing singular or wonderful. But such is every man's attention to himself, that what is common and unheeded when it is only seen, becomes remarkable and peculiar when we happen to feel it.

It is well enough known to be according to the usual process of nature that men should sicken and recover, that some designs should succeed and others miscarry, that friends should be separated and meet again, that some should be made angry by endeavours to please them, and some be pleased when no care has been used to gain their approbation; that men and women should at first come together by chance, like each other so well as to commence acquaintance, improve acquaintance into fondness, increase or extinguish fondness by marriage, and have children of different degrees of intellects and virtue, some of whom die before their parents, and others survive them.

Yet let any man tell his own story, and nothing of all this has ever befallen him according to the common order of things; something has always discriminated his case; some unusual concurrence of events has appeared which made him more happy or more miserable than other mortals; for in pleasures or calamities, however common, every one has comforts and afflictions of his own.

It is certain that without some artificial augmentations, many of the pleasures of life, and almost all its embellishments, would fall to the ground. If no man was to express more delight than he felt, those who felt most would raise little envy. If travellers were to describe the most laboured performances of art with the same coldness as they survey them, all expectations of happiness from change of place would cease. The pictures of Raphael would hang without spectators, and the gardens of Versailles might be inhabited by hermits. All the pleasure that is received ends in an opportunity of splendid falsehood, in the power of gaining notice by the display of beauties which the eye was weary of beholding, and a history of happy moments, of which, in reality, the most happy was the last.

The ambition of superior sensibility and superior eloquence disposes the lovers of arts to receive rapture at one time, and communicate it at another; and each labours first to impose upon himself, and then to propagate the imposture.

Pain is less subject than pleasure to caprices of expression. The torments of disease, and the grief for irremediable misfortunes, sometimes are such as no words can declare, and can only be signified by groans, or sobs, or inarticulate ejaculations. Man has from nature a mode of utterance peculiar to pain, but he has none peculiar to pleasure, because he never has pleasure but in such degrees as the ordinary use of language may equal or surpass.

It is nevertheless certain, that many pains as well as pleasures are heightened by rhetorical affectation, and that the picture is, for the most part, bigger than the life.

When we describe our sensations of another's sorrows, either in friendly or ceremonious condolence, the customs of the world scarcely admit of rigid veracity. Perhaps the fondest friendship would enrage oftener than comfort, were the tongue on such occasions faithfully to represent the sentiments of the heart ; and I think the strictest moralists allow forms of address to be used without much regard to their literal acceptation, when either respect or tenderness requires them, because they are universally known to denote not the degree but the species of our sentiments.

But the same indulgence cannot be allowed to him who aggravates dangers incurred or sorrow endured by himself, because he darkens the prospect of futurity, and multiplies the pains of our condition by useless terrour. Those who magnify their delights are less criminal deceivers, yet they raise hopes which are sure to be disappointed. It would be undoubtedly best, if we could see and hear every thing as it is, that nothing might be too anxiously dreaded, or too ardently pursued.

NUMB. 51.　SATURDAY, *April* 7, 1759.

IT has been commonly remarked, that eminent men are least eminent at home, that bright characters lose much of their splendour at a nearer view, and many who fill the world with their fame, excite very little reverence among those that surround them in their domestick privacies.

To blame or to suspect is easy and natural. When the fact is evident, and the cause doubtful, some accusation is always engendered between idleness and malignity. This disparity of general and familiar esteem is therefore imputed to hidden vices, and to practices indulged in secret, but carefully covered from the publick eye.

Vice will indeed always produce contempt. The dignity of Alexander, though nations fell prostrate before him, was certainly held in little veneration by the partakers of his midnight revels, who had seen him in the madness of wine, murder his friend, or set fire to the Persian palace at the instigation of a harlot ; and it is well remembered among us, that the avarice of Marlborough kept him in subjection to his wife, while he was dreaded by France as her conqueror, and honoured by the emperor as his deliverer.

But though, where there is vice there must be want of reverence, it is not reciprocally true, that when there is want of reverence there is always vice.   That awe which great actions or abilities impress will be inevitably diminished by acquaintance, though nothing either mean or criminal should be found.

Of men, as of every thing else, we must judge according to our knowledge.   When we see of a hero only his battles, or of a writer only his books, we have nothing to allay our ideas of their greatness. We consider the one only as the guardian of his country, and the other only as the instructor of mankind. We have neither opportunity nor motive to examine the minuter parts of their lives, or the less apparent peculiarities of their characters; we name them with habitual respect, and forget, what we still continue to know, that they are men like other mortals.

But such is the constitution of the world, that much of life must be spent in the same manner by the wise and the ignorant, the exalted and the low. Men, however distinguished by external accidents or intrinsick qualities, have all the same wants, the same pains, and, as far as the senses are consulted, the same pleasures.   The petty cares and petty duties are the same in every station to every understanding, and every hour brings some occasion on which we all sink to the common level.   We are all naked till we are dressed, and hungry till we are fed; and the general's triumph, and sage's disputation, end, like the humble labours of the smith or ploughman, in a dinner or in sleep.

Those notions which are to be collected by reason, in opposition to the senses, will seldom stand forward in the mind, but lie treasured in the remoter repositories of memory, to be found only when they are sought. Whatever any man may have written or done, his precepts or his valour will scarcely overbalance the unimportant uniformity which runs through his time. We do not easily consider him as great, whom our own eyes shew us to be little; nor labour to keep present to our thoughts the latent excellencies of him who shares with us all our weaknesses and many of our follies; who like us is delighted with slight amusements, busied with trifling employments, and disturbed by little vexations.

Great powers cannot be exerted, but when great exigences make them necessary. Great exigences can happen but seldom, and therefore those qualities which have a claim to the veneration of mankind, lie hid, for the most part, like subterranean treasures, over which the foot passes as on common ground, till necessity breaks open the golden cavern.

In the ancient celebration of victory, a slave was placed on the triumphal car, by the side of the general, who reminded him by a short sentence, that he was a man. Whatever danger there might be lest a leader, in his passage to the capitol, should forget the frailties of his nature, there was surely no need of such an admonition; the intoxication could not have continued long; he would have been at home but a few hours before some of his dependants would have forgot his greatness, and shewn him, that notwithstanding his laurels he was yet a man.

There are some who try to escape this domestick degradation, by labouring to appear always wise or always great; but he that strives against nature, will for ever strive in vain.   To be grave of mien and slow of utterance ; to look with solicitude and speak with hesitation, is attainable at will ; but the shew of wisdom is ridiculous when there is nothing to cause doubt, as that of valour where there is nothing to be feared.

A man who has duly considered the condition of his being, will contentedly yield to the course of things : he will not pant for distinction where distinction would imply no merit ; but though on great occasions he may wish to be greater than others, he will be satisfied in common occurrences not to be less.

NUMB. 52.   SATURDAY, *April* 14, 1759.

Responsare cupidinibus.   Hor.

THE practice of self-denial, or the forbearance of lawful pleasure, has been considered by almost every nation, from the remotest ages, as the highest exaltation of human virtue ; and all have agreed to pay respect and veneration to those who abstained from the delights of life, even when they did not censure those who enjoy them.

The general voice of mankind, civil and barbarous, confesses that the mind and body are at variance, and that neither can be made happy by its proper gratifications but at the expence of the other ; that a pampered body will darken the mind, and an enlightened mind will macerate the body.   And none have failed to confer their esteem on those who prefer intellect to sense, who controul their lower by their higher faculties, and forget the wants and desires of animal life for rational disquisitions or pious contemplations.

The earth has scarcely a country so far advanced towards political regularity as to divide the inhabitants into classes, where some orders of men or women are not distinguished by voluntary severities, and where the reputation of their sanctity is not increased in proportion to the rigour of their rules, and the exactness of their performance.

When an opinion to which there is no temptation of interest spreads wide, and continues long, it may be reasonably presumed to have been infused by nature or dictated by reason. It has been often observed that the fictions of imposture, and illusions of fancy, soon give way to time and experience; and that nothing keeps its ground but truth, which gains every day new influence by new confirmation.

But truth, when it is reduced to practice, easily becomes subject to caprice and imagination; and many particular acts will be wrong, though their general principle be right. It cannot be denied that a just conviction of the restraint necessary to be laid upon the appetites has produced extravagant and unnatural modes of mortification, and institutions, which, however favourably considered, will be found to violate nature without promoting piety.

But the doctrine of self-denial is not weakened in itself by the errours of those who misinterpret or misapply it; the encroachment of the appetites upon the understanding is hourly perceived; and the state of those, whom sensuality has enslaved, is known to be in the highest degree despicable and wretched.

The dread of such shameful captivity may justly raise alarms, and wisdom will endeavour to keep danger at a distance. By timely caution and suspicious vigilance those desires may be repressed, to which indulgence would soon give absolute dominion;

those enemies may be overcome, which, when they have been a while accustomed to victory, can no longer be resisted.

Nothing is more fatal to happiness or virtue, than that confidence which flatters us with an opinion of our own strength, and by assuring us of the power of retreat precipitates us into hazard. Some may safely venture farther than others into the regions of delight, lay themselves more open to the golden shafts of pleasure, and advance nearer to the residence of the Syrens; but he that is best armed with constancy and reason is yet vulnerable in one part or other, and to every man there is a point fixed, beyond which, if he passes, he will not easily return. It is certainly most wise, as it is most safe, to stop before he touches the utmost limit, since every step of advance will more and more entice him to go forward, till he shall at last enter into the recesses of voluptuousness, and sloth and despondency close the passage behind him.

To deny early and inflexibly, is the only art of checking the importunity of desire, and of preserving quiet and innocence. Innocent gratifications must be sometimes withheld; he that complies with all lawful desires will certainly lose his empire over himself, and in time either submit his reason to his wishes, and think all his desires lawful, or dismiss his reason as troublesome and intrusive, and resolve to snatch what he may happen to wish, without inquiring about right and wrong.

No man, whose appetites are his masters, can perform the duties of his nature with strictness and regularity; he that would be superiour to external influences must first become superiour to his own passions.

When the Roman general, sitting at supper with a plate of turnips before him, was solicited by large presents to betray his trust, he asked the messengers whether he that could sup on turnips was a man likely to sell his own country. Upon him who has reduced his senses to obedience, temptation has lost its power; he is able to attend impartially to virtue, and execute her commands without hesitation.

To set the mind above the appetites is the end of abstinence, which one of the Fathers observes to be not a virtue, but the ground-work of virtue. By forbearing to do what may innocently be done, we may add hourly new vigour or resolution, and secure the power of resistance when pleasure or interest shall lend their charms to guilt.

NUMB. 53.   SATURDAY, *April* 21, 1759.

TO THE IDLER.

SIR,

I HAVE a wife that keeps good company. You know that the word *good* varies its meaning according to the value set upon different qualities in different places. To be a good man in a college, is to be learned; in a camp, to be brave; and in the city, to be rich. By good company in the place which I have the misfortune to inhabit, we understand not only those from whom any good can be learned, whether wisdom or virtue; or by whom any good can be conferred, whether profit or reputation. Good company is the company of those whose birth is high, and whose riches are great; or of those whom the rich and noble admit to familiarity.

I am a gentleman of a fortune by no means exuberant, but more than equal to the wants of my family, and for some years equal to our desires. My wife, who had never been accustomed to splendour, joined her endeavours to mine in the superintendance of our œconomy; we lived in decent plenty, and were not excluded from moderate pleasures.

But slight causes produce great effects. All my happiness has been destroyed by change of place;

virtue is too often merely local; in some situations the air diseases the body, and in others poisons the mind. Being obliged to remove my habitation, I was led by my evil genius to a convenient house in a street where many of the nobility reside. We had scarcely ranged our furniture, and aired our rooms, when my wife began to grow discontented, and to wonder what the neighbours would think when they saw so few chairs and chariots at her door.

Her acquaintance, who came to see her from the quarter that we had left, mortified her without design, by continual inquiries about the ladies whose houses they viewed from our windows. She was ashamed to confess that she had no intercourse with them, and sheltered her distress under general answers, which always tended to raise suspicion that she knew more than she would tell; but she was often reduced to difficulties, when the course of talk introduced questions about the furniture or ornaments of their houses, which, when she could get no intelligence, she was forced to pass slightly over, as things which she saw so often that she never minded them.

To all these vexations she was resolved to put an end, and redoubled her visits to those few of her friends who visited those who kept good company; and if ever she met a lady of quality, forced herself into notice by respect and assiduity. Her advances were generally rejected; and she heard them, as they went down stairs, talk how some creatures put themselves forward.

She was not discouraged, but crept forward from

one to another; and, as perseverance will do great things, sapped her way unperceived, till, unexpectedly, she appeared at the card-table of lady Biddy Porpoise, a lethargick virgin of seventy-six, whom all the families in the next square visited very punctually when she was not at home.

This was the first step of that elevation to which my wife has since ascended. For five months she had no name in her mouth but that of lady Biddy, who, let the world say what it would, had a fine understanding, and such a command of her temper, that, whether she won or lost, she slept over her cards.

At lady Biddy's she met with lady Tawdry, whose favour she gained by estimating her ear-rings, which were counterfeit, at twice the value of real diamonds. When she had once entered two houses of distinction, she was easily admitted into more, and in ten weeks had all her time anticipated by parties and engagements. Every morning she is bespoke, in the summer, for the gardens; in the winter, for a sale; every afternoon she has visits to pay, and every night brings an inviolable appointment, or an assembly in which the best company in the town were to appear.

You will easily imagine that much of my domestick comfort is withdrawn. I never see my wife but in the hurry of preparation or the languor of weariness. To dress and to undress is almost her whole business in private, and the servants take advantage of her negligence to increase expence. But I can supply her omissions by my own diligence, and should not much regret this new course of life, if it did nothing more than transfer to me the care of our accounts. The changes which it has made are more vexatious. My wife has no longer the use of her understanding. She has no rule of action but the fashion. She has no opinion but that of the people of quality. She has no language but the dialect of her own set of company. She hates and admires in humble imitation ; and echoes the words *charming* and *detestable* without consulting her own perceptions.

If for a few minutes we sit down together, she entertains me with the repartees of lady Cackle, or the conversation of lord Whiffler and Miss Quick, and wonders to find me receiving with indifference sayings which put all the company into laughter.

By her old friends she is no longer very willing to be seen, but she must not rid herself of them all at once ; and is sometimes surprised by her best visitants in company which she would not shew, and cannot hide ; but from the moment that a countess enters, she takes care neither to hear nor see them : they soon find themselves neglected, and retire ; and she tells her ladyship that they are somehow related at a great distance, and that as they are good sort of people she cannot be rude to them.

As by this ambitious union with those that are above her, she is always forced upon disadvanta-geous comparisons of her condition with theirs, she has a constant source of misery within ; and never returns from glittering assemblies and mag-nificent apartments but she growls out her discontent and wonders why she was doomed to so indigent a state. When she attends the duchess to a sale, she always sees something that she cannot buy; and, that she may not seem wholly insignificant, she will sometimes venture to bid, and often make acquisitions which she did not want at prices which she cannot afford.

What adds to all this uneasiness is, that this expense is without use, and this vanity without honour; she forsakes houses where she might be courted, for those where she is only suffered; her equals are daily made her enemies, and her superiors will never be her friends.

I am, Sir, yours, &c.

NUMB. 54. SATURDAY, *April* 28, 1759.

TO THE IDLER.

SIR,

You have lately entertained your admirers with the case of an unfortunate husband, and thereby given a demonstrative proof you are not averse even to hear appeals and terminate differences between man and wife; I therefore take the liberty to present you with the case of an injured lady, which, as it chiefly relates to what I think the lawyers call a point of law, I shall do in as juridical a manner as I am capable, and submit it to the consideration of the learned gentlemen of that profession.

Imprimis. In the style of my marriage articles, a marriage was *had and solemnized*, about six months ago, between me and Mr. Savecharges, a gentleman possessed of a plentiful fortune of his own, and one who, I was persuaded, would improve, and not spend, mine.

Before our marriage, Mr. Savecharges had all along preferred the salutary exercise of walking on foot to the distempered ease, as he terms it, of lolling in a chariot; but, notwithstanding his fine panegyricks on walking, the great advantages the infantry were in the sole possession of, and the many dreadful dangers they escaped, he found I had very different notions of an equipage, and was not easily to be converted, or gained over to his party.

An equipage I was determined to have, whenever I married. I too well knew the disposition of my intended consort to leaving the providing one entirely to his honour, and flatter myself Mr. Savecharges has, in the articles made previous to our marriage, *agreed to keep me a coach;* but lest I should be mistaken, or the attorneys should not have done me justice in methodizing or legalizing these half dozen words, I will set about and transcribe that part of the agreement, which will explain the matter to you much better than can be done by one who is so deeply interested in the event; and show on what foundation I build my hopes of being soon under the transporting, delightful denomination of a fashionable lady, who enjoys the exalted and much-envied felicity of bowling about in her own coach.

" And further the said Solomon Savecharges, for divers good causes and considerations him hereunto moving, hath agreed, and doth hereby agree, that the said Solomon Savecharges shall and will, so soon as conveniently may be after the solemnization of the said intended marriage, at his own proper cost and charges, find and provide a *certain vehicle or four-wheel carriage, commonly called or known by the name of a coach,* which said vehicle or wheel-carriage, so called or known by the name of a coach, shall be *used and enjoyed* by the said Sukey Modish, his intended wife," [pray mind that, Mr. Idler,] " at such times and in such manner as she the said Sukey Modish shall think fit and convenient."

Such, Mr. Idler, is the agreement my *passionate admirer* entered into; and what the *dear frugal husband* calls a performance of it remains to be described.   Soon after the ceremony of signing and sealing was over, our wedding-clothes being sent home, and, in short, every thing in readiness except the coach, my own shadow was scarcely more constant than my passionate lover in his attendance on me: wearied by his perpetual importunities for what he called a completion of his bliss, I consented to make him happy; in a few days I gave him my hand, and, attended by Hymen in his saffron robes, retired to a country-seat of my husband's, where the honey-moon flew over our heads ere we had time to recollect ourselves, or think of our engagements in town.   Well, to town we came, and you may be sure, Sir, I expected to step into my coach on my arrival here; but what was my surprise and disappointment, when, instead of this, he began to sound in my ears, "That the interest of money was low, very low; and what a terrible thing it was to be incumbered with a little regiment of servants in these hard times!"   I could easily perceive what all this tended to, but would not seem to understand him; which made it highly necessary for Mr. Savecharges to explain himself more intelligibly; to harp upon and protest he dreaded the expence of keeping a coach.   And truly, for his part, he could not conceive how the pleasure resulting from such a convenience could be any way adequate to the heavy expence attending it.   I now thought it high time to speak with equal plainness, and told him, as the fortune I brought fairly entitled me to ride in my own coach, and as I was sensible his circumstances would very well afford it, he must pardon me if I insisted on a performance of his agreement.

I appeal to you, Mr. Idler, whether any thing could be more civil, more complaisant, than this? And, would you believe it, the creature in return, a few days after, accosted me, in an offended tone, with, "Madam, I can now tell you your coach is ready; and since you are so passionately fond of one, I intend you the honour of keeping a pair of horses.—You insisted upon having an article of pin-money, and horses are no part of my agreement." Base, designing wretch!—I beg your pardon, Mr. Idler, the very recital of such mean, ungentleman-like behaviour fires my blood, and lights up a flame within me. But hence, thou worst of monsters, ill-timed Rage, and let me not spoil my cause for want of temper.

Now, though I am convinced I might make a worse use of part of the pin-money, than by extending my bounty towards the support of so useful a part of the brute creation; yet, like a true-born Englishwoman, I am so tenacious of my rights and privileges, and moreover so good a friend to the gentlemen of the law, that I protest, Mr. Idler, sooner than tamely give up the point, and be quibbled out of my right, I will receive my pin-money, as it were, with one hand, and pay it to them with the other; provided they will give me, or, which is the same thing, my trustees, encouragement to commence a suit against this dear, frugal husband of mine.

And of this I can't have the least shadow of doubt, inasmuch as I have been told by very good authority, it is someway or other laid down as a rule, " * *That whenever* the law doth give any thing to one, it giveth impliedly whatever is necessary for the taking and enjoying the same." Now I would gladly know what enjoyment I, or any lady in the kingdom, can have of a coach without horses? The answer is obvious—None at all! For as Serj. Catlyne very wisely observes, " Though a coach has wheels, to the end it may thereby and by virtue thereof be enabled to move ; yet in point of utility it may as well have none, if they are not put in motion by means of its vital parts, that is, the horses."

And therefore, Sir, I humbly hope you and the learned in the law will be of opinion, that two certain animals, or quadruped creatures, commonly called or known by the name of horses, ought to be annexed to, and go along with, the coach.

SUKEY SAVECHARGES.†

* Coke on Littleton.
† An unknown correspondent.   C.

NUMB. 55.   SATURDAY, *May 5*, 1759.

TO THE IDLER.

MR. IDLER,

I HAVE taken the liberty of laying before you my complaint, and of desiring advice or consolation with the greater confidence, because I believe many other writers have suffered the same indignities with myself, and hope my quarrel will be regarded by you and your readers as the common cause of literature.

Having been long a student, I thought myself qualified in time to become an author. My inquiries have been much diversified and far extended, and not finding my genius directing me by irresistible impulse to any particular subject, I deliberated three years which part of knowledge to illustrate by my labours. Choice is more often determined by accident than by reason : I walked abroad one morning with a curious lady, and by her inquiries and observations was incited to write the natural history of the county in which I reside.

Natural history is no work for one that loves his chair or his bed. Speculation may be pursued on a soft couch, but nature must be observed in the open air. I have collected materials with indefatigable pertinacity. I have gathered glow-worms in the evening, and snails in the morning ; I have seen the daisy close and open, I have heard the owl shriek at midnight, and hunted insects in the heat of noon.

Seven years I was employed in collecting animals and vegetables, and then found that my design was yet imperfect. The subterranean treasures of the place had been passed unobserved, and another year was to be spent in mines and coal-pits. What I had already done supplied a sufficient motive to do more. I acquainted myself with the black inhabitants of metallic caverns, and, in defiance of damps and floods, wandered through the gloomy labyrinths, and gathered fossils from every fissure.

At last I began to write, and as I finished any section of my book, read it to such of my friends as were most skilful in the matter which it treated. None of them were satisfied; one disliked the disposition of the parts, another the colours of the style; one advised me to enlarge, another to abridge. I resolved to read no more, but to take my own way and write on, for by consultation I only perplexed my thoughts and retarded my work.

The book was at last finished, and I did not doubt but my labour would be repaid by profit, and my ambition satisfied with honours. I considered that natural history is neither temporary nor local, and that though I limited my inquiries to my own country, yet every part of the earth has productions common to all the rest. Civil history may be partially studied, the revolutions of one nation may be neglected by another; but after that in which all have an interest, all must be inquisitive. No man can have sunk so far into stupidity as not to consider the properties of the ground on which he walks, of the plants on which he feeds, or the animals that delight his ear, or amuse his eye ; and therefore I computed that universal curiosity would call for many editions of my book, and that in five years I should gain fifteen thousand pounds by the sale of thirty thousand copies.

When I began to write, I insured the house ; and suffered the utmost solicitude when I entrusted my book to the carrier, though I had secured it against mischances by lodging two transcripts in different places.   At my arrival, I expected that the patrons of learning would contend for the honour of a dedication, and resolved to maintain the dignity of letters by a haughty contempt of pecuniary solicitations.

I took lodgings near the house of the Royal Society, and expected every morning a visit from the president.   I walked in the Park, and wondered that I overheard no mention of the great naturalist. At last I visited a noble earl, and told him of my work : he answered, that he was under an engagement never to subscribe.   I was angry to have that refused which I did not mean to ask, and concealed my design of making him immortal.   I went next day to another, and, in resentment of my late affront, offered to prefix his name to my new book.   He said, coldly, that *he did not understand those things ;* another thought *there were too many books ;* and another would *talk with me when the races were over.*

Being amazed to find a man of learning so indecently slighted, I resolved to indulge the philosophical pride of retirement and independence.   I then sent to some of the principal booksellers the plan of my book, and bespoke a large room in the next tavern, that I might more commodiously see them together, and enjoy the contest, while they were outbidding one another. I drank my coffee, and yet nobody was come; at last I received a note from one, to tell me that he was going out of town; and from another, that natural history was out of his way. At last there came a grave man, who desired to see the work, and, without opening it, told me that a book of that size *would never do.*

I then condescended to step into shops, and mention my work to the masters. Some never dealt with authors; others had their hands full; some never had known such a dead time; others had lost by all that they had published for the last twelvemonth. One offered to print my work, if I could procure subscriptions for five hundred, and would allow me two hundred copies for my property. I lost my patience, and gave him a kick; for which he has indicted me.

I can easily perceive, that there is a combination among them to defeat my expectations; and I find it so general, that I am sure it must have been long concerted. I suppose some of my friends, to whom I read the first part, gave notice of my design, and, perhaps, sold the treacherous intelligence at a higher price than the fraudulence of trade will now allow me for my book.

Inform me, Mr. Idler, what I must do; where must knowledge and industry find their recompence, thus neglected by the high, and cheated by the low! I sometimes resolve to print my book at my own expence, and, like the Sibyl, double the price; and sometimes am tempted, in emulation of Raleigh, to throw it into the fire, and leave this sordid generation to the curses of posterity. Tell me, dear Idler, what I shall do.

I am, Sir, &c.

NUMB. 56. SATURDAY, *May* 21, 1759.

THERE is such difference between the pursuits of men, that one part of the inhabitants of a great city lives to little other purpose than to wonder at the rest. Some have hopes and fears, wishes and aversions, which never enter into the thought of others, and inquiry is laboriously exerted to gain that which those who possess it are ready to throw away.

To those who are accustomed to value every thing by its use, and have no such superfluity of time or money as may prompt them to unnatural wants or capricious emulations, nothing appears more improbable or extravagant than the love of curiosities, or that desire of accumulating trifles, which distinguishes many by whom no other distinction could have ever been obtained.

He that has lived without knowing to what height desire may be raised by vanity, with what rapture baubles are snatched out of the hands of rival collectors, how the eagerness of one raises eagerness in another, and one worthless purchase makes a second necessary, may, by passing a few hours at an auction, learn more than can be shewn by many volumes of maxims or essays.

The advertisement of a sale is a signal which at once puts a thousand hearts in motion, and brings contenders from every part to the scene of distribution. He that had resolved to buy no more, feels his constancy subdued; there is now something in the catalogue which completes his cabinet, and which he was never before able to find. He whose sober reflections inform him, that of adding collection to collection there is no end, and that it is wise to leave early that which must be left imperfect at last, yet cannot withhold himself from coming to see what it is that brings so many together, and when he comes is soon overpowered by his habitual passion; he is attracted by rarity, seduced by example, and inflamed by competition.

While the stores of pride and happiness are surveyed, one looks with longing eyes and gloomy countenance on that which he despairs to gain from a richer bidder; another keeps his eye with care from settling too long on that which he most earnestly desires; and another, with more art than virtue, depreciates that which he values most, in hope to have it at an easy rate.

The novice is often surprized to see what minute and unimportant discriminations increase or diminish value. An irregular contortion of a turbinated shell, which common eyes pass unregarded, will ten times treble its price in the imagination of philosophers. Beauty is far from operating upon collectors as upon low and vulgar minds, even where beauty might be thought the only quality that could deserve notice. Among the shells that please by their variety of colours, if one can be found accidentally deformed by a cloudy spot, it is boasted as the pride of the collection.   China is sometimes purchased for little less than its weight in gold, only because it is old, though neither less brittle, nor better painted, than the modern ; and brown china is caught up with extasy, though no reason can be imagined for which it should be preferred to common vessels of common clay.

The fate of prints and coins is equally inexplicable. Some prints are treasured up as inestimably valuable, because the impression was made before the plate was finished. Of coins the price rises not from the purity of the metal, the excellence of the workmanship, the elegance of the legend, or the chronological use.   A piece, of which neither the inscription can be read, nor the face distinguished, if there remain of it but enough to shew that it is rare, will be sought by contending nations, and dignify the treasury in which it shall be shown.

Whether this curiosity, so barren of immediate advantage, and so liable to depravation, does more harm or good, is not easily decided.   Its harm is apparent at the first view.   It fills the mind with trifling ambition ; fixes the attention upon things which have seldom any tendency towards virtue or wisdom ; employs in idle inquiries the time that is given for better purposes ; and often ends in mean and dishonest practices, when desire increases by indulgence beyond the power of honest gratification.

These are the effects of curiosity in excess; but what passion in excess will not become vicious? All indifferent qualities and practices are bad if they are compared with those which are good, and good if they are opposed to those that are bad. The pride or the pleasure of making collections, if it be restrained by prudence and morality, produces a pleasing remission after more laborious studies; furnishes an amusement not wholly unprofitable for that part of life, the greater part of many lives, which would otherwise be lost in idleness or vice; it produces an useful traffick between the industry of indigence and the curiosity of wealth; it brings many things to notice that would be neglected, and, by fixing the thoughts upon intellectual pleasures, resists the natural encroachments of sensuality, and maintains the mind in her lawful superiority.

NUMB. 57.   SATURDAY, *May* 19, 1759.

PRUDENCE is of more frequent use than any other intellectual quality ; it is exerted on slight occasions, and called into act by the cursory business of common life.

Whatever is universally necessary, has been granted to mankind on easy terms. Prudence, as it is always wanted, is without great difficulty obtained.   It requires neither extensive view nor profound search, but forces itself, by spontaneous impulse, upon a mind neither great nor busy, neither engrossed by vast designs, nor distracted by multiplicity of attention.

Prudence operates on life in the same manner as rules on composition : it produces vigilance rather than elevation, rather prevents loss than procures advantage ; and often escapes miscarriages, but seldom reaches either power or honour.   It quenches that ardour of enterprize, by which every thing is done that can claim praise or admiration ; and represses that generous temerity which often fails and often succeeds.   Rules may obviate faults, but can never confer beauties ; and prudence keeps life safe, but does not often make it happy.   The world is not amazed with prodigies of excellence, but when wit tramples upon rules, and magnanimity breaks the chains of prudence.

One of the most prudent of all that have fallen within my observation, is my old companion Sophron, who has passed through the world in quiet, by perpetual adherence to a few plain maxims, and wonders how contention and distress can so often happen.

The first principle of Sophron is to *run no hazards*. Though he loves money, he is of opinion, that frugality is a more certain source of riches than industry. It is to no purpose that any prospect of large profit is set before him; he believes little about futurity, and does not love to trust his money out of his sight, for nobody knows what may happen. He has a small estate, which he lets at the old rent, because *it is better to have a little than nothing*; but he rigorously demands payment on the stated day, for *he that cannot pay one quarter cannot pay two*. If he is told of any improvements in agriculture, he likes the old way, has observed that changes very seldom answer expectation, is of opinion that our forefathers knew how to till the ground as well as we; and concludes with an argument that nothing can overpower, that the expence of planting and fencing is immediate, and the advantage distant, and that *he is no wise man who will quit a certainty for an uncertainty*.

Another of Sophron's rules is, *to mind no business but his own*. In the state he is of no party; but hears and speaks of publick affairs with the same coldness as of the administration of some ancient republick. If any flagrant act of fraud or oppression is mentioned, he hopes that *all is not true that is told*: if misconduct or corruption puts the nation in a flame, he hopes that *every man means well*. At elections he leaves his dependants to their own choice, and declines to vote himself, for every candidate is a good man, whom he is unwilling to oppose or offend.

If disputes happen among his neighbours, he observes an invariable and cold neutrality. His punctuality has gained him the reputation of honesty, and his caution that of wisdom; and few would refuse to refer their claims to his award. He might have prevented many expensive law-suits, and quenched many a feud in its first smoke; but always refuses the office of arbitration, because he must decide against one or the other.

With the affairs of other families he is always unacquainted. He sees estates bought and sold, squandered and increased, without praising the economist, or censuring the spendthrift. He never courts the rising, lest they should fall; nor insults the fallen, lest they should rise again. His caution has the appearance of virtue, and all who do not want his help praise his benevolence; but, if any man solicits his assistance, he has just sent away all his money; and, when the petitioner is gone, declares to his family that he is sorry for his misfortunes, has always looked upon him with particular kindness, and therefore could not lend him money, lest he should destroy their friendship by the necessity of enforcing payment.

Of domestick misfortunes he has never heard. When he is told the hundredth time of a gentleman's daughter who has married the coachman, he lifts up his hands with astonishment, for he always thought her a very sober girl. When nuptial quarrels, after having filled the country with talk and laughter, at last end in separation, he never can conceive how it happened, for he looked upon them as a happy couple.

If his advice is asked, he nevers gives any particular direction, because events are uncertain, and he will bring no blame upon himself; but he takes the consulter tenderly by the hand, tells him he makes his case his own, and advises him not to act rashly, but to weigh the reasons on both sides; observes, that a man may be as easily too hasty as too slow, and that as many fail by doing too much as too little; that *a wise man has two ears and one tongue*; and that *little said is soon amended*; that he could tell him this and that, but that after all every man is the best judge of his own affairs.

With this some are satisfied, and go home with great reverence of Sophron's wisdom; and none are offended, because every one is left in full possession of his own opinion.

Sophron gives no characters. It is equally vain to tell him of vice and virtue; for he has remarked, that no man likes to be censured, and that very few are delighted with the praises of another. He has a few terms which he uses to all alike. With respect to fortune, he believes every family to be in good circumstances; he never exalts any understanding by lavish praise, yet he meets with none but very sensible people. Every man is honest and hearty; and every woman is a good creature.

Thus Sophron creeps along, neither loved nor hated, neither favoured nor opposed: he has never attempted to grow rich, for fear of growing poor; and has raised no friends, for fear of making enemies.

NUMB. 58.   SATURDAY, *May* 26, 1759.

·PLEASURE is very seldom found where it is sought.   Our brightest blazes of gladness are commonly kindled by unexpected sparks.   The flowers which scatter their odours from time to time in the paths of life, grow up without culture from seeds scattered by chance.

Nothing is more hopeless than a scheme of merriment.   Wits and humourists are brought together from distant quarters by preconcerted invitations; they come attended by their admirers prepared to laugh and to applaud; they gaze a-while on each other, ashamed to be silent, and afraid to speak; every man is discontented with himself, grows angry with those that give him pain, and resolves that he will contribute nothing to the merriment of such worthless company.   Wine inflames the general malignity, and changes sullenness to petulance, till at last none can bear any longer the presence of the rest.   They retire to vent their indignation in safer places, where they are heard with attention; their importance is restored, they recover their good humour, and gladden the night with wit and jocularity.

Merriment is always the effect of a sudden impression.   The jest which is expected is already destroyed.   The most active imagination will be sometimes torpid under the frigid influence of melancholy, and sometimes occasions will be wanting to tempt the mind, however volatile, to sallies and excursions. Nothing was ever said with uncommon felicity, but by the co-operation of chance ; and, therefore, wit as well as valour must be content to share its honours with fortune.

All other pleasures are equally uncertain ; the general remedy of uneasiness is change of place ; almost every one has some journey of pleasure in his mind, with which he flatters his expectation. He that travels in theory has no inconvenience ; he has shade and sunshine at his disposal, and wherever he alights finds tables of plenty and looks of gaiety. These ideas are indulged till the day of departure arrives, the chaise is called, and the progress of happiness begins.

A few miles teach him the fallacies of imagination. The road is dusty, the air is sultry, the horses are sluggish, and the postillion brutal. He longs for the time of dinner, that he may eat and rest. The inn is crowded, his orders are neglected, and nothing remains but that he devour in haste what the cook has spoiled, and drive on in quest of better entertainment. He finds at night a more commodious house, but the best is always worse than he expected.

He at last enters his native province, and resolves to feast his mind with the conversation of his old friends, and the recollection of juvenile frolicks. He stops at the house of his friend, whom he designs to overpower with pleasure by the unexpected interview. He is not known till he tells his name, and revives the memory of himself by a gradual explanation. He is then coldly received, and ceremoniously feasted. He hastes away to another, whom his affairs have called to a distant place, and, having seen the empty house, goes away disgusted, by a disappointment which could not be intended because it could not be foreseen. At the next house he finds every face clouded with misfortune, and is regarded with malevolence as an unreasonable intruder, who comes not to visit but to insult them.

It is seldom that we find either men or places such as we expect them. He that has pictured a prospect upon his fancy, will receive little pleasure from his eyes; he that has anticipated the conversation of a wit will wonder to what prejudice he owes his reputation. Yet it is necessary to hope, though hope should always be deluded; for hope itself is happiness, and its frustrations, however frequent, are yet less dreadful than its extinction.

Numb. 59. Saturday, *June* 2, 1759.

In the common enjoyments of life, we cannot very liberally indulge the present hour, but by anticipating part of the pleasure which might have relieved the tediousness of another day; and any uncommon exertion of strength, or perseverance in labour, is succeeded by a long interval of languor and weariness. Whatever advantage we snatch beyond the certain portion allotted us by nature, is like money spent before it is due, which at the time of regular payment will be missed and regretted.

Fame, like all other things which are supposed to give or to increase happiness, is dispensed with the same equality of distribution. He that is loudly praised will be clamorously censured; he that rises hastily into fame will be in danger of sinking suddenly into oblivion.

Of many writers who filled their age with wonder, and whose names we find celebrated in the books of their contemporaries, the works are now no longer to be seen, or are seen only amidst the lumber of libraries which are seldom visited, where they lie only to shew the deceitfulness of hope, and the uncertainty of honour.

Of the decline of reputation many causes may be assigned. It is commonly lost because it never was deserved; and was conferred at first, not by the suffrage of criticism, but by the fondness of friendship, or servility of flattery. The great and popular are very freely applauded; but all soon grow weary of echoing to each other a name which has no other claim to notice, but that many mouths are pronouncing it at once.

But many have lost the final reward of their labours, because they were too hasty to enjoy it. They have laid hold on recent occurrences, and eminent names, and delighted their readers with allusions and remarks, in which all were interested, and to which all therefore were attentive. But the effect ceased with its cause; the time quickly came when new events drove the former from memory, when the vicissitudes of the world brought new hopes and fears, transferred the love and hatred of the publick to other agents, and the writer, whose works were no longer assisted by gratitude or resentment, was left to the cold regard of idle curiosity.

He that writes upon general principles, or delivers universal truths, may hope to be often read, because his work will be equally useful at all times and in every country; but he cannot expect it to be received with eagerness, or to spread with rapidity, because desire can have no particular stimulation: that which is to be loved long must be loved with reason rather than with passion. He that lays out his labours upon temporary subjects, easily finds readers, and quickly loses them; for what should make the book valued when its subject is no more?

These observations will shew the reason why the poem of Hudibras is almost forgotten, however embellished with sentiments and diversified with allusions, however bright with wit, and however solid with truth. The hypocrisy which it detected, and the folly which it ridiculed, have long vanished from publick notice. Those who had felt the mischief of discord, and the tyranny of usurpation, read it with rapture, for every line brought back to memory something known, and gratified resentment by the just censure of something hated. But the book which was once quoted by princes, and which supplied conversation to all the assemblies of the gay and witty, is now seldom mentioned, and even by those that affect to mention it, is seldom read. So vainly is wit lavished upon fugitive topicks, so little can architecture secure duration when the ground is false.

increases; that the great art is the art of blotting; and that, according to the rule of Horace, every piece should be kept nine years.

Of the great authors he now began to display the characters, laying down as an universal position, that all had beauties and defects. His opinion was, that Shakespear, committing himself wholly to the impulse of nature, wanted that correctness which learning would have given him; and that Jonson, trusting to learning, did not sufficiently cast his eye on nature. He blamed the stanza of Spenser, and could not bear the hexameters of Sidney. Denham and Waller he held the first reformers of English numbers; and thought that if Waller could have obtained the strength of Denham, or Denham the sweetness of Waller, there had been nothing wanting to complete a poet. He often expressed his commiseration of Dryden's poverty, and his indignation at the age which suffered him to write for bread; he repeated with rapture the first lines of "All for Love," but wondered at the corruption of taste which could bear any thing so unnatural as rhyming tragedies. In Otway he found uncommon powers of moving the passions, but was disgusted by his general negligence, and blamed him for making a conspirator his hero; and never concluded his disquisition, without remarking how happily the sound of the clock is made to alarm the audience. Southern would have been his favourite, but that he mixes comick with tragick scenes, intercepts the natural course of the passions, and fills the mind with a wild confusion of mirth and melancholy. The versification of Rowe

he thought too melodious for the stage, and too little
varied in different passions.   He made it the great
fault of Congreve, that all his persons were wits, and
that he always wrote with more art than nature.   He
considered " Cato" rather as a poem than a play, and
allowed Addison to be the complete master of alle-
gory and grave humour, but paid no great defe-
rence to him as a critick.   He thought the chief
merit of Prior was in his easy tales and lighter poems,
though he allowed that his "Solomon" had many
noble sentiments elegantly expressed.   In Swift he
discovered an inimitable vein of irony, and an easiness which all would hope and few would attain.
Pope he was inclined to degrade from a poet to a
versifier, and thought his numbers rather luscious
than sweet.   He often lamented the neglect of
" Phædra and Hippolitus," and wished to see the stage
under better regulations.

These assertions passed commonly uncontradicted ;
and if now and then an opponent started up, he was
quickly repressed by the suffrages of the company,
and Minim went away from every dispute with elation of heart and increase of confidence.

He now grew conscious of his abilities, and began
to talk of the present state of dramatick poetry ;
wondered what was become of the comick genius
which supplied our ancestors with wit and pleasantry,
and why no writer could be found that durst now
venture beyond a farce.   He saw no reason for thinking that the vein of humour was exhausted, since we
live in a country where liberty suffers every character to spread itself to its utmost bulk, and which

therefore produces more originals than all the rest of
the world together.   Of tragedy he concluded business to be the soul, and yet often hinted that love
predominates too much upon the modern stage.

He was now an acknowledged critick, and had his
own seat in a coffee-house, and headed a party in the
pit.   Minim has more vanity than ill-nature, and
seldom desires to do much mischief; he will perhaps
murmur a little in the ear of him that sits next him,
but endeavours to influence the audience to favour,
by clapping when an actor exclaims, *Ye gods!* or
laments the misery of his country.

By degrees he was admitted to rehearsals ; and
many of his friends are of opinion, that our present
poets are indebted to him for their happiest thoughts ;
by his contrivance the bell was rung twice in Bar-
barossa, and by his persuasion the author of Cleone
concluded his play without a couplet ; for what can
be more absurd, said Minim, than that part of a play
should be rhymed, and part written in blank verse ?
and by what acquisition of faculties is the speaker,
who never could find rhymes before, enabled to rhyme
at the conclusion of an act ?

He is the great investigator of hidden beauties,
and is particularly delighted when he finds *the sound
an echo to the sense.*   He has read all our poets
with particular attention to this delicacy of versification, and wonders at the supineness with which their
works have been hitherto perused, so that no man
has found the sound of a drum in this distich :

> " When pulpit, drum ecclesiastic,
>   Was beat with fist instead of a stick ;"

and that the wonderful lines upon honour and a bubble have hitherto passed without notice :

> " Honour is like the glassy bubble,
>   Which costs philosophers such trouble ;
>   Where one part crack'd, the whole does fly,
>   And wits are crack'd to find out why."

In these verses, says Minim, we have two striking accommodations of the sound to the sense.   It is impossible to utter the two lines emphatically without an act like that which they describe ; *bubble* and *trouble* causing a momentary inflation of the cheeks by the retention of the breath, which is afterwards forcibly emitted, as in the practice of *blowing bubbles*. But the greatest excellence is in the third line, which is *crack'd* in the middle to express a crack, and then shivers into monosyllables.   Yet has this diamond lain neglected with common stones, and among the innumerable admirers of Hudibras the observation of this superlative passage has been reserved for the sagacity of Minim.

NUMB. 61.   SATURDAY, *June* 15, 1759.

MR. Minim had now advanced himself to the zenith of critical reputation ; when he was in the pit, every eye in the boxes was fixed upon him ; when he entered his coffee-house, he was surrounded by circles of candidates, who passed their noviciate of literature under his tuition : his opinion was asked by all who had no opinion of their own, and yet loved to debate and decide ; and no composition was supposed to pass in safety to posterity, till it had been secured by Minim's approbation.

Minim professes great admiration of the wisdom and munificence by which the academies of the continent were raised ; and often wishes for some standard of taste, for some tribunal, to which merit may appeal from caprice, prejudice, and malignity. He has formed a plan for an academy of criticism, where every work of imagination may be read before it is printed, and which shall authoritatively direct the theatres what pieces to receive or reject, to exclude or to revive.

Such an institution would, in Dick's opinion, spread the fame of English literature over Europe, and make London the metropolis of elegance and politeness, the place to which the learned and ingenious of all countries would repair for instruction and improvement, and where nothing would any longer be applauded or endured that was not conformed to the nicest rules, and finished with the highest elegance.

Till some happy conjunction of the planets shall dispose our princes or ministers to make themselves immortal by such an academy, Minim contents himself to preside four nights in a week in a critical society selected by himself, where he is heard without contradiction, and whence his judgment is disseminated through the great vulgar and the small.

When he is placed in the chair of criticism, he declares loudly for the noble simplicity of our ancestors, in opposition to the petty refinements, and ornamental luxuriance. Sometimes he is sunk in despair, and perceives false delicacy daily gaining ground, and sometimes brightens his countenance with a gleam of hope, and predicts the revival of the true sublime. He then fulminates his loudest censures against the monkish barbarity of rhyme; wonders how beings that pretend to reason can be pleased with one line always ending like another; tells how unjustly and unnaturally sense is sacrificed to sound; how often the best thoughts are mangled by the necessity of confining or extending them to the dimensions of a couplet; and rejoices that genius has, in our days, shaken off the shackles which had encumbered it so long. Yet he allows that rhyme may sometimes be borne, if the lines be often broken, and the pauses judiciously diversified.

From blank verse he makes an easy transition to Milton, whom he produces as an example of the slow advance of lasting reputation. Milton is the only writer in whose books Minim can read for ever without weariness. What cause it is that exempts this

pleasure from satiety he has long and diligently inquired and believes it to consist in the perpetual
variation of the numbers, by which the ear is gratified and the attention awakened.   The lines that
are commonly thought rugged and unmusical, he
conceives to have been written to temper the melodious luxury of the rest, or to express things by a
proper cadence: for he scarcely finds a verse that has
not this favourite beauty; he declares that he could
shiver in a hot-house when he reads that

> " the ground
> " Burns frore, and cold performs th' effect of fire; "

and that, when Milton bewails his blindness, the
verse,

> " So thick a drop serene has quench'd these orbs,"

has, he knows not how, something that strikes him
with an obscure sensation like that which he fancies
would be felt from the sound of darkness.

Minim is not so confident of his rules of judgment
as not very eagerly to catch new light from the
name of the author.   He is commonly so prudent
as to spare those whom he cannot resist, unless, as
will sometimes happen, he finds the publick combined against them.   But a fresh pretender to fame
he is strongly inclined to censure, till his own honour requires that he commend him.   Till he knows
the success of a composition, he entrenches himself
in general terms; there are some new thoughts and
beautiful passages, but there is likewise much which
he would have advised the author to expunge.   He
has several favourite epithets of which he has never

settled the meaning, but which are very commodiously applied to books which he has not read, or
cannot understand.　One is *manly*, another is *dry*,
another *stiff*, and another *flimsy;* sometimes he discovers delicacy of style, and sometimes meets with
strange expressions.

He is never so great, or so happy, as when a
youth of promising parts is brought to receive his
directions for the prosecution of his studies.　He
then puts on a very serious air; he advises the pupil
to read none but the best authors, and when he finds
one congenial to his own mind, to study his beauties,
but avoid his faults, and, when he sits down to write,
to consider how his favourite author would think at
the present time on the present occasion.　He ex-
horts him to catch those moments when he finds his
thoughts expanded and his genius exalted, but to
take care lest imagination hurry him beyond the
bounds of nature.　He holds diligence the mother
of success; yet enjoins him, with great earnestness,
not to read more than he can digest, and not to confuse his mind by pursuing studies of contrary ten-
dencies.　He tells him, that every man has his
genius, and that Cicero could never be a poet.　The
boy retires illuminated, resolves to follow his genius,
and to think how Milton would have thought: and
Minim feasts upon his own beneficence till another
day brings another pupil.

NUMB. 62.   SATURDAY, *June* 23, 1759.

TO THE IDLER.

SIR,

AN opinion prevails almost universally in the world, that he who has money has every thing. This is not a modern paradox, or the tenet of a small and obscure sect, but a persuasion which appears to have operated upon most minds in all ages, and which is supported by authorities so numerous and so cogent, that nothing but long experience could have given me confidence to question its truth.

But experience is the test by which all the philosophers of the present age agree, that speculation must be tried; and I may be therefore allowed to doubt the power of money, since I have been a long time rich, and have not yet found that riches can make me happy.

My father was a farmer neither wealthy nor indigent, who gave me a better education than was suitable to my birth, because my uncle in the city designed me for his heir, and desired that I might be bred a gentleman. My uncle's wealth was the perpetual subject of conversation in the house; and when any little misfortune befell us, or any mortification dejected us, my father always exhorted me to hold up my head, for my uncle would never marry.

My uncle, indeed, kept his promise. Having his mind completely busied between his warehouse and the 'Change, he felt no tediousness of life, nor any want of domestick amusements. When my father died, he received me kindly; but, after a few months, finding no great pleasure in the conversation of each other, we parted; and he remitted me a small annuity, on which I lived a quiet and studious life, without any wish to grow great by the death of my benefactor.

But though I never suffered any malignant impatience to take hold on my mind, I could not forbear sometimes to imagine to myself the pleasure of being rich; and, when I read of diversions and magnificence, resolved to try, when time should put the trial in my power, what pleasure they could afford.

My uncle, in the latter spring of his life, when his ruddy cheek and his firm nerves promised him a long and healthy age, died of an apoplexy. His death gave me neither joy nor sorrow. He did me good, and I regarded him with gratitude; but I could not please him, and therefore could not love him.

He had the policy of little minds, who love to surprize; and, having always represented his fortune as less than it was, had, I suppose, often gratified himself with thinking, how I should be delighted to find myself twice as rich as I expected. My wealth was such as exceeded all the schemes of expence which I had formed; and I soon began to expand my thoughts, and look round for some purchase of felicity.

The most striking effect of riches is the splendour of dress, which every man has observed to enforce respect, and facilitate reception ; and my first desire was to be fine. I sent for a taylor who was employed by the nobility, and ordered such a suit of clothes as I had often looked on with involuntary submission, and am ashamed to remember with what flutters of expectation I waited for the hour when I should issue forth in all the splendour of embroidery. The clothes were brought, and for three days I observed many eyes turned towards me as I passed : but I felt myself obstructed in the common intercourse of civility, by an uneasy consciousness of my new appearance ; as I thought myself more observed, I was more anxious about my mien and behaviour ; and the mien which is formed by care is commonly ridiculous. A short time accustomed me to myself, and my dress was without pain and without pleasure.

For a little while I tried to be a rake, but I began too late ; and having by nature no turn for a frolick, was in great danger of ending in a drunkard. A fever, in which not one of my companions paid me a visit, gave me time for reflection. I found that there was no great pleasure in breaking windows and lying in the round-house ; and resolved to associate no longer with those whom, though I had treated and bailed them, I could not make friends.

I then changed my measures, kept running horses, and had the comfort of seeing my name very often in the news. I had a chesnut horse, the grandson of *Childers*, who won four plates, and ten by-matches ;

and a bay filly, who carried off the five years old plate, and was expected to perform much greater exploits, when my groom broke her wind, because I happened to catch him selling oats for beer. This happiness was soon at an end; there was no pleasure when I lost, and when I won I could not much exalt myself by the virtues of my horse. I grew ashamed of the company of jockey-lords, and resolved to spend no more of my time in the stable.

It was now known that I had money and would spend it, and I passed four months in the company of architects, whose whole business was to persuade me to build a house. I told them that I had more room than I wanted, but could not get rid of their importunities. A new plan was brought me every morning; till at last my constancy was overpowered, and I began to build. The happiness of building lasted but a little while, for though I love to spend, I hate to be cheated; and I soon found that to build is to be robbed.

How I proceed in the pursuit of happiness, you shall hear when I find myself disposed to write.

I am Sir, &c.

Tim. Ranger.

NUMB. 63.　SATURDAY, *June* 30, 1759.

THE natural progress of the works of men is from rudeness to convenience, from convenience to elegance, and from elegance to nicety.

The first labour is enforced by necessity. The savage finds himself incommoded by heat and cold, by rain and wind; he shelters himself in the hollow of a rock, and learns to dig a cave where there was none before. He finds the sun and the wind excluded by the thicket, and when the accidents of the chace, or the convenience of pasturage leads him into more open places, he forms a thicket for himself, by planting stakes at proper distances, and laying branches from one to another.

The next gradation of skill and industry produces a house closed with doors, and divided by partitions; and apartments are multiplied and disposed according to the various degrees of power or invention; improvement succeeds improvement, as he that is free from a greater evil grows impatient of a less, till ease in time is advanced to pleasure.

The mind, set free from the importunities of natural want, gains leisure to go in search of superfluous gratifications, and adds to the uses of habitation, the delights of prospect. Then begins the reign of symmetry; orders of architecture are invented, and one part of the edifice is conformed to another, without any other reason, than that the eye may not be offended.

The passage is very short from elegance to luxury. Ionick and Corinthian columns are soon succeeded by gilt cornices, inlaid floors, and petty ornaments, which shew rather the wealth than the taste of the possessor.

Language proceeds, like every thing else, through improvement to degeneracy. The rovers who first take possession of a country, having not many ideas, and those not nicely modified or discriminated, were contented, if by general terms and abrupt sentences they could make their thoughts known to one another ; as life begins to be more regulated, and property to become limited, disputes must be decided, and claims adjusted ; the differences of things are noted, and distinctness and propriety of expression become necessary. In time, happiness and plenty give rise to curiosity, and the sciences are cultivated for ease and pleasure ; to the arts, which are now to be taught, emulation soon adds the art of teaching ; and the studious and ambitious contend not only who shall think best, but who shall tell their thoughts in the most pleasing manner.

Then begin the arts of rhetorick and poetry, the regulation of figures, the selection of words, the modulation of periods, the graces of transition, the complication of clauses, and all the delicacies of style and subtilties of composition, useful while they advance perspicuity, and laudable while they increase pleasure, but easy to be refined by needless scrupulosity till they shall more embarrass the writer than assist the reader or delight him.

The first state is commonly antecedent to the

practice of writing; the ignorant essays of imperfect diction pass away with the savage generation that uttered them. No nation can trace their language beyond the second period, and even of that it does not often happen that many monuments remain.

The fate of the English tongue is like that of others. We know nothing of the scanty jargon of our barbarous ancestors; but we have specimens of our language when it began to be adapted to civil and religious purposes, and find it such as might naturally be expected, artless and simple, unconnected and concise. The writers seem to have desired little more than to be understood, and perhaps seldom aspired to the praise of pleasing. Their verses were considered chiefly as memorial, and therefore did not differ from prose but by the measure or the rhyme.

In this state, varied a little according to the different purposes or abilities of writers, our language may be said to have continued to the time of Gower, whom Chaucer calls his master, and who, however obscured by his scholar's popularity, seems justly to claim the honour which has been hitherto denied him, of shewing his countrymen that something more was to be desired, and that English verse might be exalted into poetry.

From the time of Gower and Chaucer, the English writers have studied elegance, and advanced their language, by successive improvements, to as much harmony as it can easily receive, and as much copiousness as human knowledge has hitherto required. These advances have not been made at all times with the same diligence or the same success. Negligence has suspended the course of improvement, or affectation turned it aside; time has elapsed with little change, or change has been made without amendment. But elegance has been long kept in view with attention as near to constancy as life permits, till every man now endeavours to excel others in accuracy, or outshine them in splendour of style, and the danger is, lest care should too soon pass to affectation.

NUMB. 64.   SATURDAY, *July* 7, 1759.

TO THE IDLER.

SIR,

As nature has made every man desirous of happiness, I flatter myself, that you and your readers cannot but feel some curiosity to know the sequel of my story; for though, by trying the different schemes of pleasure, I have yet found nothing in which I could finally acquiesce; yet the narrative of my attempts will not be wholly without use, since we always approach nearer to truth as we detect more and more varieties of error.

When I had sold my racers, and put the orders of architecture out of my head, my next resolution was to be a *fine gentleman*. I frequented the polite coffee-houses, grew acquainted with all the men of humour, and gained the right of bowing familiarly to half the nobility. In this new scene of life my great labour was to learn to laugh. I had been used to consider laughter as the effect of merriment; but I soon learned that it is one of the arts of adulation, and, from laughing only to shew that I was pleased, I now began to laugh when I wished to please. This was at first very difficult. I sometimes heard the story with dull indifference, and, not exalting myself to merriment by due gradations, burst out suddenly into an awkward noise, which was not always favourably interpreted. Sometimes I was behind the rest of the company, and lost the grace of laughing by delay, and sometimes when I began at the right time was deficient in loudness or in length. But, by diligent imitation of the best models, I attained at last such flexibility of muscles, that I was always a welcome auditor of a story, and got the reputation of a good-natured fellow.

This was something; but much more was to be done, that I might be universally allowed to be a fine gentleman. I appeared at court on all publick days; betted at gaming-tables; and played at all the routs of eminence. I went every night to the opera, took a fidler of disputed merit under my protection, became the head of a musical faction, and had sometimes concerts at my own house. I once thought to have attained the highest rank of elegance, by taking a foreign singer into keeping. But my favourite fidler contrived to be arrested on the night of a concert, for a finer suit of clothes than I had ever presumed to wear, and I lost all the fame of patronage by refusing to bail him.

My next ambition was to sit for my picture. I spent a whole winter in going from painter to painter, to bespeak a whole length of one, and a half length of another; I talked of nothing but attitudes, draperies, and proper lights; took my friends to see the pictures after every sitting; heard every day of a wonderful performer in crayons and miniature, and sent my pictures to be copied; was told by the judges that they were not like, and was recommended to other artists. At length, being not able to please my friends, I grew less pleased myself, and at last resolved to think no more about it.

It was impossible to live in total idleness: and wandering about in search of something to do, I was invited to a weekly meeting of virtuosos, and felt myself instantaneously seized with an unextinguishable ardour for all natural curiosities. I ran from auction to auction, became a critick in shells and fossils, bought a *Hortus siccus* of inestimable value, and purchased a secret art of preserving insects, which made my collection the envy of the other philosophers. I found this pleasure mingled with much vexation. All the faults of my life were for nine months circulated through the town with the most active malignity, because I happened to catch a moth of peculiar variegation; and because I once out-bid all the lovers of shells, and carried off a nautilus, it was hinted that the validity of my uncle's will ought to be disputed. I will not deny that I was very proud both of the moth and of the shell, and gratified myself with the envy of my companions, perhaps more than became a benevolent being. But in time I grew weary of being hated for that which produced no advantage, gave my shells to children that wanted play-things, and suppressed the art of drying butterflies, because I would not tempt idleness and cruelty to kill them.

I now began to feel life tedious, and wished to store myself with friends, with whom I might grow old in the interchange of benevolence. I had observed that popularity was most easily gained by an open table, and therefore hired a French cook, furnished my sideboard with great magnificence, filled my cellar with wines of pompous appellations, bought every thing that was dear before it was good, and invited all those who were most famous for judging of a dinner. In three weeks my cook gave me warning, and, upon inquiry, told me that Lord Queasy, who dined with me the day before, had sent him an offer of double wages. My pride prevailed; I raised his wages, and invited his lordship to another feast. I love plain meat, and was therefore soon weary of spreading a table of which I could not partake. I found that my guests when they went away, criticised their entertainment, and censured my profusion; my cook thought himself necessary, and took upon him the direction of the house; and I could not rid myself of flatterers, or break from slavery, but by shutting up my house, and declaring my resolution to live in lodgings.

After all this, tell me, dear Idler, what I must do next; I have health, I have money, and I hope that I have understanding; yet, with all these, I have never been able to pass a single day which I did not wish at an end before sun-set. Tell me, dear Idler, what I shall do. I am

Your humble servant,

TIM. RANGER.

NUMB 65. SATURDAY, *July* 14, 1759.

THE sequel of Clarendon's history, at last happily published, is an accession to English literature equally agreeable to the admirers of elegance and the lovers of truth; many doubtful facts may now be ascertained, and many questions, after long debate, may be determined by decisive authority. He that records transactions in which himself was engaged, has not only an opportunity of knowing innumerable particulars which escape spectators, but has his natural powers exalted by that ardour which always rises at the remembrance of our own importance, and by which every man is enabled to relate his own actions better than another's.

The difficulties through which this work has struggled into light, and the delays with which our hopes have been long mocked, naturally lead the mind to the consideration of the common fate of posthumous compositions.

He who sees himself surrounded by admirers, and whose vanity is hourly feasted with all the luxuries of studied praise, is easily persuaded that his influence will be extended beyond his life; that they who cringe in his presence will reverence his memory, and that those who are proud to be numbered among his friends, will endeavour to vindicate his choice by zeal for his reputation.

With hopes like these, to the executors of Swift, was committed the history of the last years of Queen Anne, and to those of Pope, the works which remained unprinted in his closet. The performances of Pope were burnt by those whom he had perhaps selected from all mankind as most likely to publish them; and the history had likewise perished, had not a straggling transcript fallen into busy hands.

The papers left in the closet of Pieresc supplied his heirs with a whole winter's fuel; and many of the labours of the learned Bishop Lloyd were consumed in the kitchen of his descendants.

Some works, indeed, have escaped total destruction; but yet have had reason to lament the fate of orphans exposed to the frauds of unfaithful guardians. How Hale would have borne the mutilations which his " Pleas of the Crown" have suffered from the editor, they who know his character will easily conceive.

The original copy of Burnet's history, though promised to some publick * library, has been never given; and who then can prove the fidelity of the publication, when the authenticity of Clarendon's

* It would be proper to reposite, in some public place, the manuscript of Clarendon, which has not escaped all suspicion of unfaithful publication.

history, though printed with the sanction of one of the first universities of the world, had not an unexpected manuscript been happily discovered, would, with the help of factious credulity, have been brought into question by the two lowest of all human beings, a scribbler for a party, and a commissioner of excise.*

Vanity is often no less mischievous than negligence or dishonesty. He that possesses a valuable manuscript, hopes to raise its esteem by concealment, and delights in the distinction which he imagines himself to obtain by keeping the key of a treasure which he neither uses nor imparts. From him it falls to some other owner, less vain but more negligent, who considers it as useless lumber, and rids himself of the incumbrance.

Yet there are some works which the authors must consign unpublished to posterity, however uncertain be the event, however hopeless be the trust. He that writes the history of his own times, if he adheres steadily to truth, will write that which his own times will not easily endure. He must be content to reposite his book till all private passions shall cease, and love and hatred give way to curiosity.

But many leave the labours of half their life to their executors and to chance, because they will not send them abroad unfinished, and are unable to finish them, having prescribed to themselves such a degree of exactness as human diligence can scarcely attain.

* John Oldmixon and George Ducket. See a more particular history of this paper in Vol. XXXIII. of the BRITISH ESSAYISTS, Preface to the IDLER.   C.

Lloyd, says Burnet, " did not lay out his learning with the same diligence as he laid it in." He was always hesitating and enquiring, raising objections and removing them, and waiting for clearer light and fuller discovery. Baker, after many years passed in biography, left his manuscripts to be buried in a library, because that was imperfect which could never be perfected.

Of these learned men, let those who aspire to the same praise imitate the diligence, and avoid the scrupulosity. Let it be always remembered that life is short, that knowledge is endless, and that many doubts deserve not to be cleared. Let those whom nature and study have qualified to teach mankind, tell us what they have learned while they are yet able to tell it, and trust their reputation only to themselves.

NUMB. 66.   SATURDAY, *July* 21, 1759.

No complaint is more frequently repeated among the learned, than that of the waste made by time among the labours of antiquity.   Of those who once filled the civilized world with their renown, nothing is now left but their names, which are left only to raise desires that never can be satisfied, and sorrow which never can be comforted.

Had all the writings of the ancients been faithfully delivered down from age to age, had the Alexandrian library been spared, and the Palatine repositories remained unimpaired, how much might we have known of which we are now doomed to be ignorant ! how many laborious inquiries, and dark conjectures ; how many collations of broken hints and mutilated passages might have been spared ! We should have known the successions of princes, the revolutions of empire, the actions of the great, and opinions of the wise, the laws and constitutions of every state, and the arts by which publick grandeur and happiness are acquired and preserved ; we should have traced the progress of life, seen colonies from distant regions take possession of European deserts, and troops of savages settled into communities by the desire of keeping what they had acquired ; we should have traced the gradations of civility, and travelled upward to the original of things by the light of history, till in remoter times it had glimmered in fable, and at last sunk into darkness.

If the works of imagination had been less diminished, it is likely that all future times might have been supplied with inexhaustible amusement by the fictions of antiquity. The tragedies of Sophocles and Euripides would all have shown the stronger passions in all their diversities; and the comedies of Menander would have furnished all the maxims of domestick life. Nothing would have been necessary to moral wisdom but to have studied these great masters, whose knowledge would have guided doubt, and whose authority would have silenced cavils.

Such are the thoughts that rise in every student, when his curiosity is eluded, and his searches are frustrated; yet it may perhaps be doubted, whether our complaints are not sometimes inconsiderate, and whether we do not imagine more evil than we feel. Of the ancients, enough remains to excite our emulation and direct our endeavours. Many of the works which time has left us, we know to have been those that were most esteemed, and which antiquity itself considered as models; so that, having the originals, we may without much regret lose the imitations. The obscurity which the want of contemporary writers often produces, only darkens single passages, and those commonly of slight importance. The general tendency of every piece may be known; and though that diligence deserves praise which leaves nothing unexamined, yet its miscarriages are not much to be lamented; for the most useful truths are always universal, and unconnected with accidents and customs.

Such is the general conspiracy of human nature

against contemporary merit, that, if we had inherited from antiquity enough to afford employment for the laborious, and amusement for the idle, I know not what room would have been left for modern genius or modern industry; almost every subject would have been pre-occupied, and every style would have been fixed by a precedent from which few would have ventured to depart. Every writer would have had a rival, whose superiority was already acknowledged, and to whose fame his work would, even before it was seen, be marked out for a sacrifice.

We see how little the united experience of mankind hath been able to add to the heroick characters displayed by Homer, and how few incidents the fertile imagination of modern Italy has yet produced, which may not be found in the Iliad and Odyssey. It is likely, that if all the works of the Athenian philosophers had been extant, Malbranche and Locke would have been condemned to be silent readers of the ancient metaphysicians; and it is apparent, that, if the old writers had all remained, the Idler could not have written a disquisition on the loss.

NUMB. 67.   SATURDAY, *July* 28, 1759.

TO THE IDLER.

SIR,

IN the observations which you have made on the various opinions and pursuits of mankind, you must often, in literary conversations, have met with men who consider dissipation as the great enemy of the intellect; and maintain, that in proportion as the student keeps himself within the bounds of a settled plan, he will more certainly advance in science.

This opinion is, perhaps, generally true; yet when we contemplate the inquisitive nature of the human mind, and its perpetual impatience of all restraint, it may be doubted whether the faculties may not be contracted by confining the attention; and whether it may not sometimes be proper to risque the certainty of little for the chance of much. Acquisitions of knowledge, like blazes of genius, are often fortuitous. Those who had proposed to themselves a methodical course of reading, light by accident on a new book, which seizes their thoughts and kindles their curiosity, and opens an unexpected prospect, to which the way which they had prescribed to themselves would never have conducted them.

To enforce and illustrate my meaning, I have sent you a journal of three days' employment, found among the papers of a late intimate acquaintance; who, as will plainly appear, was a man of vast designs, and of vast performances, though he sometimes designed one thing, and performed another. I allow that the Spectator's inimitable productions of this kind may well discourage all subsequent journalists; but, as the subject of this is different from that of any which the Spectator has given us, I leave it to you to publish or suppress it.

Mem. The following three days I propose to give up to reading; and intend, after all the delays which have obtruded themselves upon me, to finish my "Essay on the Extent of the Mental Powers;" to revise my "Treatise on Logick;" to begin the Epick which I have long projected; to proceed in my perusal of the Scriptures with Grotius's Comment; and at my leisure to regale myself with the works of classicks, ancient and modern, and to finish my "Ode to Astronomy."

Monday.] Designed to rise at six, but, by my servant's laziness, my fire was not lighted before eight, when I dropped into a slumber that lasted till nine; at which time I arose, and, after breakfast, at ten sat down to study, proposing to begin upon my Essay; but, finding occasion to consult a passage in Plato, was absorbed in the perusal of the Republick till twelve. I had neglected to forbid company, and now enters Tom Careless, who after half an hour's chat, insisted upon my going with him to enjoy an absurd character, that he had appointed, by an advertisement, to meet him at a

particular coffee-house.   After we had for some
time entertained ourselves with him, we sallied out,
designing each to repair to his home; but, as it fell
out, coming up in the street to a man whose steel
by his side declared him a butcher, we overheard
him opening an address to a genteelish sort of
young Lady, whom he walked with : " Miss, though
your father is master of a coal-lighter, and you
will be a great fortune, 'tis true; yet I wish I
may be cut into quarters if it is not only love,
and not lucre of gain, that is my motive for
offering terms of marriage." As this lover proceeded in his speech, he misled us the length of
three streets, in admiration at the unlimited power
of the tender passion, that could soften even the
heart of a butcher.   We then adjourned to a
tavern, and from thence to one of the publick
gardens, where I was regaled with a most amusing
variety of men possessing great talents, so discoloured by affectation, that they only made them
eminently ridiculous; shallow things, who by continual dissipation, had annihilated the few ideas
nature had given them, and yet were celebrated for
wonderful pretty gentlemen; young ladies extolled
for their wit, because they were handsome; illiterate empty women as well as men, in high life,
admired for their knowledge, from their being
resolutely positive ; and women of real understanding so far from pleasing the polite million,
that they frightened them away, and were left
solitary.   When we quitted this entertaining scene,
Tom pressed me irresistibly, to sup with him.   I

reached home at twelve, and then reflected, that though indeed I had, by remarking various characters, improved my insight into human nature, yet still I had neglected the studies proposed, and accordingly took up my " Treatise on Logick," to give it the intended revisal, but found my spirits too much agitated, and could not forbear a few satirical lines, under the title of " The Evening's Walk."

Tuesday.] At breakfast, seeing my " Ode to Astronomy " lying on my desk, I was struck with a train of ideas, that I thought might contribute to its improvement. I immediately rang my bell to forbid all visitants, when my servant opened the door, with, " Sir, Mr. Jeffery Gape." My cup dropped out of one hand, and my poem out of the other. I could scarcely ask him to sit; he told me he was going to walk, but, as there was a likelihood of rain, he would sit with me; he said, he intended at first to have called at Mr. Vacant's, but, as he had not seen me a great while, he did not mind coming out of his way to wait on me; I made him a bow, but thanks for the favour stuck in my throat. I asked him if he had been to the coffee-house; he replied, two hours.

Under the oppression of this dull interruption, I sat looking wishfully at the clock; for which, to increase my satisfaction, I had chosen the inscription, " Art is long, and life is short ;" exchanging questions and answers at long intervals, and not without some hints that the weather-glass promised fair weather. At half an hour after three he told me he would trespass on me for a dinner, and desired me to send to his house for a bundle of papers, about inclosing a common upon his estate, which he would read to me in the evening. I declared myself busy, and Mr. Gape went away.

Having dined, to compose my chagrin I took up Virgil, and several other classicks, but could not calm my mind, or proceed in my scheme. At about five I laid my hand on a Bible that lay on my table, at first with coldness and insensibility ; but was imperceptibly engaged in a close attention to its sublime morality, and felt my heart expanded by warm philantbropy, and exalted to dignity of sentiment : I then censured my too great solicitude, and my disgust conceived at my acquaintance, who had been so far from designing to offend, that he only meant to shew kindness and respect. In this strain of mind I wrote " An Essay on Benevolence," and " An Elegy on Sublunary Disappointments." When I had finished these, at eleven, I supped, and recollected how little I had adhered to my plan, and almost questioned the possibility of pursuing any settled and uniform design ; however, I was not so far persuaded of the truth of these suggestions, but that I resolved to try once more at my scheme. As I observed the moon shining through my window, from a calm and bright sky spangled with innumerable stars, I indulged a pleasing meditation on the splendid scene, and finished my " Ode to Astronomy."

Wednesday.] Rose at seven, and employed three hours in perusal of the Scriptures with Grotius's Comment ;" and after breakfast fell into meditation concerning my projected Epick; and being in some doubt as to the particular lives of some heroes, whom I proposed to celebrate, I consulted Bayle and Moreri, and was engaged two hours in examining various lives and characters, but then resolved to go to my employment. When I was seated at my desk, and began to feel the glowing succession of poetical ideas, my servant brought me a letter from a lawyer, requiring my instant attendance at Gray's Inn for half an hour. I went full of vexation, and was involved in business till eight at night; and then, being too much fatigued to study, supped, and went to bed.

HERE my friend's journal concludes, which perhaps is pretty much a picture of the manner in which many prosecute their studies. I therefore resolved to send it you, imagining, that, if you think it worthy of appearing in your paper, some of your readers may receive entertainment by recognising a resemblance between my friend's conduct and their own. It must be left to the Idler accurately to ascertain the proper methods of advancing in literature; but this one position, deducible from what has been said above, may, I think, be reasonably asserted, that he who finds himself strongly attracted to any particular study, though it may happen to be out of his proposed scheme, if it is not trifling or vicious, had better continue his application to it, since it is likely that he will, with much more ease and expedition, attain that which a warm inclination stimulates him to pursue, than that at which a prescribed law compels him to toil.

I am, &c.*

* Bennet Langton, Esq. was the author of this paper: in which he evidently had in his eye the resolutions and interruptions of his friend the IDLER.   C.

NUMB. 68.　SATURDAY, *August* 4, 1759.

AMONG the studies which have exercised the ingenious and the learned for more than three centuries, none has been more diligently or more successfully cultivated than the art of translation; by which the impediments which bar the way to science are, in some measure, removed, and the multiplicity of languages becomes less incommodious.

Of every other kind of writing the ancients have left us models which all succeeding ages have laboured to imitate; but translations may justly be claimed by the moderns as their own. In the first ages of the world instruction was commonly oral, and learning traditional, and what was not written could not be translated. When alphabetical writing made the conveyance of opinions and the transmission of events more easy and certain, literature did not flourish in more than one country at once, or distant nations had little commerce with each other; and those few whom curiosity sent abroad in quest of improvement, delivered their acquisitions in their own manner, desirous perhaps to be considered as the inventors of that which they had learned from others.

The Greeks for a time travelled into Egypt, but they translated no books from the Egyptian language;

and when the Macedonians had overthrown the empire of Persia, the countries that became subject to Grecian dominion studied only the Grecian literature. The books of the conquered nations, if they had any among them, sunk into oblivion; Greece considered herself as the mistress, if not as the parent of arts, her language contained all that was supposed to be known, and, except the sacred writings of the Old Testament, I know not that the library of Alexandria adopted any thing from a foreign tongue.

The Romans confessed themselves the scholars of the Greeks, and do not appear to have expected, what has since happened, that the ignorance of succeeding ages would prefer them to their teachers. Every man, who in Rome aspired to the praise of literature, thought it necessary to learn Greek, and had no need of versions when they could study the originals. Translation, however, was not wholly neglected. Dramatick poems could be understood by the people in no language but their own, and the Romans were sometimes entertained with the tragedies of Euripides and the comedies of Menander. Other works were sometimes attempted : in an old scholiast there is mention of a Latin Iliad; and we have not wholly lost Tully's version of the poem of Aratus; but it does not appear that any man grew eminent by interpreting another, and perhaps it was more frequent to translate for exercise or amusement, than for fame.

The Arabs were the first nation who felt the ardour of translation : when they had subdued the eastern provinces of the Greek empire, they found their captives wiser than themselves, and made haste to relieve their wants by imparted knowledge. They discovered that many might grow wise by the labour of a few, and that improvements might be made with speed, when they had the knowledge of former ages in their own language. They therefore made haste to lay hold on medicine and philosophy, and turned their chief authors into Arabick. Whether they attempted the poets is not known; their literary zeal was vehement, but it was short, and probably expired before they had time to add the arts of elegance to those of necessity.

The study of ancient literature was interrupted in Europe by the irruption of the Northern nations, who subverted the Roman empire, and erected new kingdoms with new languages. It is not strange, that such confusion should suspend literary attention; those who lost, and those who gained dominion, had immediate difficulties to encounter, and immediate miseries to redress, and had little leisure, amidst the violence of war, the trepidation of flight, the distresses of forced migration, or the tumults of unsettled conquest, to inquire after speculative truth, to enjoy the amusement of imaginary adventures, to know the history of former ages, or study the events of any other lives. But no sooner had this chaos of dominion sunk into order, than learning began again to flourish in the calm of peace. When life and possessions were secure, convenience and enjoyment were soon sought, learning was found the highest gratification of the mind, and translation became one of the means by which it was imparted.

At last, by a concurrence of many causes, the European world was roused from its lethargy ; those arts which had been long obscurely studied in the gloom of monasteries became the general favorites of mankind ; every nation vied with its neighbour for the prize of learning ; the epidemical emulation spread from south to north, and curiosity and translation found their way to Britain.

NUMB. 69.   SATURDAY, *August* 11, 1759.

HE that reviews the progress of English literature, will find that translation was very early cultivated among us, but that some principles, either wholly erroneous or too far extended, hindered our success from being always equal to our diligence.

Chaucer, who is generally considered as the father of our poetry, has left a version of Boetius " on the Comforts of Philosophy," the book which seems to have been the favorite of the middle ages, which had been translated into Saxon by King Alfred, and illustrated with a copious comment ascribed to Aquinas.   It may be supposed that Chaucer would apply more than common attention to an author of so much celebrity, yet he has attempted nothing higher than a version strictly literal, and has degraded the poetical parts to prose, that the constraint of versification might not obstruct his zeal for fidelity.

T 2

Caxton taught us typography about the year 1474. The first book printed in English was a translation. Caxton was both the translator and printer of the " Destruction of Troye," a book which, in that infancy of learning, was considered as the best account of the fabulous ages, and which, though now driven out of notice by authors of no greater use or value, still continued to be read in Caxton's English to the beginning of the present century.

Caxton proceeded as he began, and except the poems of Gower and Chaucer, printed nothing but translations from the French, in which the original is so scrupulously followed, that they afford us little knowledge of our own language ; though the words are English, the phrase is foreign.

As learning advanced, new works were adopted into our language, but I think with little improvement of the art of translation, though foreign nations and other languages offered us models of a better method ; till in the age of Elizabeth we began to find that greater liberty was necessary to elegance, and that elegance was necessary to general reception ; some essays were then made upon the Italian poets, which deserve the praise and gratitude of posterity.

But the old practice was not suddenly forsaken ; Holland filled the nation with literal translation ; and, what is yet more strange, the same exactness was obstinately practised in the versions of the poets. This absurd labour of construing into rhyme was countenanced by Jonson in his version of Horace ; and whether it be that more men have learning than genius, or that the endeavours of that time were more directed towards knowledge than delight, the accuracy of Jonson found more imitators than the elegance of Fairfax; and May, Sandys, and Holiday, confined themselves to the toil of rendering line for line, not indeed with equal felicity, for May and Sandys were poets, and Holiday only a scholar and a critick.

Feltham appears to consider it as the established law of poetical translation, that the lines should be neither more nor fewer than those of the original; and so long had this prejudice prevailed, that Denham praises Fanshaw's version of Guarini as the example of a *new and noble way*, as the first attempt to break the boundaries of custom, and assert the natural freedom of the Muse.

In the general emulation of wit and genius which the festivity of the Restoration produced, the poets shook off their constraint, and considered translation as no longer confined to servile closeness. But reformation is seldom the work of pure virtue or unassisted reason. Translation was improved more by accident than conviction. The writers of the foregoing age had at least learning equal to their genius; and being often more able to explain the sentiments or illustrate the allusions of the ancients, than to exhibit their graces and transfuse their spirit, were perhaps willing sometimes to conceal their want of poetry by profusion of literature, and therefore translated literally, that their fidelity might shelter their insipidity or harshness. The wits of Charles's time had seldom more than slight and superficial views; and their care was to hide their want of learning bohind the colours of a gay imagination ; they therefore translated always with freedom, sometimes with licentiousness, and perhaps expected that their readers should accept spriteliness for knowledge, and consider ignorance and mistake as the impatience and negligence of a mind too rapid to stop at difficulties, and too elevated to descend to minuteness.

Thus was translation made more easy to the writer, and more delightful to the reader ; and there is no wonder if ease and pleasure have found their advocates.   The paraphrastick liberties have been almost universally admitted ; and Sherbourn, whose learning was eminent, and who had no need of any excuse to pass slightly over obscurities, is the only writer who in later times has attempted to justify or revive the ancient severity.

There is undoubtedly a mean to be observed. Dryden saw very early that closeness best preserved an author's sense, and that freedom best exhibited his spirit ; he therefore will deserve the highest praise, who can give a representation at once faithful and pleasing, who can convey the same thoughts with the same graces, and who, when he translates, changes nothing but the language.

NUMB. 70. SATURDAY, *August* 18, 1759.

FEW faults of style, whether real or imaginary, excite the malignity of a more numerous class of readers, than the use of hard words.

If an author be supposed to involve his thoughts in voluntary obscurity, and to obstruct, by unnecessary difficulties, a mind eager in pursuit of truth; if he writes not to make others learned, but to boast the learning which he possesses himself, and wishes to be admired rather than understood, he counteracts the first end of writing, and justly suffers the utmost severity of censure, or the more afflictive severity of neglect.

But words are only hard to those who do not understand them; and the critick ought always to inquire, whether he is incommoded by the fault of the writer, or by his own.

Every author does not write for every reader; many questions are such as the illiterate part of mankind can have neither interest nor pleasure in discussing, and which therefore it would be an useless endeavour to level with common minds, by tiresome circumlocutions or laborious explanations; and many subjects of general use may be treated in a different manner, as the book is intended for the learned or the ignorant. Diffusion and explication are necessary to the instruction of those who, being neither able nor ac-

customed to think for themselves, can learn only
what is expressly taught ; but they who can form
parallels, discover consequences, and multiply conclusions, are best pleased with involution of argument and compression of thought ; they desire only
to receive the seeds of knowledge which they may
branch out by their own power, to have the way to
truth pointed out which they can then follow without a guide.

The Guardian directs one of his pupils, " to think
with the wise, but speak with the vulgar." This is
a precept specious enough, but not always practicable.
Difference of thoughts will produce difference of language. He that thinks with more extent than another will want words of larger meaning ; he that
thinks with more subtilty will seek for terms of
more nice discrimination ; and where is the wonder,
since words are but the images of things, that he who
never knew the original should not know the copies ?

Yet vanity inclines us to find faults any where rather than in ourselves. He that reads and grows no
wiser, seldom suspects his own deficiency ; but complains of hard words and obscure sentences, and asks
why books are written which cannot be understood ?

Among the hard words which are no longer to be
used, it has been long the custom to number terms
of art. " Every man (says Swift) is more able to explain the subject of an art than its professors ; a farmer will tell you, in two words, that he has broken
his leg ; but a surgeon, after a long discourse, shall
leave you as ignorant as you were before." This
could only have been said by such an exact ob-

server of life, in gratification of malignity, or in ostentation of acuteness.   Every hour produces instances of the necessity of terms of art.   Mankind could never conspire in uniform affectation ; it is not but by necessity that every science and every trade has its peculiar language.   They that content themselves with general ideas may rest in general terms ; but those, whose studies or employments force them upon closer inspection, must have names for particular parts, and words by which they may express various modes of combination, such as none but themselves have occasion to consider.

Artists are indeed sometimes ready to suppose that none can be strangers to words to which themselves are familiar, talk to an incidental inquirer as they talk to one another, and make their knowledge ridiculous by injudicious obtrusion.   An art cannot be taught but by its proper terms, but it is not always necessary to teach the art.

That the vulgar express their thoughts clearly is far from true ; and what perspicuity can be found among them proceeds not from the easiness of their language, but the shallowness of their thoughts. He that sees a building as a common spectator, contents himself with relating that it is great or little, mean or splendid, lofty or low ; all these words are intelligible and common, but they convey no distinct or limited ideas ; if he attempts, without the terms of architecture, to delineate the parts, or enumerate the ornaments, his narration at once becomes unintelligible.   The terms, indeed, generally displease, because they are understood by few ; but they are little understood only because few, that look upon an edifice, examine its parts, or analyse its columns into their members.

The state of every other art is the same; as it is cursorily surveyed or accurately examined, different forms of expression become proper. In morality it is one thing to discuss the niceties of the casuist, and another to direct the practice of common life. In agriculture, he that instructs the farmer to plough and sow, may convey his notions without the words which he would find necessary in explaining to philosophers the process of vegetation; and if he, who has nothing to do but to be honest by the shortest way, will perplex his mind with subtile speculations; or if he, whose task is to reap and thresh, will not be contented without examining the evolution of the seed and circulation of the sap; the writers whom either shall consult are very little to be blamed, though it should sometimes happen that they are read in vain.

Numb. 71. Saturday, *August* 25, 1759.

Dick Shifter was born in Cheapside, and having passed reputably through all the classes of St. Paul's school, has been for some years a student in the Temple. He is of opinion, that intense application dulls the faculties, and thinks it necessary to temper the severity of the law by books that engage the mind, but do not fatigue it. He has therefore made a copious collection of plays, poems, and romances, to which he has recourse when he fancies himself tired with statutes and reports ; and he seldom inquires very nicely whether he is weary or idle.

Dick has received from his favourite authors very strong impressions of a country life ; and though his furthest excursions have been to Greenwich on one side, and Chelsea on the other, he has talked for several years, with great pomp of language and elevation of sentiments, about a state too high for contempt and too low for envy, about homely, quiet, and blameless simplicity, pastoral delights, and rural innocence.

His friends who had estates in the country, often invited him to pass the summer among them, but something or other had always hindered him ; and he considered, that to reside in the house of another man was to incur a kind of dependence inconsistent with that laxity of life which he had imaged as the chief good.

This summer he resolved to be happy, and procured a lodging to be taken for him at a solitary house, situated about thirty miles from London, on the banks of a small river, with corn-fields before it, and a hill on each side covered with wood. He concealed the place of his retirement, that none might violate his obscurity, and promised himself many a happy day when he should hide himself among the trees, and contemplate the tumults and vexations of the town.

He stepped into the post-chaise with his heart beating and his eyes sparkling, was conveyed through many varieties of delightful prospects, saw hills and meadows, corn-fields and pasture, succeed each other, and for four hours charged none of his poets with fiction or exaggeration. He was now within six miles of happiness, when, having never felt so much agitation before, he began to wish his journey at an end, and the last hour was passed in changing his posture, and quarrelling with his driver.

An hour may be tedious, but cannot be long. He at length alighted at his new dwelling, and was received as he expected; he looked round upon the hills and rivulets, but his joints were stiff and his muscles sore, and his first request was to see his bed-chamber.

He rested well, and ascribed the soundness of his sleep to the stillness of the country. He expected from that time nothing but nights of quiet and days of rapture, and, as soon as he had risen, wrote an account of his new state to one of his friends in the Temple.

" Dear FRANK,

" I never pitied thee before.   I am now as I could wish every man of wisdom and virtue to be, in the regions of calm content and placid meditation; with all the beauties of nature soliciting my notice, and all the diversities of pleasure courting my acceptance; the birds are chirping in the hedges, and the flowers blooming in the mead; the breeze is whistling in the wood, and the sun dancing on the water.   I can now say, with truth, that a man, capable of enjoying the purity of happiness, is never more busy than in his hours of leisure, nor ever less solitary than in a place of solitude.

" I am, dear FRANK, &c."

When he had sent away his letter, he walked into the wood, with some inconvenience, from the furze that pricked his legs, and the briars that scratched his face.   He at last sat down under a tree, and heard with great delight a shower, by which he was not wet, rattling among the branches: this, said he, is the true image of obscurity; we hear of troubles and commotions, but never feel them.

His amusement did not overpower the calls of nature, and he therefore went back to order his dinner.   He knew that the country produces whatever is eaten or drunk, and, imagining that he was now at the source of luxury, resolved to indulge himself with dainties which he supposed might be procured at a price next to nothing, if any price at all was expected; and intended to amaze the rusticks with his generosity, by paying more than they would ask. Of twenty dishes which he named, he was amazed to find that scarcely one was to be had; and heard, with astonishment and indignation, that all the fruits of the earth were sold at a higher price than in the streets of London.

His meal was short and sullen; and he retired again to his tree, to inquire how dearness could be consistent with abundance, or how fraud should be practised by simplicity. He was not satisfied with his own speculations, and, returning home early in the evening, went a while from window to window, and found that he wanted something to do.

He inquired for a newspaper, and was told that farmers never minded news, but that they could send for it from the alehouse. A messenger was dispatched, who ran away at full speed, but loitered an hour behind the hedges, and at last coming back with his feet purposely bemired, instead of expressing the gratitude which Mr. Shifter expected for the bounty of a shilling, said, that the night was wet, and the way dirty, and he hoped that his worship would not think it much to give him half-a-crown.

Dick now went to bed with some abatement of his expectations; but sleep, I know not how, revives our hopes, and rekindles our desires. He rose early in the morning, surveyed the landscape, and was pleased. He walked out, and passed from field to field, without observing any beaten path, and wondered that he had not seen the shepherd-esses dancing, nor heard the swains piping to their flocks.

At last he saw some reapers and harvest-women

at dinner. Here, said he, are the true Arcadians, and advanced courteously towards them, as afraid of confusing them by the dignity of his presence. They acknowledged his superiority by no other token than that of asking him for something to drink. He imagined that he had now purchased the privilege of discourse, and began to descend to familiar questions, endeavouring to accommodate his discourse to the grossness of rustick understandings. The clowns soon found that he did not know wheat from rye, and began to despise him; one of the boys, by pretending to shew him a bird's nest, decoyed him into a ditch; and one of the wenches sold him a bargain.

This walk had given him no great pleasure; but he hoped to find other rusticks less coarse of manners, and less mischievous of disposition. Next morning he was accosted by an attorney, who told him, that, unless he made farmer Dobson satisfaction for trampling his grass, he had orders to indict him. Shifter was offended, but not terrified; and, telling the attorney that he was himself a lawyer, talked so volubly of pettyfoggers and barraters, that he drove him away.

Finding his walks thus interrupted, he was inclined to ride, and being pleased with the appearance of a horse that was grazing in a neighbouring meadow, inquired the owner, who warranted him sound, and would not sell him, but that he was too fine for a plain man. Dick paid down the price, and, riding out to enjoy the evening, fell with his new horse into a ditch; they got out with difficulty, and, as he was going to mount again, a countryman looked at the horse, and perceived him to be blind. Dick went to the seller, and demanded back his money; but was told, that a man who rented his ground must do the best for himself, that his landlord had his rent though the year was barren, and that, whether horses had eyes or no, he should sell them to the highest bidder.

Shifter now began to be tired with rustick simplicity, and on the fifth day took possession again of his chambers, and bade farewell to the regions of calm content and placid meditation.

NUMB. 72.   SATURDAY, *September* 1, 1759.

MEN complain of nothing more frequently than of deficient memory; and, indeed, every one finds that many of the ideas which he desired to retain have slipped irretrievably away; that the acquisitions of the mind are sometimes equally fugitive with the gifts of fortune; and that a short intermission of attention more certainly lessens knowledge than impairs an estate.

To assist this weakness of our nature, many methods have been proposed, all of which may be justly suspected of being ineffectual; for no art of memory, however its effects have been boasted or admired, has been ever adopted into general use, nor have those who possessed it appeared to excel others in readiness of recollection or multiplicity of attainments.

There is another art of which all have felt the want, though Themistocles only confessed it. We suffer equal pain from the pertinacious adhesion of unwelcome images, as from the evanescence of those which are pleasing and useful ; and it may be doubted whether we should be more benefited by the art of memory or the art of forgetfulness.

Forgetfulness is necessary to remembrance. Ideas are retained by renovation of that impression which time is always wearing away, and which new images are striving to obliterate. If useless thoughts could be expelled from the mind, all the valuable parts of our knowledge would more frequently recur, and every recurrence would reinstate them in their former place.

It is impossible to consider, without some regret, how much might have been learned, or how much might have been invented by a rational and vigorous application of time, uselessly or painfully passed in the revocation of events which have left neither good nor evil behind them, in grief for misfortunes either repaired or irreparable, in resentment of injuries known only to ourselves, of which death has put the authors beyond our power.

Philosophy has accumulated precept upon precept, to warn us against the anticipation of future calamities. All useless misery is certainly folly, and he that feels evils before they come may be deservedly censured ; yet surely to dread the future is more reasonable than to lament the past. The business of life is to go forwards : he who sees evil in prospect meets it in his way ; but he who catches it by retrospection turns back to find it. That which is feared may sometimes be avoided, but that which is regretted to-day may be regretted again to-morrow.

Regret is indeed useful and virtuous, and not only allowable but necessary, when it tends to the amendment of life, or to admonition of error which we may be again in danger of committing. But a very small part of the moments spent in meditation on the past, produce any reasonable caution or salutary sorrow. Most of the mortifications that we have suffered, arose from the concurrence of local and temporary circumstances, which can never meet again; and most of our disappointments have succeeded those expectations, which life allows not to be formed a second time.

It would add much to human happiness, if an art could be taught of forgetting all of which the remembrance is at once useless and afflictive, if that pain which never can end in pleasure could be driven totally away, that the mind might perform its functions without incumbrance, and the past might no longer encroach upon the present.

Little can be done well to which the whole mind is not applied; the business of every day calls for the day to which it is assigned; and he will have no leisure to regret yesterday's vexations who resolves not to have a new subject of regret to-morrow.

But to forget or to remember at pleasure, are equally beyond the power of man. Yet as memory may be assisted by method, and the decays of knowledge repaired by stated times of recollection, so the power of forgetting is capable of improvement. Reason will, by a resolute contest, prevail over imagination, and the power may be obtained of transferring the attention as judgment shall direct.

The incursions of troublesome thoughts are often violent and importunate; and it is not easy to a mind accustomed to their inroads to expel them immediately by putting better images into motion; but this enemy of quiet is above all others weakened by every defeat; the reflexion which has been once overpowered and ejected, seldom returns with any formidable vehemence.

Employment is the great instrument of intellectual dominion. The mind cannot retire from its enemy into total vacancy, or turn aside from one object but by passing to another. The gloomy and the resentful are always found among those who have nothing to do, or who do nothing. We must be busy about good or evil, and he to whom the present offers nothing will often be looking backward on the past.

NUMB. 73.   SATURDAY, *September* 8, 1759.

THAT every man would be rich if a wish could obtain riches, is a position which I believe few will contest, at least in a nation like ours, in which commerce has kindled an universal emulation of wealth, and in which money receives all the honours which are the proper right of knowledge and of virtue.

Yet though we are all labouring for gold as for the chief good, and, by the natural effort of unwearied diligence, have found many expeditious methods of obtaining it, we have not been able to improve the art of using it, or to make it produce more happiness than it afforded in former times, when every declaimer expatiated on its mischiefs, and every philosopher taught his followers to despise it.

Many of the dangers imputed of old to exorbitant wealth are now at an end. The rich are neither way-laid by robbers, nor watched by informers; there is nothing to be dreaded from proscriptions, or seizures. The necessity of concealing treasure has long ceased; no man now needs counterfeit mediocrity, and condemn his plate and jewels to caverns and darkness, or feast his mind with the consciousness of clouded splendour, of finery which is useless till it is shewn, and which he dares not shew.

In our time the poor are strongly tempted to assume the appearance of wealth, but the wealthy very rarely desire to be thought poor; for we are all at full liberty to display riches by every mode of ostentation. We fill our houses with useless ornaments, only to shew that we can buy them; we cover our coaches with gold, and employ artists in the discovery of new fashions of expence; and yet it cannot be found that riches produce happiness.

Of riches, as of every thing else, the hope is more than the enjoyment; while we consider them as the means to be used, at some future time, for the attainment of felicity, we press on our pursuit ardently and vigorously, and that ardour secures us from weariness of ourselves; but no sooner do we sit down to enjoy our acquisitions, than we find them insufficient to fill up the vacuities of life.

One cause which is not always observed of the insufficiency of riches is, that they very seldom make their owner rich. To be rich, is to have more than is desired, and more than is wanted; to have something which may be spent without reluctance, and scattered without care, with which the sudden demands of desire may be gratified, the casual freaks of fancy indulged, or the unexpected opportunities of benevolence improved.

Avarice is always poor, but poor by her own fault. There is another poverty to which the rich are exposed with less guilt by the officiousness of others. Every man, eminent for exuberance of fortune, is surrounded from morning to evening, and from evening to midnight, by flatterers, whose art of adulation consists in exciting artificial wants, and in forming new schemes of profusion.

Tom Tranquil, when he came to age, found himself in possession of a fortune, of which the twentieth part might perhaps have made him rich. His temper is easy, and his affections soft ; he receives every man with kindness, and hears him with credulity. His friends took care to settle him by giving him a wife, whom, having no particular inclination, he rather accepted than chose, because he was told she was proper for him.

He was now to live with dignity proportionate to his fortune. What his fortune requires or admits Tom does not know, for he has little skill in computation, and none of his friends think it their interest to improve it. If he was suffered to live by his own choice, he would leave every thing as he finds it, and pass through the world distinguished only by inoffensive gentleness. But the ministers of luxury have marked him out as one at whose expence they may exercise their arts. A companion, who had just learned the names of the Italian masters, runs from sale to sale, and buys pictures, for which Mr. Tranquil pays, without inquiring where they shall be hung. Another fills his garden with statues, which Tranquil wishes away, but dares' not remove. One of his friends is learning architecture by building him a house, which he passed by, and inquired to whom it belonged ; another has been for three years digging canals and raising mounts, cutting trees down in one place, and planting them in another, on which Tranquil looks with a serene indifference,

without asking what will be the cost.   Another projector tells him that a water-work, like that of Versailles, will complete the beauties of his seat, and
lays his draughts before him ; Tranquil turns his
eyes upon them, and the artist begins his explanations ; Tranquil raises no objections, but orders
him to begin the work, that he may escape from
talk which he does not understand.

Thus a thousand hands are busy at his expence,
without adding to his ·pleasures.   He pays and receives visits, and has loitered in public or in solitude,
talking in summer of the town, and in winter of the
country, without knowing that his fortune is impaired,
till his steward told him this morning, that he could
pay the workmen no longer but by mortgaging a
manor.

NUMB. 74.   SATURDAY, *September* 15, 1759.

IN the mythological pedigree of learning, memory is made the mother of the muses, by which the masters of ancient wisdom, perhaps, meant to shew the necessity of storing the mind copiously with true notions, before the imagination should be suffered to form fictions or collect embellishments ; for the works of an ignorant poet can afford nothing higher than pleasing sound, and fiction is of no other use than to display the treasures of memory.

The necessity of memory to the acquisition of knowledge is inevitably felt and universally allowed, so that scarcely any other of the mental faculties are commonly considered as necessary to a student : he that admires the proficiency of another, always attributes it to the happiness of his memory ; and he that laments his own defects, concludes with a wish that his memory was better.

It is evident, that when the power of retention is weak, all the attempts at eminence of knowledge must be vain ; and as few are willing to be doomed to perpetual ignorance, I may, perhaps, afford consolation to some that have fallen too easily into despondence, by observing that such weakness is, in my opinion, very rare, and that few have reason to complain of nature as unkindly sparing of the gifts of memory.

In the common business of life, we find the memory of one like that of another, and honestly impute omissions not to involuntary forgetfulness, but culpable inattention ; but in literary inquiries, failure is imputed rather to want of memory than of diligence.

We consider ourselves as defective in memory, either because we remember less than we desire, or less than we suppose others to remember.

Memory is like all other human powers, with which no man can be satisfied who measures them by what he can conceive, or by what he can desire. He whose mind is most capacious, finds it much too narrow for his wishes; he that remembers most, remembers little compared with what he forgets. He therefore that, after the perusal of a book, finds few ideas remaining in his mind, is not to consider the disappointment as peculiar to himself, or to resign all hopes of improvement, because he does not retain what even the author has perhaps forgotten.

He who compares his memory with that of others, is often too hasty to lament the inequality. Nature has sometimes, indeed, afforded examples of enormous, wonderful, and gigantick memory. Scaliger reports of himself, that, in his youth, he could repeat above an hundred verses, having once read them; and Barthius declares, that he wrote his Comment upon Claudian without consulting the text. But not to have such degrees of memory is no more to be lamented, than not to have the strength of Hercules, or the swiftness of Achilles. He that, in the distribution of good, has an equal share with common men, may justly be contented. Where there is no striking disparity, it is difficult to know of two which remembers most, and still more difficult to discover which reads with greater attention, which has renewed the first impression by more frequent repetitions, or by what accidental combination of ideas either mind might have united any particular narrative or argument to its former stock.

But memory, however impartially distributed, so often deceives our trust, that almost every man attempts, by some artifice or other, to secure its fidelity.

It is the practice of many readers to note, in the margin of their books, the most important passages, the strongest arguments, or the brightest sentiments. Thus they load their minds with superfluous attention, repress the vehemence of curiosity by useless deliberation, and by frequent interruption break the current of narration or the chain of reason, and at last close the volume, and forget the passages and marks together.

Others I have found unalterably persuaded, that nothing is certainly remembered but what is transcribed; and they have therefore passed weeks and months in transferring large quotations to a common-place book. Yet, why any part of a book, which can be consulted at pleasure, should be copied, I was never able to discover. The hand has no closer correspondence with the memory than the eye. The act of writing itself distracts the thoughts, and what is read twice is commonly better remembered than what is transcribed. This method therefore consumes time without assisting memory.

The true art of memory is the art of attention. No man will read with much advantage, who is not able, at pleasure, to evacuate his mind, or who brings not to his author an intellect defecated and pure, neither turbid with care, nor agitated by pleasure. If the repositories of thought are already full, what can they receive?   If the mind is employed on the past or future, the book will be held before the eyes in vain.   What is read with delight is commonly retained, because pleasure always secures attention : but the books which are consulted by occasional necessity, and perused with impatience, seldom leave any traces on the mind.

NUMB. 75.   SATURDAY, *September 22, 1759.*

IN the time when Bassora was considered as the school of Asia, and flourished by the reputation of its professors and the confluence of its students, among the pupils that listened round the chair of Albumazar was Gelaleddin, a native of Tauris, in Persia, a young man amiable in his manners and beautiful in his form, of boundless curiosity, incessant diligence, and irresistible genius, of quick apprehension and tenacious memory, accurate without narrowness, and eager for novelty without inconstancy.

No sooner did Gelaleddin appear at Bassora, than his virtues and abilities raised him to distinction. He passed from class to class rather admired than envied by those whom the rapidity of his progress left behind ; he was consulted by his fellow-students as an oraculous guide, and admitted as a competent auditor to the conferences of the sages.

After a few years, having passed through all the exercises of probation, Gelaleddin was invited to a professor's seat, and intreated to increase the splendour of Bassora. Gelaleddin affected to deliberate on the proposal, with which, before he considered it, he resolved to comply ; and next morning retired to a garden planted for the recreation of the students, and entering a solitary walk, began to meditate upon his future life.

" If I am thus eminent," said he, " in the regions
of literature, I shall be yet more conspicuous in any
other place; if I should now devote myself to study
and retirement, I must pass my life in silence, unacquainted with the delights of wealth, the influence
of power, the pomp of greatness, and the charms of
elegance, with all that man envies and desires, with
all that keeps the world in motion, by the hope of
gaining or the fear of losing it.   I will therefore depart to Tauris, where the Persian monarch resides in
all the splendour of absolute dominion : my reputation will fly before me, my arrival will be congratulated by my kinsmen and my friends ; I shall see
the eyes of those who predict my greatness, sparkling
with exultation, and the faces of those that once
despised me clouded with envy, or counterfeiting
kindness by artificial smiles.   I will shew my wisdom
by my discourse, and my moderation by my silence ;
I will instruct the modest with easy gentleness, and
repress the ostentatious by seasonable superciliousness.
My apartments will be crowded by the inquisitive
and the vain, by those that honour and those that
rival me; my name will soon reach the court; I shall
stand before the throne of the emperor ; the judges
of the law will confess my wisdom, and the nobles
will contend to heap gifts upon me.   If I shall find
that my merit, like that of others, excites malignity,
or feel myself tottering on the seat of elevation, I
may at last retire to academical obscurity, and become, in my lowest state, a professor of Bassora."

Having thus settled his determination, he declared to his friends his design of visiting Tauris, and

saw with more pleasure than he ventured to express, the regret with which he was dismissed.   He could not bear to delay the honours to which he was destined, and therefore hastened away, and in a short time entered the capital of Persia.   He was immediately immersed in the crowd, and passed unobserved to his father's house.   He entered, and was received, though not unkindly, yet without any excess of fondness or exclamations of rapture.   His father had, in his absence, suffered many losses, and Gelaleddin was considered as an additional burden to a falling family.

When he recovered from his surprise, he began to display his acquisitions, and practised all the arts of narration and disquisition: but the poor have no leisure to be pleased with eloquence; they heard his arguments without reflection, and his pleasantries without a smile.   He then applied himself singly to his brothers and sisters, but found them all chained down by invariable attention to their own fortunes, and insensible of any other excellence than that which could bring some remedy for indigence.

It was now known in the neighbourhood that Gelaleddin was returned, and he sate for some days in expectation that the learned would visit him for consultation, or the great for entertainment.   But who will be pleased or instructed in the mansions of poverty?   He then frequented places of public resort, and endeavoured to attract notice by the copiousness of his talk.   The sprightly were silenced, and went away to censure in some other place his arrogance and his pedantry; and the dull listened quietly for a while, and then wondered why any man should take pains to obtain so much knowledge which would never do him good.

He next solicited the visiers for employment, not doubting but his service would be eagerly accepted. He was told by one that there was no vacancy in his office; by another, that his merit was above any patronage but that of the emperor; by a third, that he would not forget him; and by the chief visier, that he did not think literature of any great use in public business. He was sometimes admitted to their tables, where he exerted his wit and diffused his knowledge; but he observed, that where, by endeavour or accident, he had remarkably excelled, he was seldom invited a second time.

He now returned to Bassora, wearied and disgusted, but confident of resuming his former rank, and revelling again in satiety of praise. But he who had been neglected at Tauris, was not much regarded at Bassora; he was considered as a fugitive, who returned only because he could live in no other place; his companions found that they had formerly over-rated his abilities, and he lived long without notice or esteem.

NUMB. 76.   SATURDAY, *September* 29, 1759.

TO THE IDLER.

SIR,

I WAS much pleased with your ridicule of those shallow criticks, whose judgment, though often right as far as it goes, yet reaches only to inferiour beauties, and who, unable to comprehend the whole, judge only by parts, and from thence determine the merit of extensive works.   But there is another kind of critick still worse, who judges by narrow rules, and those too often false, and which, though they should be true, and founded on nature, will lead him but a very little way toward the just estimation of the sublime beauties in works of genius; for whatever part of an art can be executed or criticised by rules, that part is no longer the work of genius, which implies excellence out of the reach of rules. For my own part I profess myself an Idler, and love to give my judgment, such as it is, from my immediate perceptions, without much fatigue of thinking; and I am of opinion, that if a man has not those perceptions right, it will be vain for him to endeavour to supply their place by rules, which may enable him to talk more learnedly, but not to distinguish more acutely.   Another reason which has lessened my affection for the study of criticism is, that criticks, so far as I have observed, debar themselves from receiving any pleasure from the polite arts, at the same time that they profess to love and admire them : for these rules, being always uppermost, give them such a propensity to criticise, that instead of giving up the reins of their imagination into their author's hands, their frigid minds are employed in examining whether the performance be according to the rules of art.

To those who are resolved to be criticks in spite of nature, and at the same time have no great disposition to much reading and study, I would recommend to them to assume the character of connoisseur, which may be purchased at a much cheaper rate than that of a critick in poetry. The remembrance of a few names of painters, with their general characters, with a few rules of the academy, which they may pick up among the painters, will go a great way towards making a very notable connoisseur.

With a gentleman of this cast, I visited last week the Cartoons at Hampton-court ; he was just returned from Italy, a connoisseur of course, and of course his mouth full of nothing but the grace of Raffaelle, the purity of Domenichino, the learning of Poussin, the air of Guido, the greatness of taste of the Caraches, and the sublimity and grand contorno of Michael Angelo ; with all the rest of the cant of criticism, which he emitted with that volubility which generally those orators have who annex no ideas to their words.

As we were passing through the rooms, in our way to the gallery, I made him observe a whole length of Charles the First by Vandyke, as a perfect

representation of the character as well as the figure
of the man. He agreed it was very fine, but it
wanted spirit and contrast, and had not the flowing line, without which a figure could not possibly
be graceful. When we entered the gallery, I
thought I could perceive him recollecting his rules
by which he was to criticise Raffaelle. I shall
pass over his observation of the boats being too
little, and other criticisms of that kind, till we
arrived at " St. Paul preaching." " This," says he,
" is esteemed the most excellent of all the cartoons ;
what nobleness, what dignity, there is in that figure
of St. Paul ! and yet what an addition to that
nobleness could Raffaelle have given, had the art
of contrast been known in his time ! but, above
all, the flowing line which constitutes grace and
beauty ! You would not have then seen an upright figure standing equally on both legs, and
both hands stretched forward in the same direction,
and his drapery, to all appearance, without the
least art of disposition." The following picture is
the " Charge to Peter." " Here," says he, " are
twelve upright figures ; what a pity it is that Raffaelle was not acquainted with the pyramidal principle ! He would then have contrived the figures
in the middle to have been on higher ground, or
the figures at the extremities stooping or lying,
which would not only have formed the group into
the shape of a pyramid, but likewise contrasted the
standing figures. Indeed," added he, " I have
often lamented that so great a genius as Raffaelle
had not lived in this enlightened age, since the art

has been reduced to principles, and had had his education in one of the modern academies; what glorious works might we then have expected from his divine pencil !"

I shall trouble you no longer with my friend's observations, which, I suppose, you are now able to continue by yourself. It is curious to observe, that, at the same time that great admiration is pretended for a name of fixed reputation, objections are raised against those very qualities by which that great name was acquired.

Those criticks are continually lamenting that Raffaelle had not the colouring and harmony of Rubens, or the light and shadow of Rembrant, without considering how much the gay harmony of the former, and affectation of the latter, would take from the dignity of Raffaelle; and yet Rubens had great harmony, and Rembrant understood light and shadow: but what may be an excellence in a lower class of painting, becomes a blemish in a higher; as the quick, spritely turn, which is the life and beauty of epigrammatick compositions, would but ill suit with the majesty of heroick poetry.

To conclude; I would not be thought to infer, from any thing that has been said, that rules are absolutely unnecessary: but to censure scrupulosity, a servile attention to minute exactness, which is sometimes inconsistent with higher excellency, and is lost in the blaze of expanded genius.

I do not know whether you will think painting a general subject. By inserting this letter, perhaps you will incur the censure a man would deserve, whose business being to entertain a whole room, should turn his back to the company, and talk to a particular person.

I am, Sir, &c. *

NUMB. 77. SATURDAY, *October* 6, 1759.

EASY poetry is universally admired ; but I know not whether any rule has yet been fixed, by which it may be decided when poetry can be properly called easy. Horace has told us, that it is such as " every reader hopes to equal, but after long labour finds unattainable." This is a very loose description, in which only the effect is noted ; the qualities which produce this effect remain to be investigated.

Easy poetry is that in which natural thoughts are expressed without violence to the language. The discriminating character of ease consists principally in the diction ; for all true poetry requires that the sentiments be natural. Language suffers violence by harsh or by daring figures, by transposition, by unusual acceptations of words, and by any licence, which would be avoided by a writer of prose. Where any artifice appears in the construction of the verse, that verse is no longer easy. Any epithet

* By Sir Joshua Reynolds. C.

which can be ejected without diminution of the sense, any curious iteration of the same word, and all unusual, though not ungrammatical structure of speech, destroy the grace of easy poetry.

The first lines of Pope's Iliad afford examples of many licences which an easy writer must decline;

Achilles' *wrath*, to Greece the *direful spring*
Of woes unnumber'd, *heav'nly* Goddess sing,
The wrath which *hurl'd* to Pluto's *gloomy reign*
The souls of *mighty* chiefs untimely slain.

In the first couplet the language is distorted by inversions, clogged with superfluities, and clouded by a harsh metaphor; and in the second there are two words used in an uncommon sense, and two epithets inserted only to lengthen the line; all these practices may in a long work easily be pardoned, but they always produce some degree of obscurity and ruggedness.

Easy poetry has been so long excluded by ambition of ornament, and luxuriance of imagery, that its nature seems now to be forgotten. Affectation, however opposite to ease, is sometimes mistaken for it: and those who aspire to gentle elegance, collect female phrases and fashionable barbarisms, and imagine that style to be easy which custom has made familiar. Such was the idea of the poet who wrote the following verses to a *countess cutting paper:*

Pallas grew *vap'rish once and odd,*
　She would not *do the least right thing*
Either for Goddess or for God,
　Nor work, nor play, nor paint, nor sing.

Jove frown'd, and "Use (he cry'd) those eyes
So skilful, and those hands so taper;
Do something exquisite and wise"——
She bow'd, obey'd him, and cut paper.

This vexing him who gave her birth,
Thought by all Heaven a *burning shame*,
What does she next, but bids on earth
Her Burlington do just the same?

Pallas, you give yourself *strange airs*;
But sure you'll find it hard to spoil
The sense and taste of one that bears
The name of Savile and of Boyle.

Alas! one bad example shown,
How quickly all the sex pursue!
See, madam! see the arts o'erthrown
Between John Overton and *you*.

It is the prerogative of easy poetry to be understood as long as the language lasts; but modes of speech, which owe their prevalence only to modish folly, or to the eminence of those that use them, die away with their inventors, and their meaning, in a few years, is no longer known.

Easy poetry is commonly sought in petty compositions upon minute subjects; but ease, though it excludes pomp, will admit greatness. Many lines in Cato's soliloquy are at once easy and sublime:

'Tis the divinity that stirs within us;
'Tis Heaven itself that points out an hereafter,
And intimates eternity to man.
———— If there's a power above us,
And that there is all nature cries aloud
Thro' all her works, he must delight in virtue,
And that which he delights in must be happy.

Nor is ease more contrary to wit than to sublimity; the celebrated stanza of Cowley, on a lady elaborately dressed, loses nothing of its freedom by the spirit of the sentiment:

> Th' adorning thee with so much art
>   Is but a barb'rous skill,
> 'Tis like the pois'ning of a dart,
>   Too apt before to kill.

Cowley seems to have possessed the power of writing easily beyond any other of our poets; yet his pursuit of remote thought led him often into harshness of expression. Waller often attempted, but seldom attained it; for he is too frequently driven into transpositions. The poets, from the time of Dryden, have gradually advanced in embellishment, and consequently departed from simplicity and ease.

To require from any author many pieces of easy poetry, would be indeed to oppress him with too hard a task. It is less difficult to write a volume of lines swelled with epithets, brightened by figures, and stiffened by transpositions, than to produce a few couplets graced only by naked elegance and simple purity, which require so much care and skill, that I doubt whether any of our authors have yet been able, for twenty lines together, nicely to observe the true definition of easy poetry.

NUMB. 78.   SATURDAY, *October* 13, 1759.

I HAVE passed the summer in one of those places to which a mineral spring gives the idle and luxurious an annual reason for resorting, whenever they fancy themselves offended by the heat of London. What is the true motive of this periodical assembly, I have never yet been able to discover. The greater part of the visitants neither feel diseases nor fear them. What pleasure can be expected more than the variety of the journey, I know not, for the numbers are too great for privacy, and too small for diversion. As each is known to be a spy upon the rest, they all live in continual restraint; and having but a narrow range for censure, they gratify its cravings by preying on one another.

But every condition has some advantages. In this confinement, a smaller circle affords opportunities for more exact observation. The glass that magnifies its object contracts the sight to a point; and the mind must be fixed upon a single character to remark its minute peculiarities. The quality or habit which passes unobserved in the tumult of successive multitudes, becomes conspicuous when it is offered to the notice day after day; and perhaps I have, without any distinct notice, seen thousands like my late companions; for when the scene can be varied at pleasure, a slight disgust turns us aside before a deep impression can be made upon the mind.

There was a select set, supposed to be distinguished by superiority of intellects, who always passed the evening together. To be admitted to their conversation was the highest honour of the place; many youths aspired to distinction, by pretending to occasional invitations; and the ladies were often wishing to be men, that they might partake the pleasures of learned society.

I know not whether by merit or destiny, I was, soon after my arrival, admitted to this envied party, which I frequented till I had learned the art by which each endeavoured to support his character.

Tom Steady was a vehement assertor of uncontroverted truth; and by keeping himself out of the reach of contradiction had acquired all the confidence which the consciousness of irresistible abilities could have given. I was once mentioning a man of eminence, and, after having recounted his virtues, endeavoured to represent him fully, by mentioning his faults. " Sir," said Mr. Steady, " that he has faults I can easily believe, for who is without them? No man, Sir, is now alive, among the innumerable multitudes that swarm upon the earth, however wise, or however good, who has not, in some degree, his failings and his faults. If there be any man faultless, bring him forth into publick view, shew him openly, and let him be known; but I will venture to affirm, and, till the contrary be plainly shewn, shall always maintain, that no such man is to be found. Tell not me, Sir, of impeccability and perfection; such

talk is for those that are strangers in the world; I
have seen several nations, and conversed with all
ranks of people; I have known the great and the
mean, the learned and the ignorant, the old and the
young, the clerical and the lay : but I have never
found a man without a fault ; and I suppose shall die
in the opinion, that to be human is to be frail."

To all this nothing could be opposed. I listened
with a hanging head ; Mr. Steady looked round on
the hearers with triumph, and saw every eye congratulating his victory; he departed, and spent the next
morning in following those who retired from the company, and telling them, with injunctions of secrecy,
how poor Spritely began to take liberties with men
wiser than himself; but that he suppressed him by a
decisive argument, which put him totally to silence.

Dick Snug is a man of sly remark and pithy sen-
tentiousness : he never immerges himself in the stream
of conversation, but lies to catch his companions in
the eddy : he is often very successful in breaking
narratives and confounding eloquence. A gentleman, giving the history of one of his acquaintance,
made mention of a lady that had many lovers:
" Then," said Dick, " she was either handsome or
rich." This observation being well received, Dick
watched the progress of the tale ; and, hearing of a
man lost in a shipwreck, remarked, that " no man
was ever drowned upon dry land."

Will Startle is a man of exquisite sensibility,
whose delicacy of frame and quickness of discernment subject him to impressions from the slightest
causes; and who therefore passes his life between

rapture and horror, in quiverings of delight, or convulsions of disgust.   His emotions are too violent for many words ; his thoughts are always discovered by exclamations.   *Vile, odious, horrid, detestable,* and *sweet, charming, delightful, astonishing,* compose almost his whole vocabulary, which he utters with various contortions and gesticulations, not easily related or described.

Jack Solid is a man of much reading, who utters nothing but quotations ; but having been, I suppose, too confident of his memory, he has for some time neglected his books, and his stock grows every day more scanty.   Mr. Solid has found an opportunity every night to repeat, from Hudibras,

> Doubtless the pleasure is as great
> Of being cheated, as to cheat ;

and from Waller,

> Poets lose half the praise they would have got,
> Were it but known what they discreetly blot.

Dick Misty is a man of deep research, and forcible penetration.   Others are content with superficial appearances ; but Dick holds, that there is no effect without a cause, and values himself upon his power of explaining the difficult, and displaying the abstruse.   Upon a dispute among us, which of two young strangers was more beautiful, " You," says Mr. Misty, turning to me, " like Amaranthia better than Chloris.   I do not wonder at the preference, for the cause is evident ; there is in man a perception of harmony, and a sensibility of perfection, which touches the finer fibres of the mental texture; and before reason can descend from her throne, to pass her sentence upon the things compared, drives us towards the object proportioned to our faculties, by an impulse gentle, yet irresistible; for the harmonick system of the Universe, and the reciprocal magnetism of similar natures, are always operating towards conformity and union; nor can the powers of the soul cease from agitation, till they find something on which they can repose." To this nothing was opposed; and Amaranthia was acknowledged to excel Chloris.

Of the rest you may expect an account from,

Sir, yours,

ROBIN SPRITELY.

NUMB. 79.   SATURDAY, *October* 20, 1759.

TO THE IDLER.

SIR,

YOUR acceptance of a former letter on painting, gives me encouragement to offer a few more sketches on the same subject.

Amongst the painters, and the writers on painting, there is one maxim universally admitted and continually inculcated. *Imitate nature* is the invariable rule; but I know none who have explained in what manner this rule is to be understood; the consequence of which is, that every one takes it in the most obvious sense, that objects are represented naturally when they have such relief that they seem real. It may appear strange, perhaps, to hear this sense of the rule disputed; but it must be considered, that, if the excellency of a painter consisted only in this kind of imitation, painting must lose its rank, and be no longer considered as a liberal art, and sister to poetry, this imitation being merely mechanical, in which the slowest intellect is always sure to succeed best: for the painter of genius cannot stoop to drudgery, in which the understanding has no part; and what pretence has the art to claim kindred with poetry, but by its powers over the imagination? To this power the painter of genius directs his aim; in this sense he studies nature, and often arrives at his end, even by being unnatural in the confined sense of the word.

The grand style of painting requires this minute attention to be carefully avoided. and must be kept as separate from it as the style of poetry from that of history.   Poetical ornaments destroy that air of truth and plainness which ought to characterise history; but the very being of poetry consists in departing from this plain narration, and adopting every ornament that will warm the imagination.   To desire to see the excellencies of each style united, to mingle the Dutch with the Italian school, is to join contrarieties which cannot subsist together, and which destroy the efficacy of each other.   The Italian attends only to the invariable, the great and general ideas which are fixed and inherent in universal nature; the Dutch, on the contrary, to literal truth and a minute exactness in the detail, as I may say, of nature modified by accident.   The attention to these petty peculiarities is the very cause of this naturalness so much admired in the Dutch pictures, which, if we suppose it to be a beauty, is certainly of a lower order, which ought to give place to a beauty of a superior kind, since one cannot be obtained but by departing from the other.

If my opinion was asked concerning the works of Michael Angelo, whether they would receive any advantage from possessing this mechanical merit, I should not scruple to say they would not only receive no advantage, but would lose, in a great measure, the effect which they now have on every mind susceptible of great and noble ideas. His works may be said to be all genius and soul; and why should they be loaded with heavy matter, which can only counteract his purpose by retarding the progress of the imagination ?

If this opinion should be thought one of the wild extravagancies of enthusiasm, I shall only say, that those who censure it are not conversant in the works of the great masters. It is very difficult to determine the exact degree of enthusiasm that the arts of painting and poetry may admit. There may perhaps be too great an indulgence, as well as too great a restraint of imagination; and if the one produces incoherent monsters, the other produces what is full as bad, lifeless insipidity. An intimate knowledge of the passions, and good sense, but not common sense, must at last determine its limits. It has been thought, and I believe with reason, that Michael Angelo sometimes transgressed those limits; and I think I have seen figures of him of which it was very difficult to determine whether they were in the highest degree sublime or extremely ridiculous. Such faults may be said to be the ebullitions of genius; but at least he had this merit, that he never was insipid, and whatever passion his works may excite, they will always escape contempt.

What I have had under consideration is the sublimest style, particularly that of Michael Angelo, the Homer of painting. Other kinds may admit of this naturalness, which of the lowest kind is the chief merit; but in painting, as in poetry, the highest style has the least of common nature.

One may very safely recommend a little more enthusiasm to the modern painters; too much is certainly not the vice of the present age. The Italians

seem to have been continually declining in this respect from the time of Michael Angelo to that of
Carlo Maratti, and from thence to the very bathos
of insipidity to which they are now sunk; so that
there is no need of remarking, that where I mentioned the Italian painters in opposition to the
Dutch, I mean not the moderns, but the heads of
the old Roman and Bolognian schools; nor did I
mean to include in my idea of an Italian painter,
the Venetian school, which may be said to be the
Dutch part of the Italian genius.   I have only to
add a word of advice to the painters, that, however
excellent they may be in painting naturally, they
would not flatter themselves very much upon it, and
to the connoisseurs, that when they see a cat or
fiddle painted so finely, that, as the phrase is, " It
looks as if you could take it up," they would not for
that reason immediately compare the painter to
Raffaelle and Michael Angelo.*

* By Sir Joshua Reynolds.   C.

NUMB. 80.   SATURDAY, *October* 27, 1759.

THAT every day has its pains and sorrows is universally experienced, and almost universally confessed; but let us not attend only to mournful truths; if we look impartially about us, we shall find that every day has likewise its pleasures and its joys.

The time is now come when the town is again beginning to be full, and the rusticated beauty sees an end of her banishment. Those whom the tyranny of fashion had condemned to pass the summer among shades and brooks, are now preparing to return to plays, balls, and assemblies, with health restored by retirement, and spirits kindled by expectation.

Many a mind, which has languished some months without emotion or desire, now feels a sudden renovation of its faculties. It was long ago observed by Pythagoras, that ability and necessity dwell near each other. She that wandered in the garden without sense of its fragrance, and lay day after day stretched upon a couch behind a green curtain, unwilling to wake, and unable to sleep, now summons her thoughts to consider which of her last year's clothes shall be seen again, and to anticipate the raptures of a new suit; the day and the night are now filled with occupation; the laces, which were too fine to be worn among rusticks, are taken from the boxes and reviewed, and the eye is no sooner closed after its labours, than whole shops of silk busy the fancy.

But happiness is nothing if it is not known, and very little if it is not envied. Before the day of departure a week is always appropriated to the payment and reception of ceremonial visits, at which nothing can be mentioned but the delights of London. The lady who is hastening to the scene of action flutters her wings, displays her prospects of felicity, tells how she grudges every moment of delay, and, in the presence of those whom she knows condemned to stay at home, is sure to wonder by what arts life can be made supportable through a winter in the country, and to tell how often amidst the extasies of an opera, she shall pity those friends whom she has left behind. Her hope of giving pain is seldom disappointed; the affected indifference of one, the faint congratulations of another, the wishes of some openly confessed, and the silent dejection of the rest, all exalt her opinion of her own superiority.

But, however we may labour for our own deception, truth, though unwelcome, will sometimes intrude upon the mind. They who have already enjoyed the crowds and noise of the great city, know that their desire to return is little more than the restlessness of a vacant mind, that they are not so much led by hope as driven by disgust, and wish rather to leave the country than to see the town. There is commonly in every coach a passenger enwrapped in silent expectation, whose joy is more sincere and whose hopes are more exalted. The virgin whom the last summer released from her governess, and who is now going between her mother and her aunt to try the fortune of her wit and beauty, suspects no fallacy in the gay representation. She believes herself passing into another world, and images London as an elysian region, where every hour has its proper pleasure, where nothing is seen but the blaze of wealth, and nothing heard but merriment and flattery; where the morning always rises on a show, and the evening closes on a ball; where the eyes are used only to sparkle, and the feet only to dance.

Her aunt and her mother amuse themselves on the road, with telling her of dangers to be dreaded, and cautions to be observed. She hears them as they heard their predecessors, with incredulity or contempt. She sees that they have ventured and escaped; and one of the pleasures which she promises herself is to detect their falsehoods, and be freed from their admonitions.

We are inclined to believe those whom we do not know, because they have never deceived us. The fair adventurer may perhaps listen to the Idler, whom she cannot suspect of rivalry or malice; yet he scarcely expects to be credited when he tells her that her expectations will likewise end in disappointment.

The uniform necessities of human nature produce in a great measure uniformity of life, and for part of the day make one place like another; to dress and to undress, to eat and to sleep, are the same in London as in the country. The supernumerary hours have indeed a great variety both of pleasure and of pain. The stranger, gazed on by multitudes at her first appearance in the Park, is perhaps on the highest summit of female happiness; but how great is the anguish when the novelty of another face draws her worshippers away! The heart may leap for a time under a fine gown; but the sight of a gown yet finer puts an end to rapture. In the first row at an opera two hours may be happily passed in listening to the musick on the stage, and watching the glances of the company; but how will the night end in despondency when she that imagined herself the sovereign of the place, sees lords contending to lead Iris to her chair! There is little pleasure in conversation to her whose wit is regarded but in the second place; and who can dance with ease or spirit that sees Amaryllis led out before her? She that fancied nothing but a succession of pleasures, will find herself engaged without design in numberless competitions, and mortified without provocation with numberless afflictions.

But I do not mean to extinguish that ardour which I wish to moderate, or to discourage those whom I am endeavouring to restrain. To know the world is necessary, since we were born for the help of one another; and to know it early is convenient, if it be only that we may learn early to despise it. She that brings to London a mind well prepared for improvement, though she misses her hope of uninterrupted happiness, will gain in return an opportunity of adding knowledge to vivacity, and enlarging innocence to virtue.

NUMB. 81.   SATURDAY, *November* 3, 1759.

As the English army was passing towards Quebec along a soft savanna between a mountain and a lake, one of the petty chiefs of the inland regions stood upon a rock surrounded by his clan, and from behind the shelter of the bushes contemplated the art and regularity of European war. It was evening, the tents were pitched : he observed the security with which the troops rested in the night, and the order with which the march was renewed in the morning. He continued to pursue them with his eye till they could be seen no longer, and then stood for some time silent and pensive.

Then turning to his followers, " My children (said he) I have often heard from men hoary with long life, that there was a time when our ancestors were absolute lords of the woods, the meadows, and the lakes, wherever the eye can reach or the foot can pass. They fished and hunted, feasted and danced, and when they were weary lay down under the first thicket, without danger, and without fear. They changed their habitations as the seasons required, convenience prompted, or curiosity allured them ; and sometimes gathered the fruits of the mountain, and sometimes sported in canoes along the coast.

" Many years and ages are supposed to have been thus passed in plenty and security ; when, at last, a

new race of men entered our country from the great
ocean. They inclosed themselves in habitations of
stone, which our ancestors could neither enter by violence, nor destroy by fire. They issued from those
fastnesses, sometimes covered like the armadillo with
shells, from which the lance rebounded on the
striker, and sometimes carried by mighty beasts which
had never been seen in our vales or forests, of such
strength and swiftness that flight and opposition
were vain alike. Those invaders ranged over the continent, slaughtering in their rage those that resisted,
and those that submitted, in their mirth. Of those
that remained, some were buried in caverns, and condemned to dig metals for their masters; some were
employed in tilling the ground, of which foreign tyrants devour the produce; and, when the sword and
the mines have destroyed the natives, they supply
their place by human beings of another colour, brought
from some distant country to perish here under toil
and torture.

"Some there are who boast their humanity, and
content themselves to seize our chaces and fisheries,
who drive us from every track of ground where fertility and pleasantness invite them to settle, and
make no war upon us except when we intrude upon
our own lands.

"Others pretend to have purchased a right of residence and tyranny: but surely the insolence of such
bargains is more offensive than the avowed and open
dominion of force. What reward can induce the
possessor of a country to admit a stranger more pow-

erful than himself? . Fraud or terror must operate
in such contracts; either they promised protection
which they never have afforded, or instruction which
they never imparted. We hoped to be secured by
their favour from some other evil, or· to learn the
arts of Europe, by which we might be able to secure ourselves. Their power they never have exerted
in our defence, and their arts they have studiously
concealed from us. Their treaties are only to deceive, and their traffick only to defraud us. They
have a written law among them, of which they boast
as derived from Him who made the earth and sea,
and by which they profess to believe that man will be
made happy when life shall forsake him. Why is
not this law communicated to us? It is concealed
because it is violated. For how can they preach it
to an Indian nation, when I am told that one of its
first precepts forbids them to do to others what they
would not that others should do to them?

"But the time perhaps is now approaching when
the pride of usurpation shall be crushed, and the
cruelties of invasion shall be revenged. The sons of
rapacity have now drawn their swords upon each
other, and referred their claims to the decision of
war; let us look unconcerned upon the slaughter,
and remember that the death of every European delivers the country from a tyrant and a robber; for
what is the claim of either nation, but the claim of
the vulture to the leveret, of the tiger to the fawn?
Let them then continue to dispute their title to regions which they cannot people, to purchase by dan-

ger and blood the empty dignity of dominion over mountains which they will never climb, and rivers which they will never pass. Let us endeavour, in the mean time, to learn their discipline, and to forge their weapons; and, when they shall be weakened with mutual slaughter, let us rush down upon them, force their remains to take shelter in their ships, and reign once more in our native country."

NUMB. 82. SATURDAY, *November* 10, 1759.

TO THE IDLER.

SIR,

DISCOURSING in my last letter on the different practice of the Italian and Dutch painters, I observed, that " the Italian painter attends only to the invariable, the great and general ideas which are fixed and inherent in universal nature."

I was led into the subject of this letter by endeavouring to fix the original cause of this conduct of the Italian masters. If it can be proved that by this choice they selected the most beautiful part of the creation, it will shew how much their principles are founded on reason, and, at the same time, discover the origin of our ideas of beauty.

I suppose it will be easily granted, that no man can judge whether any animal be beautiful in its kind, or deformed, who has seen only one of that species : this is as conclusive in regard to the human figure ; so that if a man, born blind, was to recover his sight, and the most beautiful woman was brought before him, he could not determine whether she was handsome or not ; nor, if the most beautiful and most deformed were produced, could he any better determine to which he should give the preference, having seen only those two. To distinguish beauty, then, implies the having seen many individuals of that species. If it is asked, how is more skill acquired by the observation of greater numbers ? I answer that, in consequence of having seen many, the power is acquired, even without seeking after it, of distinguishing between accidental blemishes and excrescences which are continually varying the surface of Nature's works, and the invariable general form which Nature most frequently produces, and always seems to intend in her productions.

Thus amongst the blades of grass or leaves of the same tree, though no two can be found exactly alike, yet the general form is invariable : A naturalist, before he chose one as a sample, would examine many, since, if he took the first that occurred, it might have, by accident or otherwise, such a form as that it would scarcely be known to belong to that species ; he selects, as the painter does, the most beautiful, that is, the most general form of nature.

Every species of the animal as well as the vegetable creation may be said to have a fixed or determinate form towards which nature is continually inclining, like various lines terminating in the centre ; or it may be compared to pendulums vibrating in different directions over one central point, and as they all cross the centre, though only one passes through any other point, so it will be found that perfect beauty is oftener produced by nature than deformity ; I do not mean than deformity in general, but than any one kind of deformity. To instance in a particular part of a feature : the line that forms the ridge of the nose is beautiful when it is straight ; this then is the central form, which is oftener found than either concave, convex, or any other irregular form that shall be proposed.   As we are then more accustomed to beauty than deformity, we may conclude that to be the reason why we approve and admire it, as we approve and admire customs and fashions of dress for no other reason than that we are used to them, so that though habit and custom cannot be said to be the cause of beauty, it is certainly the cause of our liking it ; and I have no doubt but that, if we were more used to deformity than beauty, deformity would then lose the idea now annexed to it, and take that of beauty ; as, if the whole world should agree that *yes* and *no* should change their meanings, *yes* would then deny, and *no* would affirm.

Whoever undertakes to proceed further in this argument, and endeavours to fix a general criterion of beauty respecting different species, or to shew why one species is more beautiful than another, it will be required from him first to prove that one species is really more beautiful than another.   That we prefer one to the other, and with very good reason, will be readily granted ; but it does not follow from thence that we think it a more beautiful form ; for we have no criterion of form by which to determine our judgment.   He who says a swan is more beautiful than a dove, means little more than that he has more pleasure in seeing a swan than a dove, either from the stateliness of its motions, or its being

a more rare bird; and he who gives the preference
to the dove, does it from some association of ideas
of innocence that he always annexes to the dove;
but, if he pretends to defend the preference he gives
to one or the other by endeavouring to prove that
this more beautiful form proceeds from a particular
gradation of magnitude, undulation of a curve,
or direction of a line, or whatever other conceit
of his imagination he shall fix on as a criterion of
form, he will be continually contradicting himself,
and find at last that the great Mother of Nature
will not be subjected to such narrow rules.   Among
the various reasons why we prefer one part of her
works to another, the most general, I believe, is habit and custom; custom makes, in a certain sense,
white black, and black white; it is custom alone
determines our preference of the colour of the Europeans to the Æthiopians; and they, for the same
reason, prefer their own colour to ours.   I suppose
nobody will doubt, if one of their painters were to
paint the goddess of beauty, but that he would
represent her black, with thick lips, flat nose, and
woolly hair; and, it seems to me, he would act very
unnaturally if he did not; for by what criterion
will any one dispute the propriety of his idea?   We,
indeed, say, that the form and colour of the European is preferable to that of the Æthiopian; but I
know of no reason we have for it, but that we are
more accustomed to it.   It is absurd to say, that
beauty is possessed of attractive powers, which irresistibly seize the corresponding mind with love and
admiration, since that argument is equally conclusive in favour of the white and the black philosopher.

The black and white nations must, in respect of beauty, be considered as of different kinds, at least a different species of the same kind; from one of which to the other, as I observed, no inference can be drawn.

Novelty is said to be one of the causes of beauty : that novelty is a very sufficient reason why we should admire, is not denied; but because it is uncommon, is it therefore beautiful ? The beauty that is produced by colour, as when we prefer one bird to another, though of the same form, on account of its colour, has nothing to do with this argument, which reaches only to form. I have here considered the word *beauty* as being properly applied to form alone. There is a necessity of fixing this confined sense ; for there can be no argument, if the sense of the word is extended to every thing that is approved. A rose may as well be said to be beautiful, because it has a fine smell, as a bird because of its colour. When we apply the word *beauty* we do not mean always by it a more beautiful form, but something valuable on account of its rarity, usefulness, colour, or any other property. A horse is said to be a beautiful animal ; but, had a horse as few good qualities as a tortoise, I do not imagine that he would be then esteemed beautiful.

A fitness to the end proposed, is said to be another cause of beauty; but supposing we were proper judges of what form is the most proper in an animal to constitute strength or swiftness, we always determine concerning its beauty, before we exert our understanding to judge of its fitness.

From what has been said, it may be inferred, that the works of nature, if we compare one species with another, are all equally beautiful; and that preference is given from custom, or some association of ideas: and that, in creatures of the same species, beauty is the medium or centre of all various forms.

To conclude, then, by way of corollary: if it has been proved, that the painter, by attending to the invariable and general ideas of nature, produces beauty, he must, by regarding minute particularities and accidental discriminations, deviate from the universal rule, and pollute his canvass with deformity. *

* By Sir Joshua Reynolds.   C.

NUMB. 83.   SATURDAY, *November* 17, 1759.

TO THE IDLER.

SIR,

I SUPPOSE you have forgotten that many weeks ago I promised to send you an account of my companions at the Wells.   You would not deny me a place among the most faithful votaries of idleness, if you knew how often I have recollected my engagement, and contented myself to delay the performance for some reason which I durst not examine because I knew it to be false; how often I have sat down to write, and rejoiced at interruption; and how often I have praised the dignity of resolution, determined at night to write in the morning, and deferred it in the morning to the quiet hours of night.

I have at last begun what I have long wished at an end, and find it more easy than I expected to continue my narration.

Our assembly could boast of no such constellation of intellects as Clarendon's band of associates.   We had among us no Selden, Falkland, or Waller; but we had men not less important in their own eyes, though less distinguished by the public; and many a time have we lamented the partiality of mankind, and agreed that men of the deepest inquiry sometimes let their discoveries die away in silence, that

the most comprehensive observers have seldom opportunities of imparting their remarks, and that modest
merit passes in the crowd unknown and unheeded.

One of the greatest men of the society was Sim
Scruple, who lives in a continual equipoise of
doubt, and is a constant enemy to confidence and
dogmatism. Sim's favourite topick of conversation
is the narrowness of the human mind, the fallaci-
ousness of our senses, the prevalence of early prejudice, and the uncertainty of appearances. Sim
has many doubts about the nature of death, and is
sometimes inclined to believe that sensation may
survive motion, and that a dead man may feel
though he cannot stir. He has sometimes hinted
that man might perhaps have been naturally a
quadruped; and thinks it would be very proper,
that at the Foundling Hospital some children should
be inclosed in an apartment in which the nurses
should be obliged to walk half upon four and half
upon two, that the younglings, being bred without
the prejudice of example, might have no other
guide than nature, and might at last come forth
into the world as genius should direct, erect or
prone, on two legs or on four.

The next in dignity of mien and fluency of talk
was Dick Wormwood, whose sole delight is to
find every thing wrong. Dick never enters a room
but he shews that the door and the chimney are ill-
placed. He never walks into the fields but he finds
ground ploughed which is fitter for pasture. He is
always an enemy to the present fashion. He holds
that all the beauty and virtue of women will soon

be destroyed by the use of tea. He triumphs when he talks on the present system of education, and tells us with great vehemence, that we are learning words when we should learn things. He is of opinion that we suck in errors at the nurse's breast, and thinks it extremely ridiculous that children should be taught to use the right hand rather than the left.

Bob Sturdy considers it as a point of honour to say again what he has once said, and wonders how any man that has been known to alter his opinion, can look his neighbours in the face. Bob is the most formidable disputant of the whole company; for without troubling himself to search for reasons, he tires his antagonist with repeated affirmations. When Bob has been attacked for an hour with all the powers of eloquence and reason, and his position appears to all but himself utterly untenable, he always closes the debate with his first declaration, introduced by a stout preface of contemptuous civility. "All this is very judicious; you may talk, Sir, as you please; but I will still say what I said at first." Bob deals much in universals, which he has now obliged us to let pass without exceptions. He lives on an annuity, and holds that *there are as many thieves as traders;* he is of loyalty unshaken, and always maintains, that *he who sees a Jacobite sees a rascal.*

Phil Gentle is an enemy to the rudeness of contradiction and the turbulence of debate. Phil has no notions of his own, and therefore willingly catches from the last speaker such as he shall drop. This inflexibility of ignorance is easily accommodated to any tenet; his only difficulty is, when the disputants grow zealous, how to be of two contrary opinions at once. If no appeal is made to his judgment, he has the art of distributing his attention and his smiles in such a manner, that each thinks him of his own party; but if he is obliged to speak, he then observes that the question is difficult; that he never received so much pleasure from a debate before; that neither of the controvertists could have found his match in any other company; that Mr. Wormwood's assertion is very well supported, and yet there is great force in what Mr. Scruple advanced against it. By this indefinite declaration both are commonly satisfied; for he that has prevailed is in good humour; and he that has felt his own weakness is very glad to have escaped so well.

I am, Sir, yours, &c.

ROBIN SPRITELY.

NUMB. 84. SATURDAY, *November* 24, 1759.

BIOGRAPHY is, of the various kinds of narrative writing, that which is most eagerly read, and most easily applied to the purposes of life.

In romances, when the wild field of possibility lies open to invention, the incidents may easily be made more numerous, the vicissitudes more sudden, and the events more wonderful; but from the time of life when fancy begins to be over-ruled by reason and corrected by experience, the most artful tale raises little curiosity when it is known to be false; though it may, perhaps, be sometimes read as a model of a neat or elegant style, not for the sake of knowing what it contains, but how it is written; or those that are weary of themselves, may have recourse to it as a pleasing dream, of which, when they awake, they voluntarily dismiss the images from their minds.

The examples and events of history press, indeed, upon the mind with the weight of truth; but when they are reposited in the memory, they are oftener employed for shew than use, and rather diversify conversation than regulate life. Few are engaged in such scenes as give them opportunities of growing wiser by the downfal of statesmen or the defeat of generals. The stratagems of war, and the intrigues of courts, are read by far the greater part of mankind with the same indifference as the adventures of fabled heroes, or the revolutions of a fairy

region. Between falsehood and useless truth there
is little difference. As gold which he cannot spend
will make no man rich, so knowledge which he cannot apply will make no man wise.

The mischievous consequences of vice and folly,
of irregular desires and predominant passions, are
best discovered by those relations which are levelled
with the general surface of life, which tell not how
any man became great, but how he was made happy ;
not how he lost the favour of his prince, but how he
became discontented with himself.

Those relations are therefore commonly of most
value in which the writer tells his own story. He
that recounts the life of another, commonly dwells
most upon conspicuous events, lessens the familiarity
of his tale to increase its dignity, shews his favourite at a distance, decorated and magnified like the
ancient actors in their tragick dress, and endeavours
to hide the man that he may produce a hero.

But if it be true, which was said by a French
prince, " That no man was a hero to the servants of
his chamber," it is equally true, that every man is
yet less a hero to himself. He that is most elevated above the crowd by the importance of his employments, or the reputation of his genius, feels himself affected by fame or business but as they influence
his domestick life. The high and low, as they have
the same faculties and the same senses, have no less
similitude in their pains and pleasures. The sensations are the same in all, though produced by very
different occasions. The prince feels the same pain
when an invader seizes a province, as the farmer

when a thief drives away his cow.. Men thus equal in themselves will appear equal in honest and impartial biography; and those whom fortune or nature place at the greatest distance may afford instruction to each other.

The writer of his own life has at least the first qualification of an historian, the knowledge of the truth; and though it may be plausibly objected that his temptations to disguise it are equal to his opportunities of knowing it, yet I cannot but think that impartiality may be expected with equal confidence from him that relates the passages of his own life, as from him that delivers the transactions of another.

Certainty of knowledge not only excludes mistake, but fortifies veracity. What we collect by conjecture, and by conjecture only can one man judge of another's motives or sentiments, is easily modified by fancy or by desire; as objects imperfectly discerned take forms from the hope or fear of the beholder. But that which is fully known cannot be falsified but with reluctance of understanding, and alarm of conscience: of understanding, the lover of truth; of conscience, the sentinel of virtue.

He that writes the life of another is either his friend or his enemy, and wishes either to exalt his praise or aggravate his infamy; many temptations to falsehood will occur in the disguise of passions, too specious to fear much resistance. Love of virtue will animate panegyrick, and hatred of wickedness imbitter censure. The zeal of gratitude, the ardour of patriotism, fondness for an opinion, or fidelity to a party, may easily overpower the vigilance of a mind habitually well disposed, and prevail over unassisted and unfriended veracity.

But he that speaks of himself has no motive to falsehood or partiality except self-love, by which all have so often been betrayed, that all are on the watch against its artifices.   He that writes an apology for a single action, to confute an accusation, to recommend himself to favour, is indeed always to be suspected of favouring his own cause; but he that sits down calmly and voluntarily to review his life for the admonition of posterity, or to amuse himself, and leaves this account unpublished, may be commonly presumed to tell truth, since faslehood cannot appease his own mind, and fame will not be heard beneath the tomb.

NUMB. 85. SATURDAY, *December* 1, 1759.

ONE of the peculiarities which distinguish the present age is the multiplication of books. Every day brings new advertisements of literary undertakings, and we are flattered with repeated promises of growing wise on easier terms than our progenitors.

How much either happiness or knowledge is advanced by this multitude of authors, it is not very easy to decide.

He that teaches us any thing which we knew not before, is undoubtedly to be reverenced as a master.

He that conveys knowledge by more pleasing ways, may very properly be loved as a benefactor; and he that supplies life with innocent amusement, will be certainly caressed as a pleasing companion.

But few of those who fill the world with books, have any pretensions to the hope either of pleasing or instructing. They have often no other task than to lay two books before them, out of which they compile a third, without any new materials of their own, and with very little application of judgment to those which former authors have supplied.

That all compilations are useless I do not assert. Particles of science are often very widely scattered. Writers of extensive comprehension have incidental remarks upon topicks very remote from the principal subject, which are often more valuable than formal treatises, and which yet are not known because they are not promised in the title. He that collects those under proper heads is very laudably employed, for though he exerts no great abilities in the work, he facilitates the progress of others, and by making that easy of attainment which is already written, may give some mind, more vigorous or more adventurous than his own, leisure for new thoughts and original designs.

But the collections poured lately from the press have been seldom made at any great expence of time or inquiry, and therefore only serve to distract choice without supplying any real want.

It is observed that " a corrupt society has many laws ;" I know not whether it is not equally true, that " an ignorant age has many books." When the treasures of ancient knowledge lie unexamined, and original authors are neglected and forgotten, compilers and plagiaries are encouraged, who give us again what we had before, and grow great by setting before us what our own sloth had hidden from our view.

Yet are not even these writers to be indiscriminately censured and rejected. Truth like beauty varies its fashions, and is best recommended by different dresses to different minds ; and he that recalls the attention of mankind to any part of learning which time has left behind it, may be truly said to advance the literature of his own age. As the manners of nations vary, new topicks of persuasion become necessary, and new combinations of imagery are produced ; and he that can accommodate himself to the reigning taste, may always have readers who perhaps would not have looked upon better performances.

To exact of every man who writes that he should say something new, would be to reduce authors to a small number ; to oblige the most fertile genius to say only what is new would be to contract his volumes to a few pages.   Yet, surely, there ought to be some bounds to repetition ; libraries ought no more to be heaped for ever with the same thoughts differently expressed, than with the same books differently decorated.

The good or evil which these secondary writers produce is seldom of any long duration.   As they owe their existence to change of fashion, they commonly disappear when a new fashion becomes prevalent.   The authors that in any nation last from age to age are very few, because there are very few that have any other claim to notice than that they catch hold on present curiosity, and gratify some accidental desire, or produce some temporary conveniency.

But however the writers of the day may despair of future fame, they ought at least to forbear any present mischief.   Though they cannot arrive at eminent heights of excellence, they might keep themselves harmless.   They might take care to inform themselves before they attempt to inform others, and exert the little influence which they have for honest purposes.

But such is the present state of our literature, that the ancient sage, who thought *a great book a great evil*, would now think the multitude of books a multitude of evils.   He would consider a bulky writer who engrossed a year, and a swarm of pamphleteers who stole each an hour, as equal wasters of human life, and would make no other difference between them, than between a beast of prey and a flight of locusts.

***

NUMB. 86.   SATURDAY, *December* 8, 1759.

TO THE IDLER.

SIR,

I AM a young lady newly married to a young gentleman. Our fortune is large, our minds are vacant, our dispositions gay, our acquaintances numerous, and our relations splendid. We considered that marriage, like life, has its youth; that the first year is the year of gaiety and revel, and resolved to see the shows and feel the joys of London before the increase of our family should confine us to domestick cares and domestick pleasures.

Little time was spent in preparation; the coach was harnessed, and a few days brought us to London, and we alighted at a lodging provided for us by Miss Biddy Trifle, a maiden niece of my husband's father, where we found apartments on a second floor, which my cousin told us would serve us till we could please ourselves with a more commodious and elegant habitation, and which she had taken at a very high price, because it was not worth the while to make a hard bargain for so short a time.

Here I intended to lie concealed till my new clothes were made, and my new lodging hired; but Miss Trifle had so industriously given notice of our arrival to all her acquaintance, that I had the mortification next day of seeing the door thronged with painted coaches and chairs with coronets, and was obliged to receive all my husband's relations on a second floor.

Inconveniences are often balanced by some advantage: the elevation of my apartments furnished a subject for conversation, which, without some such help, we should have been in danger of wanting. Lady Stately told us how many years had passed since she climbed so many steps. Miss Airy ran to the window, and thought it charming to see the walkers so little in the street; and Miss Gentle went to try the same experiment, and screamed to find herself so far above the ground.

They all knew that we intended to remove, and therefore all gave me advice about a proper choice. One street was recommended for the purity of its air, another for its freedom from noise, another for its nearness to the Park, another because there was but a step from it to all places of diversion, and another, because its inhabitants enjoyed at once the town and country.

I had civility enough to hear every recommendation with a look of curiosity while it was made, and of acquiescence when it was concluded, but in my heart felt no other desire than to be free from the disgrace of a second floor, and cared little where I should fix, if the apartments were spacious and splendid.

Next day a chariot was hired, and Miss Trifle was dispatched to find a lodging. She returned in the afternoon with an account of a charming place, to which my husband went in the morning to make the contract. Being young and inexperienced, he took with him his friend Ned Quick, a gentleman of great skill in rooms and furniture, who sees, at a single glance, whatever there is to be commended or censured. Mr. Quick, at the first view of the house, declared that it could not be inhabited, for the sun in the afternoon shone with full glare on the windows of the dining-room.

Miss Trifle went out again and soon discovered another lodging, which Mr. Quick went to survey, and found, that, whenever the wind should blow from the east, all the smoke of the city would be driven upon it.

A magnificent set of rooms was then found in one of the streets near Westminster-Bridge, which Miss Trifle preferred to any which she had yet seen; but Mr. Quick, having mused upon it for a time, concluded that it would be too much exposed in the morning to the fogs that rise from the river.

Thus Mr. Quick proceeded to give us every day new testimonies of his taste and circumspection; sometimes the street was too narrow for a double range of coaches; sometimes it was an obscure place, not inhabited by persons of quality. Some places were dirty, and some crowded; in some houses the furniture was ill-suited, and in others the stairs were too narrow. He had such fertility of objections that Miss Trifle was at last tired, and desisted from all attempts for our accommodation.

In the mean time I have still continued to see my company on a second floor, and am asked twenty times a day when I am to leave those odious lodgings, in which I live tumultuously without pleasure, and expensively without honour. My husband thinks so highly of Mr. Quick, that he cannot be persuaded to remove without his approbation ; and Mr. Quick thinks his reputation raised by the multiplication of difficulties.

In this distress to whom can I have recourse ? I find my temper vitiated by daily disappointment, by the sight of pleasures which I cannot partake, and the possession of riches which I cannot enjoy. Dear Mr. Idler, inform my husband that he is trifling away, in superfluous vexation, the few months which custom has appropriated to delight ; that matrimonial quarrels are not easily reconciled between those that have no children ; that wherever we settle he must always find some inconvenience ; but nothing is so much to be avoided as a perpetual state of inquiry and suspence.

I am Sir,
Your humble servant,
PEGGY HEARTLESS.

NUMB. 87.   SATURDAY, *December* 15, 1759.

OF what we know not, we can only judge by what
we know.   Every novelty appears more wonderful
as it is more remote from any thing with which experience or testimony have hitherto acquainted us;
and if it passes further beyond the notions that we
have been accustomed to form, it becomes at last incredible.

We seldom consider that human knowledge is very
narrow, that national manners are formed by chance,
that uncommon conjunctures of causes produce rare
effects, or that what is impossible at one time or place
may yet happen in another.   It is always easier to deny
than to inquire.   To refuse credit confers for a moment
an appearance of superiority, which every little mind is
tempted to assume when it may be gained so cheaply
as by withdrawing attention from evidence, and declining the fatigue of comparing probabilities.   The
most pertinacious and vehement demonstrator may
be wearied in time by continual negation; and incredulity, which an old poet, in his address to Raleigh, calls *the wit of fools*, obtunds the argument
which it cannot answer, as woolsacks deaden arrows
though they cannot repel them.

Many relations of travellers have been slighted as
fabulous, till more frequent voyages have confirmed

their veracity; and it may reasonably be imagined, that many ancient historians are unjustly suspected of falsehood, because our own times afford nothing that resembles what they tell.

Had only the writers of antiquity informed us that there was once a nation in which the wife lay down upon the burning pile only to mix her ashes with those of her husband, we should have thought it a tale to be told with that of Endymion's commerce with the moon.   Had only a single traveller related that many nations of the earth were black, we should have thought the accounts of the Negroes and of the Phœnix equally credible.   But of black men the numbers are too great who are now repining under English cruelty, and the custom of voluntary cremation is not yet lost among the ladies of India.

Few narratives will either to men or women appear more incredible than the histories of the Amazons; of female nations of whose constitution it was the essential and fundamental law, to exclude men from all participation either of publick affairs or domestick business; where female armies marched under female captains, female farmers gathered the harvest, female partners danced together, and female wits diverted one another.

Yet several ages of antiquity have transmitted accounts of the Amazons of Caucasus; and of the Amazons of America, who have given their name to the greatest river in the world, Condamine lately found such memorials, as can be expected among erratick and unlettered nations, where events are recorded only by tradition, and new swarms settling in the country from time to time, confuse and efface all traces of former times.

To die with husbands, or to live without them, are the two extremes which the prudence and moderation of European ladies have, in all ages, equally declined; they have never been allured to death by the kindness or civility of the politest nations, nor has the roughness and brutality of more savage countries ever provoked them to doom their male associates to irrevocable banishment. The Bohemian matrons are said to have made one short struggle for superiority, but instead of banishing the men they contented themselves with condemning them to servile offices; and their constitution thus left imperfect, was quickly overthrown.

There is, I think, no class of English women from whom we are in any danger of Amazonian usurpation. The old maids seem nearest to independence, and most likely to be animated by revenge against masculine authority; they often speak of men with acrimonious vehemence, but it is seldom found that they have any settled hatred against them, and it is yet more rarely observed that they have any kindness for each other. They will not easily combine in any plot; and if they should ever agree to retire and fortify themselves in castles or in mountains, the sentinel will betray the passes in spite, and the garrison will capitulate upon easy terms, if the besiegers have handsome swordknots, and are well supplied with fringe and lace.

The gamesters, if they were united, would make a formidable body; and since they consider men only as beings that are to lose their money, they might live

live together without any wish for the officiousness
of gallantry or the delights of diversified conversation.
But as nothing would hold them together but the
hope of plundering one another, their government
would fail from the defect of its principles ; the men
would need only to neglect them, and they would
perish in a few weeks by a civil war.

I do not mean to censure the ladies of England
as defective in knowledge or in spirit, when I suppose them unlikely to revive the military honours
of their sex.   The character of the ancient Amazons
was rather terrible than lovely ;   the hand could not
be very delicate that was only employed in drawing
the bow and brandishing the battle-axe ; their power
was maintained by cruelty, their courage was deformed by ferocity, and their example only shews that
men and women live best together.

NUMB. 88.   SATURDAY, *December* 22, 1759.

WHEN the philosophers of the last age were first congregated into the Royal Society, great expectations were raised of the sudden progress of useful arts ; the time was supposed to be near, when engines should turn by a perpetual motion, and health be secured by the universal medicine ; when learning should be facilitated by a real character, and commerce extended by ships which could reach their ports in defiance of the tempest.

But improvement is naturally slow.   The Society met and parted without any visible diminution of the miseries of life.   The gout and stone were still painful, the ground that was not ploughed brought no harvest, and neither oranges nor grapes would grow upon the hawthorn.   At last, those who were disappointed began to be angry ; those likewise who hated innovation were glad to gain an opportunity of ridiculing men who had depreciated, perhaps with too much arrogance, the knowledge of antiquity. And it appears from some of their earliest apologies, that the philosophers felt with great sensibility the unwelcome importunities of those who were daily asking, " What have ye done ?"

The truth is, that little had been done compared with what fame had been suffered to promise ; and the question could only be answered by general apologies and by new hopes, which, when they were frustrated, gave a new occasion to the same vexatious inquiry.

This fatal question has disturbed the quiet of many other minds. He that in the latter part of his life too strictly enquires what he has done, can very seldom receive from his own heart such an account as will give him satisfaction.

We do not indeed so often disappoint others as ourselves. We not only think more highly than others of our own abilities, but allow ourselves to form hopes which we never communicate, and please our thoughts with employments which none ever will allot us, and with elevations to which we are never expected to rise ; and when our days and years have passed away in common business or common amusements, and we find at last that we have suffered our purposes to sleep till the time of action is past, we are reproached only by our own reflections ; neither our friends nor our enemies wonder that we live and die like the rest of mankind ; that we live without notice, and die without memorial ; they know not what task we had proposed, and therefore cannot discern whether it is finished.

He that compares what he has done with what he has left undone, will feel the effect which must always follow the comparison of imagination with reality : he will look with contempt on his own unimportance, and wonder to what purpose he came into the world ; he will repine that he shall leave behind him no evidence of his having been, that he has added nothing to the system of life, but has glided from youth to age among the crowd, without any effort for distinction.

Man is seldom willing to let fall the opinion of his own dignity, or to believe that he does little only because every individual is a very little being. He is better content to want diligence than power, and sooner confesses the depravity of his will than the imbecility of his nature.

From this mistaken notion of human greatness it proceeds, that many who pretend to have made great advances in wisdom so loudly declare that they despise themselves. If I had ever found any of the self-contemners much irritated or pained by the consciousness of their meanness, I should have given them consolation by observing, that a little more than nothing is as much as can be expected from a being, who with respect to the multitudes about him is himself little more than nothing. Every man is obliged by the Supreme Master of the universe to improve all the opportunities of good which are afforded him, and to keep in continual activity such abilities as are bestowed upon him. But he has no reason to repine, though his abilities are small and his opportunities few. He that has improved the virtue, or advanced the happiness of one fellow-creature, he that has ascertained a single moral proposition, or added one useful experiment to natural knowledge, may be contented with his own performance, and, with respect to mortals like himself, may demand, like Augustus, to be dismissed at his departure with applause.

NUMB. 89.   SATURDAY, *December* 29, 1759.

'Ανίχου καὶ ἀπίχου.   EPICT.

How evil came into the world; for what reason it is that life is overspread with such boundless varieties of misery; why the only thinking being of this globe is doomed to think merely to be wretched, and to pass his time from youth to age in fearing or in suffering calamities, is a question which philosophers have long asked, and which philosophy could never answer.

Religion informs us that misery and sin were produced together. The depravation of human will was followed by a disorder of the harmony of nature; and by that providence which often places antidotes in the neighbourhood of poisons, vice was checked by misery, lest it should swell to universal and unlimited dominion.

A state of innocence and happiness is so remote from all that we have ever seen, that though we can easily conceive it possible, and may therefore hope to attain it, yet our speculations upon it must be general and confused. We can discover that where there is universal innocence, there will probably be universal happiness; for why should afflictions be permitted to infest beings who are not in danger of corruption from blessings, and where there is no use of terrour nor cause of punishment? But in a world like ours, where our senses assault us, and our hearts betray us, we should pass on from crime to crime, heedless and remorseless, if misery did not stand in our way, and our own pains admonish us of our folly.

Almost all the moral good which is left among us, is the apparent effect of physical evil.

Goodness is divided by divines into soberness, righteousness, and godliness. Let it be examined how each of these duties would be practised if there were no physical evil to enforce it.

Sobriety, or temperance, is nothing but the forbearance of pleasure; and if pleasure was not followed by pain, who would forbear it? We see every hour those in whom the desire of present indulgence overpowers all sense of past and all foresight of future misery. In a remission of the gout, the drunkard returns to his wine, and the glutton to his feast; and if neither disease nor poverty were felt or dreaded, every one would sink down in idle sensuality, without any care of others, or of himself. To eat and drink, and lie down to sleep, would be the whole business of mankind.

Righteousness, or the system of social duty, may be subdivided into justice and charity. Of justice one of the Heathen sages has shewn, with great acuteness, that it was impressed upon mankind only by the inconveniences which injustice had produced. " In the first ages," says he, " men acted without any rule but the impulse of desire; they practised injustice upon others, and suffered it from others in their turn; but in time it was discovered, that the pain of suffering wrong was greater than the pleasure of doing it; and mankind, by a general compact, submitted to the restraint of laws, and resigned the pleasure to escape the pain."

Of charity it is superfluous to observe, that it could have no place if there were no want; for of a virtue which could not be practised, the omission could not be culpable. Evil is not only the occasional but the efficient cause of charity; we are incited to the relief of misery by the consciousness that we have the same nature with the sufferer, that we are in danger of the same distresses, and may sometimes implore the same assistance.

Godliness, or piety, is elevation of the mind towards the Supreme Being, and extension of the thoughts to another life. The other life is future, and the Supreme Being is invisible. None would have recourse to an invisible power, but that all other subjects have eluded their hopes. None would fix their attention upon the future, but that they are discontented with the present. If the senses were feasted with perpetual pleasure, they would always keep the mind in subjection. Reason has no authority over us, but by its power to warn us against evil.

In childhood, while our minds are yet unoccupied, religion is impressed upon them, and the first years of almost all who have been well educated are passed in a regular discharge of the duties of piety. But as we advance forward into the crowds of life, innumerable delights solicit our inclinations, and innumerable cares distract our attention; the time of youth is passed in noisy frolicks; manhood is led on from

hope to hope, and from project to project; the disso-
luteness of pleasure, the inebriation of success, the
ardour of expectation, and the vehemence of competition, chain down the mind alike to the present
scene, nor is it remembered how soon this mist of
trifles must be scattered, and the bubbles that float
upon the rivulet of life be lost for ever in the gulph
of eternity. To this consideration scarcely any man
is awakened but by some pressing and resistless evil.
The death of those from whom he derived his pleasures, or to whom he destined his possessions, some
disease which shews him the vanity of all external
acquisitions, or the gloom of age, which intercepts
his prospects of long enjoyment, forces him to fix his
hopes upon another state; and when he has con-
tended with the tempests of life till his strength fails
him, he flies at last to the shelter of religion.

That misery does not make all virtuous, experience too certainly informs us; but it is no less certain that of what virtue there is, misery produces far
the greater part. Physical evil may be therefore endured with patience, since it is the cause of moral
good; and patience itself is one virtue by which we
are prepared for that state in which evil shall be no
more.

NUMB. 90.   SATURDAY, *January* 5, 1760.

IT is a complaint which has been made from time
to time, and which seems to have lately become more
frequent, that English oratory, however forcible in
argument, or elegant in expression, is deficient and
inefficacious, because our speakers want the grace and
energy of action.

Among the numerous projectors who are desirous
to refine our manners, and improve our faculties,
some are willing to supply the deficiency of our
speakers. We have had more than one exhortation
to study the neglected art of moving the passions,
and have been encouraged to believe that our tongues,
however feeble in themselves, may, by the help of
our hands and legs, obtain an uncontroulable dominion over the most stubborn audience, animate the
insensible, engage the careless, force tears from the
obdurate, and money from the avaricious.

If by slight of hand, or nimbleness of foot, all
these wonders can be performed, he that shall neglect to attain the free use of his limbs may be justly
censured as criminally lazy. But I am afraid that no
specimen of such effects will easily be shewn. If I
could once find a speaker in Change-Alley raising
the price of stocks by the power of persuasive gestures,
I should very zealously recommend the study of his

art ; but having never seen any action by which language was much assisted, I have been hitherto inclined to doubt whether my countrymen are not blamed too hastily for their calm and motionless utterance.

Foreigners of many nations accompany their speech with action ; but why should their example have more influence upon us than ours upon them ? Customs are not to be changed but for better. Let those who desire to reform us shew the benefits of the change proposed. When the Frenchman waves his hands and writhes his body in recounting the revolutions of a game at cards, or the Neapolitan, who tells the hour of the day, shews upon his fingers the number which he mentions ; I do not perceive that their manual exercise is of much use, or that they leave any image more deeply impressed by their bustle and vehemence of communication.

Upon the English stage there is no want of action ; but the difficulty of making it at once various and proper, and its perpetual tendency to become ridiculous, notwithstanding all the advantages which art and show, and custom and prejudice, can give it, may prove how little it can be admitted into any other place, where it can have no recommendation but from truth and nature.

The use of English oratory is only at the bar, in the parliament, and in the church. Neither the judges of our laws nor the representatives of our people would be much affected by laboured gesticulation, or believe any man the more because he rolled his eyes, or puffed his cheeks, or spread abroad his arms, or stamped the ground, or thumped his breast, or turned his eyes sometimes to the ceiling and sometimes to the floor. Upon men intent only upon truth, the arm of an orator has little power; a credible testimony, or a cogent argument, will overcome all the art of modulation, and all the violence of contortion.

It is well known that, in the city which may be called the parent of oratory, all the arts of mechanical persuasion were banished from the court of supreme judicature. The judges of the Areopagus considered action and vociferation as a foolish appeal to the external senses, and unworthy to be practised before those who had no desire of idle amusement, and whose only pleasure was to discover right.

Whether action may not be yet of use in churches, where the preacher addresses a mingled audience, may deserve inquiry. It is certain that the senses are more powerful as the reason is weaker; and that he whose ears convey little to his mind, may sometimes listen with his eyes till truth may gradually take possession of his heart. If there be any use of gesticulation, it must be applied to the ignorant and rude, who will be more affected by vehemence than delighted by propriety. In the pulpit little action can be proper, for action can illustrate nothing but that to which it may be referred by nature or by custom. He that imitates by his hand a motion which he describes, explains it by natural similitude; he that lays his hand on his breast, when he expresses pity, enforces his words by a customary illusion. But theology has few topics to which action can be appropriated; that action which is vague and indeterminate will at last settle into habit, and habitual peculiarities are quickly ridiculous.

It is perhaps the character of the English to despise trifles; and that art may surely be accounted a trifle which is at once useless and ostentatious, which can seldom be practised with propriety, and which, as the mind is more cultivated, is less powerful. Yet as all innocent means are to be used for the propagation of truth, I would not deter those who are employed in preaching to common congregations from any practice which they may find persuasive: for, compared with the conversion of sinners, propriety and elegance are less than nothing.

NUMB. 91. SATURDAY, *January* 12, 1760.

IT is common to overlook what is near, by keeping the eye fixed upon something remote. In the same manner present opportunities are neglected, and attainable good is slighted, by minds busied in extensive ranges, and intent upon future advantages. Life, however short, is made still shorter by waste of time, and its progress towards happiness, though naturally slow, is yet retarded by unnecessary labour.

The difficulty of obtaining knowledge is universally confessed. To fix deeply in the mind the principles of science, to settle their limitations, and deduce the long succession of their consequences ; to comprehend the whole compass of complicated systems, with all the arguments, objections, and solutions, and to reposite in the intellectual treasury the numberless facts, experiments, apophthegms, and positions, which must stand single in the memory, and of which none has any perceptible connexion with the rest, is a task which, though undertaken with ardour and pursued with diligence, must at last be left unfinished by the frailty of our nature.

To make the way to learning either less short or less smooth, is certainly absurd ; yet this is the apparent effect of the prejudice which seems to prevail among us in favour of foreign authors, and of the contempt of our native literature, which this excursive curiosity must necessarily produce.   Every man is more speedily instructed by his own language, than by any other ; before we search the rest of the world for teachers, let us try whether we may not spare our trouble by finding them at home.

The riches of the English language are much greater than they are commonly supposed.   Many useful and valuable books lie buried in shops and libraries, unknown and unexamined, unless some lucky compiler opens them by chance, and finds an easy spoil of wit and learning.   I am far from intending to insinuate, that other languages are not necessary to him who aspires to eminence, and whose whole life is devoted to study ; but to him who reads only for amusement, or whose purpose is not to deck himself with the honours of literature, but to be qualified for domestic usefulness, and sit down content with subordinate reputation, we have authors sufficient to fill up all the vacancies of his time, and gratify most of his wishes for information.

Of our poets I need say little, because they are perhaps the only authors to whom their country has done justice. We consider the whole succession from Spenser to Pope as superior to any names which the continent can boast; and therefore the poets of other nations, however familiarly they may be sometimes mentioned, are very little read, except by those who design to borrow their beauties.

There is, I think, not one of the liberal arts which may not be competently learned in the English language. He that searches after mathematical knowledge may busy himself among his own countrymen, and will find one or other able to instruct him in every part of those abstruse sciences. He that is delighted with experiments, and wishes to know the nature of bodies from certain and visible effects, is happily placed where the mechanical philosophy was first established by a public institution, and from which it was spread to all other countries.

The more airy and elegant studies of philology and criticism have little need of any foreign help. Though our language, not being very analogical, gives few opportunities for grammatical researches, yet we have not wanted authors who have considered the principles of speech; and with critical writings we abound sufficiently to enable pedantry to impose rules which can seldom be observed, and vanity to talk of books which are seldom read.

But our own language has, from the Reformation

to the present time, been chiefly dignified and adorned by the works of our divines, who, considered as commentators, controvertists, or preachers, have undoubtedly left all other nations far behind them. No vulgar language can boast such treasures of theological knowledge, or such multitudes of authors at once learned, elegant, and pious. Other countries and other communions have authors perhaps equal in abilities and diligence to ours; but if we unite number with excellence, there is certainly no nation which must not allow us to be superior. Of morality little is necessary to be said, because it is comprehended in practical divinity, and is perhaps better taught in English sermons than in any other books ancient and modern. Nor shall I dwell on our excellence in metaphysical speculations, because he that reads the works of our divines will easily discover how far human subtilty has been able to penetrate.

Political knowledge is forced upon us by the form of our constitution; and all the mysteries of government are discovered in the attack or defence of every minister. The original law of society, the rights of subjects, and the prerogatives of kings, have been considered with the utmost nicety, sometimes profoundly investigated, and sometimes familiarly explained.

Thus copiously instructive is the English language; and thus needless is all recourse to foreign writers. Let us not therefore make our neighbours proud by soliciting help which we do not want, nor discourage our own industry by difficulties which we need not suffer.

NUMB. 92.   SATURDAY, *January* 19, 1760.

WHATEVER is useful or honourable will be desired by many who never can obtain it; and that which cannot be obtained when it is desired, artifice or folly will be diligent to counterfeit. Those to whom fortune has denied gold and diamonds decorate themselves with stones and metals, which have something of the show, but little of the value; and every moral excellence or intellectual faculty has some vice or folly which imitates its appearance.

Every man wishes to be wise, and they who cannot be wise are almost always cunning. The less is the real discernment of those whom business or conversation brings together, the more illusions are practised; nor is caution ever so necessary as with associates or opponents of feeble minds.

Cunning differs from wisdom as twilight from open day. He that walks in the sunshine goes boldly forward by the nearest way; he sees that where the path is straight and even, he may proceed in security, and where it is rough and crooked he easily complies with the turns, and avoids the obstructions. But the traveller in the dusk fears more as he sees less; he knows there may be danger, and therefore suspects that he is never safe, tries every step before he fixes his foot, and shrinks at every noise lest violence should approach him. Wisdom comprehends at once the end and the means, estimates easiness or difficulty, and is cautious or confident in due proportion. Cunning discovers little at a time, and has no other means of certainty than multiplication of stratagems and superfluity of suspicion. The man of cunning always considers that he can never be too safe, and therefore always keeps himself enveloped in a mist, impenetrable, as he hopes, to the eye of rivalry or curiosity.

Upon this principle, Tom Double has formed a habit of eluding the most harmless question. What he has no inclination to answer, he pretends sometimes not to hear, and endeavours to divert the inquirer's attention by some other subject; but if he be pressed hard by repeated interrogation, he always evades a direct reply. Ask him whom he likes best on the stage; he is ready to tell that there are several excellent performers. Inquire when he was last at the coffee-house; he replies, that the weather has been bad lately. Desire him to tell the age of any of his acquaintance; he immediately mentions another who is older or younger.

Will Puzzle values himself upon a long reach. He foresees every thing before it will happen, though he never relates his prognostications till the event is past. Nothing has come to pass for these twenty years of which Mr. Puzzle had not given broad hints, and told at least that it was not proper to tell. Of those predictions, which every conclusion will equally verify, he always claims the credit, and wonders that his friends did not understand them. He supposes very truly that much may be known which he knows not, and therefore pretends to know much of which he and all mankind are equally ignorant. I desired his opinion yesterday of the German war, and was told, that if the Prussians were well supported, something great may be expected; but that they have very powerful enemies to encounter; that the Austrian general has long experience, and the Russians are hardy and resolute; but that no human power is invincible. I then drew the conversation to our own affairs, and invited him to balance the probabilities of war and peace. He told me that war requires courage, and negociation judgment, and that the time will come when it will be seen whether our skill in treaty is equal to our bravery in battle. To this general prattle he will appeal hereafter, and will demand to have his foresight applauded, whoever shall at last be conquered or victorious.

With Ned Smuggle all is a secret. He believes himself watched by observation and malignity on every side, and rejoices in the dexterity by which he has escaped snares that never were laid. Ned holds that a man is never deceived if he never trusts, and therefore will not tell the name of his taylor or his hatter. He rides out every morning for the air, and pleases himself with thinking that nobody knows where he has been. When he dines with a friend, he never goes to his house the nearest way, but walks up a bye-street to perplex the scent. When he has a coach called, he never tells him at the door the true place to which he is going, but stops him in the way that he may give him directions where nobody can hear him. The price of what he buys or sells is always concealed.   He often takes lodgings in the country by a wrong name, and thinks that the world is wondering where he can be hid.   All these transactions he registers in a book, which, he says, will some time or other amaze posterity.

It is remarked by Bacon, that many men try to procure reputation only by objections, of which, if they are once admitted, the nullity never appears, because the design is laid aside.   " This false feint of wisdom," says he, " is the ruin of business."   The whole power of cunning is privative ; to say nothing, and to do nothing, is the utmost of its reach.   Yet men thus narrow by nature, and mean by art, are sometimes able to rise by the miscarriages of bravery and the openness of integrity ; and by watching failures and snatching opportunities, obtain advantages which belong properly to higher characters.

NUMB. 93.   SATURDAY, *January* 26, 1760.

SAM SOFTLY was bred a sugar-baker; but succeeding to a considerable estate on the death of his elder brother, he retired early from business, married a fortune, and settled in a country house near Kentish-town. Sam, who formerly was a sportsman, and in his apprenticeship used to frequent Barnet races, keeps a high chaise, with a brace of seasoned geldings. During the summer months, the principal passion and employment of Sam's life is to visit, in this vehicle, the most eminent seats of the nobility and gentry in different parts of the kingdom, with his wife and some select friends. By these periodical excursions Sam gratifies many important purposes. He assists the several pregnancies of his wife; he shews his chaise to the best advantage; he indulges his insatiable curiosity for finery, which, since he has turned gentleman, has grown upon him to an extraordinary degree; he discovers taste and spirit, and, what is above all, he finds frequent opportunities of displaying to the party, at every house he sees, his knowledge of family connection. At first, Sam was contented with driving a friend between London and his villa. Here he prided himself in pointing out the boxes of the citizens on each side of the road, with an accurate detail of their respective failures or successes in trade; and harangued on the several equipages that were accidentally passing. Here, too, the seats interspersed on the surrounding hills, afforded ample matter for Sam's curious discoveries. For one, he told his companion, a rich Jew had offered money; and that a retired widow was courted at another, by an eminent dry-salter. At the same time he discussed the utility, and enumerated the expences, of the Islington turnpike. But Sam's ambition is at present raised to nobler undertakings.

When the happy hour of the annual expedition arrives, the seat of the chaise is furnished with Ogilvy's " Book of Roads," and a choice quantity of cold tongues. The most alarming disaster which can happen to our hero, who thinks he *throws a whip* admirably well, is to be overtaken in a road which affords no *quarter* for wheels. Indeed, few men possess more skill or discernment for concerting and conducting a *party of pleasure.* When a seat is to be surveyed, he has a peculiar talent in selecting some shady bench in the park, where the company may most commodiously refresh themselves with cold tongue, chicken, and French rolls; and is very sagacious in discovering what cool temple in the garden will be best adapted for drinking tea, brought for this purpose, in the afternoon, and from which the chaise may be resumed with the greatest convenience. In viewing the house itself, he is principally attracted by the chairs and beds, concerning the cost of which his minute inquiries generally gain the clearest information. An agate table easily diverts his eyes from the most capital strokes of Rubens, and a Turkey carpet has more charms than a Titian.

Sam, however, dwells with some attention on the family portraits, particularly the most modern ones; and as this is a topick on which the house-keeper usually harangues in a more copious manner, he takes this opportunity of improving his knowledge of intermarriages. Yet, notwithstanding this appearance of satisfaction, Sam has some objection to all he sees. One house has too much gilding; at another, the chimney-pieces are all monuments; at a third, he conjectures that the beautiful canal must certainly be dried up in a hot summer. He despises the statues at Wilton, because he thinks he can see much better carving at Westminster Abbey. But there is one general objection which he is sure to make at almost every house, particularly at those which are most distinguished. He allows that all the apartments are extremely fine, but adds, with a sneer, that they are too fine to be inhabited.

Misapplied genius most commonly proves ridiculous. Had Sam, as Nature intended, contentedly continued in the calmer and less conspicuous pursuits of sugar-baking, he might have been a respectable and useful character. At present he dissipates his life in a specious idleness, which neither improves himself nor his friends. Those talents which might have benefited society, he exposes to contempt by false pretensions. He affects pleasures which he cannot enjoy, and is acquainted only with those subjects on which he has no right to talk, and which it is no merit to understand.*

* By Mr. Thomas Warton.　C.

Numb. 94. Saturday, *February* 2, 1760.

It is common to find young men ardent and diligent in the pursuit of knowledge; but the progress of life very often produces laxity and indifference; and not only those who are at liberty to chuse their business and amusements, but those likewise whose professions engage them in literary inquiries, pass the latter part of their time without improvement, and spend the day rather in any other entertainment than that which they might find among their books.

This abatement of the vigour of curiosity is sometimes imputed to the insufficiency of learning. Men are supposed to remit their labours, because they find their labours to have been vain; and to search no longer after truth and wisdom, because they at last despair of finding them.

But this reason is for the most part very falsely assigned. Of learning, as of virtue, it may be affirmed, that it is at once honoured and neglected. Whoever forsakes it will for ever look after it with longing, lament the loss which he does not endeavour to repair, and desire the good which he wants resolution to seize and keep. The idler never applauds his own idleness, nor does any man repent of the diligence of his youth.

So many hindrances may obstruct the acquisition of knowledge, that there is little reason for wondering that it is in a few hands. To the greater part of mankind the duties of life are inconsistent with much study; and the hours which they would spend upon letters must be stolen from their occupations and their families.   Many suffer themselves to be lured by more spritely and luxurious pleasures from the shades of contemplation, where they find seldom more than a calm delight, such as, though greater than all others, if its certainty and its duration be reckoned with its power of gratification, is yet easily quitted for some extemporary joy, which the present moment offers, and another perhaps will put out of reach.

It is the great excellence of learning, that it borrows very little from time or place; it is not confined to season or to climate, to cities or to the country, but may be cultivated and enjoyed where no other pleasure can be obtained.   But this quality, which constitutes much of its value, is one occasion of neglect; what may be done at all times with equal propriety, is deferred from day to day, till the mind is gradually reconciled to the omission, and the attention is turned to other objects.   Thus habitual idleness gains too much power to be conquered, and the soul shrinks from the idea of intellectual labour and intenseness of meditation.

That those who profess to advance learning sometimes obstruct it, cannot be denied; the continual multiplication of books not only distracts choice, but disappoints inquiry.   To him that has moderately stored his mind with images, few writers afford any novelty; or what little they have to add to the common stock of learning, is so buried in the mass of general notions, that, like silver mingled with the ore of lead, it is too little to pay for the labour of separation; and he that has often been deceived by the promise of a title, at last grows weary of examining, and is tempted to consider all as equally fallacious.

There are indeed some repetitions always lawful, because they never deceive. He that writes the history of past times, undertakes only to decorate known facts by new beauties of method or of style, or at most to illustrate them by his own reflexions. The author of a system, whether moral or physical, is obliged to nothing beyond care of selection and regularity of disposition. But there are others who claim the name of authors merely to disgrace it, and fill the world with volumes only to bury letters in their own rubbish. The traveller, who tells, in a pompous folio, that he saw the Pantheon at Rome, and the Medicean Venus at Florence; the natural historian, who, describing the productions of a narrow island, recounts all that it has in common with every other part of the world; the collector of antiquities, that accounts every thing a curiosity which the ruins of Herculaneum happen to emit, though an instrument already shewn in a thousand repositories, or a cup common to the ancients, the moderns, and all mankind; may be justly censured as the persecutors of students, and the thieves of that time which never can be restored.

TO THE IDLER.

MR. IDLER,

IT is, I think, universally agreed, that seldom any good is gotten by complaint; yet we find that few forbear to complain, but those who are afraid of being reproached as the authors of their own miseries. I hope therefore for the common permission to lay my case before you and your readers, by which I shall disburden my heart, though I cannot hope to receive either assistance or consolation.

I am a trader, and owe my fortune to frugality and industry. I began with little; but by the easy and obvious method of spending less than I gain, I have every year added something to my stock, and expect to have a seat in the common-council at the next election.

My wife, who was as prudent as myself, died six years ago, and left me one son and one daughter, for whose sake I resolved never to marry again, and rejected the overtures of Mrs. Squeeze, the broker's widow, who had ten thousand pounds at her own disposal.

I bred my son at a school near Islington; and when he had learned arithmetick, and wrote a good hand, I took him into the shop, designing, in about ten years, to retire to Stratford or Hackney, and leave him established in the business.

For four years he was diligent and sedate, entered the shop before it was opened, and when it was shut, always examined the pins of the window. In any intermission of business it was his constant practice to peruse the ledger. I had always great hopes of him, when I observed how sorrowfully he would shake his head over a bad debt, and how eagerly he would listen to me when I told him that he might at one time or other become an alderman.

We lived together with mutual confidence, till unluckily a visit was paid him by two of his school-fellows who were placed, I suppose, in the army, because they were fit for nothing better: they came glittering in their military dress, accosted their old acquaintance, and invited him to a tavern, where, as I have been since informed, they ridiculed the meanness of commerce, and wondered how a youth of spirit could spend the prime of life behind a counter.

I did not suspect any mischief. I knew my son was never without money in his pocket, and was better able to pay his reckoning than his compa-nions; and expected to see him return triumphing in his own advantages, and congratulating himself that he was not one of those who expose their heads to a musquet bullet for three shillings a day.

He returned sullen and thoughtful; I supposed him sorry for the hard fortune of his friends; and tried to comfort him, by saying that the war would soon be at an end, and that, if they had any honest occupation, half-pay would be a pretty help. He looked at me with indignation; and snatching up his candle, told me, as he went up stairs, that *he hoped to see a battle yet.*

Why he should hope to see a battle, I could not conceive, but let him go quietly to sleep away his folly. Next day he made two mistakes in the first bill, disobliged a customer by surly answers, and dated all his entries in the journal in a wrong month. At night he met his military companions again, came home late, and quarrelled with the maid.

From this fatal interview he has gradually lost all his laudable passions and desires. He soon grew useless in the shop, where, indeed, I did not willingly trust him any longer : for he often mistook the price of goods to his own loss, and once gave a promissory note instead of a receipt.

I did not know to what degree he was corrupted, till an honest taylor gave me notice that he had bespoke a laced suit, which was to be left for him at a house kept by the sister of one of my journeymen. I went to this clandestine lodging, and found, to my amazement, all the ornaments of a fine gentleman, which he has taken upon credit, or purchased with money subducted from the shop.

This detection has made him desperate. He now openly declares his resolution to be a gentleman ; says that his soul is too great for a counting-house ; ridicules the conversation of city taverns ; talks of new plays, and boxes and ladies ; gives duchesses for his toasts ; carries silver, for readiness, in his waistcoat-pocket ; and comes home at night in a chair, with such thunders at the door, as have more than once brought the watchmen from their stands.

Little expences will not hurt us; and I could forgive a few juvenile frolicks, if he would be careful of the main; but his favorite topick is contempt of money, which, he says, is of no use but to be spent. Riches, without honour, he holds empty things; and once told me to my face, that wealthy plodders were only purveyors to men of spirit.

He is always impatient in the company of his old friends, and seldom speaks till he is warmed with wine; he then entertains us with accounts that we do not desire to hear, of intrigues among lords and ladies, and quarrels between officers of the guards; shews a miniature on his snuff-box, and wonders that any man can look upon the new dancer without rapture.

All this is very provoking; and yet all this might be borne, if the boy could support his pretensions. But, whatever he may think, he is yet far from the accomplishments which he has endeavoured to purchase at so dear a rate. I have watched him in publick places. He sneaks in like a man that knows he is where he should not be; he is proud to catch the slightest salutation, and often claims it when it is not intended. Other men receive dignity from dress, but my booby looks always more meanly for his finery. Dear Mr. Idler, tell him what must at last become of a fop, whom pride will not suffer to be a trader, and whom long habits in a shop forbid to be a gentleman.

I am, Sir, &c.

TIM WAINSCOT.

NUMB. 96.   SATURDAY, *February* 16, 1760.

HACHO, a king of Lapland, was in his youth the
most renowned of the Northern warriors.   His martial atchievements remain engraved on a pillar of
flint in the rocks of Hanga, and are to this day
solemnly carolled to the harp by the Laplanders,
at the fires with which they celebrate their night-
ly festivities.   Such was his intrepid spirit, that
he ventured to pass the lake Vether to the isle of
Wizards, where he descended alone into the dreary
vault in which a magician had been kept bound for
six ages, and read the Gothick characters inscribed
on his brazen mace.   His eye was so piercing, that,
as ancient chronicles report, he could blunt the weapons of his enemies only by looking at them.   At
twelve years of age he carried an iron vessel of a pro-
digious weight, for the length of five furlongs, in the
presence of all the chiefs of his father's castle.

Nor was he less celebrated for his prudence and
wisdom.   Two of his proverbs are yet remembered
and repeated among Laplanders.   To express the
vigilance of the Supreme Being, he was wont to
say, *Odin's belt is always buckled.*   To shew that
the most prosperous condition of life is often
hazardous, his lesson was, *When you slide on the
smoothest ice, beware of pits beneath.*   He consoled
his countrymen, when they were once preparing

to leave the frozen desarts of Lapland, and resolved to seek some warmer climate, by telling them, that the Eastern nations, notwithstanding their boasted fertility, passed every night amidst the horrors of anxious apprehension, and were inexpressibly affrighted, and almost stunned, every morning, with the noise of the sun while he was rising.

His temperance and severity of manners were his chief praise. In his early years he never tasted wine; nor would he drink out of a painted cup. He constantly slept in his armour, with his spear in his hand; nor would he use a battle-axe whose handle was inlaid with brass. He did not, however, persevere in this contempt of luxury; nor did he close his days with honour.

One evening, after hunting the Gulos, or wild-dog, being bewildered in a solitary forest, and having passed the fatigues of the day without any interval of refreshment, he discovered a large store of honey in the hollow of a pine. This was a dainty which he had never tasted before; and being at once faint and hungry, he fed greedily upon it. From this unusual and delicious repast he received so much satisfaction, that, at his return home, he commanded honey to be served up at his table every day. His palate, by degrees, became refined and vitiated; he began to lose his native relish for simple fare, and contracted a habit of indulging himself in delicacies; he ordered the delightful gardens of his castle to be thrown open, in which the most luscious fruits had been suffered to ripen and decay, unobserved and untouched, for many revolving autumns, and gratified his appetite with luxurious desserts. At length he found it expedient to introduce wine, as an agreeable improvement, or a necessary ingredient, to his new way of living ; and having once tasted it, he was tempted, by little and little, to give a loose to the excesses of intoxication. His general simplicity of life was changed ; he perfumed his apartments by burning the wood of the most aromatick fir, and commanded his helmet to be ornamented with beautiful rows of the teeth of the rein-deer. Indolence and effeminacy stole upon him by pleasing and imperceptible gradations, relaxed the sinews of his resolution, and extinguished his thirst of military glory.

While Hacho was thus immersed in pleasure and in repose, it was reported to him, one morning, that the preceding night, a disastrous omen had been discovered, and that bats and hideous birds had drunk up the oil which nourished the perpetual lamp in the temple of Odin. About the same time, a messenger arrived to tell him that the king of Norway had invaded his kingdom with a formidable army. Hacho, terrified as he was with the omen of the night, and enervated with indulgence, rouzed himself from his voluptuous lethargy, and recollecting some faint and few sparks of veteran valour, marched forward to meet him. Both armies joined battle in the forest where Hacho had been lost after hunting ; and it so happened, that the king of Norway challenged him to single combat, near the place where he had tasted the honey. The Lapland chief, languid and long disused to arms, was soon overpowered; he fell to the ground; and before his insulting adversary struck his head from his body, uttered this exclamation, which the Laplanders still use as an early lesson to their children : " The vicious man should date his destruction from the first temptation. How justly do I fall a sacrifice to sloth and luxury, in the place where I first yielded to those allurements which seduced me to deviate from temperance and innocence! The honey which I tasted in this forest, and not the hand of the king of Norway, conquers Hacho."*

* By Mr. Thomas Warton. C

NUMB. 97.   SATURDAY, *February* 23, 1760.

IT may, I think, be justly observed, that few books disappoint their readers more than the narrations of travellers.   One part of mankind is naturally curious to learn the sentiments, manners, and condition of the rest; and every mind that has leisure or power to extend its views, must be desirous of knowing in what proportion Providence has distributed the blessings of nature, or the advantages of art, among the several nations of the earth.

This general desire easily procures readers to every book from which it can expect gratification.   The adventurer upon unknown coasts, and the describer of distant regions, is always welcomed as a man who has laboured for the pleasure of others, and who is able to enlarge our knowledge and rectify our opinions; but when the volume is opened, nothing is found but such general accounts as leave no distinct idea behind them, or such minute enumerations as few can read with either profit or delight.

Every writer of travels should consider, that, like all other authors, he undertakes either to instruct or please, or to mingle pleasure with instruction.   He that instructs must offer to the mind something to be imitated, or something to be avoided; he that pleases must offer new images to his reader, and enable him to form a tacit comparison of his own state with that of others.

The greater part of travellers tell nothing, because their method of travelling supplies them with nothing to be told.　He that enters a town at night and surveys it in the morning, and then hastens away to another place, and guesses at the manners of the inhabitants by the entertainment which his inn afforded him, may please himself for a time with a hasty change of scenes, and a confused remembrance of palaces and churches; he may gratify his eye with a variety of landscapes, and regale his palate with a succession of vintages; but let him be contented to please himself without endeavouring to disturb others. Why should he record excursions by which nothing could be learned, or wish to make a shew of knowledge, which, without some power of intuition unknown to other mortals, he never could attain?

Of those who crowd the world with their itineraries, some have no other purpose than to describe the face of the country; those who sit idle at home, and are curious to know what is done or suffered in distant countries, may be informed by one of these wanderers, that on a certain day he set out early with the caravan, and in the first hour's march saw, towards the south, a hill covered with trees, then passed over a stream, which ran northward with a swift course, but which is probably dry in the summer months; that an hour after he saw something to the right which looked at a distance like a castle with towers, but which he discovered afterwards to be a craggy rock; that he then entered a valley, in which he saw several trees tall and flourishing, watered by a rivulet not marked in the maps, of which he was

not able to learn the name ; that the road afterward
grew stony, and the country uneven, where he observed among the hills many hollows worn by torrents,
and was told that the road was passable only part of
the year ; that going on they found the remains of a
building, once, perhaps, a fortress to secure the pass,
or to restrain the robbers, of which the present inhabitants can give no other account than that it is
haunted by fairies; that they went to dine at the foot
of a rock, and travelled the rest of the day along the
banks of a river, from which the road turned aside
towards evening, and brought them within sight of
a village, which was once a considerable town, but
which afforded them neither good victuals nor commodious lodging.

Thus he conducts his reader through wet and dry,
over rough and smooth, without incidents, without
reflection ; and, if he obtains his company for another day, will dismiss him again at night, equally
fatigued with a like succession of rocks and streams,
mountains and ruins.

This is the common style of those sons of enterprise, who visit savage countries, and range through
solitude and desolation ; who pass a desart, and tell
that it is sandy ; who cross a valley and find that it
is green.   There are others of more delicate sensibility, that visit only the realms of elegance and
softness ; that wander through Italian palaces, and
amuse the gentle reader with catalogues of pictures ;
that hear masses in magnificent churches, and recount the number of the pillars or variegations of
the pavement.   And there are yet others, who, in

disdain of trifles, copy inscriptions elegant and rude, ancient and modern ; and transcribe into their book the walls of every edifice, sacred or civil. He that reads these books must consider his labour as its own reward ; for he will find nothing on which attention can fix, or which memory cau retain.

He that would travel for the entertainment of others, should remember that the great object of remark is human life. Every nation has something particular in its manufactures, its works of genius, its medicines, its agriculture, its customs, and its policy. He only is a useful traveller, who brings home something by which his country may be benefited ; who procures some supply of want, or some mitigation of evil, which may enable his readers to compare their condition with that of others, to improve it whenever it is worse, and whenever it is better to enjoy it.

NUMB. 98.   SATURDAY, *March* 1, 1760.

TO THE IDLER.

SIR,

I AM the daughter of a gentleman, who during his life-time enjoyed a small income which arose from a pension from the court, by which he was enabled to live in a genteel and comfortable manner.

By the situation of life in which he was placed, he was frequently introduced into the company of those of much greater fortunes than his own, among whom he was always received with complaisance, and treated with civility.

At six years of age I was sent to a boarding-school in the country, at which I continued till my father's death.   This melancholy event happened at a time when I was by no means of sufficient age to manage for myself, while the passions of youth continued unsubdued, and before experience could guide my sentiments or my actions.

I was then taken from school by an uncle, to the care of whom my father had committed me on his dying-bed.   With him I lived several years: and as he was unmarried, the management of his family was committed to me.   In this character I always endeavoured to acquit myself, if not with applause, at least without censure.

At the age of twenty-one, a young gentleman of some fortune paid his addresses to me, and offered me terms of marriage. This proposal I should readily have accepted, because from vicinity of residence, and from many opportunities of observing his behaviour, I had in some sort contracted an affection for him. My uncle, for what reason I do not know, refused his consent to this alliance, though it would have been complied with by the father of the young gentleman; and as the future condition of my life was wholly dependant on him, I was not willing to disoblige him, and therefore, though unwillingly, declined the offer.

My uncle, who possessed a plentiful fortune, frequently hinted to me in conversation, that at his death I should be provided for in such a manner that I should be able to make my future life comfortable and happy. As this promise was often repeated, I was the less anxious about any provision for myself. In a short time my uncle was taken ill, and though all possible means were made use of for his recovery, in a few days he died.

The sorrow arising from the loss of a relation, by whom I had been always treated with the greatest kindness, however grievous, was not the worst of my misfortunes. As he enjoyed an almost uninterrupted state of health, he was the less mindful of his dissolution, and died intestate; by which means his whole fortune devolved to a nearer relation, the heir at law.

Thus excluded from all hopes of living in the manner with which I have so long flattered myself, I am doubtful what method I shall take to procure a decent maintenance.   I have been educated in a manner that has set me above a state of servitude, and my situation renders me unfit for the company of those with whom I have hitherto conversed.   But, though disappointed in my expectations, I do not despair.   I will hope that assistance may still be obtained for innocent distress, and that friendship, though rare, is yet not impossible to be found.

I am, Sir,

Your humble servant,

SOPHIA HEEDFUL.*

* By an unknown Correspondent.   C.

NUMB. 99.   SATURDAY, *March* 8, 1760.

As Ortogrul of Basra was one day wandering along the streets of Bagdat, musing on the varieties of merchandise which the shops offered to his view, and observing the different occupations which busied the multitudes on every side, he was awakened from the tranquillity of meditation by a crowd that obstructed his passage.   He raised his eyes, and saw the chief visier, who, having returned from the divan, was entering his palace.

Ortogrul mingled with the attendants, and being supposed to have some petition for the visier, was permitted to enter.   He surveyed the spaciousness of the apartments, admired the walls hung with golden tapestry, and the floors covered with silken carpets, and despised the simple neatness of his own little habitation.

Surely, said he to himself, this palace is the seat of happiness, where pleasure succeeds to pleasure, and discontent and sorrow can have no admission. Whatever Nature has provided for the delight of sense, is here spread forth to be enjoyed.   What can mortals hope or imagine, which the master of this palace has not obtained?   The dishes of Luxury cover his table, the voice of Harmony lulls him in his bowers; he breathes the fragrance of the groves of Java, and sleeps upon the down of the cygnets of

Ganges. He speaks, and his mandate is obeyed; he wishes, and his wish is gratified; all whom he sees obey him, and all whom he hears flatter him. How different, Ortogrul, is thy condition, who art doomed to the perpetual torments of unsatisfied desire, and who hast no amusement in thy power that can withhold thee from thy own reflections! They tell thee that thou art wise; but what does wisdom avail with poverty? None will flatter the poor, and the wise have very little power of flattering themselves. That man is surely the most wretched of the sons of wretchedness, who lives with his own faults and follies always before him, and who has none to reconcile him to himself by praise and veneration. I have long sought content, and have not found it; I will from this moment endeavour to be rich.

Full of his new resolution, he shut himself in his chamber for six months, to deliberate how he should grow rich; he sometimes proposed to offer himself as a counseller to one of the kings of India, and sometimes resolved to dig for diamonds in the mines of Golconda. One day, after some hours passed in violent fluctuation of opinion, sleep insensibly seized him in his chair; he dreamed that he was ranging a desert country in search of some one that might teach him to grow rich; and as he stood on the top of a hill shaded with cypress, in doubt whither to direct his steps, his father appeared on a sudden standing before him. Ortogrul, said the old man, I know thy perplexity; listen to thy father; turn thine eye on the opposite mountain. Ortogrul looked, and saw a torrent tumbling down the rocks, roaring with the noise of thunder, and scattering its foam on the impending woods. Now, said his father, behold the valley that lies between the hills. Ortogrul looked, and espied a little well, out of which issued a small rivulet. Tell me now, said his father, dost thou wish for sudden affluence, that may pour upon thee like the mountain torrent, or for a slow and gradual encrease, resembling the rill gliding from the well? Let me be quickly rich, said Ortogrul; let the golden stream be quick and violent. Look round thee, said his father, once again. Ortogrul looked, and perceived the channel of the torrent dry and dusty; but following the rivulet from the well, he traced it to a wide lake, which the supply, slow and constant, kept always full. He waked, and determined to grow rich by silent profit and persevering industry.

Having sold his patrimony, he engaged in merchandise, and in twenty years purchased lands, on which he raised a house, equal in sumptuousness to that of the visier, to which he invited all the ministers of pleasure, expecting to enjoy all the felicity which he had imagined riches able to afford. Leisure soon made him weary of himself, and he longed to be persuaded that he was great and happy. He was courteous and liberal; he gave all that approached him hopes of pleasing him, and all who should please him hopes of being rewarded. Every art of praise was tried, and every source of adulatory fiction was exhausted. Ortogrul heard his flatterers without delight, because he found himself unable to believe them. His own heart told him its frailties, his own understanding reproached him with his faults. How long, said he, with a deep sigh, have I been labouring in vain to amass wealth which at last is useless! Let no man hereafter wish to be rich, who is already too wise to be flattered.

NUMB. 100. SATURDAY, *March* 15, 1760.

TO THE IDLER.

SIR,

THE uncertainty and defects of language have produced very frequent complaints among the learned; yet there still remain many words among us undefined, which are very necessary to be rightly understood, and which produce very mischievous mistakes when they are erroneously interpreted.

I lived in a state of celibacy beyond the usual time. In the hurry first of pleasure, and afterwards of business, I felt no want of a domestic companion; but becoming weary of labour, I soon grew more weary of idleness, and thought it reasonable to follow the custom of life, and to seek some solace of my cares in female tenderness, and some amusement of my leisure in female chearfulness.

The choice which has been long delayed is commonly made at last with great caution. My resolution was, to keep my passions neutral, and to marry only in compliance with my reason. I drew upon a page of my pocket-book a scheme of all female virtues and vices, with the vices which border upon every virtue, and the virtues which are allied to every vice. I considered that wit was sarcastick, and magnanimity imperious; that avarice was œconomical, and ignorance obsequious; and having estimated the good and evil of every quality, employed my own diligence, and that of my friends, to find the lady in whom nature and reason had reached that happy mediocrity which is equally remote from exuberance and deficience.

Every woman had her admirers and her censurers; and the expectations which one raised were by another quickly depressed; yet there was one in whose favour almost all suffrages concurred. Miss Gentle was universally allowed to be a good sort of woman. Her fortune was not large, but so prudently managed, that she wore finer clothes, and saw more company, than many who were known to be twice as rich. Miss Gentle's visits were every where welcome; and whatever family she favoured with her company, she always left behind her such a degree of kindness as recommended her to others. Every day extended her acquaintance; and all who knew her declared that they never met with a better sort of woman.

To Miss Gentle I made my addresses, and was received with great equality of temper. She did not in the days of courtship assume the privilege of imposing rigorous commands, or resenting slight offences. If I forgot any of her injunctions, I was gently reminded; if I missed the minute of appointment, I was easily forgiven. I foresaw nothing in marriage but a halcyon calm, and longed for the happiness which was to be found in the inseparable society of a good sort of woman.

The jointure was soon settled by the intervention of friends, and the day came in which Miss Gentle was made mine for ever. The first month was passed easily enough in receiving and repaying the civilities of our friends. The bride practised with great exactness all the niceties of ceremony, and distributed her notice in the most punctilious proportions to the friends who surrounded us with their happy auguries.

But the time soon came when we were left to ourselves, and were to receive our pleasures from each other, and I then began to perceive that I was not formed to be much delighted by a good sort of woman. Her great principle is, that the order of a family must not be broken. Every hour of the day has its employment inviolably appropriated; nor will any importunity persuade her to walk in the garden at the time which she has devoted to her needle-work, or to sit up stairs in that part of the forenoon which she has accustomed herself to spend in the back parlour. She allows herself to sit half an hour after breakfast, and an hour after dinner; while I am talking or reading to her, she keeps her eye upon her watch, and when the minute of departure comes, will leave an argument unfinished, or the intrigue of a play unravelled. She once called me to supper when I was watching an eclipse, and summoned me at another time to bed when I was going to give directions at a fire.

Her conversation is so habitually cautious, that she never talks to me but in general terms, as to one whom it is dangerous to trust. For discriminations of character she has no names : all whom she mentions are honest men and agreeable women. She smiles not by sensation, but by practice. Her laughter is never excited but by a joke, and her notion of a joke is not very delicate. The repetition of a good joke does not weaken its effect; if she has laughed once, she will laugh again.

She is an enemy to nothing but ill-nature and pride ; but she has frequent reason to lament that they are so frequent in the world. All who are not equally pleased with the good and the bad, with the elegant and gross, with the witty and the dull, all who distinguish excellence from defect, she considers as ill-natured ; and she condemns as proud all who repress impertinence or quell presumption, or expect respect from any other eminence than that of fortune, to which she is always willing to pay homage.

There are none whom she openly hates, for if once she suffers, or believes herself to suffer, any contempt or insult, she never dismisses it from her mind, but takes all opportunities to tell how easily she can forgive. There are none whom she loves much better than others; for when any of her acquaintance decline in the opinion of the world, she always finds it inconvenient to visit them ; her affection continues unaltered, but it is impossible to be intimate with the whole town.

She daily exercises her benevolence by pitying every misfortune that happens to every family within her circle of notice ; she is in hourly terrors lest one should catch cold in the rain, and another be frighted by the high wind. Her charity she shews by lamenting that so many poor wretches should languish in the streets, and by wondering what the great can think on that they do so little good with such large estates.

Her house is elegant, and her table dainty, though she has little taste of elegance, and is wholly free from vicious luxury ; but she comforts herself that nobody can say that her house is dirty, or that her dishes are not well drest.

This, Mr. Idler, I have found by long experience to be the character of a good sort of woman, which I have sent you for the information of those by whom a *good sort of woman* and a *good woman,* may happen to be used as equivalent terms, and who may suffer by the mistake, like

Your humble servant,
TIM WARNER.

Numb. 101.   Saturday, *March* 22, 1760.

Omar, the son of Hassan, had passed seventy-five years in honour and prosperity. The favour of three successive califs had filled his house with gold and silver; and whenever he appeared, the benedictions of the people proclaimed his passage.

Terrestrial happiness is of short continuance The brightness of the flame is wasting its fuel; the fragrant flower is passing away in its own odours. The vigour of Omar began to fail, the curls of beauty fell from his head, strength departed from his hands, and agility from his feet. He gave back to the calif the keys of trust and the seals of secrecy; and sought no other pleasure for the remains of life than the converse of the wise, and the gratitude of the good.

The powers of his mind were yet unimpaired. His chamber was filled by visitants, eager to catch the dictates of experience, and officious to pay the tribute of admiration. Caled, the son of the viceroy of Egypt, entered every day early, and retired late. He was beautiful and eloquent; Omar admired his wit, and loved his docility. Tell me, said Caled, thou to whose voice nations have listened, and whose wisdom is known to the extremities of Asia, tell me how I may resemble Omar the prudent. The arts by which you have gained power

and preserved it, are to you no longer necessary
or useful; impart to me the secret of your conduct,
and teach me the plan upon which your wisdom has
built your fortune.

Young man, said Omar, it is of little use to form
plans of life. When I took my first survey of the
world, in my twentieth year, having considered the
various conditions of mankind, in the hour of solitude I said thus to myself, leaning against a cedar
which spread its branches over my head: Seventy
years are allowed to man; I have yet fifty remaining: ten years I will allot to the attainment of
knowledge, and ten I will pass in foreign countries;
I shall be learned, and therefore shall be honoured;
every city will shout at my arrival, and every student will solicit my friendship. Twenty years thus
passed will store my mind with images which I
shall be busy through the rest of my life in combin-
ing and comparing. I shall revel in inexhaustible
accumulations of intellectual riches; I shall find
new pleasures for every moment, and shall never
more be weary of myself. I will, however, not
deviate too far from the beaten track of life, but
will try what can be found in female delicacy. I
will marry a wife beautiful as the Houries, and wise
as Zobeide; with her I will live twenty years within
the suburbs of Bagdat, in every pleasure that wealth
can purchase, and fancy can invent. I will then
retire to a rural dwelling, pass my last days in obscurity and contemplation, and lie silently down on
the bed of death. Through my life it shall be my
settled resolution, that I will never depend upon

the smile of princes; that I will never stand exposed to the artifices of courts; I will never pant for publick honours, nor disturb my quiet with affairs of state. Such was my scheme of life, which I impressed indelibly upon my memory.

The first part of my ensuing time was to be spent in search of knowledge; and I know not how I was diverted from my design. I had no visible impediments without, nor any ungovernable passions within. I regarded knowledge as the highest honour and the most engaging pleasure; yet day stole upon day, and month glided after month, till I found that seven years of the first ten had vanished, and left nothing behind them. I now postponed my purpose of travelling; for why should I go abroad while so much remained to be learned at home? I immured myself for four years, and studied the laws of the empire. The fame of my skill reached the judges; I was found able to speak upon doubtful questions, and was commanded to stand at the footstool of the calif. I was heard with attention, I was consulted with confidence, and the love of praise fastened on my heart.

I still wished to see distant countries, listened with rapture to the relations of travellers, and resolved some time to ask my dismission, that I might feast my soul with novelty; but my presence was always necessary, and the stream of business hurried me along. Sometimes I was afraid lest I should be charged with ingratitude; but I still proposed to travel, and therefore would not confine myself by marriage.

In my fiftieth year I began to suspect that the time of travelling was past, and thought it best to lay hold on the felicity yet in my power, and indulge myself in domestick pleasures. But at fifty no man easily finds a woman beautiful as the Houries, and wise as Zobeide. I inquired and rejected, consulted and deliberated, till the sixty-second year made me ashamed of gazing upon girls. I had now nothing left but retirement, and for retirement I never found a time, till disease forced me from publick employment.

Such was my scheme, and such has been its consequence. With an insatiable thirst for knowledge, I trifled away the years of improvement; with a restless desire of seeing different countries, I have always resided in the same city; with the highest expectation of connubial felicity, I have lived unmarried; and with unalterable resolutions of contemplative retirement, I am going to die within the walls of Bagdat.

NUMB. 102. SATURDAY, *March* 29, 1760.

IT very seldom happens to man that his business is his pleasure. What is done from necessity is so often to be done when against the present inclination, and so often fills the mind with anxiety, that an habitual dislike steals upon us, and we shrink involuntarily from the remembrance of our task. This is the reason why almost every one wishes to quit his employment; he does not like another state, but is disgusted with his own.

From this unwillingness to perform more than is required of that which is commonly performed with reluctance, it proceeds that few authors write their own lives. Statesmen, courtiers, ladies, generals, and seamen, have given to the world their own stories, and the events with which their different stations have made them acquainted. They retired to the closet as to a place of quiet and amusement, and pleased themselves with writing, because they could lay down the pen whenever they were weary. But the author, however conspicuous, or however important, either in the publick eye or in his own, leaves his life to be related by his successors, for he cannot gratify his vanity but by sacrifieing his ease.

It is commonly supposed that the uniformity of a studious life affords no matter for a narration: but the truth is, that of the most studious life a great part passes without study. An author par-

takes of the common condition of humanity ; he is
born and married like another man ; he has hopes
and fears, expectations and disappointments, griefs
and joys, and friends and enemies, like a courtier
or a statesman ; nor can I conceive why his affairs
should not excite curiosity as much as the whisper of
a drawing-room, or the factions of a camp.

Nothing detains the reader's attention more powerfully than deep involutions of distress, or sudden
vicissitudes of fortune ; and these might be abun-
dantly afforded by memoirs of the sons of literature.
They are entangled by contracts which they know
not how to fulfil, and obliged to write on subjects
which they do not understand. Every publication
is a new period of time, from which some increase or
declension of fame is to be reckoned. The gradations of a hero's life are from battle to battle, and of
an author's from book to book.

Success and miscarriage have the same effects in
all conditions. The prosperous are feared, hated,
and flattered ; and the unfortunate avoided, pitied,
and despised. No sooner is a book published than
the writer may judge of the opinion of the world.
If his acquaintance press round him in publick
places, or salute him from the other side of the
street ; if invitations to dinner come thick upon him,
and those with whom he dines keep him to supper ;
if the ladies turn to him when his coat is plain, and
the footmen serve him with attention and alacrity ;
he may be sure that his work has been praised by
some leader of literary fashions.

Of declining reputation the symptoms are not

less easily observed.   If the author enters a coffee-
house, he has a box to himself; if he calls at a book-
seller's, the boy turns his back; and what is the most
fatal of all prognosticks, authors will visit him in a
morning, and talk to him hour after hour of the malevolence of criticks, the neglect of merit, the bad
taste of the age, and the candour of posterity.

All this, modified and varied by accident and
custom, would form very amusing scenes of biography, and might recreate many a mind which is
very little delighted with conspiracies or battles,
intrigues of a court, or debates of a parliament;
to this might be added all the changes of the countenance of a patron, traced from the first glow which
flattery raises in his cheek, through ardour of fondness, vehemence of promise, magnificence of praise,
excuse of delay, and lamentation of inability, to the
last chill look of final dismission, when the one grows
weary of soliciting, and the other of hearing solicitation.

Thus copious are the materials which have been
hitherto suffered to lie neglected, while the repositories of every family that has produced a soldier or
a minister are ransacked, and libraries are crowded
with useless folios of state papers which will never
be read, and which contribute nothing to valuable
knowledge.

I hope the learned will be taught to know their
own strength and their value, and instead of de-
voting their lives to the honour of those who seldom
thank them for their labours, resolve at last to do
justice to themselves.

NUMB. 103. SATURDAY, *April 5*, 1760.

Respicere ad longæ jussit spatia ultima τitæ. JUV.

MUCH of the pain and pleasure of mankind arises from the conjectures which every one makes of the thoughts of others; we all enjoy praise which we do not hear, and resent contempt which we do not see. The Idler may therefore be forgiven, if he suffers his imagination to represent to him what his readers will say or think when they are informed that they have now his last paper in their hands.

Value is more frequently raised by scarcity than by use. That which lay neglected when it was common, rises in estimation as its quantity becomes less. We seldom learn the true want of what we have till it is discovered that we can have no more.

This essay will, perhaps, be read with care even by those who have not yet attended to any other; and he that finds this late attention recompensed, will not forbear to wish that he had bestowed it sooner.

Though the Idler and his readers have contracted no close friendship, they are perhaps both unwilling to part. There are few things not purely evil, of which we can say, without some emotion of uneasiness, *this is the last.* Those who never could agree together, shed tears when mutual discontent has determined them to final separation ; of a place which has been frequently visited, though without pleasure, the last look is taken with heaviness of heart; and the Idler, with all his chillness of tranquillity, is not wholly unaffected by the thought that his last essay is now before him.

This secret horror of the last is inseparable from a thinking being, whose life is limited, and to whom death is dreadful. We always make a secret comparison between a part and the whole; the termination of any period of life reminds us that life itself has likewise its termination; when we have done any thing for the last time, we involuntarily reflect that a part of the days allotted us is past, and that as more is past there is less remaining.

It is very happily and kindly provided, that in every life there are certain pauses and interruptions, which force consideration upon the careless, and seriousness upon the light; points of time where one course of action ends, and another begins; and by vicissitudes of fortune, or alteration of employment, by change of place or loss of friendship, we are forced to say of something, *this is the last.*

An even and unvaried tenour of life always hides from our apprehension the approach of its end. Succession is not perceived but by variation; he that lives to-day as he lived yesterday, and expects that, as the present day is, such will be the morrow, easily conceives time as running in a circle and returning to itself. The uncertainty of our duration is impressed commonly by dissimilitude of condition; it is only by finding life changeable that we are reminded of its shortness.

This conviction, however forcible at every new impression, is every moment fading from the mind; and partly by the inevitable incursion of new images, and partly by voluntary exclusion of unwelcome thoughts, we are again exposed to the universal fallacy; and we must do another thing for the last time, before we consider that the time is nigh when we shall do no more.

As the last Idler is published in that solemn week which the Christian world has always set apart for the examination of the conscience, the review of life, the extinction of earthly desires, and the renovation of holy purposes; I hope that my readers are already disposed to view every incident with seriousness, and improve it by meditation; and that, when they see this series of trifles brought to a conclusion, they will consider that, by outliving the Idler, they have passed weeks, months, and years, which are now no longer in their power; that an end must in time be put to every thing great as to every thing little; that to life must come its last hour, and to this system of being its last day, the hour at which probation ceases, and repentance will be vain; the day in which every work of the hand and imagination of the heart shall be brought to judgment, and an everlasting futurity shall be determined by the past.

THE IDLER. Numb. 22.*

MANY naturalists are of opinion, that the animals which we commonly consider as mute, have the power of imparting their thoughts to one another. That they can express general sensations is very certain; every being that can utter sounds, has a different voice for pleasure and for pain. The hound informs his fellows when he scents his game; the hen calls her chickens to their food by her cluck, and drives them from danger by her scream.

Birds have the greatest variety of notes; they have indeed a variety, which seems almost sufficient to make a speech adequate to the purposes of a life, which is regulated by instinct, and can admit little change or improvement. To the cries of birds, curiosity or superstition has been always attentive; many have studied the language of the feathered tribes, and some have boasted that they understood it.

The most skilful or most confident interpreters of the sylvan dialogues have been commonly found among

* This was the original No. 22, but on the republication of the work in volumes, Dr. Johnson substituted what now stands under that head. C.

the philosophers of the east, in a country where the calmness of the air, and the mildness of the seasons, allow the student to pass a great part of the year in groves and bowers. But what may be done in one place by peculiar opportunities, may be performed in another by peculiar diligence. A shepherd of Bohemia has, by long abode in the forests, enabled himself to understand the voice of birds; at least he relates with great confidence a story, of which the credibility is left to be considered by the learned.

As I was sitting (said he) within a hollow rock, and watching my sheep that fed in the valley, I heard two vultures interchangeably crying on the summit of the cliff. Both voices were earnest and deliberate. My curiosity prevailed over my care of the flock; I climbed slowly and silently from crag to crag, concealed among the shrubs, till I found a cavity where I might sit and listen without suffering, or giving disturbance.

I soon perceived, that my labour would be well repaid; for an old vulture was sitting on a naked prominence, with her young about her, whom she was instructing in the arts of a vulture's life, and preparing, by the last lecture, for their final dismission to the mountains and the skies.

My children, said the old vulture, you will the less want my instructions, because you have had my practice before your eyes; you have seen me snatch from the farm the household fowl, you have seen me seize the leveret in the bush, and the kid in the pasture; you know how to fix your talons, and how to balance your flight when you are laden with your prey. But you remember the taste of more delicious food ; I have often regaled you with the flesh of man. Tell us, said the young vultures, where man may be found, and how he may be known ; his flesh is surely the natural food of a vulture. Why have you never brought a man in your talons to the nest ? He is too bulky, said the mother ; when we find a man, we can only tear away his flesh, and leave his bones upon the ground. Since man is so big, said the young ones, how do you kill him ? You are afraid of the wolf and of the bear, by what power are vultures superior to man ? is man more defenceless than a sheep? We have not the strength of man, returned the mother, and I am sometimes in doubt whether we have the subtilty ; and the vultures would seldom feast upon his flesh, had not nature, that devoted him to our uses, infused into him a strange ferocity, which I have never observed in any other being that feeds upon the earth. Two herds of men will often meet and shake the earth with noise, and fill the air with fire. When you hear noise and see fire, with flashes along the ground, hasten to the place with your swiftest wing, for men are surely destroying one another ; you will then find the ground smoking with blood, and covered with carcasses, of which many are dismembered and mangled for the convenience of the vulture. But when men have killed their prey, said the pupil, why do they not eat it ? When the wolf has killed a sheep, he suffers not the vulture to touch it till he has satisfied himself. Is not man another kind of wolf? Man, said the mother, is the only beast who kills that which he does not devour, and this quality makes him so much a

benefactor to our species.   If men kill our prey and
lay it in our way, said the young one, what need
shall we have of labouring for ourselves?   Because
man will, sometimes, replied the mother, remain for
a long time quiet in his den.   The old vultures will
tell you when you are to watch his motions.   When
you see men in great numbers moving close together,
like a flight of storks, you may conclude that they are
hunting, and that you will soon revel in human blood.
But still, said the young one, I would gladly know
the reason of this mutual slaughter.   I could never kill
what I could not eat.   My child, said the mother,
this is a question which I cannot answer, though I
am reckoned the most subtile bird of the mountain.
When I was young, I used frequently to visit the
ayry of an old vulture, who dwelt upon the Carpa-
thian rocks; he had made many observations; he
knew the places that afforded prey round his habitation, as far in every direction as the strongest wing
can fly between the rising and setting of the summer
sun; he had fed year after year on the entrails of
men.   His opinion was, that men had only the appearance of animal life, being really vegetables with
a power of motion; and that as the boughs of an oak
are dashed together by the storm, that swine may
fatten upon the falling acorns, so men are by some
unaccountable power driven one against another, till
they lose their motion, that vultures may be fed.
Others think they have observed something of contrivance and policy among these mischievous beings;
and those that hover more closely round them, pretend, that there is, in every herd, one that gives di-

rections to the rest, and seems to be more eminently delighted with a wide carnage.   What it is that entitles him to such pre-eminence we know not; he is seldom the biggest or the swiftest, but he shews by his eagerness and diligence that he is, more than any of the others, a friend to vultures.

THE

HISTORY

OF

RASSELAS,

PRINCE OF ABISSINIA.

This work was published in March or April 1759. Dr. Johnson wrote it in order to defray the expences of his mother's funeral, and pay some little debts which she had left. He told Sir Joshua Reynolds that he composed it in the evenings of one week, sent it to the press in portions as it was written, and had never since read it over. Mr. Strahan, Mr. Johnston, and Mr. Dodsley, purchased it for a hundred pounds, but afterwards paid him twenty-five pounds more, when it came to a second edition. None of his writings has been so extensively diffused over Europe: for it has been translated into most, if not all, of the modern languages. Boswell.

THE

HISTORY

OF

R A S S E L A S,

PRINCE OF ABISSINIA.

CHAP. I.

DESCRIPTION OF A PALACE IN A VALLEY.

Ye who listen with credulity to the whispers of
fancy, and pursue with eagerness the phantoms of
hope ; who expect that age will perform the promises
of youth, and that the deficiencies of the present day
will be supplied by the morrow ; attend to the history of Rasselas, Prince of Abissinia.

Rasselas was the fourth son of the mighty emperour, in whose dominions the Father of Waters
begins his course ; whose bounty pours down the
streams of plenty, and scatters over half the world the
harvests of Egypt.

According to the custom which has descended from
age to age among the monarchs of the torrid zone,
Rasselas was confined in a private palace, with the
other sons and daughters of Abissinian royalty, till
the order of succession should call him to the throne.

The place which the wisdom or policy of antiquity had destined for the residence of the Abissinian princes, was a spacious valley in the kingdom of Amhara, surrounded on every side by mountains, of which the summits overhang the middle part. The only passage, by which it could be entered, was a cavern that passed under a rock, of which it has long been disputed whether it was the work of nature or of human industry. The outlet of the cavern was concealed by thick wood, and the mouth which opened into the valley was closed with gates of iron, forged by the artificers of ancient days, so massy that no man could without the help of engines open or shut them.

From the mountains on every side, rivulets descended that filled all the valley with verdure and fertility, and formed a lake in the middle inhabited by fish of every species, and frequented by every fowl whom nature has taught to dip the wing in water. This lake discharged its superfluities by a stream which entered a dark cleft of the mountain on the northern side, and fell with dreadful noise from precipice to precipice till it was heard no more.

The sides of the mountains were covered with trees, the banks of the brooks were diversified with flowers ; every blast shook spices from the rocks, and every month dropped fruits upon the ground. All animals that bite the grass, or browse the shrub, whether wild or tame, wandered in this extensive circuit, secured from beasts of prey by the mountains which confined them. On one part were flocks and herds feeding in the pastures, on another all the beasts of chase frisking in the lawns ; the sprightly kid was bounding on the rocks, the subtle monkey frolicking in the trees, and the solemn elephant reposing in the shade. All the diversities of the world were brought together, the blessings of nature were collected, and its evils extracted and excluded.

The valley, wide and fruitful, supplied its inhabitants with the necessaries of life; and all delights and superfluities were added at the annual visit which the emperour paid his children, when the iron gate was opened to the sound of musick; and during eight days every one that resided in the valley was required to propose whatever might contribute to make seclusion pleasant, to fill up the vacancies of attention, and lessen the tediousness of time. Every desire was immediately granted. All the artificers of pleasure were called to gladden the festivity; the musicians exerted the power of harmony, and the dancers showed their activity before the princes, in hope that they should pass their lives in this blissful captivity, to which those only were admitted, whose performance was thought able to add novelty to luxury. Such was the appearance of security and delight which this retirement afforded, that they, to whom it was new, always desired that it might be perpetual; and as those, on whom the iron gate had once closed, were never suffered to return, the effect of long experience could not be known. Thus every year produced new schemes of delight, and new competitors for imprisonment.

The palace stood on an eminence raised about thirty paces above the surface of the lake. It was divided into many squares or courts, built with greater or less magnificence, according to the rank of those for whom they were designed. The roofs were turned into arches of massy stone, joined by a cement that grew harder by time, and the building stood from century to century deriding the solstitial rains and equinoctial hurricanes, without need of reparation.

This house, which was so large as to be fully known to none but some ancient officers who successively inherited the secrets of the place, was built as if suspicion herself had dictated the plan. To every room there was an open and secret passage, every square had a communication with the rest, either from the upper stories by private galleries, or by subterranean passages from the lower apartments. Many of the columns had unsuspected cavities, in which a long race of monarchs had reposited their treasures. They then closed up the opening with marble, which was never to be removed but in the utmost exigencies of the kingdom ; and recorded their accumulations in a book which was itself concealed in a tower not entered but by the emperour, attended by the prince who stood next in succession.

CHAP. II.

THE DISCONTENT OF RASSELAS IN THE HAPPY VALLEY.

HERE the sons and daughters of Abissinia lived only to know the soft vicissitudes of pleasure and repose, attended by all that were skilful to delight, and gratified with whatever the senses can enjoy. They wandered in gardens of fragrance, and slept in the fortresses of security. Every art was practised to make them pleased with their own condition. The sages who instructed them, told them of nothing but the miseries of publick life, and described all beyond the mountains as regions of calamity, where discord was always raging, and where man preyed upon man.

To heighten their opinion of their own felicity, they were daily entertained with songs, the subject of which was the *happy valley.* Their appetites were excited by frequent enumerations of different enjoyments, and revelry and merriment was the business of every hour from the dawn of morning to the close of even.

These methods were generally successful ; few of the princes had ever wished to enlarge their bounds, but passed their lives in full conviction that they had all within their reach that art or nature could bestow, and pitied those whom fate had excluded from this seat of tranquillity, as the sport of chance and the slaves of misery.

Thus they rose in the morning and lay down at night, pleased with each other and with themselves, all but Rasselas, who in the twenty-sixth year of his age began to withdraw himself from their pastimes and assemblies, and to delight in solitary walks and silent meditation. He often sat before tables covered with luxury, and forgot to taste the dainties that were placed before him : he rose abruptly in the midst of the song, and hastily retired beyond the sound of musick. His attendants observed the change, and endeavoured to renew his love of pleasure : he neglected their officiousness, repulsed their invitations, and spent day after day on the banks of rivulets sheltered with trees, where he sometimes listened to the birds in the branches, sometimes observed the fish playing in the stream, and anon cast his eyes upon the pastures and mountains filled with animals, of which some were biting the herbage, and some sleeping among the bushes.

This singularity of his humour made him much observed. One of the Sages, in whose conversation he had formerly delighted, followed him secretly, in. hope of discovering the cause of his disquiet. Rasselas, who knew not that any one was near him, having for some time fixed his eyes upon the goats that were browsing among the rocks, began to compare their condition with his own.

" What, said he, makes the difference between man and all the rest of the animal creation? Every beast that strays beside me has the same corporal necessities with myself; he is hungry and crops the grass, he is thirsty and drinks the stream, his thirst and hunger are appeased, he is satisfied and sleeps: he rises again and is hungry, he is again fed and is at rest. I am hungry and thirsty like him, but when thirst and hunger cease I am not at rest; I am, like him, pained with want, but am not, like him, satisfied with fulness. The intermediate hours are tedious and gloomy; I long again to be hungry that I may again quicken my attention. The birds peck the berries or the corn, and fly away to the groves, where they sit in seeming happiness on the branches, and waste their lives in tuning one unvaried series of sounds. I likewise can call the lutanist and the singer, but the sounds that pleased me yesterday weary me to-day, and will grow yet more wearisome to-morrow. I can discover within me no power of perception which is not glutted with its proper plea-

sure, yet I do not feel myself delighted. Man surely
has some latent sense for which this place affords no
gratification, or he has some desires distinct from
sense, which must be satisfied before he can be
happy."

After this he lifted up his head, and seeing the
moon rising, walked towards the palace. As he
passed through the fields, and saw the animals around
him, " Ye, said he, are happy, and need not envy
me that walk thus among you, burdened with myself;
nor do I, ye gentle beings, envy your felicity; for it
is not the felicity of man. I have many distresses from
which ye are free; I fear pain when I do not feel it;
I sometimes shrink at evils recollected, and sometimes
start at evils anticipated : surely the equity of Providence has balanced peculiar sufferings with peculiar
enjoyments."

With observations like these the prince amused
himself as he returned, uttering them with a plaintive
voice, yet with a look that discovered him to feel some
complacence in his own perspicacity, and to receive
some solace of the miseries of life, from consciousness
of the delicacy with which he felt, and the eloquence
with which he bewailed them. He mingled cheerfully in the diversions of the evening, and all rejoiced
to find that his heart was lightened.

CHAP. III.

THE WANTS OF HIM THAT WANTS NOTHING.

ON the next day his old instructor, imagining that
he had now made himself acquainted with his disease
of mind, was in hope of curing it by counsel, and offi-

ciously sought an opportunity of conference, which the prince, having long considered him as one whose intellects were exhausted, was not very willing to afford : " Why, said he, does this man thus obtrude upon me ? shall I be never suffered to forget those lectures which pleased only while they were new, and to become new again must be forgotten ?" He then walked into the wood, and composed himself to his usual meditations, when before his thoughts had taken any settled form, he perceived his pursuer at his side, and was at first prompted by his impatience to go hastily away ; but being unwilling to offend a man whom he had once reverenced and still loved, he invited him to sit down with him on the bank.

The old man thus encouraged, began to lament the change which had been lately observed in the prince, and to inquire why he so often retired from the pleasures of the palace, to loneliness and silence. " I fly from pleasure, said the prince, because pleasure has ceased to please ; I am lonely because I am miserable, and am unwilling to cloud with my presence the happiness of others." " You, Sir, said the sage, are the first who has complained of misery in the *happy valley*. I hope to convince you that your complaints have no real cause. You are here in full possession of all that the emperour of Abissinia can bestow ; here is neither labour to be endured nor danger to be dreaded, yet here is all that labour or danger can procure or purchase. Look round and tell me which of your wants is without supply : if you want nothing, how are you unhappy ?"

" That I want nothing, said the prince, or that I

know not what I want, is the cause of my complaint ; if I had any known want, I should have a certain wish ; that wish would excite endeavour, and I should not then repine to see the sun move so slowly towards the western mountain, or lament when the day breaks and sleep will no longer hide me from myself. When I see the kids and the lambs chasing one another, I fancy that I should be happy if I had something to pursue. But, possessing all that I can want, I find one day and one hour exactly like another, except that the latter is still more tedious than the former. Let your experience inform me how the day may now seem as short as in my childhood, while nature was yet fresh, and every moment showed me what I never had observed before. I have already enjoyed too much ; give me something to desire."

The old man was surprised at this new species of affliction, and knew not what to reply, yet was unwilling to be silent. " Sir, said he, if you had seen the miseries of the world, you would know how to value your present state." " Now, said the prince, you have given me something to desire ; I shall long to see the miseries of the world, since the sight of them is necessary to happiness."

CHAP. IV.

THE PRINCE CONTINUES TO GRIEVE AND MUSE.

At this time the sound of musick proclaimed the hour of repast, and the conversation was concluded. The old man went away sufficiently discontented, to find that his reasonings had produced the only conclusion which they were intended to prevent. But in the decline of life shame and grief are of short duration ; whether it be that we bear easily what we have borne long, or that, finding ourselves in age less regarded, we less regard others; or that we look with slight regard upon afflictions, to which we know that the hand of death is about to put an end.

The prince, whose views were extended to a wider space, could not speedily quiet his emotions. He had been before terrified at the length of life which nature promised him, because he considered that in a long time much must be endured ; he now rejoiced in his youth, because in many years much might be done.

This first beam of hope, that had been ever darted into his mind, rekindled youth in his cheeks, and doubled the lustre of his eyes. He was fired with the desire of doing something, though he knew not yet with distinctness, either end or means.

He was now no longer gloomy and unsocial; but, considering himself as master of a secret stock of happiness, which he could enjoy only by concealing it, he affected to be busy in all schemes of diversion, and endeavoured to make others pleased with the state of which he himself was weary. But pleasures never can be so multiplied or continued, as not to leave much of life unemployed ; there were many hours, both of the night and day, which he could spend without suspicion in solitary thought. The load of life was much lightened : he went eagerly into the assemblies, because he supposed the frequency of his presence necessary to the success of his purposes ; he retired gladly to privacy, because he had now a subject of thought.

His chief amusement was to picture to himself that world which he had never seen ; to place himself in various conditions ; to be entangled in imaginary difficulties, and to be engaged in wild adventures : but his benevolence always terminated his projects in the relief of distress, the detection of fraud, the defeat of oppression, and the diffusion of happiness.

Thus passed twenty months of the life of Rasselas. He busied himself so intensely in visionary bustle, that he forgot his real solitude, and, amidst hourly preparations for the various incidents of human affairs, neglected to consider by what means he should mingle with mankind.

One day, as he was sitting on a bank, he feigned to himself an orphan virgin robbed of her little portion by a treacherous lover, and crying after him for restitution and redress. So strongly was the image impressed upon his mind, that he started up in the maid's defence, and ran forward to seize the plunderer with all the eagerness of real pursuit. Fear naturally quickens the flight of guilt. Rasselas could not catch the fugitive with his utmost efforts ; but, resolving to weary by perseverance, him whom he could not surpass in speed, he pressed on till the foot of the mountain stopped his course.

Here he recollected himself, and smiled at his own useless impetuosity. Then raising his eyes to the mountain, " This, said he, is the fatal obstacle that hinders at once the enjoyment of pleasure, and the exercise of virtue. How long is it that my hopes and wishes have flown beyond this boundary of my life, which yet I never have attempted to surmount !"

Struck with this reflection, he sat down to muse;
and remembered, that since he first resolved to escape
from his confinement, the sun had passed twice over
him in his annual course.   He now felt a degree of
regret with which he had never been before acquainted.
He considered how much might have been done in
the time which had passed, and left nothing real behind it. He compared twenty months with the life of
man.   " In life, said he, is not to be counted the ignorance of infancy, or imbecility of age.   We are
long before we are able to think, and we soon cease
from the power of acting. The true period of human
existence may be reasonably estimated at forty years,
of which I have mused away the four and twentieth
part.   What I have lost was certain, for I have certainly possessed it ; but of twenty months to come who
can assure me ?"

The consciousness of his own folly pierced him
deeply, and he was long before he could be reconciled to himself.   " The rest of my time, said he,
has been lost by the crime or folly of my ancestors,
and the absurd institutions of my country ; I remember it with disgust, yet without remorse : but
the months that have passed since new light darted
into my soul, since I formed a scheme of reasonable
felicity, have been squandered by my own fault.
I have lost that which can never be restored : I
have seen the sun rise and set for twenty months,
an idle gazer on the light of heaven : In this time
the birds have left the nest of their mother, and committed themselves to the woods and to the skies :
the kid has forsaken the teat, and learned by

degrees to climb the rocks in quest of independent sustenance. I only have made no advances, but am still helpless and ignorant. The moon, by more than twenty changes, admonished me of the flux of life ; the stream that rolled before my feet upbraided my inactivity. I sat feasting on intellectual luxury, regardless alike of the examples of the earth, and the instructions of the planets. Twenty months are passed, who shall restore them ?"

These sorrowful meditations fastened upon his mind ; he passed four months in resolving to lose no more time in idle resolves, and was awakened to more vigorous exertion, by hearing a maid, who had broken a porcelain cup, remark, that what cannot be repaired is not to be regretted.

This was obvious ; and Rasselas reproached himself that he had not discovered it, having not known, or not considered, how many useful hints are obtained by chance, and how often the mind, hurried by her own ardour to distant views, neglects the truths that lie open before her. He, for a few hours, regretted his regret, and from that time bent his whole mind upon the means of escaping from the valley of happiness.

CHAP. V.

THE PRINCE MEDITATES HIS ESCAPE.

HE now found that it would be very difficult to effect that which it was very easy to suppose effected. When he looked round about him, he saw himself confined by the bars of nature which had never yet been broken, and by the gate through which none that once had passed it were ever able to return. He was now impatient as an eagle in a grate. He passed week after week in clambering the mountains, to see if there was any aperture which the bushes might conceal, but found all the summits inaccessible by their prominence. The iron gate he despaired to open ; for it was not only secured with all the power of art, but was always watched by successive sentinels, and was by its position exposed to the perpetual observation of all the inhabitants.

He then examined the cavern through which the waters of the lake were discharged ; and, looking down at a time when the sun shone strongly upon its mouth, he discovered it to be full of broken rocks, which though they permitted the stream to flow through many narrow passages, would stop any body of solid bulk. He returned discouraged and dejected ; but having now known the blessing of hope, resolved never to despair.

In these fruitless searches he spent ten months. The time, however, passed cheerfully away : in the morning he rose with new hope, in the evening applauded his own diligence, and in the night slept sound after his fatigue. He met a thousand amusements which beguiled his labour, and diversified his thoughts. He discerned the various instincts of animals and properties of plants, and found the place replete with wonders, of which he purposed to solace himself with the contemplation, if he should never be able to accomplish his flight ; rejoicing that his endeavours, though yet unsuccessful, had supplied him with a source of inexhaustible inquiry.

But his original curiosity was not yet abated ; he

resolved to obtain some knowledge of the ways of men. His wish still continued, but his hope grew less. He ceased to survey any longer the walls of his prison, and spared to search by new toils for interstices which he knew could not be found, yet determined to keep his design always in view, and lay hold on any expedient that time should offer.

CHAP VI.

A DISSERTATION ON THE ART OF FLYING.

AMONG the artists that had been allured into the happy valley to labour for the accommodation and pleasure of its inhabitants, was a man eminent for his knowledge of the mechanick powers, who had contrived many engines both of use and recreation. By a wheel, which the stream turned, he forced the water into a tower, whence it was distributed to all the apartments of the palace. He erected a pavilion in the garden, around which he kept the air always cool by artificial showers. One of the groves, appropriated to the ladies, was ventilated by fans, to which the rivulet that ran through it gave a constant motion ; and instruments of soft musick were placed at proper distances, of which some played by the impulse of the wind, and some by the power of the stream.

This artist was sometimes visited by Rasselas, who was pleased with every kind of knowledge, imagining that the time would come when all his acquisitions should be of use to him in the open world. He came one day to amuse himself in his usual manner, and found the master busy in building a sailing chariot: he saw that the design was practicable upon a level surface, and with expressions of great esteem solicited its completion. The workman was pleased to find himself so much regarded by the prince, and resolved to gain yet higher honours. " Sir, said he, you have seen but a small part of what the mechanick sciences can perform. I have been long of opinion, that instead of the tardy conveyance of ships and chariots, man might use the swifter migration of wings; that the fields of air are open to knowledge, and that only ignorance and idleness need crawl upon the ground."

This hint rekindled the prince's desire of passing the mountains; having seen what the mechanist had already performed, he was willing to fancy that he could do more; yet resolved to inquire further, before he suffered hope to afflict him by disappointment. " I am afraid, said he to the artist, that your imagination prevails over your skill, and that you now tell me rather what you wish, than what you know. Every animal has his element assigned him; the birds have the air, and man and beasts the earth." " So replied the mechanist, fishes have the water, in which yet beasts can swim by nature, and men by art. He that can swim needs not despair to fly: to swim is to fly in a grosser fluid, and to fly is to swim in a subtler. We are only to proportion our power of resistance to the different density of matter through which we are to pass. You will be necessarily upborne by the air, if you can renew any impulse upon it, faster than the air can recede from the pressure."

" But the exercise of swimming, said the prince, is very laborious; the strongest limbs are soon wearied; I am afraid the act of flying will be yet more violent, and wings will be of no great use, unless we can fly further than we can swim."

" The labour of rising from the ground, said the artist, will be great, as we see it in the heavier domestick fowls, but as we mount higher, the earth's attraction, and the body's gravity, will be gradually diminished till we shall arrive at a region where the man will float in the air without any tendency to fall; no care will then be necessary but to move forwards, which the gentlest impulse will effect. You, Sir, whose curiosity is so extensive, will easily conceive with what pleasure a philosopher, furnished with wings, and hovering in the sky, would see the earth, and all its inhabitants, rolling beneath him, and presenting to him successively, by its diurnal motion, all the countries within the same parallel. How must it amuse the pendent spectator to see the moving scene of land and ocean, cities and deserts ! To survey with equal security the marts of trade, and the fields of battle; mountains infested by barbarians, and fruitful regions gladdened by plenty, and lulled by peace ? How easily shall we then trace the Nile through all his passage; pass over to distant regions, and examine the face of nature from one extremity of the earth to the other !"

"All this, said the prince, is much to be desired; but I am afraid that no man will be able to breathe in these regions of speculation and tranquillity. I have been told, that respiration is difficult upon lofty mountains, yet from these precipices, though so high as to produce great tenuity of air, it is very easy to fall: therefore I suspect, that from any height, where life can be supported, there may be danger of too quick descent."

" Nothing, replied the artist, will ever be attempted, if all possible objections must be first overcome. If you will favour my project, I will try the first flight at my own hazard. I have considered the structure of all volant animals, and find the folding continuity of the bat's wings most easily accommodated to the human form. Upon this model I shall begin my task to-morrow, and in a year expect to tower into the air beyond the malice and pursuit of man. But I will work only on this condition, that the art shall not be divulged, and that you shall not require me to make wings for any but ourselves."

" Why, said Rasselas, should you envy others so great an advantage? All skill ought to be exerted for universal good; every man has owed much to others, and ought to repay the kindness that he has received."

" If men were all virtuous, returned the artist, I should with great alacrity teach them all to fly. But what would be the security of the good if the bad could at pleasure invade them from the sky? Against an army sailing through the clouds, neither walls, nor mountains, nor seas, could afford any security. A flight of northern savages might hover in the wind, and light at once with irresistible violence upon the capital of a fruitful region that was rolling under them. Even this valley, the retreat of princes, the abode of happiness, might be violated by the sudden descent of some of the naked nations that swarm on the coast of the southern sea."

The prince promised secrecy, and waited for the performance, not wholly hopeless of success. He visited the work from time to time, observed its progress, and remarked many ingenious contrivances to facilitate motion, and unite levity with strength. The artist was every day more certain that he should leave vultures and eagles behind him, and the contagion of his confidence seized upon the prince.

In a year the wings were finished, and, on a morning appointed, the maker appeared furnished for flight on a little promontory : he waved his pinions a while to gather air, then leaped from his stand, and in an instant dropped into the lake. His wings, which were of no use in the air, sustained him in the water, and the prince drew him to land, half dead with terrour and vexation.

CHAP. VII.

THE PRINCE FINDS A MAN OF LEARNING.

THE prince was not much afflicted by this disaster, having suffered himself to hope for a happier event, only because he had no other means of escape in view. He still persisted in his design to leave the happy valley by the first opportunity.

His imagination was now at a stand ; he had no prospect of entering into the world ; and notwithstanding all his endeavours to support himself, discontent by degrees preyed upon him, and he began again to lose his thoughts in sadness, when the rainy season, which in these countries is periodical, made it inconvenient to wander in the woods.

The rain continued longer and with more violence than had been ever known : the clouds broke on the surrounding mountains, and the torrents streamed into the plain on every side, till the cavern was too narrow to discharge the water. The lake overflowed its banks, and all the level of the valley was covered with the inundation. The eminence, on which the palace was built, and some other spots of rising ground, were all that the eye could now discover. The herds and flocks left the pastures, and both the wild beasts and the tame retreated to the mountains.

This inundation confined all the princes to domestick amusements, and the attention of Rasselas was particularly seized by a poem, which Imlac rehearsed, upon the various conditions of humanity. He commanded the poet to attend him in his apartment, and recite his verses a second time; then entering into familiar talk, he thought himself happy in having found a man who knew the world so well, and could so skilfully paint the scenes of life. He asked a thousand questions about things, to which, though common to all other mortals, his confinement from childhood had kept him a stranger. The poet pitied his ignorance, and loved his curiosity, and entertained him from day to day with novelty and instruction, so that the prince regretted the necessity of sleep, and longed till the morning should renew his pleasure.

As they were sitting together, the prince commanded Imlac to relate his history, and to tell by what accident he was forced, or by what motive induced, to close his life in the happy valley. As he was going to begin his narrative, Rasselas was called to a concert, and obliged to restrain his curiosity till the evening.

CHAP. VIII.

THE HISTORY OF IMLAC.

THE close of the day is, in the regions of the torrid zone, the only season of diversion and entertainment, and it was therefore midnight before the musick ceased, and the princesses retired. Rasselas then called for his companion, and required him to begin the story of his life.

"Sir, said Imlac, my history will not be long: the life that is devoted to knowledge passes silently away, and is very little diversified by events. To talk in publick, to think in solitude, to read and to hear, to inquire, and answer inquiries, is the business of a scholar. He wanders about the world without pomp or terrour, and is neither known nor valued but by men like himself.

"I was born in the kingdom of Goiama, at no great distance from the fountain of the Nile. My father was a wealthy merchant, who traded between the inland countries of Africk and the ports of the Red Sea. He was honest, frugal, and diligent, but of mean sentiments, and narrow comprehension: he desired only to be rich, and to conceal his riches, lest he should be spoiled by the governours of the province."

"Surely, said the prince, my father must be neg-

ligent of his charge, if any man in his dominions
dares take that which belongs to another. Does he
not know that kings are accountable for injustice
permitted as well as done? If I were emperour, not
the meanest of my subjects should be oppressed with
impunity. My blood boils when I am told that a
merchant durst not enjoy his honest gains for fear of
losing them by the rapacity of power. Name the
governour who robbed the people, that I may declare
his crimes to the emperour."

"Sir, said Imlac, your ardour is the natural effect
of virtue animated by youth: the time will come
when you will acquit your father, and perhaps hear
with less impatience of the governour. Oppression is,
in the Abissinian dominions, neither frequent nor
tolerated; but no form of government has been yet
discovered, by which cruelty can be wholly prevented.
Subordination supposes power on one part, and subjection on the other; and if power be in the hands of
men, it will sometimes be abused. The vigilance of
the supreme magistrate may do much, but much will
still remain undone. He can never know all the
crimes that are committed, and can seldom punish all
that he knows."

"This, said the prince, I do not understand, but
I had rather hear thee than dispute. Continue thy
narration."

"My father, proceeded Imlac, originally intended
that I should have no other education than such as
might qualify me for commerce; and discovering in
me great strength of memory, and quickness of apprehension, often declared his hope that I should be
some time the richest man in Abissinia."

" Why, said the prince, did thy father desire the increase of his wealth, when it was already greater than he durst discover or enjoy? I am unwilling to doubt thy veracity, yet inconsistencies cannot both be true."

" Inconsistencies, answered Imlac, cannot both be right, but, imputed to man, they may both be true. Yet diversity is not inconsistency. My father might expect a time of greater security. However, some desire is necessary to keep life in motion, and he, whose real wants are supplied, must admit those of fancy."

" This, said the prince, I can in some measure conceive. I repent that I interrupted thee."

" With this hope, proceeded Imlac, he sent me to school; but when I had once found the delight of knowledge, and felt the pleasure of intelligence and the pride of invention, I began silently to despise riches, and determined to disappoint the purpose of my father, whose grossness of conception raised my pity. I was twenty years old before his tenderness would expose me to the fatigue of travel, in which time I had been instructed, by successive masters, in all the literature of my native country. As every hour taught me something new, I lived in a continual course of gratifications; but as I advanced towards manhood, I lost much of the reverence with which I had been used to look on my instructors; because, when the lesson was ended, I did not find them wiser or better than common men.

" At length my father resolved to initiate me in commerce, and opening one of his subterranean treasuries, counted out ten thousand pieces of gold. This, young man, said he, is the stock with which you must negociate. I began with less than the fifth part, and you see how diligence and parsimony have increased it. This is your own, to waste or to improve. If you squander it by negligence or caprice, you must wait for my death before you will be rich: if, in four years, you double your stock, we will thenceforward let subordination cease, and live together as friends and partners; for he shall always be equal with me, who is equally skilled in the art of growing rich.

" We laid our money upon camels, concealed in bales of cheap goods, and travelled to the shore of the Red Sea. When I cast my eye on the expanse of waters, my heart bounded like that of a prisoner escaped. I felt an unextinguishable curiosity kindle in my mind, and resolved to snatch this opportunity of seeing the manners of other nations, and of learning sciences unknown in Abissinia.

" I remembered that my father had obliged me to the improvement of my stock, not by a promise which I ought not to violate, but by a penalty which I was at liberty to incur; and therefore determined to gratify my predominant desire, and by drinking at the fountains of knowledge, to quench the thirst of curiosity.

" As I was supposed to trade without connexion with my father, it was easy for me to become acquainted with the master of a ship, and procure a passage to some other country. I had no motives of choice to regulate my voyage; it was sufficient for me that wherever I wandered, I should see a country which I had not seen before. I therefore entered a ship bound for Surat, having left a letter for my father declaring my intention.

CHAP. IX.

THE HISTORY OF IMLAC CONTINUED.

" WHEN I first entered upon the world of waters, and lost sight of land, I looked round about me with pleasing terrour, and thinking my soul enlarged by the boundless prospect, imagined that I could gaze round for ever without satiety ; but, in a short time, I grew weary of looking on barren uniformity, where I could only see again what I had already seen. I then descended into the ship, and doubted for a while whether all my future pleasures would not end like this, in disgust and disappointment. Yet, surely, said I, the ocean and the land are very different ; the only variety of water is rest and motion, but the earth has mountains and valleys, deserts and cities : it is inhabited by men of different customs and contrary opinions ; and I may hope to find variety in life, though I should miss it in nature.

" With this thought I quieted my mind, and amused myself during the voyage, sometimes by learning from the sailors the art of navigation, which I have never practised, and sometimes by forming schemes for my conduct in different situations, in not one of which I have been ever placed.

" I was almost weary of my naval amusements when we landed safely at Surat. I secured my money, and purchasing some commodities for show, joined myself to a caravan that was passing into the inland country. My companions, for some reason or other, conjecturing that I was rich, and, by my inquiries and admiration, finding that I was ignorant, considered me as a novice whom they had a right to cheat, and who was to learn, at the usual expence, the art of fraud. They exposed me to the theft of servants, and the exaction of officers, and saw me plundered upon false pretences, without any advantage to themselves, but that of rejoicing in the superiority of their own knowledge."

" Stop a moment, said the prince. Is there such depravity in man, as that he should injure another without benefit to himself? I can easily conceive that all are pleased with superiority: but your ignorance was merely accidental, which being neither your crime nor your folly, could afford them no reason to applaud themselves; and the knowledge which they had, and which you wanted, they might as effectually have shown by warning, as betraying you."

" Pride, said Imlac, is seldom delicate, it will please itself with very mean advantages; envy feels not its own happiness, but when it may be compared with the misery of others. They were my enemies, because they grieved to think me rich; and my oppressors, because they delighted to find me weak."

" Proceed, said the prince: I doubt not of the facts which you relate, but imagine that you impute them to mistaken motives."

"In this company, said Imlac, I arrived at Agra, the capital of Indostan, the city in which the Great Mogul commonly resides. I applied myself to the language of the country, and in a few months was able to converse with the learned men; some of whom I found morose and reserved, and others easy and communicative; some were unwilling to teach another what they had with difficulty learned themselves; and some showed that the end of their studies was to gain the dignity of instructing.

" To the tutor of the young princes I recommended myself so much, that I was presented to the emperour as a man of uncommon knowledge. The emperour asked me many questions concerning my country and my travels; and though I cannot now recollect any thing that he uttered above the power of a common man, he dismissed me astonished at his wisdom, and enamoured of his goodness.

" My credit was now so high, that the merchants, with whom I had travelled, applied to me for recommendations to the ladies of the court. I was surprised at their confidence of solicitation, and gently reproached them with their practices on the road. They heard me with cold indifference, and showed no tokens of shame or sorrow.

" They then urged their request with the offer of a bribe ; but what I would not do for kindness, I would not do for money ; and refused them, not because they had injured me, but because I would not enable them to injure others ; for I knew they would have made use of my credit to cheat those who should buy their wares.

" Having resided at Agra till there was no more to be learned, I travelled into Persia, where I saw many remains of ancient magnificence, and observed many new accommodations of life. The Persians are a nation eminently social, and their assemblies afforded me daily opportunities of remarking characters and manners, and of tracing human nature through all its variations.

" From Persia I passed into Arabia, where I saw a nation at once pastoral and warlike ; who live without any settled habitation; whose only wealth is their flocks and herds; and who have yet carried on, through all ages, an hereditary war with all mankind, though they neither covet nor envy their possessions."

CHAP. X.

IMLAC'S HISTORY CONTINUED. A DISSERTATION UPON POETRY.

" WHEREVER I went, I found that poetry was considered as the highest learning, and regarded with a veneration somewhat approaching to that which man would pay to the Angelick Nature. And yet it fills me with wonder, that, in almost all countries, the most ancient poets are considered as the best : whether it be that every other kind of knowledge is an acquisition gradually attained, and poetry is a gift conferred at once ; or that the first poetry of every nation surprised them as a novelty, and retained the credit by consent which it received by accident at first : or whether, as the province of poetry is to describe Nature and Passion, which are always the same, the first writers took possession of the most striking objects for description, and the most probable occurrences for fiction, and left nothing to those that followed them, but transcription of the same events, and new combinations of the same images. Whatever be the reason, it is commonly observed that the early writers are in possession of

nature, and their followers of art: that the first excel
in strength and invention, and the latter in elegance
and refinement.

" I was desirous to add my name to this illustrious
fraternity. I read all the poets of Persia and Arabia,
and was able to repeat by memory the volumes that
are suspended in the mosque of Mecca. But I soon
found that no man was ever great by imitation. My
desire of excellence impelled me to transfer my attention to nature and to life. Nature was to be my
subject, and men to be my auditors : I could never
describe what I had not seen : I could not hope to
move those with delight or terrour, whose interests
and opinions I did not understand.

" Being now resolved to be a poet, I saw every
thing with a new purpose ; my sphere of attention
was suddenly magnified : no kind of knowledge was
to be overlooked. I ranged mountains and deserts
for images and resemblances, and pictured upon my
mind every tree of the forest and flower of the valley.
I observed with equal care the crags of the rock and
the pinnacles of the palace. Sometimes I wandered
along the mazes of the rivulet, and sometimes watched
the changes of the summer clouds. To a poet nothing can be useless. Whatever is beautiful, and
whatever is dreadful, must be familiar to his imagination : he must be conversant with all that is aw-
fully vast or elegantly little. The plants of the garden, the animals of the wood, the minerals of the
earth, and meteors of the sky, must all concur to
store his mind with inexhaustible variety: for every
idea is useful for the enforcement or decoration of

moral or religious truth; and he, who knows most, will have most power of diversifying his scenes, and of gratifying his reader with remote allusions and unexpected instruction.

"All the appearances of nature I was therefore careful to study, and every country which I have surveyed, has contributed something to my poetical powers."

"In so wide a survey, said the prince, you must surely have left much unobserved. I have lived till now, within the circuit of these mountains, and yet cannot walk abroad without the sight of something which I had never beheld before, or never heeded."

"The business of a poet, said Imlac, is to examine, not the individual, but the species; to remark general properties and large appearances: he does not number the streaks of the tulip, or describe the different shades in the verdure of the forest. He is to exhibit in his portraits of nature such prominent and striking features as recall the original to every mind; and must neglect the minuter discriminations, which one may have remarked, and another have neglected, for those characteristicks which are alike obvious to vigilance and carelessness.

"But the knowledge of nature is only half the task of a poet; he must be acquainted likewise with all the modes of life. His character requires that he estimate the happiness and misery of every condition; observe the power of all the passions in all their combinations, and trace the changes of the human mind as they are modified by various institutions, and accidental influences, of climate or custom, from the sprightliness of infancy to the despondence of decrepitude. He must divest himself of the prejudices of his age or country; he must consider right and wrong in their abstracted and invariable state; he must disregard present laws and opinions, and rise to general and transcendental truths, which will always be the same; he must therefore content himself with the slow progress of his name; contemn the applause of his own time, and commit his claims to the justice of posterity. He must write as the interpreter of nature, and the legislator of mankind, and consider himself as presiding over the thoughts and manners of future generations; as being superiour to time and place.

"His labour is not yet at an end: he must know many languages and many sciences; and, that his style may be worthy of his thoughts, must, by incessant practice, familiarize to himself every delicacy of speech and grace of harmony."

CHAP. XI.

IMLAC'S NARRATIVE CONTINUED.   A HINT ON PILGRIMAGE.

IMLAC now felt the enthusiastick fit, and was proceeding to aggrandize his own profession, when the prince cried out, "Enough! thou hast convinced me, that no human being can ever be a poet. Proceed with thy narration."

"To be a poet, said Imlac, is indeed very difficult."
"So difficult, returned the prince, that I will at present hear no more of his labours. Tell me whither you went when you had seen Persia."

"From Persia, said the poet, I travelled through

Syria, and for three years resided in Palestine, where I conversed with great numbers of the northern and western nations of Europe; the nations which are now in possession of all power and all knowledge; whose armies are irresistible, and whose fleets command the remotest parts of the globe. When I compared these men with the natives of our own kingdom, and those that surround us, they appeared almost another order of beings. In their countries it is difficult to wish for any thing that may not be obtained: a thousand arts, of which we never heard, are continually labouring for their convenience and pleasure; and whatever their own climate has denied them is supplied by their commerce."

" By what means, said the prince, are the Europeans thus powerful, or why, since they can so easily visit Asia and Africa for trade or conquest, cannot the Asiaticks and Africans invade their coasts, plant colonies in their ports, and give laws to their natural princes? The same wind that carries them back would bring us thither."

" They are more powerful, Sir, than we, answered Imlac, because they are wiser; knowledge will always predominate over ignorance, as man governs the other animals. But why their knowledge is more than ours, I know not what reason can be given, but the unsearchable will of the Supreme Being."

"When, said the prince with a sigh, shall I be able to visit Palestine, and mingle with this mighty confluence of nations? Till that happy moment shall arrive, let me fill up the time with such representations as thou canst give me. I am not ignorant of the motive that assembles such numbers in that place, and cannot but consider it as the centre of wisdom and piety, to which the best and wisest men of every land must be continually resorting."

" There are some nations, said Imlac, that send few visitants to Palestine: for many numerous and learned sects in Europe concur to censure pilgrimage as superstitious, or deride it as ridiculous."

" You know, said the prince, how little my life has made me acquainted with diversity of opinions; it will be too long to hear the arguments on both sides; you, that have considered them, tell me the result."

" Pilgrimage, said Imlac, like many other acts of piety, may be reasonable or superstitious, according to the principles upon which it is performed. Long journeys in search of truth are not commanded. Truth, such as is necessary to the regulation of life, is always found where it is honestly sought. Change of place is no natural cause of the increase of piety, for it inevitably produces dissipation of mind. Yet, since men go every day to view the fields where great actions have been performed, and return with stronger impressions of the event, curiosity of the same kind may naturally dispose us to view that country whence our religion had its beginning; and I believe no man surveys those awful scenes without some confirmation of holy resolutions. That the Supreme Being may be more easily propitiated in one place than in another, is the dream of idle superstition; but that some places may operate upon our own minds in an uncommon manner, is an opinion which hourly experience will justify. He who supposes that his vices may be more successfully combated in Palestine, will, perhaps, find himself mistaken, yet he may go thither without folly; he who thinks they will be more freely pardoned, dishonours at once his reason and religion."

" These, said the prince, are European distinctions. I will consider them another time. What have you found to be the effect of knowledge? Are those nations happier than we?"

" There is so much infelicity, said the poet, in the world, that scarce any man has leisure from his own distresses to estimate the comparative happiness of others. Knowledge is certainly one of the means of pleasure, as is confessed by the natural desire which every mind feels of increasing its ideas. Ignorance is mere privation, by which nothing can be produced; it is a vacuity in which the soul sits motionless and torpid for want of attraction; and, without knowing why, we always rejoice when we learn, and grieve when we forget. I am therefore inclined to conclude, that if nothing counteracts the natural consequence of learning, we grow more happy as our minds take a wider range.

" In enumerating the particular comforts of life, we shall find many advantages on the side of the Europeans. They cure wounds and diseases with which we languish and perish. We suffer inclemencies of weather which they can obviate. They have engines for the dispatch of many laborious works, which we must perform by manual industry. There is such communication between distant places, that one friend can hardly be said to be absent from

another.   Their policy removes all public inconve-
niencies : they have roads cut through their mountains, and bridges laid upon their rivers.   And if we
descend to the privacies of life, their habitations are
more commodious, and their possessions are more
secure."

"They are surely happy, said the prince, who
have all these conveniencies, of which I envy none
so much as the facility with which separated friends
interchange their thoughts."

"The Europeans, answered Imlac, are less unhappy than we, but they are not happy.   Human
life is every where a state in which much is to be endured, and little to be enjoyed."

CHAP. XII.

THE STORY OF IMLAC CONTINUED.

"I AM not yet willing, said the prince, to suppose that happiness is so parsimoniously distributed
to mortals ; nor can believe but that, if I had the
choice of life, I should be able to fill every day with
pleasure.   I would injure no man, and should pro-
voke no resentment : I would relieve every distress,
and should enjoy the benedictions of gratitude.   I
would chuse my friends among the wise, and my wife
among the virtuous ; and therefore should be in no
danger from treachery or unkindness.   My children
should, by my care, be learned and pious, and would
repay to my age what their childhood had received.

What would dare to molest him who might call on every side to thousands enriched by his bounty, or assisted by his power? And why should not life glide quietly away in the soft reciprocation of protection and reverence? All this may be done without the help of European refinements, which appear by their effects to be rather specious than useful. Let us leave them, and pursue our journey."

" From Palestine, said Imlac, I passed through many regions of Asia; in the more civilized kingdoms as a trader, and among the barbarians of the mountains as a pilgrim. At last I began to long for my native country, that I might repose after my travels and fatigues, in the places where I had spent my earliest years, and gladden my old companions with the recital of my adventures. Often did I figure to myself those with whom I had sported away the gay hours of dawning life, sitting round me in its evening, wondering at my tales, and listening to my counsels.

" When this thought had taken possession of my mind, I considered every moment as wasted which did not bring me nearer to Abissinia. I hastened into Egypt, and notwithstanding my impatience, was detained ten months in the contemplation of its ancient magnificence, and in inquiries after the remains of its ancient learning. I found in Cairo a mixture of all nations; some brought thither by the love of knowledge, some by the hope of gain, and many by the desire of living after their own manner without observation, and of lying hid in the obscurity of multitudes: for in a city, populous as Cairo, it is possible to obtain at the same time the gratifications of society, and the secrecy of solitude.

" From Cairo I travelled to Suez, and embarked on the Red Sea, passing along the coast till I arrived at the port from which I had departed twenty years before. Here I joined myself to a caravan, and re-entered my native country.

" I now expected the caresses of my kinsmen, and the congratulations of my friends, and was not without hope that my father, whatever value he had set upon riches, would own with gladness and pride a son who was able to add to the felicity and honour of the nation. But I was soon convinced that my thoughts were vain. My father had been dead fourteen years, having divided his wealth among my brothers, who were removed to some other provinces. Of my companions the greater part was in the grave; of the rest, some could with difficulty remember me, and some considered me as one corrupted by foreign manners.

" A man used to vicissitudes is not easily dejected. I forgot, after a time, my disappointment, and endeavoured to recommend myself to the nobles of the kingdom; they admitted me to their tables, heard my story, and dismissed me. I opened a school, and was prohibited to teach. I then resolved to sit down in the quiet of domestick life, and addressed a lady that was fond of my conversation, but rejected my suit, because my father was a merchant.

" Wearied at last with solicitation and repulses, I resolved to hide myself for ever from the world, and depend no longer on the opinion or caprice of others.

I waited for the time when the gate of the *happy valley* should open, that I might bid farewell to hope and fear : the day came ; my performance was distinguished with favour, and I resigned myself with joy to perpetual confinement."

" Hast thou here found happiness at last ? said Rasselas. Tell me without reserve ; art thou content with thy condition ? or, dost thou wish to be again wandering and inquiring ? All the inhabitants of this valley celebrate their lot, and at the annual visit of the emperour, invite others to partake of their felicity."

" Great prince, said Imlac, I shall speak the truth ; I know not one of all your attendants who does not lament the hour when he entered this retreat. I am less unhappy than the rest, because I have a mind replete with images, which I can vary and combine at pleasure. I can amuse my solitude by the renovation of the knowledge which begins to fade from my memory, and by recollection of the accidents of my past life. Yet all this ends in the sorrowful consideration, that my acquirements are now useless, and that none of my pleasures can be again enjoyed. The rest, whose minds have no impression but of the present moment, are either corroded by malignant passions, or sit stupid in the gloom of perpetual vacancy."

" What passions can infest those, said the prince, who have no rivals? We are in a place where impotence precludes malice, and where all envy is repressed by community of enjoyments."

" There may be community, said Imlac, of material possessions, but there can never be community of love or of esteem. It must happen that one will please more than another; he that knows himself despised will always be envious; and still more envious and malevolent, if he is condemned to live in the presence of those who despise him. The invitations, by which they allure others to a state which they feel to be wretched, proceed from the natural malignity of hopeless misery. They are weary of themselves, and of each other, and expect to find relief in new companions. They envy the liberty which their folly has forfeited, and would gladly see all mankind imprisoned like themselves.

" From this crime, however, I am wholly free. No man can say that he is wretched by my persuasion. I look with pity on the crowds who are annually soliciting admission to captivity, and wish that it were lawful for me to warn them of their danger."

" My dear Imlac, said the prince, I will open to thee my whole heart. I have long meditated an escape from the happy valley. I have examined the mountains on every side, but find myself insuperably barred : teach me the way to break my prison ; thou shalt be the companion of my flight, the guide of my rambles, the partner of my fortune, and my sole director in the *choice of life.*"

" Sir, answered the poet, your escape will be difficult, and, perhaps, you may soon repent your curiosity. The world, which you figure to yourself smooth and quiet as the lake in the valley, you will find a sea foaming with tempests, and boiling with whirlpools : you will be sometimes overwhelmed by the waves of violence, and sometimes dashed against the rocks of treachery. Amidst wrongs and frauds, competitions and anxieties, you will wish a thousand times for these seats of quiet, and willingly quit hope to be free from fear."

" Do not seek to deter me from my purpose, said the prince : I am impatient to see what thou hast seen ; and, since thou art thyself weary of the valley, it is evident that thy former state was better than this. Whatever be the consequence of my experiment, I am resolved to judge, with mine own eyes, of the various conditions of men, and then to make deliberately my *choice of life*."

" I am afraid, said Imlac, you are hindered by stronger restraints than my persuasions ; yet, if your determination is fixed, I do not counsel you to despair. Few things are impossible to diligence and skill."

CHAP. XIII.

RASSELAS DISCOVERS THE MEANS OF ESCAPE.

THE prince now dismissed his favourite to rest, but the narrative of wonders and novelties filled his mind with perturbation. He revolved all that he had heard, and prepared innumerable questions for the morning.

Much of his uneasiness was now removed. He had a friend to whom he could impart his thoughts, and whose experience could assist him in his designs. His heart was no longer condemned to swell with silent vexation. He thought that even the *happy valley* might be endured with such a companion, and that if they could range the world together, he should have nothing further to desire.

In a few days the water was discharged, and the ground dried. The prince and Imlac then walked out together to converse without the notice of the rest. The prince, whose thoughts were always on the wing, as he passed by the gate, said, with a countenance of sorrow, "Why art thou so strong, and why is man so weak?"

"Man is not weak," answered his companion; "knowledge is more than equivalent to force. The master of mechanicks laughs at strength. I can burst the gate, but cannot do it secretly. Some other expedient must be tried."

As they were walking on the side of the mountain, they observed that the conies, which the rain had ·driven from their burrows, had taken shelter among the bushes, and formed holes behind them, tending upwards in an oblique line. "It has been the opinion of antiquity, said Imlac, that human reason borrowed many arts from the instinct of animals; let us, therefore, not think ourselves degraded by learning from the coney. We may escape by piercing the mountain in the same direction. We will begin where the summit hangs over the middle part, and labour upwards till we shall issue up beyond the prominence."

The eyes of the prince, when he heard this proposal, sparkled with joy. The execution was easy, and the success certain.

No time was now lost. They hastened early in the morning to chuse a place proper for their mine.

They clambered with great fatigue among crags and brambles, and returned without having discovered any part that favoured their design. The second and the third day were spent in the same manner, and with the same frustration. But, on the fourth, they found a small cavern, concealed by a thicket, where they resolved to make their experiment.

Imlac procured instruments proper to hew stone and remove earth, and they fell to their work on the next day with more eagerness than vigour. They were presently exhausted by their efforts, and sat down to pant upon the grass. The prince, for a moment, appeared to be discouraged. " Sir, said his companion, practice will enable us to continue our labour for a longer time ; mark, however, how far we have advanced, and you will find that our toil will sometime have an end. Great works are performed, not by strength, but perseverance: yonder palace was raised by single stones, yet you see its height and spaciousness. He that shall walk with vigour three hours a day, will pass in seven years a space equal to the circumference of the globe."

They returned to their work day after day, and, in a short time, found a fissure in the rock, which enabled them to pass far with very little obstruction. This Rasselas considered as a good omen. " Do not disturb your mind," said Imlac, " with other hopes or fears than reason may suggest ; if you are pleased with prognosticks of good, you will be terrified likewise with tokens of evil, and your wnole life will be a prey to superstition. Whatever facilitates our work is more than an omen, it is a cause of success. This is one of those pleasing surprises which often happen to active resolution. Many things difficult to design prove easy to performance."

CHAP. XIV.

RASSELAS AND IMLAC RECEIVE AN UNEXPECTED VISIT.

THEY had now wrought their way to the middle, and solaced their toil with the approach of liberty, when the prince, coming down to refresh himself with air, found his sister Nekayah standing before the mouth of the cavity. He started and stood confused, afraid to tell his design, and yet hopeless to conceal it. A few moments determined him to repose on her fidelity, and secure her secrecy by a declaration without reserve.

" Do not imagine, said the princess, that I came hither as a spy : I had long observed from my window that you and Imlac directed your walk every day towards the same point, but I did not suppose you had any better reason for the preference than a cooler shade, or more fragrant bank ; nor followed you with any other design than to partake of your conversation. Since then not suspicion but fondness has detected you, let me not lose the advantage of my discovery. I am equally weary of confinement with yourself, and not less desirous of knowing what is done or suffered in the world. Permit me to fly with you from this tasteless tranquillity, which will yet grow more loathsome when you have left me. You may deny me to accompany you, but cannot hinder me from following."

The prince, who loved Nekayah above his other sisters, had no inclination to refuse her request, and grieved that he had lost an opportunity of showing his confidence by a voluntary communication. It was therefore agreed that she should leave the valley with them; and that, in the mean time, she should watch, lest any other straggler should, by chance or curiosity, follow them to the mountain.

At length their labour was at an end; they saw light beyond the prominence, and, issuing to the top of the mountain, beheld the Nile, yet a narrow current, wandering beneath them.

The prince looked round with rapture, anticipated all the pleasures of travel, and in thought was already transported beyond his father's dominions. Imlac, though very joyful at his escape, had less expectation of pleasure in the world, which he had before tried, and of which he had been weary.

Rasselas was so much delighted with a wider horizon, that he could not soon be persuaded to return into the valley. He informed his sister that the way was open, and that nothing now remained but to prepare for their departure.

CHAP. XV.

THE PRINCE AND PRINCESS LEAVE THE VALLEY, AND SEE MANY WONDERS.

The prince and princess had jewels sufficient to make them rich whenever they came into a place of commerce, which, by Imlac's direction, they hid in their clothes, and, on the night of the next full moon, all left the valley. The princess was followed only by a single favourite, who did not know whither she was going.

They clambered through the cavity, and began to go down on the other side. The princess and her maid turned their eyes towards every part, and, seeing nothing to bound their prospect, considered themselves as in danger of being lost in a dreary vacuity. They stopped and trembled. " I am almost afraid, said the princess, to begin a journey of which I cannot perceive an end, and to venture into this immense plain, where I may be approached on every side by men whom I never saw." The prince felt nearly the same emotions, though he thought it more manly to conceal them.

Imlac smiled at their terrours, and encouraged them to proceed; but the princess continued irresolute till she had been imperceptibly drawn forward too far to return.

In the morning they found some shepherds in the field, who set milk and fruits before them. The princess wondered that she did not see a palace ready for her reception, and a table spread with delicacies; but being faint and hungry, she drank the milk and eat the fruits, and thought them of a higher flavour than the produce of the valley.

They travelled forward by easy journeys, being all unaccustomed to toil or difficulty, and knowing, that though they might be missed, they could not be pursued. In a few days they came into a more populous region, where Imlac was diverted with the admiration which his companions expressed at the diversity of manners, stations, and employments.

Their dress was such as might not bring upon them the suspicion of having any thing to conceal, yet the prince, wherever he came, expected to be obeyed, and the princess was frightened, because those that came into her presence did not prostrate themselves before her. Imlac was forced to observe them with great vigilance, lest they should betray their rank by their unusual behaviour, and detained them several weeks in the first village, to accustom them to the sight of common mortals.

By degrees the royal wanderers were taught to understand that they had for a time laid aside their dignity, and were to expect only such regard as liberality and courtesy could procure. And Imlac having, by many admonitions, prepared them to endure the tumults of a port, and the ruggedness of the commercial race, brought them down to the sea-coast.

The prince and his sister, to whom every thing was new, were gratified equally at all places, and therefore remained for some months at the port without any inclination to pass further. Imlac was content with their stay, because he did not think it safe to expose them, unpractised in the world, to the hazards of a foreign country.

At last he began to fear lest they should be discovered, and proposed to fix a day for their departure. They had no pretensions to judge for themselves, and referred the whole scheme to his direction. He therefore took passage in a ship to Suez; and, when the time came, with great difficulty prevailed on the princess to enter the vessel. They had a quick and prosperous voyage, and from Suez travelled by land to Cairo.

CHAP. XVI.

THEY ENTER CAIRO, AND FIND EVERY MAN HAPPY.

As they approached the city, which filled the strangers with astonishment, " This, said Imlac to the prince, is the place where travellers and merchants assemble from all corners of the earth. You will here find men of every character, and every occupation. Commerce is here honourable: I will act as a merchant, and you shall live as strangers, who have no other end of travel than curiosity; it will soon be observed that we are rich; our reputation will procure us access to all whom we shall desire to know; you will see all the conditions of humanity, and enable yourself at leisure to make your *choice of life*."

They now entered the town, stunned by the noise, and offended by the crowds. Instruction had not yet so prevailed over habit, but that they wondered to see themselves pass undistinguished along the street, and met by the lowest of the people without reverence or notice. The princess could not at first bear the thought of being levelled with the vulgar, and for some days, continued in her chamber, where she was served by her favourite Pekuah as in the palace of the valley.

Imlac, who understood traffic, sold part of the jewels the next day, and hired a house, which he adorned with such magnificence, that he was immediately considered as a merchant of great wealth. His politeness attracted many acquaintance, and his generosity made him courted by many dependants. His

2 H 2

table was crowded by men of every nation, who all admired his knowledge, and solicited his favour. His companions, not being able to mix in the conversation could make no discovery of their ignorance or surprise, and were gradually initiated in the world as they gained knowledge of the language.

The prince had, by frequent lectures, been taught the use and nature of money; but the ladies could not, for a long time, comprehend what the merchants did with small pieces of gold and silver, or why things of so little use should be received as equivalent to the necessaries of life.

They studied the language two years, while Imlac was preparing to set before them the various ranks and conditions of mankind. He grew acquainted with all who had any thing uncommon in their fortune or conduct. He frequented the voluptuous and the frugal, the idle and the busy, the merchants and the men of learning.

The prince being now able to converse with fluency, and having learned the caution necessary to be observed in his intercourse with strangers, began to accompany Imlac to places of resort, and to enter into all assemblies, that he might make his *choice of life*.

For some time he thought choice needless, because all appeared to him equally happy. Wherever he went he met gaiety and kindness, and heard the song of joy or the laugh of carelessness. He began to believe that the world overflowed with universal plenty, and that nothing was withheld either from want or merit; that every hand showered liberality, and every heart melted with benevolence; " and who then, says he, will be suffered to be wretched?"

Imlac permitted the pleasing delusion, and was unwilling to crush the hope of inexperience, till one day having sat a while silent, " I know not, said the prince, what can be the reason that I am more unhappy than any of our friends. I see them perpetually and unalterably cheerful, but feel my own mind restless and uneasy. I am unsatisfied with those pleasures which I seem most to court; I live in the crowds of jollity, not so much to enjoy company, as to shun myself, and am only loud and merry to conceal my sadness."

" Every man, said Imlac, may, by examining his own mind, guess what passes in the minds of others: when you feel that your own gaiety is counterfeit, it may justly lead you to suspect that of your companions not to be sincere. Envy is commonly reciprocal. We are long before we are convinced that happiness is never to be found, and each believes it possessed by others, to keep alive the hope of obtaining it for himself. In the assembly, where you passed the last night, there appeared such sprightliness of air, and volatility of fancy, as might have suited beings of an higher order, formed to inhabit serener regions, inaccessible to care or sorrow: yet, believe me, prince, there was not one who did not dread the moment when solitude should deliver him to the tyranny of reflection."

" This, said the prince, may be true of others, since it is true of me; yet, whatever be the general infelicity of man, one condition is more happy than another, and wisdom surely directs us to take the least evil in the *choice of life*."

" The causes of good and evil, answered Imlac, " are so various and uncertain, so often entangled with each other, so diversified by various relations, and so much subject to accidents which cannot be foreseen, that he who would fix his condition upon incontestable reasons of preference, must live and die inquiring and deliberating."

" But surely, said Rasselas, the wise men, to whom we listen with reverence and wonder, chose that mode of life for themselves which they thought most likely to make them happy."

" Very few, said the poet, live by choice. Every man is placed in his present condition by causes which acted without his foresight, and with which he did not always willingly co-operate; and therefore you will rarely meet one who does not think the lot of his neighbour better than his own."

" I am pleased to think, said the prince, that my birth has given me at least one advantage over others, by enabling me to determine for myself. I have here the world before me; I will review it at leisure : surely happiness is somewhere to be found."

CHAP. XVII.

THE PRINCE ASSOCIATES WITH YOUNG MEN OF SPIRIT AND GAIETY.

RASSELAS rose next day, and resolved to begin his experiments upon life. " Youth, cried he, is the time of gladness : I will join myself to the young men, whose only business is to gratify their desires, and whose time is all spent in a succession of enjoyments."

To such societies he was readily admitted, but a few days brought him back weary and disgusted. Their mirth was without images; their laughter without motive; their pleasures were gross and sensual, in which the mind had no part; their conduct was at once wild and mean; they laughed at order and at law, but the frown of power dejected, and the eye of wisdom abashed them.

The prince soon concluded, that he should never be happy in a course of life of which he was ashamed. He thought it unsuitable to a reasonable being to act without a plan, and to be sad or cheerful only by chance. "Happiness, said he, must be something solid and permanent, without fear and without uncertainty."

But his young companions had gained so much of his regard by their frankness and courtesy, that he could not leave them without warning and remonstrance. "My friends, said he, I have seriously considered our manners and our prospects, and find that we have mistaken our own interest. The first years of man must make provision for the last. He that never thinks never can be wise. Perpetual levity must end in ignorance; and intemperance, though it may fire the spirits for an hour, will make life short or miserable. Let us consider that youth is of no long duration, and that in maturer age, when the enchantments of fancy shall cease, and phantoms of delight dance no more about us, we shall have no

comforts but the esteem of wise men, and the means
of doing good.   Let us, therefore, stop, while to stop
is in our power : let us live as men who are sometime
to grow old, and to whom it will be the most dreadful
of all evils to count their past years by follies, and to
be reminded of their former luxuriance of health only
by the maladies which riot has produced."

They stared a while in silence one upon another,
and at last drove him away by a general chorus of
continued laughter.

The consciousness that his sentiments were just,
and his intentions kind, was scarcely sufficient to support him against the horror of derision.   But he recovered his tranquillity, and pursued his search.

CHAP XVIII.

THE PRINCE FINDS A WISE AND HAPPY MAN.

As he was one day walking in the street, he saw a
spacious building which all were, by the open doors,
invited to enter : he followed the stream of people,
and found it a hall or school of declamation, in
which professors read lectures to their auditory.
He fixed his eye upon a sage raised above the rest,
who discoursed with great energy on the government of the passions.   His look was venerable, his
action graceful, his pronunciation clear, and his
diction elegant.   He showed with great strength
of sentiment, and variety of illustration, that human nature is degraded and debased, when the
lower faculties predominate over the higher ; that
when fancy, the parent of passion, usurps the do-

minion of the mind, nothing ensues but the natural effect of unlawful government, perturbation and confusion; that she betrays the fortresses of the intellect to rebels, and excites her children to sedition against reason, their lawful sovereign. He compared reason to the sun, of which the light is constant, uniform, and lasting; and fancy to a meteor, of bright but transitory lustre, irregular in its motion, and delusive in its direction.

He then communicated the various precepts given from time to time for the conquest of passion, and displayed the happiness of those who had obtained the important victory, after which man is no longer the slave of fear, nor the fool of hope; is no more emaciated by envy, inflamed by anger, emasculated by tenderness, or depressed by grief; but walks on calmly through the tumults or privacies of life, as the sun pursues alike his course through the calm or the stormy sky.

He enumerated many examples of heroes immovable by pain or pleasure, who looked with indifference on those modes or accidents to which the vulgar give the names of good and evil. He exhorted his hearers to lay aside their prejudices, and arm themselves against the shafts of malice or misfortune, by invulnerable patience, concluding, that this state only was happiness, and that this happiness was in every one's power.

Rasselas listened to him with the veneration due to the instructions of a superiour being, and, waiting for him at the door, humbly implored the liberty of visiting so great a master of true wisdom. The lecturer hesitated a moment, when Rasselas put a purse of gold into his hand, which he received with a mixture of joy and wonder.

"I have found, said the prince, at his return to Imlac, a man who can teach all that is necessary to be known, who, from the unshaken throne of rational fortitude, looks down on the scenes of life changing beneath him. He speaks, and attention watches his lips. He reasons, and conviction closes his periods. This man shall be my future guide : I will learn his doctrines, and imitate his life."

"Be not too hasty, said Imlac, to trust, or to admire the teachers of morality : they discourse like angels, but they live like men."

Rasselas, who could not conceive how any man could reason so forcibly without feeling the cogency of his own arguments, paid his visit in a few days, and was denied admission. He had now learned the power of money, and made his way by a piece of gold to the inner apartment, where he found the philosopher in a room half darkened, with his eyes misty, and his face pale. "Sir, said he, you are come at a time when all human friendship is useless ; what I suffer cannot be remedied, what I have lost cannot be supplied. My daughter, my only daughter, from whose tenderness I expected all the comforts of my age, died last night of a fever. My views, my purposes, my hopes are at an end : I am now a lonely being disunited from society."

"Sir, said the prince, mortality is an event by which a wise man can never be surprised : we know that death is always near, and it should therefore always be expected." " Young man, answered the philosopher, you speak like one that has never felt the pangs of separation." " Have you then forgot the precepts, said Rasselas, which you so powerfully enforced? Has wisdom no strength to arm the heart against calamity? Consider, that external things are naturally variable, but truth and reason are always the same." " What comfort, said the mourner, can truth and reason afford me? of what effect are they now, but to tell me, that my daughter will not be restored?"

The prince, whose humanity would not suffer him to insult misery with reproof, went away convinced of the emptiness of rhetorical sound, and the inefficacy of polished periods and studied sentences.

CHAP. XIX.

A GLIMPSE OF PASTORAL LIFE.

HE was still eager upon the same inquiry: and having heard of a hermit, that lived near the lowest cataract of the Nile, and filled the whole country with the fame of his sanctity, resolved to visit his retreat, and inquire whether that felicity which public life could not afford, was to be found in solitude; and whether a man whose age and virtue made him venerable, could teach any peculiar art of shunning evils, or enduring them?

Imlac and the princess agreed to accompany him, and, after the necessary preparations, they began their journey. Their way lay through the fields, where shepherds tended their flocks, and the lambs were playing upon the pasture. " This, said the poet,

of Imlac caught his attention, and the lofty courtesy of the princess excited his respect. When they offered to depart he entreated their stay, and was the next day still more unwilling to dismiss them than before. They were easily persuaded to stop, and civility grew up in time to freedom and confidence.

The prince now saw all the domesticks cheerful, and all the face of nature smiling round the place, and could not forbear to hope that he should find here what he was seeking ; but when he was congratulating the master upon his possessions, he answered with a sigh, " My condition has indeed the appearance of happiness, but appearances are delusive. My prosperity puts my life in danger ; the Bassa of Egypt is my enemy, incensed only by my wealth and popularity. 1 have been hitherto protected against him by the princes of the country ; but, as the favour of the great is uncertain, I know not how soon my defenders may be persuaded to share the plunder with the Bassa. I have sent my treasures into a distant country, and, upon the first alarm, am prepared to follow them. Then will my enemies riot in my mansion, and enjoy the gardens which I have planted."

They all joined in lamenting his danger, and deprecating his exile : and the princess was so much disturbed with the tumult of grief and indignation, that she retired to her apartment. They continued with their kind inviter a few days longer, and then went forward to find the hermit.

CHAP. XXI.

THE HAPPINESS OF SOLITUDE, THE HERMIT'S HISTORY.

THEY came on the third day, by the direction of the peasants, to the hermit's cell : it was a cavern in the side of a mountain, over-shadowed with palm-trees ; at such a distance from the cataract, that nothing more was heard than a gentle uniform murmur, such as composed the mind to pensive meditation, especially when it was assisted by the wind whistling among the branches. The first rude essay of nature had been so much improved by human labour, that the cave contained several apartments appropriated to different uses, and often afforded lodging to travellers, whom darkness or tempests happened to overtake.

The hermit sat on a bench at the door, to enjoy the coolness of the evening. On one side lay a book with pens and papers, on the other mechanical instruments of various kinds. As they approached him unregarded, the princess observed that he had not the countenance of a man that had found, or could teach the way to happiness.

They saluted him with great respect, which he repaid like a man not unaccustomed to the forms of courts. "My children, said he, if you have lost your way, you shall be willingly supplied with such conveniencies for the night as this cavern will afford. I have all that nature requires, and you will not expect delicacies in a hermit's cell."

They thanked him, and, entering, were pleased with the neatness and regularity of the place. The hermit set flesh and wine before them, though he fed only upon fruits and water. His discourse was cheerful without levity, and pious without enthusiasm. He soon gained the esteem of his guests, and the princess repented of her hasty censure.

At last Imlac began thus : " I do not now wonder that your reputation is so far extended ; we have heard at Cairo of your wisdom, and came hither to implore your direction for this young man and maiden in the *choice of life*."

" To him that lives well, answered the hermit, every form of life is good ; nor can I give any other rule for choice, than to remove from all apparent evil."

" He will remove most certainly from evil, said the prince, who shall devote himself to that solitude which you have recommended by your example."

" I have indeed lived fifteen years in solitude, said the hermit, but have no desire that my example should gain any imitators. In my youth I professed arms, and was raised by degrees to the highest military rank. I have traversed wide countries at the head of my troops, and seen many battles and sieges. At last, being disgusted by the preferments of a younger officer, and feeling that my vigour was beginning to decay, I was resolved to close my life in peace, having found the world full of snares, discord, and misery. I had once escaped from the pursuit of the enemy by the shelter of this cavern, and therefore chose it for my final residence. I employed artificers to form it into chambers, and stored it with all that I was likely to want.

"For some time after my retreat, I rejoiced like a tempest-beaten sailor at his entrance into the harbour, being delighted with the sudden change of the noise and hurry of war to stillness and repose. When the pleasure of novelty went away, I employed my hours in examining the plants which grow in the valley, and the minerals which I collected from the rocks. But that inquiry is now grown tasteless and irksome. I have been for some time unsettled and distracted: my mind is disturbed with a thousand perplexities of doubt, and vanities of imagination, which hourly prevail upon me because I have no opportunities of relaxation or diversion. I am sometimes ashamed to think that I could not secure myself from vice, but by retiring from the exercise of virtue, and begin to suspect that I was rather impelled by resentment, than led by devotion, into solitude. My fancy riots in scenes of folly, and I lament that I have lost so much, and have gained so little. In solitude, if I escape the example of bad men, I want likewise the counsel and conversation of the good. I have been long comparing the evils with the advantages of society, and resolve to return into the world to-morrow. The life of a solitary man will be certainly miserable, but not certainly devout."

They heard his resolution with surprise, but after a short pause, offered to conduct him to Cairo. He dug up a considerable treasure which he had hid among the rocks, and accompanied them to the city, on which, as he approached it, he gazed with rapture.

CHAP. XXII.

THE HAPPINESS OF A LIFE LED ACCORDING TO NATURE.

RASSELAS went often to an assembly of learned men, who met at stated times to unbend their minds, and compare their opinions. Their manners were somewhat coarse, but their conversation was instructive, and their disputations acute, though sometimes too violent, and often continued till neither controvertist remembered upon what question they began. Some faults were almost general among them ; every one was desirous to dictate to the rest, and every one was pleased to hear the genius or knowledge of another depreciated.

In this assembly Rasselas was relating his interview with the hermit, and the wonder with which he heard him censure a course of life which he had so deliberately chosen, and so laudably followed. The sentiments of the hearers were various. Some were of opinion, that the folly of his choice had been justly punished by condemnation to perpetual perseverance. One of the youngest among them, with great vehemence, pronounced him an hypocrite. Some talked of the right of society to the labour of individuals, and considered retirement as a desertion of duty. Others readily allowed, that there was a time when the claims of the publick were satisfied, and when a man might properly sequester himself, to review his life, and purify his heart.

One, who appeared more affected with the narrative than the rest, thought it likely, that the hermit would, in a few years, go back to his retreat, and, perhaps, if shame did not restrain, or death intercept him, return once more from his retreat into the world : " For the hope of happiness, said he, is so strongly impressed, that the longest experience is not able to efface it. Of the present state, whatever it be, we feel, and are forced to confess, the misery ; yet, when the same state is again at a distance, imagination paints it as desirable. But the time will surely come, when desire will be no longer our torment, and no man shall be wretched but by his own fault."

" This, said a philosopher, who had heard him with tokens of great impatience, is the present condition of a wise man. The time is already come, when none are wretched but by their own fault. Nothing is more idle, than to inquire after happiness, which nature has kindly placed within our reach. The way to be happy is to live according to nature, in obedience to that universal and unalterable law with which every heart is originally impressed ; which is not written on it by precept, but engraven by destiny, not instilled by education, but infused at our nativity. He that lives according to nature will suffer nothing from the delusions of hope, or importunities of desire : he will receive and reject with equability of temper ; and act or suffer as the reason of things shall alternately prescribe. Other men may amuse themselves with subtle definitions, or intricate ratiocinations. Let them learn to be wise by easier means : let them observe the hind of the forest, and the linnet of the grove : let them consider the life of animals, whose motions are regulated by instinct; they obey their guide, and are happy. Let us therefore, at length, cease to dispute, and learn to live; throw away the incumbrance of precepts, which they who utter them with so much pride and pomp do not understand, and carry with us this simple and intelligible maxim, That deviation from nature is deviation from happiness."

When he had spoken, he looked round him with a placid air, and enjoyed the consciousness of his own beneficence. " Sir, said the prince, with great modesty, as I, like all the rest of mankind, am desirous of felicity, my closest attention has been fixed upon your discourse : I doubt not the truth of a position which a man so learned has so confidently advanced. Let me only know what it is to live according to nature."

" When I find young men so humble and so docile, said the philosopher, I can deny them no information which my studies have enabled me to afford. To live according to nature, is to act always with due regard to the fitness arising from the relations and qualities of causes and effects; to concur with the great and unchangeable scheme of universal felicity; to co-operate with the general disposition and tendency of the present system of things."

The prince soon found that this was one of the sages whom he should understand less as he heard him longer. He therefore bowed and was silent, and the philosopher, supposing him satisfied, and the rest vanquished, rose up and departed with the air of a man that had co-operated with the present system.

CHAP. XXIII.

THE PRINCE AND HIS SISTER DIVIDE BETWEEN THEM THE WORK OF OBSERVATION.

RASSELAS returned home full of reflections, doubtful how to direct his future steps. Of the way to happiness he found the learned and simple equally ignorant; but, as he was yet young, he flattered himself that he had time remaining for more experiments, and further inquiries. He communicated to Imlac his observations and his doubts, but was answered by him with new doubts, and remarks that gave him no comfort. He therefore discoursed more frequently and freely with his sister, who had yet the same hope with himself, and always assisted him to give some reason why, though he had been hitherto frustrated, he might succeed at last.

" We have hitherto, said she, known but little of the world : we have never yet been either great or mean. In our own country, though we had royalty, we had no power, and in this we have not yet seen the private recesses of domestick peace. Imlac favours not our search, lest we should in time find him mistaken. We will divide the task between us : you shall try what is to be found in the splendour of courts, and I will range the shades of humbler life. Perhaps command and authority may be the supreme blessings, as they afford most opportunities of doing good : or, perhaps, what this world can give may be found in the modest habitations of middle fortune ; too low for great designs, and too high for penury and distress."

CHAP. XXIV.

THE PRINCE EXAMINES THE HAPPINESS OF HIGH STATIONS.

RASSELAS applauded the design, and appeared next day with a splendid retinue at the court of the Bassa. He was soon distinguished for his magnificence, and admitted as a prince whose curiosity had brought him from distant countries, to an intimacy with the great officers, and frequent conversation with the Bassa himself.

He was at first inclined to believe, that the man must be pleased with his own condition, whom all approached with reverence, and heard with obedience, and who had the power to extend his edicts to a whole kingdom. "There can be no pleasure, said he, equal to that of feeling at once the joy of thousands all made happy by wise administration. Yet, since by the law of subordination, this sublime delight can be in one nation but the lot of one, it is surely reasonable to think, that there is some satisfaction more popular and accessible, and that millions can hardly be subjected to the will of a single man, only to fill his particular breast with incommunicable content."

These thoughts were often in his mind, and he found no solution of the difficulty. But as presents and civilities gained him more familiarity, he found that almost every man who stood high in employment hated all the rest, and was hated by them, and that their lives were a continual succession of plots and detections, stratagems and escapes, faction and treachery. Many of those who surrounded the Bassa, were sent only to watch and report his conduct ; every tongue was muttering censure, and every eye was searching for a fault.

At last the letters of revocation arrived, the Bassa was carried in chains to Constantinople, and his name was mentioned no more.

" What are we now to think of the prerogatives of power? said Rasselas to his sister ; is it without any efficacy to good? or, is the subordinate degree only dangerous, and the supreme safe and glorious? Is the Sultan the only happy man in his dominions ? or, is the Sultan himself subject to the torments of suspicion, and the dread of enemies ?"

In a short time the second Bassa was deposed. The Sultan, that had advanced him, was murdered by the Janisaries, and his successour had other views and different favourites.

CHAP. XXV.

THE PRINCESS PURSUES HER INQUIRY WITH MORE DILIGENCE THAN SUCCESS.

THE princess, in the mean time, insinuated herself into many families; for there are few doors, through which liberality, joined with good-humour, cannot find its way. The daughters of many houses were airy and cheerful, but Nekayah had been too long accustomed to the conversation of Imlac and her brother to be much pleased with childish levity, and prattle which had no meaning. She found their thoughts narrow, their wishes low, and their merriment often artificial. Their pleasures, poor as they were, could not be preserved pure; but were embittered by petty competitions and worthless emulation. They were always jealous of the beauty of each other; of a quality to which solicitude can add nothing, and from which detraction can take nothing away. Many were in love with triflers like themselves, and many fancied that they were in love when in truth they were only idle. Their affection was not fixed on sense or virtue, and therefore seldom ended but in vexation. Their grief, however, like their joy, was transient; every thing floated in their mind unconnected with the past or future, so that one desire easily gave way to another, as a second stone cast into the water effaces and confounds the circles of the first.

With these girls she played as with inoffensive animals, and found them proud of her countenance, and weary of her company.

But her purpose was to examine more deeply, and her affability easily persuaded the hearts that were swelling with sorrow, to discharge their secrets in her ear: and those whom hope flattered, or prosperity delighted, often courted her to partake their pleasures.

The princess and her brother commonly met in the evening in a private summer-house on the bank of the Nile, and related to each other the occurrences of the day. As they were sitting together, the princess cast her eyes upon the river that flowed before her. "Answer, said she, great father of waters, thou that rollest thy floods through eighty nations, to the invocations of the daughter of thy native king. Tell me if thou waterest, through all thy course, a single habitation from which thou dost not hear the murmurs of complaint ?"

" You are then, said Rasselas, not more successful in private houses than I have been in courts." " I have, since the last partition of our provinces, said the princess, enabled myself to enter familiarly into many families, where there was the fairest show of prosperity and peace, and know not one house that is not haunted by some fury that destroys their quiet.

" I did not seek ease among the poor, because I concluded that there it could not be found. But I saw many poor whom I had supposed to live in affluence. Poverty has, in large cities, very different appearances : it is often concealed in splendour, and often in extravagance. It is the care of a very great part of mankind to conceal their indigence from the rest : they support themselves by temporary expedients, and every day is lost in contriving for the morrow.

" This, however, was an evil, which, though frequent, I saw with less pain, because I could relieve it. Yet some have refused my bounties ; more offended with my quickness to detect their wants, than pleased with my readiness to succour them : and others, whose exigencies compelled them to admit my kindness, have never been able to forgive their benefactress. Many, however, have been sincerely grateful, without the ostentation of gratitude, or the hope of other favours."

CHAP. XXVI.

THE PRINCESS CONTINUES HER REMARKS UPON PRIVATE LIFE.

NEKAYAH perceiving her brother's attention fixed, proceeded in her narrative.

" In families, where there is or is not poverty, there is commonly discord : if a kingdom be, as Imlac tells us, a great family, a family likewise is a little kingdom, torn with factions, and exposed to revolutions. An unpractised observer expects the love of parents and children to be constant and equal ; but this kindness seldom continues beyond the years of infancy ; in a short time the children become rivals to their parents. Benefits are allayed by reproaches, and gratitude debased by envy.

" Parents and children seldom act in concert : each child endeavours to appropriate the esteem or fondness of the parents, and the parents, with yet less temptation, betray each other to their children ; thus some place their confidence in the father, and some in the mother, and by degrees, the house is filled with artifices and feuds.

" The opinions of children and parents, of the young and the old, are naturally opposite, by the contrary effects of hope and despondence, of expectation and experience, without crime or folly on either side. The colours of life in youth and age appear different, as the face of nature in spring and winter. And how can children credit the assertions of parents, which their own eyes show them to be false ?

" Few parents act in such a manner as much to enforce their maxims by the credit of their lives. The old man trusts wholly to slow contrivance and gradual progression : the youth expects to force his way by genius, vigour, and precipitance. The old man pays regard to riches, and the youth reverences virtue. The old man deifies prudence : the youth commits himself to magnanimity and chance. The young man who intends no ill, believes that none is intended, and therefore acts with openness and candour : but his father, having suffered the injuries of fraud, is impelled to suspect, and too often allured to practise it. Age looks with anger on the temerity of youth, and youth with contempt on the scrupulosity of age. Thus parents and children, for the greatest part, live on to love less and less : and, if those whom nature has thus closely united are the torments of each other, where shall we look for tenderness and consolation ?"

" Surely, said the prince, you must have been unfortunate in your choice of acquaintance : I am unwilling to believe, that the most tender of all relations is thus impeded in its effects by natural necessity."

" Domestick discord, answered she, is not inevitably and fatally necessary ; but yet it is not easily avoided. We seldom see that a whole family is virtuous : the good and evil cannot well agree : and the evil can yet less agree with one another : even the virtuous fall sometimes to variance, when their virtues are of different kinds, and tending to extremes. In general, those parents have most reverence who most deserve it : for he that lives well cannot be despised.

" Many other evils infest private life. Some are the slaves of servants whom they have trusted with their affairs. Some are kept in continual anxiety to the caprice of rich relations, whom they cannot please, and dare not offend. Some husbands are imperious, and some wives perverse : and, as it is always more easy to do evil than good, though the wisdom or virtue of one can very rarely make many happy, the folly or vice of one may often make many miserable."

" If such be the general effect of marriage, said the prince, I shall, for the future, think it dangerous to connect my interest with that of another, lest I should be unhappy by my partner's fault."

" I have met, said the princess, with many who live single for that reason ; but I never found that their prudence ought to raise envy. They dream away their time without friendship, without fondness, and are driven to rid themselves of the day, for which they have no use, by childish amusements, or vicious delights. They act as beings under the constant sense of some known inferiority, that fills their minds with rancour, and their tongues with censure. They are peevish at home, and malevolent abroad ; and, as the outlaws of human nature, make it their business and their pleasure to disturb that society which debars them from its privileges. To live without feeling or exciting sympathy, to be fortunate without adding to the felicity of others, or afflicted without tasting the balm of pity, is a state more gloomy than solitude: it is not retreat, but exclusion from mankind. Marriage has many pains, but celibacy has no pleasures."

" What then is to be done? said Rasselas; the more we inquire, the less we can resolve. Surely he is most likely to please himself, that has no other inclination to regard."

CHAP. XXVII.

DISQUISITION UPON GREATNESS.

THE conversation had a short pause. The prince, having considered his sister's observations, told her that she had surveyed life with prejudice, and supposed misery where she did not find it. " Your narrative, says he, throws yet a darker gloom upon the prospects of futurity: the predictions of Imlac were but faint sketches of the evils painted by Nekayah. I have been lately convinced that quiet is not the daughter of grandeur, or of power: that her presence is not to be bought by wealth, nor enforced by conquest. It is evident, that as any man acts in a wider compass, he must be more exposed to opposition from enmity, or miscarriage from chance; whoever has many to please or to govern, must use the ministry of many agents, some of whom will be wicked, and some ignorant; by some he will be misled, and by others betrayed. If he gratifies one he will offend another: those that are not favoured will think themselves injured; and, since favours can be conferred but upon few, the greater number will be always discontented."

" The discontent, said the princess, which is thus unreasonable, I hope that I shall always have spirit to despise, and you power to repress."

" Discontent, answered Rasselas, will not always be without reason under the most just and vigilant administration of publick affairs. None, however attentive, can always discover that merit which indigence or faction may happen to obscure; and none, however powerful, can always reward it. Yet, he that sees inferiour desert advanced above him will naturally impute that preference to partiality or caprice; and, indeed, it can scarcely be hoped that any man, however magnanimous by nature, or exalted by condition, will be able to persist for ever in the fixed and inexorable justice of distribution; he will sometimes indulge his own affections, and sometimes those of his favourites; he will permit some to please him who can never serve him ; he will discover in those whom he loves, qualities which in reality they do not possess; and to those, from whom he receives pleasure, he will in his turn endeavour to give it. Thus will recommendations sometimes prevail which were purchased by money, or by the more destructive bribery of flattery and servility.

" He that has much to do will do something wrong, and of that wrong must suffer the consequences; and, if it were possible that he should always act rightly, yet when such numbers are to judge of his conduct, the bad will censure and obstruct him by malevolence, and the good sometimes by mistake.

" The highest stations cannot therefore hope to be the abodes of happiness, which I would willingly believe to have fled from thrones and palaces to seats of humble privacy and placid obscurity. For what can hinder the satisfaction, or intercept the expectations, of him whose abilities are adequate to his employments, who sees with his own eyes the whole circuit of his influence, who chooses by his own knowledge all whom he trusts, and whom none are tempted to deceive by hope or fear? Surely he has nothing to do but to love and to be loved, to be virtuous and to be happy."

" Whether perfect happiness would be procured by perfect goodness, said Nekayah, this world will never afford an opportunity of deciding. But this, at least, may be maintained, that we do not always find visible happiness in proportion to visible virtue. All natural, and almost all political evils, are incident alike to the bad and good: they are confounded in the misery of a famine, and not much distinguished in the fury of a faction; they sink together in a tempest, and are driven together from their country by invaders. All that virtue can afford is quietness of conscience, a steady prospect of a happier state; this may enable us to endure calamity with patience; but remember that patience must suppose pain.

CHAP XXVIII.

RASSELAS AND NEKAYAH CONTINUE THEIR CONVERSATION.

" DEAR Princess, said Rasselas, you fall into the common errours of exaggeratory declamation, by producing, in a familiar disquisition, examples of national calamities, and scenes of extensive misery, which are found in books rather than in the world, and which, as they are horrid, are ordained to be rare. Let us not imagine evils which we do not feel, nor injure life by misrepresentations. I cannot bear that querulous eloquence which threatens every city with a siege like that of Jerusalem, that makes famine attend on every flight of locusts, and suspends pestilence on the wing of every blast that issues from the south.

" On necessary and inevitable evils, which overwhelm kingdoms at once, all disputation is vain : when they happen they must be endured. But it is evident, that these bursts of universal distress are more dreaded than felt; thousands and ten thousands flourish in youth, and wither in age, without the knowledge of any other than domestick evils, and share the same pleasures and vexations, whether their kings are mild or cruel, whether the armies of their country pursue their enemies, or retreat before them. While courts are disturbed with intestine competitions, and ambassadors are negociating in foreign countries, the smith still plies his anvil, and the husbandman drives his plough forward; the necessaries of life are required and obtained; and the successive business of the seasons continues to make its wonted revolutions.

" Let us cease to consider what, perhaps, may never happen, and what, when it shall happen, will laugh at human speculation. We will not endeavour to modify the motions of the elements, or to fix the destiny of kingdoms. It is our business to consider what beings like us may perform; each labouring for his own happiness, by promoting within his circle, however narrow, the happiness of others.

" Marriage is evidently the dictate of nature; men and women are made to be companions of each other, and therefore I cannot be persuaded but that marriage is one of the means of happiness."

" I know not, said the princess, whether marriage be more than one of the innumerable modes of human misery. When I see and reckon the various forms of connubial infelicity, the unexpected causes of lasting discord, the diversities of temper, the oppositions of opinion, the rude collisions of contrary desire where both are urged by violent impulses, the obstinate contests of disagreeable virtues, where both are supported by consciousness of good intention; I am sometimes disposed to think with the severer casuists of most nations, that marriage is rather permitted than approved, and that none, but by the instigation of a passion too much indulged, entangle themselves with indissoluble compacts."

" You seem to forget, replied Rasselas, that you have, even now, represented celibacy as less happy than marriage. Both conditions may be bad, but they cannot both be worst. Thus it happens when wrong opinions are entertained, that they mutually destroy each other, and leave the mind open to truth."

" I did not expect, answered the princess, to hear that imputed to falsehood which is the consequence only of frailty. To the mind, as to the eye, it is difficult to compare with exactness objects vast in their extent, and various in their parts. Where we see or conceive the whole at once, we readily note the discriminations, and decide the preference : but of two systems, of which neither can be surveyed by any human being in its full compass of magnitude and multiplicity of complication, where is the wonder that judging of the whole by parts, I am alternately affected by one and the other as either presses on my memory or fancy ? We differ from ourselves just as we differ from each other, when we see only part of the question, as in the multifarious relations of politicks and morality; but when we perceive the whole at once, as in numerical computations, all agree in one judgment, and none ever varies his opinion."

"Let us not add, said the prince, to the other evils of life, the bitterness of controversy, nor endeavour to vie with each other in subtilties of argument. We are employed in a search, of which both are equally to enjoy the success, or suffer by the miscarriage. It is therefore fit that we assist each other. You surely conclude too hastily from the infelicity of marriage against its institution : will not the misery of life prove equally that life cannot be the gift of Heaven ? The world must be peopled by marriage, or peopled without it."

"How the world is to be peopled, returned Ne-kayah, is not my care, and needs not be yours. I see no danger that the present generation should omit to leave successours behind them: we are not now inquiring for the world, but for ourselves."

CHAP. XXIX.
THE DEBATE ON MARRIAGE CONTINUED.

"The good of the whole, says Rasselas, is the same with the good of all its parts. If marriage be best for mankind, it must be evidently best for individuals, or a permanent and necessary duty must be the cause of evil, and some must be inevitably sacrificed to the convenience of others. In the estimate which you have made of the two states, it appears that the incommodities of a single life are, in a great measure, necessary and certain, but those of the conjugal state accidental and avoidable.

"I cannot forbear to flatter myself, that prudence and benevolence will make marriage happy. The general folly of mankind is the cause of general complaint. What can be expected but disappointment and repentance from a choice made in the immaturity of youth, in the ardour of desire, without judgment, without foresight, without inquiry after conformity of opinions, similarity of manners, rectitude of judgment, or purity of sentiment?

"Such is the common process of marriage. A youth or maiden meeting by chance, or brought together by artifice, exchange glances, reciprocate civilities, go home, and dream of one another. Having little to divert attention, or diversify thought, they find themselves uneasy when they are apart, and therefore conclude that they shall be happy together. They marry, and discover what nothing but voluntary blindness before had concealed; they wear out life in altercations, and charge nature with cruelty.

" From those early marriages proceeds likewise the rivalry of parents and children : the son is eager to enjoy the world before the father is willing to forsake it, and there is hardly room at once for two generations. The daughter begins to bloom before the mother can be content to fade, and neither can forbear to wish for the absence of the other.

" Surely all these evils may be avoided by that deliberation and delay which prudence prescribes to irrevocable choice. In the variety and jollity of youthful pleasures, life may be well enough supported without the help of a partner. Longer time will increase experience, and wider views will allow better opportunities of inquiry and selection : one advantage, at least, will be certain ; the parents will be visibly older than their children."

" What reason cannot collect, said Nekayah, and what experiment has not yet taught, can be known only from the report of others. I have been told that late marriages are not eminently happy. This is a question too important to be neglected, and I have often proposed it to those, whose accuracy of remark, and comprehensiveness of knowledge, made their suffrages worthy of regard. They have generally determined, that it is dangerous for a man and woman to suspend their fate upon each other, at a time when opinions are fixed, and habits are established : when friendships have been contracted on both sides, when life has been planned into method, and the mind has long enjoyed the contemplation of its own prospects.

" It is scarcely possible that two travelling through the world under the conduct of chance, should have been both directed to the same path, and it will not often happen that either will quit the track which custom has made pleasing. When the desultory levity of youth has settled into regularity, it is soon succeeded by pride ashamed to yield, or obstinacy delighting to contend. And even though mutual esteem produces mutual desire to please, time itself, as it modifies unchangeably the external mien, determines likewise the direction of the passions, and gives an inflxeible rigidity to the manners. Long customs are not easily broken: he that attempts to change the course of his own life, very often labours in vain; and how shall we do that for others, which we are seldom able to do for ourselves?"

" But surely, interposed the prince, you suppose the chief motive of choice forgotten or neglected. Whenever I shall seek a wife, it shall be my first question, whether she be willing to be led by reason?"

" Thus it is, said Nekayah, that philosophers are deceived. There are a thousand familiar disputes which reason never can decide ; questions that elude investigation, and make logick ridiculous; cases where something must be done, and where little can be said. Consider the state of mankind, and inquire how few can be supposed to act upon any occasions, whether small or great, with all the reasons of action present to their minds. Wretched would be the pair above all names of wretchedness, who should be doomed to adjust by reason, every morning, all the minute detail of a domestick day.

"Those who marry at an advanced age, will probably escape the encroachments of their children ; but, in diminution of this advantage, they will be likely to leave them, ignorant and helpless, to a guardian's mercy ; or, if that should not happen, they must at least go out of the world before they see those whom they love best either wise or great.

"From their children, if they have less to fear, they have less also to hope, and they lose, without equivalent, the joys of early love, and the convenience of uniting with manners pliant, and minds susceptible of new impressions, which might wear away their dissimilitudes by long cohabitation, as soft bodies, by continual attrition, conform their surfaces to each other.

"I believe it will be found that those who marry late are best pleased with their children, and those who marry early with their partners."

"The union of these two affections, said Rasselas, would produce all that could be wished. Perhaps there is a time when marriage might unite them, a time neither too early for the father, nor too late for the husband." ·

"Every hour, answered the princess, confirms my prejudice in favour of the position so often uttered by the mouth of Imlac, ' That nature sets her gifts on the right hand and on the left.' Those conditions, which flatter hope and attract desire, are so constituted, that as we approach one, we recede from

another.   There are goods so opposed that we cannot seize both, but, by too much prudence, may
pass between them at too great a distance to reach
either.   This is often the fate of long consideration ;
he does nothing who endeavours to do more than is
allowed to humanity.   Flatter not yourself with contrarieties of pleasure.   Of the blessings set before
you, make your choice and be content.   No man
can taste the fruits of autumn while he is delighting
his scent with the flowers of the spring ; no man can,
at the same time, fill his cup from the source and
from the mouth of the Nile."

CHAP. XXX.

IMLAC ENTERS, AND CHANGES THE CONVER-
SATION.

HERE Imlac entered, and interrupted them.   " Imlac, said Rasselas, I have been taking from the
princess the dismal history of private life, and am almost discouraged from further search."

" It seems to me, said Imlac, that while you are
making the choice of life, you neglect to live.   You
wander about a single city, which, however large and
diversified, can now afford few novelties, and forget
that you are in a country, famous among the earliest
monarchies for the power and wisdom of its inhabitants ; a country where the sciences first dawned that
illuminate the world, and beyond which the arts
cannot be traced of civil society or domestick life.

" The old Egyptians have left behind them monuments of industry and power before which all Euro-

pean magnificence is confessed to fade away. The
ruins of their architecture are the schools of modern
builders ; and from the wonders which time has
spared, we may conjecture, though uncertainly, what
it has destroyed."

" My curiosity, said Rasselas, does not very
strongly lead me to survey piles of stone, or mounds
of earth ; my business is with man. I came hither
not to measure fragments of temples, or trace choaked
aqueducts, but to look upon the various scenes of
the present world."

" The things that are now before us, said the
princess, require attention and deserve it. What
have I to do with the heroes or the monuments of
ancient times ? with times which never can return,
and heroes, whose form of life was different from
all that the present condition of mankind requires or
allows."

" To know any thing, returned the poet, we must
know its effects ; to see men we must see their
works, that we may learn what reason has dictated
or passion has incited, and find what are the most
powerful motives of action. To judge rightly of the
present we must oppose it to the past ; for all judgment is comparative, and of the future nothing can
be known. The truth is, that no mind is much employed upon the present : recollection and anticipation fill up almost all our moments. Our passions
are joy and grief, love and hatred, hope and fear.
Of joy and grief the past is the object, and the future of hope and fear ; even love and hatred respect
the past, for the cause must have been before the
effect.

" The present state of things is the consequence of the former, and it is natural to inquire what were the sources of the good that we enjoy, or the evil that we suffer. If we act only for ourselves, to neglect the study of history is not prudent: if we are intrusted with the care of others, it is not just. Ignorance, when it is voluntary, is criminal; and he may properly be charged with evil, who refused to learn how he might prevent it.

" There is no part of history so generally useful as that which relates the progress of the human mind, the gradual improvement of reason, the successive advances of science, the vicissitudes of learning and ignorance, which are the light and darkness of thinking beings, the extinction and resuscitation of arts, and the revolutions of the intellectual world. If accounts of battles and invasions are peculiarly the business of princes, the useful or elegant arts are not to be neglected; those who have kingdoms to govern, have understandings to cultivate.

" Example is always more efficacious than precept. A soldier is formed in war, and a painter must copy pictures. In this, contemplative life has the advantage: great actions are seldom seen, but the labours of art are always at hand for those who desire to know what art has been able to perform.

" When the eye or the imagination is struck with an uncommon work, the next transition of an active mind is to the means by which it was performed. Here begins the true use of such contemplation; we enlarge our comprehension by new ideas, and perhaps recover some art lost to mankind, or learn what is less perfectly known in our own country. At least we compare our own with former times, and either rejoice at our improvements, or, what is the first motion towards good, discover our defects."

" I am willing, said the prince, to see all that can deserve my search." " And I, said the princess, shall rejoice to learn something of the manners of antiquity."

" The most pompous monument of Egyptian greatness, and one of the most bulky works of manual industry, said Imlac, are the pyramids ; fabricks raised before the time of history, and of which the earliest narratives afford us only uncertain traditions. Of these, the greatest is still standing very little injured by time."

" Let us visit them to-morrow, said Nekayah. I have often heard of the pyramids, and shall not rest till I have seen them within and without with my own eyes."

CHAP. XXXI.

THEY VISIT THE PYRAMIDS.

THE resolution being thus taken, they set out the next day. They laid tents upon their camels, being resolved to stay among the pyramids till their curiosity was fully satisfied. They travelled gently, turned aside to every thing remarkable, stopped from time to time and conversed with the inhabitants, and observed the various appearances of towns ruined and inhabited, of wild and cultivated nature.

When they came to the great pyramid, they were astonished at the extent of the base, and the height of the top.   Imlac explained to them the principles upon which the pyramidal form was chosen for a fabrick, intended to co-extend its duration with that of the world : he showed that its gradual diminution gave it such stability, as defeated all the common attacks of the Elements, and could scarcely be overthrown by earthquakes themselves, the least resistible of natural violence.   A concussion that should shatter the pyramid would threaten the dissolution of the continent.

They measured all its dimensions, and pitched their tents at its foot. Next day they prepared to enter its interior apartments, and having hired the common guides, climbed up to the first passage, when the favourite of the Princess, looking into the cavity, stepped back and trembled. " Pekuah, said the princess, of what art thou afraid ?"   " Of the narrow entrance, answered the lady, and of the dreadful gloom.   I dare not enter a place which must surely be inhabited by unquiet souls.   The original possessors of these dreadful vaults will start up before us, and perhaps shut us in for ever."   She spoke, and threw her arms round the neck of her mistress.

" If all your fear be of apparitions, said the prince, I will promise you safety : there is no danger from the dead ; he that is once buried will be seen no more."

" That the dead are seen no more, said Imlac, I will not undertake to maintain, against the concurrent and unvaried testimony of all ages and of all nations. There is no people, rude or learned, among whom apparitions of the dead are not related and believed. This opinion, which perhaps prevails as far as human nature is diffused, could become universal only by its truth: those that never heard of one another, would not have agreed in a tale which nothing but experience can make credible. That it is doubted by single cavillers, can very little weaken the general evidence; and some who deny it with their tongues confess it by their fears.

" Yet I do not mean to add new terrours to those which have already seized upon Pekuah. There can be no reason why spectres should haunt the pyramid more than other places, or why they should have power or will to hurt innocence and purity. Our entrance is no violation of their privileges; we can take nothing from them, how then can we offend them ?"

" My dear Pekuah, said the princess, I will always go before you, and Imlac shall follow you. Remember that you are the companion of the princess of Abissinia."

" If the princess is pleased that her servant should die, returned the lady, let her command some death less dreadful than enclosure in this horrid cavern. You know I dare not disobey you: I must go if you command me; but, if I once enter, I never shall come back."

The princess saw that her fear was too strong for expostulation or reproof, and embracing her, told her that she should stay in the tent till their return. Pekuah was yet not satisfied, but entreated the princess not to pursue so dreadful a purpose as that of entering the recesses of the pyramid. "Though I cannot teach courage, said Nekayah, I must not learn cowardice; nor leave at last undone what I came hither only to do."

CHAP. XXXII.

THEY ENTER THE PYRAMID.

PEKUAH descended to the tents, and the rest entered the pyramid : they passed through the galleries, surveyed the vaults of marble, and examined the chest in which the body of the founder is supposed to have been reposited. They then sat down in one of the most spacious chambers to rest a while before they attempted to return.

"We have now, said Imlac, gratified our minds with an exact view of the greatest work of man, except the wall of China.

"Of the wall it is very easy to assign the motive. It secured a wealthy and timorous nation from the incursions of barbarians, whose unskilfulness in arts made it easier for them to supply their wants by rapine than by industry, and who from time to time poured in upon the habitations of peaceful commerce, as vultures descend upon domestick fowl. Their celerity and fierceness made the wall necessary, and their ignorance made it efficacious.

"But for the pyramids no reason has ever been given adequate to the cost and labour of the work. The narrowness of the chambers proves that it could afford no retreat from enemies, and treasures might have been reposited at far less expence with

equal security.   It seems to have been erected only
in compliance with that hunger of imagination
which preys incessantly upon life, .and must be
always appeased by some employment.   Those who
have already all that they can enjoy, must enlarge
their desires.   He that has built for use, till use is
supplied, must begin to build for vanity, and extend
his plan to the utmost power of human performance,
that he may not be soon reduced to form another wish.

" I consider this mighty structure as a monument
of the insufficiency of human enjoyments. A king,
whose power is unlimited, and whose treasures surmount all real and imaginary wants, is compelled to
solace, by the erection of a pyramid, the satiety
of dominion and tastelessness of pleasures, and to
amuse the tediousness of declining life, by seeing
thousands labouring without end, and one stone, for
no purpose, laid upon another. Whoever thou art,
that, not content with a moderate condition, imaginest happiness in royal magnificence, and dreamest
that command or riches can feed the appetite of
novelty with perpetual gratifications, survey the pyramids, and confess thy folly !"

CHAP. XXXIII.

THE PRINCESS MEETS WITH AN UNEXPECTED MISFORTUNE.

THEY rose up, and returned through the cavity at
which they had entered, and the princess prepared
for her favourite a long narrative of dark labyrinths,

and costly rooms, and of the different impressions which the varieties of the way had made upon her. But when they came to their train, they found every one silent and dejected : the men discovered shame and fear in their countenances, and the women were weeping in the tents.

What had happened they did not try to conjecture, but immediately inquired. " You had scarcely entered into the pyramid, said one of the attendants, when a troop of Arabs rushed upon us ; we were too few to resist them, and too slow to escape. They were about to search the tents, set us on our camels, and drive us along before them, when the approach of some Turkish horsemen put them to flight : but they seized the lady Pekuah with her two maids, and carried them away : the Turks are now pursuing them by our instigation, but I fear they will not be able to overtake them."

The princess was overpowered with surprise and grief. Rasselas, in the first heat of his resentment, ordered his servants to follow him, and prepared to pursue the robbers with his sabre in his hand. " Sir, said Imlac, what can you hope from violence or valour ? the Arabs are mounted on horses trained to battle and retreat ; we have only beasts of burden. By leaving our present station we may lose the princess, but cannot hope to regain Pekuah."

In a short time the Turks returned, having not been able to reach the enemy. The princess burst out into new lamentations, and Rasselas could scarcely forbear to reproach them with cowardice ; but Imlac was of opinion, that the escape of the Arabs was no addition to their misfortune, for perhaps they would have killed their captives rather than have resigned them.

CHAP. XXXIV.

THEY RETURN TO CAIRO WITHOUT PEKUAH.

THERE was nothing to be hoped from longer stay. They returned to Cairo repenting of their curiosity, censuring the negligence of the government, lamenting their own rashness which had neglected to procure a guard, imagining many expedients by which the loss of Pekuah might have been prevented, and resolving to do something for her recovery, though none could find any thing proper to be done.

Nekayah retired to her chamber, where her women attempted to comfort her, by telling her that all had their troubles, and that lady Pekuah had enjoyed much happiness in the world for a long time, and might reasonably expect a change of fortune. They hoped that some good would befall her wheresoever she was, and that their mistress would find another friend who might supply her place.

The princess made them no answer, and they continued the form of condolence, not much grieved in their hearts that the favourite was lost.

Next day the prince presented to the Bassa a memorial of the wrong which he had suffered, and a petition for redress. The Bassa threatened to punish the robbers, but did not attempt to catch them, nor indeed, could any account or description be given by which he might direct the pursuit.

It soon appeared that nothing would be done by authority. Governours, being accustomed to hear of more crimes than they can punish, and more wrongs than they can redress, set themselves at ease by indiscriminate negligence, and presently forget the request when they lose sight of the petitioner.

Imlac then endeavoured to gain some intelligence by private agents. He found many who pretended to an exact knowledge of all the haunts of the Arabs, and to regular correspondence with their chiefs, and who readily undertook the recovery of Pekuah. Of these, some were furnished with money for their journey, and came back no more; some were liberally paid for accounts which a few days discovered to be false. But the princess would not suffer any means, however improbable, to be left untried. While she was doing something, she kept her hope alive. As one expedient failed, another was suggested; when one messenger returned unsuccessful, another was dispatched to a different quarter.

Two months had now passed, and of Pekuah nothing had been heard; the hopes which they had endeavoured to raise in each other grew more languid, and the princess, when she saw nothing more to be tried, sunk down inconsolable in hopeless dejection. A thousand times she reproached herself with the easy compliance, by which she permitted her favourite to stay behind her. " Had not my fondness, said she, lessened my authority, Pekuah had not dared to talk of her terrours. She ought to have feared me more than spectres. A severe look would have overpowered her; a peremptory command would have compelled obedience. Why did foolish indulgence prevail upon me? Why did I not speak, and refuse to hear?"

"Great Princess, said Imlac, do not reproach yourself for your virtue, or consider that as blameable by which evil has accidentally been caused. Your tenderness for the timidity of Pekuah, was generous and kind. When we act according to our duty, we commit the event to him by whose laws our actions are governed, and who will suffer none to be finally punished for obedience. When, in prospect of some good, whether natural or moral, we break the rules prescribed us, we withdraw from the direction of superiour wisdom, and take all consequences upon ourselves. Man cannot so far know the connexion of causes and events, as that he may venture to do wrong in order to do right. When we pursue our end by lawful means, we may always console our miscarriage by the hope of future recompence. When we consult only our own policy, and attempt to find a nearer way to good, by overleaping the settled boundaries of right and wrong, we cannot be happy even by success, because we cannot escape the consciousness of our fault; but, if we miscarry, the disappointment is irremediably embittered. How comfortless is the sorrow of him who feels at once the pangs of guilt, and the vexation of calamity which guilt has brought upon him?

"Consider, Princess, what would have been your condition, if the lady Pekuah had entreated to accompany you, and being compelled to stay in the tents, had been carried away; or how would you have borne the thought, if you had forced her into the pyramid, and she had died before you in agonies of terrour ?"

" Had either happened, said Nekayah, I could not have endured life till now : I should have been tortured to madness by the remembrance of such cruelty, or must have pined away in abhorrence of myself."

" This at least, said Imlac, is the present reward of virtuous conduct, that no unlucky consequence can oblige us to repent it."

CHAP. XXXV.

THE PRINCESS LANGUISHES FOR WANT OF PEKUAH.

NEKAYAH being thus reconciled to herself, found that no evil is insupportable but that which is accompanied with consciousness of wrong. She was, from that time, delivered from the violence of tempestuous sorrow, and sunk into silent pensiveness and gloomy tranquillity. She sat from morning to evening recollecting all that had been done or said by her Pekuah, treasured up with care every trifle on which Pekuah had set an accidental value, and which might recall to mind any little incident or careless conversation. The sentiments of her, whom she now expected to see no more, were treasured in her memory as rules of life, and she deliberated to no other end than to conjecture on any occasion what would have been the opinion and counsel of Pekuah.

The women, by whom she was attended, knew nothing of her real condition, and therefore she could not talk to them but with caution and reserve. She began to remit her curiosity, having no great care to collect notions which she had no convenience of uttering. Rasselas endeavoured first to comfort, and afterwards to divert her; he hired musicians, to whom she seemed to listen, but did not hear them, and procured masters to instruct her in various arts, whose lectures, when they visited her again, were again to be repeated. She had lost her taste of pleasure, and her ambition of excellence. And her mind, though forced into short excursions, always recurred to the image of her friend.

Imlac was every morning earnestly enjoined to renew his inquiries, and was asked every night whether he had yet heard of Pekuah, till, not being able to return the princess the answer that she desired, he was less and less willing to come into her presence. She observed his backwardness, and commanded him to attend her. " You are not, said she, to confound impatience with resentment, or to suppose that I charge you with negligence, because I repine at your unsuccessfulness. I do not much wonder at your absence; I know that the unhappy are never pleasing, and that all naturally avoid the contagion of misery. To hear complaints is wearisome alike to the wretched and the happy; for who would cloud, by adventitious grief, the short gleams of gaiety which life allows us ? or who, that is struggling under his own evils, will add to them the miseries of another?

" The time is at hand, when none shall be disturbed any longer by the sighs of Nekayah: my search after happiness is now at an end. I am resolved to retire from the world with all its flatteries and deceits, and will hide myself in solitude without any other care than to compose my thoughts, and regulate my hours by a constant succession of innocent occupations, till with a mind purified from all earthly desires, I shall enter into that state, to which all are hastening, and in which I hope again to enjoy the friendship of Pekuah."

"Do not entangle your mind, said Imlac, by irrevocable determinations, nor increase the burden of life by a voluntary accumulation of misery: the weariness of retirement will continue or increase when the loss of Pekuah is forgotten. That you have been deprived of one pleasure, is no very good reason for rejection of the rest."

"Since Pekuah was taken from me, said the princess, I have no pleasure to reject or to retain. She that has no one to love or trust has little to hope. She wants the radical principle of happiness. We may, perhaps, allow that what satisfaction this world can afford, must arise from the conjunction of wealth, knowledge, and goodness: wealth is nothing but as it is bestowed, and knowledge nothing but as it is communicated: they must therefore be imparted to others, and to whom could I now delight to impart them? Goodness affords the only comfort which can be enjoyed without a partner, and goodness may be practised in retirement."

"How far solitude may admit goodness, or advance it, I shall not, replied Imlac, dispute at present. Remember the confession of the pious hermit. You will wish to return into the world, when the image of your companion has left your thoughts."

"That time, said Nekayah, will never come. The

generous frankness, the modest obsequiousness, and the faithful secrecy of my dear Pekuah, will always be more missed, as I shall live longer to see vice and folly."

"The state of a mind oppressed with a sudden calamity, said Imlac, is like that of the fabulous inhabitants of the new created earth, who, when the first night came upon them, supposed that day would never return. When the clouds of sorrow gather over us, we see nothing beyond them, nor can imagine how they will be dispelled : yet a new day succeeded to the night, and sorrow is never long without a dawn of ease. But they who restrain themselves from receiving comfort, do as the savages would have done, had they put out their eyes when it was dark. Our minds, like our bodies, are in continual flux ; something is hourly lost, and something acquired. To lose much at once is inconvenient to either, but while the vital powers remain uninjured, nature will find the means of reparation. Distance has the same effect on the mind as on the eye, and while we glide along the stream of time, whatever we leave behind us is always lessening, and that which we approach increasing in magnitude. Do not suffer life to stagnate ; it will grow muddy for want of motion : commit yourself again to the current of the world ; Pekuah will vanish by degrees; you will meet in your way some other favourite, or learn to diffuse yourself in general conversation."

"At least, said the prince, do not despair before all remedies have been tried : the inquiry after the unfortunate lady is still continued, and shall be carried on with yet greater diligence, on condition that you will promise to wait a year for the event, without any unalterable resolution."

Nekayah thought this a reasonable demand, and made the promise to her brother, who had been advised by Imlac to require it. Imlac had, indeed, no great hope of regaining Pekuah, but he supposed, that if he could secure the interval of a year, the princess would be then in no danger of a cloister.

CHAP. XXXVI.

PEKUAH IS STILL REMEMBERED. THE PROGRESS OF SORROW.

NEKAYAH, seeing that nothing was omitted for the recovery of her favourite, and having, by her promise, set her intention of retirement at a distance, began imperceptibly to return to common cares and common pleasures. She rejoiced without her own consent at the suspension of her sorrows, and sometimes caught herself with indignation in the act of turning away her mind from the remembrance of her, whom yet she resolved never to forget.

She then appointed a certain hour of the day for meditation on the merits and fondness of Pekuah, and for some weeks retired constantly at the time fixed, and returned with her eyes swollen and her countenance clouded. By degrees she grew less scrupulous, and suffered any important and pressing avocation to delay the tribute of daily tears. She then yielded to less occasions; sometimes forgot what she was indeed afraid to remember, and, at last, wholly released herself from the duty of periodical affliction.

Her real love of Pekuah was yet not diminished. A thousand occurrences brought her back to memory, and a thousand wants, which nothing but the confidence of friendship can supply, made her frequently regretted. She, therefore, solicited Imlac never to desist from inquiry, and to leave no art of intelligence untried, that, at least, she might have the comfort of knowing that she did not suffer by negligence or sluggishness. " Yet what, said she, is to be expected from our pursuit of happiness, when we find the state of life to be such, that happiness itself is the cause of misery ? Why should we endeavour to attain that, of which the possession cannot be secured ? I shall henceforward fear to yield my heart to excellence, however bright, or to fondness, however tender, lest I should lose again what I have lost in Pekuah."

CHAP. XXXVII.

THE PRINCESS HEARS NEWS OF PEKUAH.

IN seven months, one of the messengers, who had been sent away upon the day when the promise was drawn from the princess, returned, after many unsuccessful rambles, from the borders of Nubia, with an account that Pekuah was in the hands of an Arab chief, who possessed a castle or fortress on the extremity of Egypt. The Arab, whose revenue was plunder, was willing to restore her, with her two attendants, for two hundred ounces of gold.

The price was no subject of debate. The princess was in ecstacies when she heard that her favourite was alive, and might so cheaply be ransomed. She could not think of delaying for a moment Pekuah's happiness or her own, but entreated her brother to send back the messenger with the sum required. Imlac being consulted, was not very confident of the veracity of the relator, and was still more doubtful of the Arab's faith, who might, if he were too liberally trusted, detain at once the money and the captives. He thought it dangerous to put themselves in the power of the Arab, by going into his district, and could not expect that the Rover would so much expose himself as to come into the lower country, where he might be seized by the forces of the Bassa.

It is difficult to negociate where neither will trust. But Imlac, after some deliberation, directed the messenger to propose that Pekuah should be conducted by ten horsemen, to the monastery of St. Antony, which is situated in the deserts of Upper Egypt, where she should be met by the same number and her ransom should be paid.

That no time might be lost, as they expected that the proposal would not be refused, they immediately began their journey to the monastery; and when they arrived, Imlac went forward with the former messenger to the Arab's fortress. Rasselas was desirous to go with them; but neither his sister nor Imlac would consent. The Arab, according to the custom of his nation, observed the laws of hospitality with great exactness to those who put themselves into his power, and, in a few days, brought Pekuah with her maids, by easy journeys, to the place appointed, where receiving the stipulated price, he restored her with great respect to liberty and her friends, and undertook to conduct them back towards Cairo beyond all danger of robbery or violence.

The princess and her favourite embraced each other with transport too violent to be expressed, and went out together to pour the tears of tenderness in secret, and exchange professions of kindness and gratitude. After a few hours they returned into the refectory of the convent, where, in the presence of the prior and his brethren, the prince required of Pekuah the history of her adventures.

CHAP. XXXVIII.

THE ADVENTURES OF THE LADY PEKUAH.

" At what time, and in what manner I was forced away, said Pekuah, your servants have told you. The suddenness of the event struck me with surprise, and I was at first rather stupified than agitated with any passion of either fear or sorrow. My confusion was increased by the speed and tumult of our flight, while we were followed by the Turks, who, as it seemed, soon despaired to overtake us, or were afraid of those whom they made a show of menacing.

" When the Arabs saw themselves out of danger they slackened their course, and as I was less harassed by external violence, I began to feel more uneasiness in my mind. After some time we stopped near a spring shaded with trees in a pleasant meadow, where we were set upon the ground, and offered such refreshments as our masters were partaking. I was suffered to sit with my maids apart from the rest, and none attempted to comfort or insult us. Here I first began to feel the full weight of my misery. The girls sat weeping in silence, and from time to time looked on me for succour. I knew not to what condition we were doomed, nor could conjecture where would be the place of our captivity, or whence to draw any hope of deliverance. I was in the hands of robbers and savages, and had no reason to suppose that their pity was more than their justice, or that they would forbear the gratification of any ardour of desire, or caprice of cruelty. I, however, kissed my maids, and endeavoured to pacify them by remarking, that we were yet treated with decency, and that, since we were now carried beyond pursuit, there was no danger of violence to our lives.

" When we were to be set again on horseback, my maids clung round me, and refused to be parted, but I commanded them not to irritate those who had us in their power. We travelled the remaining part of the day through an unfrequented and pathless country, and came by moon-light to the side of a hill, where the rest of the troop was stationed. Their tents were pitched, and their fires kindled, and our chief was welcomed as a man much beloved by his dependants.

" We were received into a large tent, where we found women who had attended their husbands in the expedition. They set before us the supper which

they had provided, and I eat it rather to encourage
my maids than to comply with any appetite of my
own.   When the meat was taken away, they spread
the carpets for repose.   I was weary, and hoped to
find in sleep that remission of distress which nature
seldom denies.   Ordering myself therefore to be un-
drest, I observed that the women looked very earnestly upon me, not expecting, I suppose, to see me
so submissively attended.   When my upper vest was
taken off, they were apparently struck with the splendour of my clothes, and one of them timorously laid
her hand upon the embroidery.   She then went out,
and in a short time came back with another woman,
who seemed to be of higher rank and greater authority.   She did, at her entrance, the usual act of reverence, and taking me by the hand, placed me in a
smaller tent, spread with finer carpets, where I spent
the night quietly with my maids.

"In the morning, as I was sitting on the grass,
the chief of the troop came towards me.   I rose up
to receive him, and he bowed with great respect.
"Illustrious lady, said he, my fortune is better than
I had presumed to hope; I am told by my women,
that I have a princess in my camp."   "Sir, answered I, your women have deceived themselves
and you; I am not a princess, but an unhappy
stranger who intended soon to have left this country, in which I am now to be imprisoned for ever."
"Whoever, or whencesoever, you are, returned the
Arab, your dress, and that of your servants, show
your rank to be high, and your wealth to be
great. Why should you, who can so easily procure

your ransom, think yourself in danger of perpetual captivity? The purpose of my incursions is to increase my riches, or, more properly, to gather tribute. The sons of Ishmael are the natural and hereditary lords of this part of the continent, which is usurped by late invaders, and low-born tyrants, from whom we are compelled to take by the sword what is denied to justice. The violence of war admits no distinction: the lance that is lifted at guilt and power, will sometimes fall on innocence and gentleness."

" How little, said I, did I expect that yesterday it should have fallen upon me!"

" Misfortunes, answered the Arab, should always be expected. If the eye of hostility could learn reverence or pity, excellence like yours had been exempt from injury. But the angels of affliction spread their toils alike for the virtuous and the wicked, for the mighty and the mean. Do not be disconsolate: I am not one of the lawless and cruel rovers of the desert; I know the rules of civil life: I will fix your ransom, give a passport to your messenger, and perform my stipulation with nice punctuality."

" You will easily believe that I was pleased with his courtesy: and finding that his predominant passion was desire of money, I began now to think my danger less, for I knew that no sum would be thought too great for the release of Pekuah. I told him, that he should have no reason to charge me with ingratitude, if I was used with kindness, and that any ransom which could be expected for a maid of common rank, would be paid; but that he must not persist to rate me as a princess. He said he would consider what he should demand, and then smiling, bowed and retired.

" Soon after the women came about me, each contending to be more officious than the other, and my maids themselves were served with reverence. We travelled onwards by short journeys. On the fourth day the chief told me, that my ransom must be two hundred ounces of gold ; which I not only promised him, but told him, that I would add fifty more, if I and my maids were honourably treated.

" I never knew the power of gold before. From that time I was the leader of the troop. The march of every day was longer or shorter as I commanded, and the tents were pitched where I chose to rest. We now had camels and other conveniencies for travel, my own women were always at my side, and I amused myself with observing the manners of the vagrant nations, and with viewing remains of ancient edifices, with which these deserted countries appear to have been, in some distant age, lavishly embellished.

" The chief of the band was a man far from illiterate : he was able to travel by the stars or the compass, and had marked in his erratick expeditions, such places as are most worthy the notice of a passenger. He observed to me, that buildings are always best preserved in places little frequented, and difficult of access : for, when once a country declines from its primitive splendour, the more inhabitants are left, the quicker ruin will be made. Walls supply stones more easily than quarries, and palaces and temples will be demolished, to make stables of granite, and cottages of porphyry.

CHAP. XXXIX.

THE ADVENTURES OF PEKUAH CONTINUED.

" WE wandered about in this manner for some
weeks, whether, as our chief pretended, for my gratification, or, as I rather suspected, for some convenience of his own. I endeavoured to appear contented where sullenness and resentment would have
been of no use, and that endeavour conduced much
to the calmness of my mind: but my heart was always with Nekayah, and the troubles of the night
much overbalanced the amusements of the day. My
women, who threw all their cares upon their mistress,
set their minds at ease from the time when they saw
me treated with respect, and gave themselves up to
the incidental alleviations of our fatigue without solicitude or sorrow. I was pleased with their pleasure
and animated with their confidence. My condition
had lost much of its terrour, since I found that the
Arab ranged the country merely to get riches. Avarice is an uniform and tractable vice: other intellectual distempers are different in different constitutions of mind; that which sooths the pride of one
will offend the pride of another; but to the favour of
the covetous there is a ready way; bring money and
nothing is denied.

" At last we came to the dwelling of our chief, a
strong and spacious house, built with stone in an
island of the Nile, which lies, as I was told, under
the tropick. " Lady, said the Arab, you shall rest
after your journey a few weeks in this place, where

you are to consider yourself as sovereign.   My occupation is war : I have therefore chosen this obscure
residence, from which I can issue unexpected, and to
which I can retire unpursued.   You may now repose
in security : here are few pleasures, but here is no
danger."   He then led me into the inner apartments,
and seating me on the richest couch, bowed to the
ground.   His women, who considered me as a rival,
looked on me with malignity ; but being soon informed that I was a great lady detained only for my
ransom, they began to vie with each other in obsequiousness and reverence.

   " Being again comforted with new assurances of
speedy liberty, I was for some days diverted from
impatience by the novelty of the place.   The turrets
overlooked the country to a great distance, and afforded a view of many windings of the stream.   In
the day I wandered from one place to another, as the
course of the sun varied the splendour of the prospect, and saw many things which I had never seen
before.   The crocodiles and river-horses are common in this unpeopled region, and I often looked
upon them with terrour, though I knew that they
could not hurt me.   For some time I expected to
see mermaids and tritons, which, as Imlac has told
me, the European travellers have stationed in the
Nile, but no such beings ever appeared, and the
Arab, when I inquired after them, laughed at my
credulity.

   " At night the Arab always attended me to a
tower set apart for celestial observations, where he
endeavoured to teach me the names and courses of
the stars.   I had no great inclination to this study,

but an appearance of attention was necessary to
please my instructor, who valued himself for his skill;
and in a little while, I found some employment requisite to beguile the tediousness of time, which was
to be passed always amidst the same objects. I was
weary of looking in the morning on things from
which I had turned away weary in the evening: I
therefore was at last willing to observe the stars rather than do nothing, but could not always compose
my thoughts, and was very often thinking on Nekayah, when others imagined me contemplating the
sky. Soon after the Arab went upon another expedition, and then my only pleasure was to talk with
my maids about the accident by which we were carried away, and the happiness that we should all
enjoy at the end of our captivity."

"There were women in your Arab's fortress, said
the princess, why did you not make them your companions, enjoy their conversation, and partake their
diversions? In a place where they found business
or amusement, why should you alone sit corroded
with idle melancholy? or why could not you bear,
for a few months, that condition to which they were
condemned for life?"

"The diversions of the women, answered Pekuah,
were only childish play, by which the mind, accustomed to stronger operations, could not be kept busy.
I could do all which they delighted in doing by
powers merely sensitive, while my intellectual faculties were flown to Cairo. They ran from room to
room as a bird hops from wire to wire in his cage.
They danced for the sake of motion, as lambs frisk

in a meadow.   One sometimes pretended to be hurt, that the rest might be alarmed ; or hid herself, that another might seek her.   Part of their time passed in watching the progress of light bodies that floated on the river, and part in marking the various forms into which clouds broke in the sky.

" Their business was only needle-work, in which I and my maids sometimes helped them; but you know that the mind will easily straggle from the fingers, nor will you suspect that captivity and absence from Nekayah, could receive solace from silken flowers.

" Nor was much satisfaction to be hoped from their conversation : for of what could they be expected to talk ?   They had seen nothing ; for they had lived from early youth in that narrow spot : of what they had not seen they could have no knowledge, for they could not read.   They had no ideas but of the few things that were within their view, and had hardly names for any thing but their clothes and their food. As I bore a superiour character, I was often called to terminate their quarrels, which I decided as equitably as I could.   If it could have amused me to hear the complaints of each against the rest, I might have been often detained by long stories; but the motives of their animosity were so small, that I could not listen without intercepting the tale."

" How, said Rasselas, can the Arab, whom you represented as a man of more than common accomplishments, take any pleasure in his seraglio when it is filled only with women like these ?   Are they exquisitely beautiful ?"

" They do not, said Pekuah, want that unaffecting and ignoble beauty which may subsist without spriteliness or sublimity, without energy of thought or dignity of virtue. But to a man like the Arab, such beauty was only a flower casually plucked and carelessly thrown away. Whatever pleasures he might find among them, they were not those of friendship or society. When they were playing about him, he looked on them with inattentive superiority : when they vied for his regard, he sometimes turned away disgusted. As they had no knowledge, their talk could take nothing from the tediousness of life : as they had no choice, their fondness, or appearance of fondness, excited in him neither pride nor gratitude ; he was not exalted in his own esteem by the smiles of a woman who saw no other man, nor was much obliged by that regard, of which he could never know the sincerity, and which he might often perceive to be exerted, not so much to delight him as to pain a rival. That which he gave, and they received, as love, was only a careless distribution of superfluous time, such love as man can bestow upon that which he despises, such as has neither hope nor fear, neither joy nor sorrow."

" You have reason, lady, to think yourself happy, said Imlac, that you have been thus easily dismissed. How could a mind, hungry for knowledge, be willing, in an intellectual famine, to lose such a banquet as Pekuah's conversation ?"

" I am inclined to believe, answered Pekuah, that he was for some time in suspense ; for, notwithstanding his promise, whenever I proposed to dis-

2 M 2

patch a messenger to Cairo, he found some excuse for delay. While I was detained in his house he made many incursions into the neighbouring countries, and, perhaps, he would have refused to discharge me, had his plunder been equal to his wishes. He returned always courteous, related his adventures, delighted to hear my observations, and endeavoured to advance my acquaintance with the stars. When I importuned him to send away my letters, he soothed me with professions of honour and sincerity; and, when I could be no longer decently denied, put his troop again in motion, and left me to govern in his absence. I was much afflicted by this studied procrastination, and was sometimes afraid that I should be forgotten; that you would leave Cairo, and I must end my days in an island of the Nile.

" I grew at last hopeless and dejected, and cared so little to entertain him, that he for a while more frequently talked with my maids. That he should fall in love with them, or with me, might have been equally fatal, and I was not much pleased with the growing friendship. My anxiety was not long: for, as I recovered some degree of cheerfulness, he returned to me, and I could not forbear to despise my former uneasiness.

" He still delayed to send for my ransom, and would, perhaps, never have determined, had not your agent found his way to him. The gold which he would not fetch, he could not reject when it was offered. He hastened to prepare for our journey hither, like a man delivered from the pain of an intestine conflict. I took leave of my companions in the house, who dismissed me with cold indifference."

· Nekayah having heard her favourite's relation, rose and embraced her, and Rasselas gave her an hundred ounces of gold, which she presented to the Arab for the fifty that were promised.

CHAP XL.

THE HISTORY OF A MAN OF LEARNING.

THEY returned to Cairo, and were so well pleased at finding themselves together, that none of them went much abroad. The prince began to love learning, and one day declared to Imlac, that he intended to devote himself to science, and pass the rest of his days in literary solitude.

" Before you make your final choice, answered Imlac, you ought to examine its hazards, and converse with some of those who are grown old in the company of themselves. I have just left the observatory of one of the most learned astronomers in the world, who has spent forty years in unwearied attention to the motions and appearances of the celestial bodies, and has drawn out his soul in endless calculations. He admits a few friends once a month to hear his deductions and enjoy his discoveries. I was introduced as a man of knowledge worthy of his notice. Men of various ideas, and fluent conversation, are commonly welcome to those whose thoughts have been long fixed upon a single point, and who find the images of other things stealing away. I delighted him with my remarks; he smiled at the narrative of my travels, and was glad to forget the constellations, and descend for a moment into the lower world.

" On the next day of vacation I renewed my visit, and was so fortunate as to please him again. He relaxed from that time the severity of his rule, and permitted me to enter at my own choice. I found him always busy, and always glad to be relieved. As each knew much which the other was desirous of learning, we exchanged our notions with great delight. I perceived that I had every day more of his confidence, and always found new cause of admiration in the profundity of his mind. His comprehension is vast, his memory capacious and retentive, his discourse is methodical, and his expression clear.

" His integrity and benevolence are equal to his learning. His deepest researches and most favourite studies, are willingly interrupted for any opportunity of doing good by his counsel or his riches. To his closest retreat, at his most busy moments, all are admitted that want his assistance : ' For though I exclude idleness and pleasure, I will never, says he, bar my doors against charity. To man is permitted the contemplation of the skies, but the practice of virtue is commanded.'"

" Surely, said the princess, this man is happy."

" I visited him, said Imlac, with more and more frequency, and was every time more enamoured of his conversation : he was sublime without haughtiness, courteous without formality, and communicative without ostentation. I was at first, great princess, of your opinion, thought him the happiest of mankind, and often congratulated him on the blessing that he enjoyed.   He seemed to hear nothing with indifference but the praises of his condition, to which he always returned a general answer, and diverted the conversation to some other topick.

"Amidst this willingness to be pleased, and labour to please, I had quickly reason to imagine that some painful sentiment pressed upon his mind.   He often looked up earnestly towards the sun, and let his voice fall in the midst of his discourse.   He would sometimes, when we were alone, gaze upon me in silence with the air of a man who longed to speak what he was yet resolved to suppress.   He would often send for me with vehement injunctions of haste, though, when I came to him, he had nothing extraordinary to say.   And sometimes, when I was leaving him, would call me back, pause a few moments, and then dismiss me."

CHAP. XLI.

THE ASTRONOMER DISCOVERS THE CAUSE OF HIS UNEASINESS.

"At last the time came when the secret burst his reserve.   We were sitting together last night in the turret of his house, watching the emersion of a satellite of Jupiter.   A sudden tempest clouded the sky, and disappointed our observation.   We sat a while silent in the dark, and then he addressed himself to me in these words: "Imlac, I have long considered thy friendship as the greatest blessing of my life.   Integrity without knowledge is weak and useless, and knowledge without integrity is dangerous and dreadful.   I have found in thee all the qualities requisite for trust, benevolence, experience, and fortitude. I have long discharged an office which I must soon quit at the call of nature, and shall rejoice in the hour of imbecility and pain to devolve it upon thee."

" I thought myself honoured by this testimony, and protested that whatever could conduce to his happiness would add likewise to mine."

" Hear, Imlac, what thou wilt not without difficulty credit. I have possessed for five years the regulation of weather, and the distribution of the seasons : the sun has listened to my dictates, and passed from tropick to tropick by my direction ; the clouds, at my call, have poured their waters, and the Nile has overflowed at my command ; I have restrained the rage of the dog-star, and mitigated the fervours of the crab. The winds alone, of all the elemental powers, have hitherto refused my authority, and multitudes have perished by equinoctial tempests, which I found myself unable to prohibit or restrain. I have administered this great office with exact justice, and made to the different nations of the earth an impartial dividend of rain and sunshine. What must have been the misery of half the globe, if I had limited the clouds to particular regions, or confined the sun to either side of the equator !"

CHAP. XLII.

THE OPINION OF THE ASTRONOMER IS EXPLAINED AND JUSTIFIED.

" I SUPPOSE he discovered in me, through the obscurity of the room, some tokens of amazement and doubt, for, after a short pause, he proceeded thus :

" Not to be easily credited will neither surprize nor offend me ; for I am, probably, the first of human beings to whom this trust has been imparted. Nor do I know whether to deem this distinction a reward or punishment ; since I have possessed it I have been far less happy than before, and nothing but the consciousness of good intention could have enabled me to support the weariness of unremitted vigilance."

" How long, Sir, said I, has this great office been in your hands ?"

" About ten years ago, said he, my daily observations of the changes of the sky led me to consider, whether, if I had the power of the seasons, I could confer greater plenty upon the inhabitants of the earth. This contemplation fastened on my mind, and I sat days and nights in imaginary dominion, pouring upon this country and that the showers of fertility, and seconding every fall of rain with a due proportion of sunshine. I had yet only the will to do good, and did not imagine that I should ever have the power.

" One day, as I was looking on the fields withering with heat, I felt in my mind a sudden wish that I could send rain on the southern mountains, and raise the Nile to an inundation. In the hurry of my imagination I commanded rain to fall, and by comparing the time of my command with that of the inundation, I found that the clouds had listened to my lips."

" Might not some other cause, said I, produce this concurrence ? the Nile does not always rise on the same day."

" Do not believe, said he, with impatience, that such objections could escape me : I reasoned long against my own conviction, and laboured against truth with the utmost obstinacy. I sometimes suspected myself of madness, and should not have dared to impart this secret but to a man like you, capable of distinguishing the wonderful from the impossible, and the incredible from the false."

" Why, Sir, said I, do you call that incredible, which you know, or think you know, to be true ?"

" Because, said he, I cannot prove it by any external evidence ; and I know too well the laws of demonstration to think that my conviction ought to influence another, who cannot, like me, be conscious of its force. I, therefore, shall not attempt to gain credit by disputation. It is sufficient that I feel this power, that I have long possessed, and every day exerted it. But the life of man is short, the infirmities of age increase upon me, and the time will soon come, when the regulator of the year must mingle with the dust. The care of appointing a successor has long disturbed me ; the night and the day have been spent in comparisons of all the characters which have come to my knowledge, and I have yet found none so worthy as thyself."

CHAP. XLIII.

THE ASTRONOMER LEAVES IMLAC HIS DIRECTIONS.

" HEAR, therefore, what I shall impart with attention, such as the welfare of a world requires. If the task of a king be considered as difficult, who has the care only of a few millions, to whom he cannot do much good or harm, what must be the anxiety of him, on whom depends the action of the elements, and the great gifts of light and heat!—Hear me therefore with attention.

" I have diligently considered the position of the earth and sun, and formed innumerable schemes in which I changed their situation. I have sometimes turned aside the axis of the earth, and sometimes varied the ecliptick of the sun : but I have found it impossible to make a disposition by which the world may be advantaged; what one region gains, another loses by an imaginable alteration, even without considering the distant parts of the solar system with which we are unacquainted. Do not, therefore, in thy administration of the year, indulge thy pride by innovation ; do not please thyself with thinking that thou canst make thyself renowned to all future ages, by disordering the seasons. The memory of mischief is no desirable fame. Much less will it become thee to let kindness or interest prevail. Never rob other countries of rain to pour it on thine own. For us the Nile is sufficient."

" I promised, that when I possessed the power, I would use it with inflexible integrity ; and he dismissed me, pressing my hand. " My heart, said

he, will be now at rest, and my benevolence will no
more destroy my quiet : I have found a man of wisdom and virtue, to whom I can cheerfully bequeath
the inheritance of the sun."

The prince heard this narration with very serious
regard ; but the princess smiled, and Pekuah con-
vulsed herself with laughter. "Ladies, said Imlac,
to mock the heaviest of human afflictions is neither
charitable nor wise. Few can attain this man's
knowledge, and few practise his virtues ; but all may
suffer his calamity. Of the uncertainties of our present state, the most dreadful and alarming is the
uncertain continuance of reason."

The princess was recollected, and the favourite was
abashed. Rasselas, more deeply affected, inquired
of Imlac, whether he thought such maladies of the
mind frequent, and how they were contracted ?

CHAP. XLIV.

THE DANGEROUS PREVALENCE OF IMAGINATION.

"DISORDERS of intellect, answered Imlac, happen much more often than superficial observers will
easily believe. Perhaps, if we speak with rigorous
exactness, no human mind is in its right state.
There is no man whose imagination does not sometimes predominate over his reason, who can regulate his attention wholly by his will, and whose
ideas will come and go at his command. No man
will be found in whose mind airy notions do not
sometimes tyrannize, and force him to hope or fear
beyond the limits of sober probability. All power

of fancy over reason is a degree of insanity; but while this power is such as we can controul and repress, it is not visible to others, nor considered as any depravation of the mental faculties: it is not pronounced madness, but when it becomes ungovernable, and apparently influences speech or action.

"To indulge the power of fiction, and send imagination out upon the wing, is often the sport of those who delight too much in silent speculation. When we are alone we are not always busy; the labour of excogitation is too violent to last long; the ardour of inquiry will sometimes give way to idleness or satiety. He who has nothing external that can divert him, must find pleasure in his own thoughts, and must conceive himself what he is not; for who is pleased with what he is? He then expatiates in boundless futurity, and culls from all imaginable conditions that which for the present moment he should most desire, amuses his desires with impossible enjoyments, and confers upon his pride unattainable dominion. The mind dances from scence to scene, unites all pleasures in all combinations, and riots in delights, which nature and fortune, with all their bounty, cannot bestow.

"In time, some particular train of ideas fixes the attention, all other intellectual gratifications are rejected, the mind, in weariness or leisure, recurs constantly to the favourite conception, and feasts on the luscious falsehood, whenever she is offended with the bitterness of truth. By degrees the reign of fancy is confirmed; she grows first imperious, and in time despotick. Then fictions begin to operate as realities, false opinions fasten upon the mind, and life passes in dreams of rapture or of anguish.

"This, Sir, is one of the dangers of solitude, which the hermit has confessed not always to promote goodness, and the astronomer's misery has proved to be not always propitious to wisdom."

"I will no more, said the favourite, imagine myself the queen of Abissinia. I have often spent the hours, which the princess gave to my own disposal, in adjusting ceremonies and regulating the court : I have repressed the pride of the powerful, and granted the petitions of the poor ; I have built new palaces in more happy situations, planted groves upon the tops of mountains, and have exulted in the beneficence of royalty, till, when the princess entered, I had almost forgotten to bow down before her."

"And I, said the princess, will not allow myself any more to play the shepherdess in my waking dreams. I have often soothed my thoughts with the quiet and innocence of pastoral employments, till I have in my chamber heard the winds whistle, and the sheep bleat : sometimes freed the lamb entangled in the thicket, and sometimes with my crook encountered the wolf. I have a dress like that of the village maids, which I put on to help my imagination, and a pipe on which I play softly, and suppose myself followed by my flocks."

"I will confess, said the prince, an indulgence of fantastick delight more dangerous than yours. I have frequently endeavoured to image the possibility of a perfect government, by which all wrong should be restrained, all vice reformed, and all the subjects preserved in tranquillity and innocence. This thought produced innumerable schemes of reformation, and dictated many useful regulations and salutary edicts. This has been the sport, and sometimes the labour, of my solitude ; and I start, when I think with how little anguish I once supposed the death of my father and my brothers."

" Such, said Imlac, are the effects of visionary schemes: when we first form them we know them to be absurd, but familiarize them by degrees, and in time lose sight of their folly."

CHAP. XLV.

THEY DISCOURSE WITH AN OLD MAN.

THE evening was now far past, and they rose to return home. As they walked along the bank of the Nile, delighted with the beams of the moon quivering on the water, they saw at a small distance an old man, whom the prince had often heard in the assembly of the sages. " Yonder, said he, is one whose years have calmed his passions, but not clouded his reason: let us close the disquisitions of the night, by inquiring what are his sentiments of his own state, that we may know whether youth alone is to struggle with vexation, and whether any better hope remains for the latter part of life.

Here the sage approached and saluted them. They invited him to join their walk, and prattled a while, as acquaintance that had unexpectedly met one another. The old man was cheerful and talkative, and the way seemed short in his company. He was pleased to find himself not disregarded, accompanied them to their house, and, at the prince's request, entered with them. They placed him in the seat of honour, and set wine and conserves before him.

" Sir, said the princess, an evening walk must give to a man of learning, like you, pleasures which ignorance and youth can hardly conceive. You know the qualities and the causes of all that you behold, the laws by which the river flows, the periods in which the planets perform their revolutions. Every thing must supply you with contemplation, and renew the consciousness of your own dignity."

" Lady, answered he, let the gay and the vigorous expect pleasure in their excursions ; it is enough that age can obtain ease. To me the world has lost its novelty : I look round, and see what I remember to have seen in happier days. I rest against a tree, and consider that in the same shade I once disputed upon the annual overflow of the Nile with a friend who is now silent in the grave. I cast my eyes upwards, fix them on the changing moon, and think with pain on the vicissitudes of life. I have ceased to take much delight in physical truth ; for what have I to do with those things which I am soon to leave ?"

" You may at last recreate yourself, said Imlac, with the recollection of an honourable and useful life, and enjoy the praise which all agree to give you."

" Praise, said the sage, with a sigh, is to an old man an empty sound. I have neither mother to be delighted with the reputation of her son, nor wife to partake the honours of her husband. I have out-lived my friends and my rivals. Nothing is now of much importance; for I cannot extend my interest beyond myself. Youth is delighted with applause, because it is considered as the earnest of some future good, and because the prospect of life is far ex-tended: but to me, who am now declining to decrepi-tude, there is little to be feared from the malevolence of men, and yet less to be hoped from their affection or esteem. Something they may yet take away, but they can give me nothing. Riches would now be useless, and high employment would be pain. My retrospect of life recalls to my view many opportu-nies of good neglected, much time squandered upon trifles, and more lost in idleness and vacancy. I leave many great designs unattempted, and many great attempts unfinished. My mind is burdened with no heavy crime, and therefore I compose myself to tranquillity; endeavour to abstract my thoughts from hopes and cares, which, though reason knows them to be vain, still try to keep their old possession of the heart; expect with serene humility, that hour which nature cannot long delay; and hope to possess, in a better state, that happiness which here I could not find, and that virtue which here I have not attained."

He rose and went away, leaving his audience not much elated with the hope of long life. The prince consoled himself with remarking, that it was not reasonable to be disappointed by this account; for age had never been considered as the season of feli-city, and if it was possible to be easy in decline and weakness, it was likely that the days of vigour and alacrity might be happy: that the noon of life might be bright, if the evening could be calm.

The princess suspected that age was querulous and malignant, and delighted to repress the expectations of those who had newly entered the world. She had seen the possessors of estates look with envy on their heirs, and known many who enjoyed pleasure no longer than they can confine it to themselves.

Pekuah conjectured, that the man was older than he appeared, and was willing to impute his complaints to delirious dejection: or else supposed that he had been unfortunate, and was therefore discontented: " For nothing, said she, is more common than to call our own condition, the condition of life."

Imlac, who had no desire to see them depressed, smiled at the comforts which they could so readily procure to themselves, and remembered, that at the same age, he was equally confident of unmingled prosperity, and equally fertile of consolatory expedients. He forbore to force upon them unwelcome knowledge, which time itself would too soon impress. The princess and her lady retired; the madness of the astronomer hung upon their minds, and they desired Imlac to enter upon his office, and delay next morning the rising of the sun.

CHAP. XLVI.

THE PRINCESS AND PEKUAH VISIT THE ASTRO-
NOMER.

THE princess and Pekuah having talked in private
of Imlac's astronomer, thought his character at once
so amiable and so strange, that they could not be
satisfied without a nearer knowledge; and Imlac was
requested to find the means of bringing them together.

This was somewhat difficult; the philosopher had
never received any visits from women, though he
lived in a city that had in it many Europeans who
followed the manners of their own countries, and
many from other parts of the world, that lived there
with European liberty. The ladies would not be
refused, and several schemes were proposed for the
accomplishment of their design. It was proposed to
introduce them as strangers in distress, to whom the
sage was always accessible; but after some deliberation, it appeared, that by this artifice, no acquaintance could be formed, for their conversation would
be short, and they could not decently importune him
often. "This, said Rasselas, is true; but I have
yet a stronger objection against the misrepresentation
of your state. I have always considered it as treason
against the great republick of human nature, to
make any man's virtues the means of deceiving him,
whether on great or little occasions. All imposture
weakens confidence, and chills benevolence. When
the sage finds that you are not what you seemed, he
will feel the resentment natural to a man who, con-

scious of great abilities, discovers that he has been
tricked by understandings meaner than his own,
and, perhaps, the distrust, which he can never afterwards wholly lay aside, may stop the voice of counsel, and close the hand of charity; and where will
you find the power of restoring his benefactions to
mankind, or his peace to himself?"

To this no reply was attempted, and Imlac began
to hope that their curiosity would subside; but, next
day, Pekuah told him, she had now found an honest
pretence for a visit to the astronomer, for she would
solicit permission to continue under him the studies
in which she had been initiated by the Arab, and
the princess might go with her either as a fellow-
student, or because a woman could not decently come
alone. " I am afraid, said Imlac, that he will be
soon weary of your company : men advanced far in
knowledge do not love to repeat the elements of their
art, and I am not certain that even of the elements,
as he will deliver them connected with inferences,
and mingled with reflections, you are a very capable
auditress." " That, said Pekuah, must be my care:
I ask of you only to take me thither. My knowledge is, perhaps, more than you imagine it, and, by
concurring always with his opinions, I shall make
him think it greater than it is."

The astronomer, in pursuance of this resolution,
was told, that a foreign lady travelling in search
of knowledge, had heard of his reputation, and
was desirous to become his scholar. · The uncom-
monness of the proposal raised at once his surprize
and curiosity; and when, after a short deliberation,

he consented to admit her, he could not stay without impatience till the next day.

The ladies dressed themselves magnificently, and were attended by Imlac to the astronomer, who was pleased to see himself approached with respect by persons of so splendid an appearance. In the exchange of the first civilities he was timorous and bashful; but when the talk became regular, he recollected his powers, and justified the character which Imlac had given. Inquiring of Pekuah, what could have turned her inclination towards astronomy? he received from her a history of her adventure at the pyramid, and of the time passed in the Arab's island. She told her tale with ease and elegance, and her conversation took possession of his heart. The discourse was then turned to astronomy; Pekuah displayed what she knew: he looked upon her as a prodigy of genius, and entreated her not to desist from a study which she had so happily begun.

They came again, and again, and were every time more welcome than before. The sage endeavoured to amuse them, that they might prolong their visits, for he found his thoughts grow brighter in their company; the clouds of solicitude vanished by degrees, as he forced himself to entertain them, and he grieved when he was left at their departure to his old employment of regulating the seasons.

The princess and her favourite had now watched his lips for several months, and could not catch a single word from which they could judge whether he continued, or not, in the opinion of his preternatural commission. They often contrived to bring him to an open declaration ; but he easily eluded all their attacks, and on which side soever they pressed him, escaped from them to some other topick.

As their familiarity increased, they invited him often to the house of Imlac, where they distinguished him by extraordinary respect. He began gradually to delight in sublunary pleasures. He came early, and departed late; laboured to recommend himself by assiduity and compliance ; excited their curiosity after new arts, that they might still want his assistance ; and when they made any excursion of pleasure or inquiry, entreated to attend them.

By long experience of his integrity and wisdom, the prince and his sister were convinced that he might be trusted without danger ; and lest he should draw any false hopes from the civilities which he received, discovered to him their condition, with the motives of their journey ; and required his opinion on the choice of life.

" Of the various conditions which the world spreads before you, which you shall prefer, said the sage, I am not able to instruct you. I can only tell that I have chosen wrong. I have passed my time in study without experience; in the attainment of sciences which can, for the most part, be but remotely useful to mankind. I have purchased knowledge at the expence of all the common comforts of life: I have missed the endearing elegance of female friendship, and the happy commerce of domestick tenderness. If I have obtained any prerogatives above other students, they have been accompanied with fear, disquiet, and scrupulosity ; but even of these prerogatives, whatever they were, I have, since my thoughts have been diversified by more intercourse with the world, begun to question the reality. When I have been for a few days lost in pleasing dissipation, I am always tempted to think that my inquiries have ended in errour, and that I have suffered much and suffered it in vain."

Imlac was delighted to find that the sage's understanding was breaking through its mists, and resolved to detain him from the planets till he should forget his task of ruling them, and reason should recover its original influence.

From this time the astronomer was received into familiar friendship, and partook of all their projects and pleasures : his respect kept him attentive, and the activity of Rasselas did not leave much time unengaged. Something was always to be done ; the day was spent in making observations which furnished talk for the evening, and the evening was closed with a scheme for the morrow.

The sage confessed to Imlac, that since he had mingled in the gay tumults of life, and divided his hours by a succession of amusements, he found the conviction of his authority over the skies fade gradually from his mind, and began to trust less to an opinion which he never could prove to others, and which he now found subject to variation, from causes in which reason had no part. " If I am accidentally left alone for a few hours, said he, my inveterate persuasion rushes upon my soul, and my thoughts are chained down by some irresistible violence ; but they are soon disentangled by the prince's conversation, and instantaneously released at the entrance of Pe-

kuah.   I am like a man habitually afraid of spectres,
who is set at ease by a lamp, and wonders at the dread
which harassed him in the dark ; yet, if his lamp be
extinguished, feels again the terrours which he knows
that when it is light he shall feel no more.   But I
am sometimes afraid lest I indulge my quiet by criminal negligence, and voluntarily forget the great
charge with which I am intrusted.   If I favour myself in a known errour, or am determined by my own
case in a doubtful question of this importance, how
dreadful is my crime !"

"No disease of the imagination, answered Imlac,
is so difficult of cure, as that which is complicated
with the dread of guilt : fancy and conscience then
act interchangeably upon us, and so often shift their
places, that the illusions of one are not distinguished
from the dictates of the other.   If fancy presents
images not moral or religious, the mind drives them
away when they give it pain, but when melancholick
notions take the form of duty, they lay hold on the
faculties without opposition, because we are afraid to
exclude or banish them.   For this reason the superstitious are often melancholy, and the melancholy almost always superstitious.

"But do not let the suggestions of timidity overpower your better reason : the danger of neglect
can be but as the probability of the obligation,
which, when you consider it with freedom, you find
very little, and that little growing every day less.
Open your heart to the influence of the light,
which from time to time breaks in upon you :
when scruples importune you, which you in your
lucid moments know to be vain, do not stand to

parley, but fly to business or to Pekuah, and keep this thought always prevalent, that you are only one atom of the mass of humanity, and have neither such virtue nor vice, as that you should be singled out for supernatural favours or afflictions."

CHAP. XLVII.

THE PRINCE ENTERS, AND BRINGS A NEW TOPICK.

"ALL this, said the Astronomer, I have often thought, but my reason has been so long subjugated by an uncontrolable and overwhelming idea, that it durst not confide in its own decisions. I now see how fatally I betrayed my quiet, by suffering chimeras to prey upon me in secret ; but melancholy shrinks from communication, and I never found a man before, to whom I could impart my troubles, though I had been certain of relief. I rejoice to find my own sentiments confirmed by yours, who are not easily deceived, and can have no motive or purpose to deceive. I hope that time and variety will dissipate the gloom that has so long surrounded me, and the latter part of my days will be spent in peace."

"Your learning and virtue, said Imlac, may justly give you hopes."

Rasselas then entered with the Princess and Pekuah, and inquired, whether they had contrived any new diversion for the next day? "Such, said Nekayah, is the state of life, that none are happy but by the anticipation of change: the change itself is nothing: when we have made it, the next wish is to change again. The world is not yet exhausted; let me see something to-morrow which I never saw before."

"Variety, said Rasselas, is so necessary to content, that even the Happy Valley disgusted me by the recurrence of its luxuries; yet I could not forbear to reproach myself with impatience, when I saw the monks of St. Anthony support, without complaint, a life not of uniform delight, but uniform hardship."

"Those men, answered Imlac, are less wretched in their silent convent than the Abissinian princes in their prison of pleasure. Whatever is done by the monks is incited by an adequate and reasonable motive. Their labour supplies them with necessaries; it therefore cannot be omitted, and is certainly rewarded. Their devotion prepares them for another state, and reminds them of its approach, while it fits them for it. Their time is regularly distributed; one duty succeeds another, so that they are not left open to the distraction of unguided choice, nor lost in the shades of listless inactivity. There is a certain task to be performed at an appropriated hour; and their toils are cheerful, because they consider them as acts of piety, by which they are always advancing *towards* endless felicity."

"Do you think, said Nekayah, that the monastick rule is a more holy and less imperfect state than any other? May not he equally hope for future happiness who converses openly with mankind, who succours the distressed by his charity, instructs the ignorant by his learning, and contributes by his industry to the general system of life; even though he should omit some of the mortifications which are practised in the cloister, and allow himself such harmless delights as his condition may place within his reach ?"

" This, said Imlac, is a question which has long divided the wise, and perplexed the good. I am afraid to decide on either part. He that lives well in the world is better than he that lives well in a monastery. But, perhaps, every one is not able to stem the temptations of publick life ; and if he cannot conquer, he may properly retreat. Some have little power to do good, and have likewise little strength to resist evil. Many are weary of their conflicts with adversity, and are willing to eject those passions which have long busied them in vain. And many are dismissed by age and diseases from the more laborious duties of society. In monasteries the weak and timorous may be happily sheltered, the weary may repose, and the penitent may meditate. Those retreats of prayer and contemplation have something so congenial to the mind of man, that, perhaps, there is scarcely one that does not propose to close his life in pious abstraction with a few associates serious as himself."

" Such, said Pekuah, has often been my wish, and I have heard the princess declare, that she should not willingly die in a crowd."

" The liberty of using harmless pleasures, proceeded Imlac, will not be disputed ; but it is still to be examined what pleasures are harmless. The evil of any pleasure that Nekayah can image is not in the act itself, but in its consequences. Pleasure, in itself harmless, may become mischievous, by en-

dearing to us a state which we know to be transient
and probatory, and withdrawing our thoughts from
that, of which every hour brings us nearer to the beginning, and of which no length of time will bring
us to the end.   Mortification is not virtuous in itself,
nor has any other use, but that it disengages us from
the allurements of sense.   In the state of future perfection, to which we all aspire, there will be pleasure
without danger, and security without restraint."

The princess was silent, and Rasselas, turning to
the Astronomer, asked him, whether he could not
delay her retreat, by showing her something which
she had not seen before.

" Your curiosity, said the sage, has been so general, and your pursuit of knowledge so vigorous, that
novelties are not now very easily to be found : but
what you can no longer procure from the living may
be given by the dead.   Among the wonders of this
country are the Catacombs, or the ancient repositories, in which the bodies of the earliest generations
were lodged, and where, by the virtue of the gums
which embalmed them, they yet remain without corruption."

" I know not, said Rasselas, what pleasure the
sight of the Catacombs can afford ; but, since nothing
else offers, I am resolved to view them, and shall
place this with many other things which I have done,
because I would do something."

They hired a guard of horsemen, and the next
day visited the Catacombs.   When they were about
to descend into the sepulchral caves, " Pekuah,
said the princess, we are now again invading the

habitations of the dead; I know that you will stay behind; let me find you safe when I return." " No, I will not be left, answered Pekuah; I will go down between you and the prince."

They then all descended, and roved with wonder through the labyrinth of subterraneous passages, where the bodies were laid in rows on either side.

CHAP. XLVIII.

IMLAC DISCOURSES ON THE NATURE OF THE SOUL.

" WHAT reason, said the Prince, can be given, why the Egyptians should thus expensively preserve those carcases which some nations consume with fire, others lay to mingle with the earth, and all agree to remove from their sight, as soon as decent rites can be performed ?"

" The original of ancient customs, said Imlac, is commonly unknown; for the practice often continues when the cause has ceased; and concerning superstitious ceremonies it is vain to conjecture; for what reason did not dictate, reason cannot explain. I have long believed that the practice of embalming arose only from tenderness to the remains of relations or friends, and to this opinion I am more inclined, because it seems impossible that this care should have been general : had all the dead been embalmed, their repositories must in time have been more spacious than the dwellings of the living. I suppose only the rich or honourable were secured from corruption, and the rest left to the course of nature.

" But it is commonly supposed that the Egyptians believed the soul to live as long as the body continued undissolved, and therefore tried this method of eluding death."

" Could the wise Egyptians, said Nekayah, think so grossly of the soul? If the soul could once survive its separation, what could it afterwards receive or suffer from the body?"

" The Egyptians would doubtless think erroneously, said the astrouomer, in the darkness of heathenism, and the first dawn of philosophy. The nature of the soul is still disputed amidst all our opportunities of clearer knowledge: some yet say, that it may be material, who, nevertheless, believe it to be immortal."

" Some, answered Imlac, have indeed said that the soul is material, but I can scarcely believe that any man has thought it, who knew how to think; for all the conclusions of reason enforce the immateriality of mind, and all the notices of sense and investigations of science concur to prove the unconsciousness of matter.

" It was never supposed that cogitation is inherent in matter, or that every particle is a thinking being. Yet, if any part of matter be devoid of thought, what part can we suppose to think? Matter can differ from matter only in form, density, bulk, motion, and direction of motion: to which of these, however varied or combined, can consciousness be annexed? To be round or square, to be solid or fluid, to be great or little, to be moved slowly or swiftly one way or another, are modes of material existence, all equally alien from the nature of cogitation. If matter be once without thought, it can only be made to think by some new modification, but all the modifications which it can admit are equally unconnected with cogitative powers."

" But the materialists, said the astronomer, urge that matter may have qualities with which we are unacquainted."

" He who will determine, returned Imlac, against that which he knows, because there may be something, which he knows not; he that can set hypothetical possibility against acknowledged certainty, is not to be admitted among reasonable beings. All that we know of matter is, that matter is inert, senseless, and lifeless; and if this conviction cannot be opposed but by referring us to something that we know not, we have all the evidence that human intellect can admit. If that which is known may be overruled by that which is unknown, no being not omniscient, can arrive at certainty."

" Yet let us not, said the astronomer, too arrogantly limit the Creator's power."

" It is no limitation of Omnipotence, replied the poet, to suppose that one thing is not consistent with another, that the same proposition cannot be at once true and false, that the same number cannot be even and odd, that cogitation cannot be conferred on that which is created incapable of cogitation."

" I know not, said Nekayah, any great use of this question. Does that immateriality, which, in my opinion, you have sufficiently proved, necessarily include eternal duration?"

" Of immateriality, said Imlac, our ideas are negative, and therefore obscure. Immateriality

seems to imply a natural power of perpetual duration, as a consequence of exemption from all causes
of decay : whatever perishes is destroyed by the resolution of its contexture, and separation of its parts ;
nor can we conceive how that which has no parts,
and therefore admits no solution, can be naturally
corrupted or impaired."

"I know not, said Rasselas, how to conceive any
thing without extension ; what is extended must
have parts, and you allow, that whatever has parts
may be destroyed."

"Consider your own conceptions, replied Imlac,
and the difficulty will be less. You will find sub-
stance without extension. An ideal form is no
less real than material bulk : yet an ideal form has
no extension. It is no less certain, when you
think on a pyramid, that your mind possesses the
idea of a pyramid, than that the pyramid itself is
standing. What space does the idea of a pyramid
occupy more than the idea of a grain of corn ? or
how can either idea suffer laceration ? As is the effect,
such is the cause : as thought, such is the power that
thinks ; a power impassive and indiscerptible."

"But the Being, said Nekayah, whom I fear to
name, the Being which made the soul, can destroy it."

"He, surely, can destroy it, answered Imlac,
since, however unperishable, it receives from a
superiour .nature its power of duration. That it
will not perish by any inherent cause of decay, or
principle of corruption, may be shewn by philosophy ; but philosophy can tell no more. That it

will not be annihilated by Him that made it, we must humbly learn from higher authority."

The whole assembly stood awhile silent and collected. "Let us return, said Rasselas, from this scene of mortality. How gloomy would be these mansions of the dead to him who did not know that he should never die; that what now acts shall continue its agency, and what now thinks shall think on for ever. Those that lie here stretched before us, the wise and the powerful of ancient times, warn us to remember the shortness of our present state: they were, perhaps, snatched away while they were busy like us in the choice of life."

"To me, said the princess, the choice of life is become less important; I hope hereafter to think only on the choice of eternity."

They then hastened out of the caverns, and, under the protection of their guard, returned to Cairo.

CHAP. XLIX.

THE CONCLUSION, IN WHICH NOTHING IS CONCLUDED.

It was now the time of the inundation of the Nile: a few days after their visit to the catacombs, the river began to rise.

They were confined to their house. The whole region being under water gave them no invitation to any excursions, and, being well supplied with materials for talk, they diverted themselves with comparisons of the different forms of life which they had observed, and with various schemes of happiness, which each of them had formed.

Pekuah was never so much charmed with any place as the convent of St. Anthony, where the Arab restored her to the Princess, and wished only to fill it with pious maidens, and to be made prioress of the order: she was weary of expectation and disgust, and would gladly be fixed in some unvariable state.

The Princess thought, that of all sublunary things knowledge was the best: she desired first to learn all sciences, and then purposed to found a college of learned women, in which she would preside, that, by conversing with the old, and educating the young, she might divide her time between the acquisition and communication of wisdom, and raise up for the next age models of prudence, and patterns of piety.

The Prince desired a little kingdom, in which he might administer justice in his own person, and see all the parts of government with his own eyes; but he could never fix the limits of his dominion, and was always adding to the number of his subjects.

Imlac and the Astronomer were contented to be driven along the stream of life, without directing their course to any particular port.

Of these wishes that they had formed they well knew that none could be obtained. They deliberated awhile what was to be done, and resolved, when the inundation should cease, to return to Abissinia.

END OF THE FIFTH VOLUME.

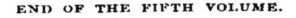

LONDON:
PRINTED BY S. AND R. BENTLEY, DORSET STREET.